MAGAZINE

FEATURE

WRITING

MAGAZINE

FEATURE

WRITING

Rick Wilber

University of South Florida

ST. MARTIN'S PRESS
New York

This book is dedicated to my family. My wife Robin's support, advice, and encouragement were crucial during the long months of interviewing, writing, and polishing. My fine son, Richard Jr., offered innumerable happy smiles and pats on the back, and my bright, beautiful, and delightful daughter, Samantha, already a voracious magazine reader at age three, always seemed ready with a hug when the work went slowly.

Editor: SUZANNE PHELPS WEIR
Managing editor: PATRICIA MANSFIELD PHELAN
Project editor: DIANA PUGLISI
Production supervisor: ALAN FISCHER
Art director: SHEREE GOODMAN
Text design: PATRICE SHERIDAN
Graphics: HAYDEL STUDIOS
Cover design: MAREK ANTONIAK

Library of Congress Catalog Card Number: 92-62729

Manufactured in the United States of America.

9 8 7 6 5
f e d c b a

For information, write:
St. Martin's Press, Inc.
175 Fifth Avenue
New York, NY 10010

ISBN: 0-312-07262-7

Acknowledgments

Acknowledgments and copyrights can be found at the back of the book on page 411, which constitutes an extension of the copyright page.

PREFACE

Magazine Feature Writing introduces beginning writers to the craft and art of writing for magazines. It is filled with examples from published writers, some of them beginners when these stories first appeared in print, some of them award-winning writers whose work is nationally known and respected. In addition to presenting this broad spectrum of work, this book also includes interviews in which most of these writers speak about how they wrote their articles. These interviews serve to reinforce concepts and give students a sense of magazine writing and editing as a career.

The book helps beginning writers move from the basics through increasingly advanced forms of magazine writing, and even includes material on some of the techniques used by successful poets and short-story writers that are valuable for the ambitious nonfiction writer. Increased interest from magazine and newspaper editors in the narrative form of storytelling makes this material particularly useful.

To provide the comprehensive instruction needed to prepare staff writers and freelancers for both today's magazines and those of the future, the book follows a certain logic in its organization; however, you may choose to change the order of the chapters to suit your own needs or to use chapters as a source for particular material.

I have chosen to begin with chapters on interviewing and research since they cover the background preparation needed before the actual writing begins. These tools are immensely important, and how well writers use them to acquire information can help determine the quality of the final story.

Chapters three and four deal with basic writing necessities, including one standard story format, reminders about the importance of grammar and spelling, and guidance on getting your reader involved in the story right from the start by using a powerful hook.

As a college journalism professor, I hope that students at the college level won't need much of a reminder about the importance of clean copy and a professional appearance. But this book is aimed at nonacademic beginning writers, too, and most of those beginners may well benefit from a chapter that highlights certain essentials, such as spelling, agreement, and punctuation.

Chapter five gives solid structural guidance on building a story. It discusses anecdotes, transitions, background, and quotes, along with other critical elements, and tells how to weave them together into a marketable story.

Chapter six takes the reader to the next level of writing, discussing the techniques an ambitious writer can use to strive for real style and write stories that go beyond the basics.

Chapter seven closes out the book's broad discussion of research and writing skills by addressing not only how writers can revise their own work but also how they can work effectively with an editor during the revision process.

Chapter eight explains the process of marketing a story, focusing on query and cover letters and their crucial function for freelance writers.

Chapter nine is the first that focuses on a particular kind of story — the travel piece. Travel writing holds special appeal for many beginners (and veterans as well!), and the chapter describes the three kinds of travel writing most typically available to writers. In addition, it should be noted that the skills practiced by the successful travel writer — such as the use of vivid description, accuracy of detail, characterization, and revealing anecdotes — are applicable to most magazine stories. Writing a few travel stories is good practice for any beginner, whether interested in the field as a career or not.

Similarly, chapter ten's discussion of personality profiles has a use for beginners far beyond its immediate focus on writing entertaining, informative profiles. This chapter helps beginning writers to discover those people worth writing about and then to find the best ways to write about them. Skills that help a writer uncover what makes someone — or something — special are useful to magazine writers for most of the stories they will write. So, like travel stories, in-depth personality profiles provide good practice for any beginner.

Chapter eleven, about essay writing, discusses a form that offers an elevated, challenging task for the nonfiction writer, requiring special concentration and attention to detail. Understanding how the mind of the essayist works is crucial to learning how the essay is written. Again, the skills learned in essay writing can be carried over to general feature writing.

Chapter twelve is a preliminary career guide for students interested in magazine writing, and discusses both staff and freelance opportunities. It includes some thoughtful advice from several top editors and writers.

Chapter thirteen is an introduction to the future of the magazine business, a future that is likely to bring profound change to the current production and distribution systems of most magazines. A beginning writer needs to be both aware of those upcoming changes and ready to take full advantage of them.

Chapter fourteen is a necessary basic primer on copyright, libel, and ethics for the beginning magazine writer.

Finally, the afterword contains various thoughts on magazine writing, including discussions about other specific kinds of articles that can be written and about the merits of reading and writing fiction and poetry as well as nonfiction. The writer who takes on the challenge of producing fiction and poetry, the afterword points out, will gain much from the experience. A reprinted short story and a few reprinted poems are included at the end of the afterword, and are referred to in several of the exercise and discussion sections in earlier chapters.

At the end of each chapter, there are exercises to help beginners put into practice the techniques and information garnered from the text. There are also discussion points, which should prompt beginning writers to deal with some of the field's pressing issues, as well as to discuss their own work and their careers.

I offer my deepest thanks and gratitude to all the writers and editors who were so willing to share their work with beginning writers by taking part in *Magazine Feature Writing*. Each one of them found the time to wade through lengthy telephone interviews with me and then to read and revise chapters in which their work was mentioned. Many of them offered me advice and encouragement as the manuscript progressed, and I deeply appreciate their comments.

I wish to thank Donna Dickerson, Director of the School of Mass Communications at the University of South Florida, for her complete support of the time and effort involved in my work on this text. Professor Randy Miller of the School of Mass Communications at USF was always willing to read through any number of drafts, chapter after chapter, and deserves special thanks (and some pity). Faculty member Tilden Counts and editor/writer Richard Gilliam were also extremely helpful, offering thoughtful comments and useful advice. An editor who offered especially insightful guidance was the late Murray Cox of *Omni* magazine.

At St. Martin's Press, I thank editors Suzanne Phelps Weir, Nancy

Lyman, Jane Lambert, and, most especially, Cathy Pusateri; Cathy started the whole process during a meeting in my office in which she convinced me that with my background in fiction and nonfiction I ought to write this book.

A special word of thanks is due to associate editor Elizabeth Toomey, who worked closely with me to develop the manuscript, offering wise suggestions and helping to shape its final form. Project editor Diana Puglisi made valuable contributions during the final stages of production as well. Elizabeth's and Diana's sharp eyes, calm demeanors, and judicious advice in the face of impending deadlines helped me immeasurably. The conscientious efforts of the copyeditor, Paula Williams, are also appreciated.

In addition, I thank the following reviewers for their valuable comments: David Abrahamson, New York University; Stephen G. Bloom, University of Iowa; Vicki Hesterman, Point Loma Nazarene College; Sammye Johnson, Trinity University; Marion Lewenstein, Stanford University; Jack Nelson, Brigham Young University; and Kathryn News, Temple University.

Finally, a full teaching load and the normal faculty duties of committee service, advising, and creative activity meant that the bulk of this text was written over a wealth of weekends and semester breaks. A very special thanks, therefore, to a most understanding and supportive family.

Rick Wilber
University of South Florida

CONTENTS

INTRODUCTION

There are more than 11,000 magazines published in the United States, with a total circulation of some 350 million. Those numbers are a bit inexact, not only because circulations rise and fall but also because dozens of new magazines start up every year and a dismayingly large number of magazines fail, too. But despite the losses, the magazine industry is a healthy one, with a generally steady rise in the number of magazines since 1952—a handy year to use as a starting point for a brief history of the contemporary magazine.

In 1952, the Federal Communications Commission ended a four-year freeze on new station allocations for the then new medium of television, and TV started its rapid rise to mass media dominance. As a result of television's success, other media, including magazines, were forced to change. The general interest magazine, for instance, had been an American staple for a century or more, but didn't last long as a competitor for advertising dollars against television's broad-based appeal. And the fiction that many magazines offered prior to 1952 made less and less sense to most magazine editors as television began to offer a wide range of visual fiction—situation comedies, dramas, westerns, science fiction, and many more.[1]

So magazines changed and, for reasons primarily economic, became increasingly specialized, appealing to narrower and narrower audiences.

---

[1]The other major media went through similar changes. Radio dropped its drama content and went to the playing of music. Newspapers became more visually appealing. Movies tried everything from 3-D productions to wide-screen extravaganzas. All of these media survived, but they had to accommodate to the reality of television to do so.

1

The logic was simple. While magazines couldn't offer the huge numbers that television could to advertisers, magazines *could* offer something even better: a select readership that meant very little waste of the advertising dollar. Here's why. An advertiser interested in selling widgets knew that most of television's viewers were never going to be interested in widgets, and so the ad was wasted on most of the people viewing it. A full-page ad in *Widget International* magazine, however, might reach far fewer people, but every one of those readers was a potential customer.

Specialization worked.

Specialization didn't necessarily mean small circulation, or small profits, by the way. In a country as huge as the United States, even a relatively narrow market can hold millions of readers. *Modern Maturity* magazine's circulation, for instance, is more than 22 million—and yet the readership is specialized in the sense that it is composed primarily of people older than 55 years of age.

Over the years, that trend toward specialized magazines has continued. For example, during the 1950s and 1960s, readers interested in sports had a number of magazines that catered to them. Later, even more narrowly specialized magazines were added to the field, appealing specifically to fans of a particular sport. Today, many of those sports magazines are still around and there are new ones, too—magazines that have narrowed the target yet again by appealing to fans of particular teams. In fact, some of the established magazines now produce various versions of their current issue for different regions, appealing to particular regional interests.

And the future seems to promise more of the same trend. The new technologies offer the possibility of magazines aimed directly at the interests of a specific fan, for example, individualized publications appealing directly to the sports interests of a particular reader. You may well be able to tell your home computer what kind of sports stories you'd like to read and in a few minutes' time have those stories available to you.

Obviously, these new technologies—on-line magazines, home access to databases, interactive CD-ROMs, and more—apply to much more than just the area of sports. They cover the whole spectrum of magazine writing. So the homemaker, the working woman, the amateur athlete, the priest, the CEO of a large corporation, the student, the teacher—everyone—will have access to a huge range of magazines. Some of these will be new publications, aimed directly at readers in the new Information Age. Others will be new versions of current magazines, many of which are on-line now or have plans to get on-line soon.

It's an exciting future, but what do the coming changes mean for the writer of magazine features? Happily, for writers they mean a steady increase in the number of magazines and, perhaps, a great increase in the number of stories (and in the depth of each story) that a magazine can offer.

Unhappily, by the way, the pay scale for freelancers hasn't improved much over the years, and the future doesn't seem to hold much change in that regard. The magazines that commonly paid a few hundred dollars for a story still seem to pay the same, even though those dollars aren't worth what they were in, say, the mid-1970s. Regrettably, the magazines that pay thousands of dollars for a story remain relatively rare.

Still, for the beginner, the thought that the markets are out there is enough to keep up the hopes of making a sale. Though the competition is tough—there are many, many thousands of writers or would-be writers—the opportunities exist if you have talent, are willing to learn, and continue to work hard to improve.

And the changes in technology, at least for the near future, do not change the basic skills you need as a magazine writer: interviewing and research skills, writing skills, a willingness to revise, and some ability to market your work.

Magazine Feature Writing is meant to give you a good start on a magazine article writing career, part-time or full-time. It offers advice by a variety of professional writers and editors, from major award winners to raw beginners who have made that all-important first sale.

There is logic to the order of the chapters, beginning with reporting skills, moving on to writing skills, adding in some marketing skills, turning then to some particular types of stories, and ending with career advice and the legal and ethical information that every magazine writer should know.

The idea is to prepare you for a start in the field, and in that sense this text is meant to be useful for any beginning writer, from a typical traditional undergraduate college student to a determined retiree eager to begin telling a lifetime of accumulated stories.

But this is only the beginning, of course. By the time you are done with this text, you will have done some research and interviewing, written a few stories, prepared a few queries, worked on your revision skills, and shared a few months of useful discourse with your classmates or others in your writing group. With a little luck you may have sold a story or had a positive response to a query. If not, you will at least have begun trying, and learning, and improving.

And that is the key, ultimately, to writing successful magazine features. Get started, and keep trying.

C H A P T E R   1

IN-DEPTH INTERVIEWING
FOR MAGAZINES

▼

DO YOUR HOMEWORK FIRST

REMEMBER WHO'S IN CHARGE

GET THE SIGHTS AND SOUNDS

FOLLOW UP

▲

Adrian Nicole LeBlanc's technique for in-depth interviewing is to ask the subject to help her find the truth.

John Calderazzo talks to people on their own turf, raising their comfort level and getting better quotes as a result.

Karima A. Haynes spends long hours preparing before the interview ever takes place. When there isn't a lot of time available for interviewing, she will be able to ask the right questions.

And Michael Bane establishes a relationship with the subject. Bane would like it to be friendship, but hatred will do just as well.

There is nothing more important to the beginning magazine writer than learning how to run an effective in-depth interview. The process, after all, is at the very core of information gathering for the writer. A great interview leaves the writer with a wealth of material that can be built into an entertaining and informative story. A poor interview leaves the writer gasping for something to say.

4

DO YOUR HOMEWORK FIRST

The process begins when writers do the background research that prepares them for the story. Most magazine writers aren't operating under the severe time constraints of the daily newspaper reporter, so the magazine editor is free to have high expectations for the depth and quality of the author's background work as well as for the interview itself.

The smart magazine writer, then, spends not only the time it takes to get the interview done right—hours or days in many cases—but also the time it takes to get the background material that's necessary before the interview ever takes place.

Then, once writers have accumulated enough background material to feel they already know the person they're going to interview, they jot down those specific topic areas they definitely want to cover once the interview starts.

Some writers write down actual questions they want to be certain to ask, but there's a problem that can arise from doing too much of that. A series of formal, careful questions is likely to result in an interview filled with formal, careful responses, and frequently that's not the sort of conversational quote material that one wants.

The idea, instead, is to engage the interviewee in a conversation, in which he or she opens up and talks freely about the subject at hand. Having a few important topic areas jotted down at the top of your notes will simply help you make sure you keep the conversation roughly centered on that topic, though a good interview may occasionally wander freely.

If you have the time, let that wandering occur, because there's always the chance that some fresh, interesting material will result. But remember that there are certain things you have to cover in the interview, and don't be afraid to redirect the conversation when you need to.

If you don't have the time—say you're interviewing a celebrity and there's a strict half-hour time limit on the conversation—then the list of topics at the top of your notepad becomes even more important. Through your research you know that these are the most important items to talk about, so you'll keep the conversation tightly focused until each one has been discussed. Then, if there's a bit of time left over at the end, go ahead and let the talk digress for a few minutes.

All of this can mean many pages of notes—both background and interview notes—that never make it into print. But that's a sign of the kind of hard work that results in top-quality writing. As a general rule, if you've used more than half of your notes in the story, you probably haven't done enough reporting. You limit yourself as a writer if, for instance, you have only one quote that you can use in a given spot in your story. Your choice, in that case, is to either change the story's direction to meet the needs of that one quote or to build a clumsy transition that gets you into the quote. If, however, you have three or four quotes that logically fit into that spot, you can pick the one that makes the most sense and doesn't require a tricky transition.

Multiply that kind of decision making throughout an entire story, and you can see that the writer who has spent the time up front in background and interview work is repaid with high-quality writing.

For Adrian Nicole LeBlanc, formerly a senior editor at *Seventeen* magazine, the background work began during a writing class in the spring semester of her senior year at Smith College, when she decided to write a story on a cluster of suicides in Leominster, Massachusetts.

"I did the whole first draft from newspaper clips," LeBlanc recalls. "Just from that information there was so much material that when I added in the later interviews and on-site reporting, I had fifty or sixty pages of first-draft manuscript."

It was several drafts later before LeBlanc was able to pare down her multiple-interview story into the form you see at the end of this chapter. Hard work? Sure, and a major sale for a beginning writer, too.

John Calderazzo, a freelancer, essayist, and fiction writer who teaches writing at Colorado State University, likes to do his background work on-site as well as through library research or through examination of the local newspaper's clip files.

"I like to go there and just walk around first, soaking up atmosphere, and then later get around to talking to people. It seems to me it's good to let your subjects talk to you on their own turf, especially when they are not used to talking to the media. They're more comfortable that way, and you're likely to get a better interview," he says.

Calderazzo, whose book *Writing from Scratch: Freelancing* (Rowman & Littlefield, 1990) emphasizes the interview process and its importance, adds, "I like to talk to two or three other people first about the person I'm interviewing. Then, when I know something about the individual and his or her turf, I'll do the face-to-face. After that, I follow up on the phone with any other questions, or just to clarify."

Writer Karima A. Haynes of *Ebony* was assigned an interview story on political candidate Carol Moseley Braun. Haynes says, "I spent almost three weeks doing the background reading for that forty-five-minute interview. I spent a lot of time reading magazine pieces, reading newspaper articles, reading anything I could about her. I knew I had to be prepared with information on her—both her biographical and her professional background—and have that ready at my command when I actually had the opportunity to do the interview."

Most of the research these writers did, of course, never made it into their stories, but doing the research first accomplished some important things for them and will do the same for you.

1. *The research establishes a context for the interview.* The more you know about your subject, the better you'll understand him or her and the better the questions you'll know to ask. This kind of in-depth background research is something that newspaper reporters are often unable to do enough of because of their deadline pressure.

   In LeBlanc's case, for instance, after she had read the clips she better understood the details of the town's teen suicides, including important names and places, what the police and local officials had to say about the deaths, and how the victims' friends and families had reacted.

2. *The research notifies the subject that you are prepared.* The subject who realizes you are prepared to ask good, specific questions will respond to you with better, more thoughtful responses. The person you are interviewing will appreciate and respect your hard work in getting ready for the meeting, and that kind of respect raises the level of the conversation. That is exactly the kind of snowball effect that you want with the subject, where mutual respect can grow and a productive, informative (and enjoyable) interview can take place. 1) conversation first to relax subject
   2)

REMEMBER WHO'S IN CHARGE

One of the mistakes some beginning magazine writers make is to forget who controls the interview. This may be because they're interviewing a celebrity or a famous athlete or a top politician whose forceful personality takes control of the conversation. Or it may be merely that the writer is the shy type who prefers to let the subject set the agenda.

But, whatever the reason, if you let the subject control the action, that means you aren't getting the information you need; you're getting the information the subject wants to give you. And your story will suffer as a result.

It is very much a matter of manipulation. You are trying to get the subject to say things that are useful and important to you in the story you are about to write. Some subjects, on the other hand, are trying to steer the conversation away from difficult areas and into areas they find safer, less controversial, or just more enjoyable.

Sometimes an interview seems downright fun and easy, but be wary when that happens. Wise writers worry that they are being manipulated by a subject smart enough to win them over with smiles and praise. You have to remember just exactly who's in charge. You're the writer, and you're being paid to spend the time and energy necessary to get the information you need.

Different writers have different techniques for running an effective, informative interview. John Calderazzo, for instance, often presents himself in an unassuming way. He makes it clear that he's a reporter doing a magazine story, but for the first few minutes he doesn't take out his notebook or tape recorder; this gives the subject time to get comfortable with the conversation first.

"I tend to write about people who are not used to being interviewed," he explains. "I like to make them as comfortable as possible. I want them to stay in their voice, you might say, and not feel they have to be formal."

In other words, Calderazzo makes a point of making everyday people feel comfortable so that they don't sound artificial or contrived in print. Instead, they sound like real people in the real world.

Listen to this brief section from Calderazzo's *Ohio Magazine* story, "Come Spring and High Water," (reprinted on page 100) a piece on the Maumee River's flooding of Grand Rapids, Ohio:

> Small and worried-looking, Nick Weaver . . . stands at the edge of the old canal that runs behind his land, midway between Front Street and the river, and squints through the warm September sun upstream at the spillway, where a few fishermen wade hip deep in the gently purling water.
>
> "Three times I've stood here and watched the river push over that dam like it was bulldozing boulders," he says. "It sounded like a million windshields being smashed. Then it came into my place, and there wasn't a thing anybody could do about it."
>
> Weaver walks to the front of his building and stops before a drain in the street. "And here's where your water comes up first," he says, idly kicking the metal grate as though that might seal it. "Your water comes boiling out and then follows that curve down the street, crosses over and starts filling up them stores over there one by one."

Calderazzo took the time to get to know Weaver first, to set him at ease. The result is a quote that sounds natural, unpolished, unpracticed, and very real. For certain kinds of stories, especially those involving ordinary people, Calderazzo's technique is perfect. Later, in chapter five, we'll talk about how Calderazzo's writing style takes the best advantage of this interviewing technique.

With celebrities or other public figures, however, many of whom are not only quite used to being interviewed but well schooled in "handling" reporters who are digging for information, other techniques are called for.

Michael Bane, a freelancer who has several books to his credit as well as hundreds of magazine pieces, has done dozens of magazine interviews with celebrities and political figures. His technique is to recognize that "Celebrity interviews are somewhere between a war and a game. You've been hired to extract a certain amount of information from them, and you can never, ever lose sight of that, even when you find you like them, or even when they've had so much practice that they're really dry and careful in what they say.

"It's important to establish a relationship with the subject, and it doesn't really matter what that relationship is. I can be your friend; that works fine. I can be your enemy; that works fine, too. Love me, hate me, it doesn't matter, as long as we avoid that worst-case scene where there's no emotion at all."

Bane admits that establishing that emotional contact with somebody who's toughened to interviewing sometimes isn't easy, or comfortable for that matter. But it has to be done.

During your preinterview research, you may discover something you share with your subject, for example, a common school or hometown. If you have both recently experienced major changes, such as a new career or the birth of a child, a routine interview can become a personal discussion in which you discover a whole new angle for your story. As Bane says, "Look, you need that relationship. I'll sympathize, I'll overtly make you mad, I'll find a subject we have in common—something, so long as there's interaction and emotion."

In a piece for *Country Music* magazine on singer-songwriter Randy Travis, Bane makes it clear that his relationship with Travis is one of friendship.

> We talk for a while about singing, about technique. His singing strength has improved since he was diagnosed as having an allergy to a number of common foods, including dairy products. The result is a very strict, low cholesterol, no-sweets diet that is, by his own admission, tough to stick to on the road.
>
> "Like for Thanksgiving, I ate whatever I wanted," he says, "and I felt really, really bad. But, you know, after two years on the diet, it's getting easier and easier to sing. When I started singing, I thought you just *sang,* you know, like you talked. Boy, forget that! Technique, practice, learn more technique."

Bane, having earned a level of friendliness with Travis through previous interviews, now is able to get the singer to talk about some of his problems as well as his successes. For the *Country Music* reader, hungry to read about the "real" Randy Travis, those kinds of details are important.

Adrian LeBlanc found out how difficult it can be to interview people in the midst of tragedy but managed to keep the interviews focused on the information she needed for her piece on teen suicide for *New England Monthly* magazine.

A college senior when she wrote this story, LeBlanc quickly developed a technique that was useful under such tragic circumstances. She purposefully enlisted the aid of the subjects in uncovering the "real" truth about the suicides, something previous newspaper reporters had been unable to do.

"I found that many of these people—the parents, the friends—really wanted to talk if you gave them the chance. There was a tremendous amount of national coverage for this, but I made it clear I wanted to build trust with them, and I wasn't in a rush like the newspaper reporters. I could stay there for six hours with them if I needed to. They appreciated that."

LeBlanc found that after one or two face-to-face interviews, phone interviews worked fine for follow-ups to verify quotes or ask more questions. By then, the subjects knew and trusted her.

With one young friend of a victim, in fact, LeBlanc had several long conversations. The girl wound up sharing with LeBlanc her letters and notes from the victim, and some of this material found its way into the story, a particularly telling piece called "You Wanna Die with Me?"

> A couple of days before her death, Melissa's mood began to pick up. For the first time in months, Melissa seemed happy, upbeat.
>
> "I thought to myself, 'Melissa's finally happy,' " says her friend, Andrea. "Her problems are finally over." But despite Melissa's abrupt mood swing, the suicidal symptoms were still apparent: Melissa gave Andrea some brand-new clothes she hadn't worn yet. Melissa wouldn't make plans with Andrea for that afternoon. Melissa had written this poem to Andrea just one week before:
> Andrea Happy Andrea,
>> Joyful Andrea,
>> I Love Andrea,
>> I shall miss her,
> She will hurt but will heal,
>> Andrea is strong
>> Andrea is brave
> Andrea has helped a great deal
>> She will pull through
> She always knew this would

be the way
The end of the day!
My end.

The power of that poem, and of Andrea's memories of her friend,
come from LeBlanc's patient work as an interviewer, making good use of
the great advantage that magazine writers often have over newspaper reporters—time. See pages 160–161 for a discussion of Time and Space for
magazine writers. LeBlanc's story is reprinted at the end of this chapter.

GET THE SIGHTS AND SOUNDS

One of the things that many veteran magazine writers do is take notes on
everything but the actual interview itself. They let a tape recorder handle
the actual words being spoken, and they busy themselves taking notes on
all of the sights and sounds that surround the interview. Other writers focus tightly on the interview and then come back later to take notes on
the ambience.

The key, in either case, is to make sure you've reported on the surroundings of the interview as well as the interview itself.

Why? First, those surroundings help bring the interview alive for the
reader by establishing a visual context for the quotes. This makes the
subject part of the real world, not just some isolated person being interviewed in a sterile, nondescript room.

Second, sights-and-sounds description helps you clarify the real
meaning of the quotes by bringing in the body language, vocal intona-
tion, and facial expressions that are not conveyed through words on paper, no matter how accurate the rendition.

"I take notes about description all along the line," says Calderazzo.
"In fact, I write down about ten or fifteen times more than I can possibly
use. Those kinds of specific details render the character of people and
places, and they add a lot of verisimilitude. The reader believes you when
you have them there."

In the excerpt of Calderazzo's story given earlier, note how a descriptive expression such as "Small and worried-looking" helps make the subject a real person for the reader and how the physical act of Weaver's "idly
kicking the metal grate as though that might seal it" helps the reader visualize Weaver as he speaks.

Calderazzo also has Weaver himself use sound description to good effect when he quotes the subject as saying, "It sounded like a million

BOX 1.1

TO TAPE OR NOT

The cassette or tape recorder brings with it some real advantages and some problems, too.

Some writers feel that the person they are interviewing is likely to be intimidated by the presence of the recorder, that taping people makes them too aware of what they're saying, too careful. A notebook and a pencil, those writers feel, are simply less intrusive and so make for a better interview.

Many newspaper reporters, also, don't use a recorder, because transcription of tapes is time-consuming, and newspaper reporters often find time in short supply. Also, they say, most of the transcription isn't going to make it into the story anyway, so why bother?

The alternative to transcribing is to fast-forward or rewind to find the right quote in the tape to use, and many find that process clumsy and time-consuming as well, even when using the counter on the recorder. In addition, to a newspaper reporter pressed for time, the process seems redundant. A good reporter would have jotted down that good quote during the actual interview and not have to go searching for it again on the tape.

Finally, newspaper reporters learn to trust their handwritten notes, including the quotes. And if they often don't get the words exactly right (ask them, and they'll admit this), reporters are confident they are essentially accurate and aren't burdened with the hassles of recording.

All of that is true. But many magazine writers have their own reasons for coming to a very different conclusion. Most people being interviewed become used to the recorder, and the intimidation factor quickly fades, these writers say. After a few minutes of interviewing, the subjects seem every bit as open as they would be without the conversation's being taped.

For the magazine writer, the transcription process, though it may take an extra hour or two, is not the bother it is for a newspaper reporter. Transcribing, after all, not only puts *all* the quotes from the interview down on paper (compared to the newspaper reporter's highlights) for note-taking purposes but also gives the writer an extra chance to hear the interview take place and make newer, sometimes better, decisions about which quotes to use.

In addition, readers of magazines are even less likely than

readers of newspapers to be forgiving of inaccuracies. The magazine writer, after all, cannot plead the pressure of daily deadlines as an excuse for mistakes. And a tape recorder guarantees the complete accuracy of a quote.

The magazine writer, too, is often able to use considerably more quotes from the interview than the newspaper reporter. The recorder is extremely helpful in situations when whole paragraphs (or more) of the interview are going to make it into print.

Finally, by using a tape recorder, the magazine writer is freed from some of the note-taking duties and able to jot down the important sights and sounds surrounding the interview. For the magazine writer, those descriptive elements of the interview may be as important as the words being spoken.

Conclusion: Get a recorder and learn to use it well. For magazine writing, the benefits far outweigh the problems.

---

windshields being smashed." The simile gives the reader a vibrant idea of the river's raw power by way of comparison to a loud, violent act.

Similarly, in the following section of LeBlanc's story that talks about a suicide prevention group's lecture to an assembly of bored high school students, the writer surrounds many of her quotes with bits of supportive description that help establish a sense of visual reality for the reader:

> "This is a tough scene, and it's tough to cope," says the Samaritan onstage now, her passé language causing you to roll your eyes. Your neighbor picks lint off his jeans; another stretches and yawns. "Oh, Christ," a student behind you mutters, "here we go again." There's hissing. One girl writes a note to her friend. "You must be mad that you live in Leominster," the Samaritan continues, "because it's only known for one thing these days. Suicide."

The physical acts of the students, like picking lint off jeans or stretching and yawning, make clear their boredom, so that LeBlanc is never forced to come right out and say the students are bored. The students' actions speak for them instead. Those actions also stand in sharp contrast to the earnest pleas of the suicide-prevention expert, and this helps give extra strength to the quotes, which are meant to be effective in sending students a strong antisuicide message, but, instead, sadly, seem ignored.

Karima A. Haynes often finds sights-and-sounds reporting crucial to her work for *Ebony*. For her piece on Carol Moseley Braun, Haynes tagged along on a campaign swing through downstate Illinois.

"I had a chance at one point to step back and watch, so I just let the tape recorder roll to get her speech and the sound of the crowd. Then I took notes on all the color and atmosphere. It was everything that I witnessed with my own eyes."

The result was a polished piece on Braun that focused on the candidate's broad appeal, not by telling the reader about it, but by showing it.

As Haynes explains, "I think you just let readers figure it out for themselves, through inference and indirect writing, without your having to say it directly. I didn't say 'Carol Moseley Braun shocked the political establishment with her victory.' I just stepped back and showed the reader who she is."

You can see how Haynes manages this in her story on page 16.

Because they had taken plenty of notes, Calderazzo, LeBlanc, and Haynes could be confident they would have just the right bit of description available to flesh out a quote. Too many beginning writers take a minimum of notes on the surroundings and are forced to use whatever they have. If you're smart enough to maximize sights-and-sounds reporting, you'll find yourself with options other writers don't have.

Protect yourself as a writer, and be prepared. Then, when that quote you thought wasn't important winds up being critical to your story, you'll have three or four descriptive passages about it to choose from. That means you can use the best one, not the only one, or, in the worst case, not have one at all.

In short, you're never more happy about having taken the time to jot down those one or two "extra" bits of description than when you see them in your story.

Just like with your background research, this can mean many pages of notes that never make it into print. But, once again, that's the kind of hard work that gives you the writing options later that result in a top-quality story.

FOLLOW UP

Ask any veteran magazine writer about the importance of follow-up interviews to either check on quote accuracy or to get more information, and you'll hear the same message: Follow up every time you can. There are several reasons for this.

First, the follow-up not only ensures that your quotes are accurate but also is likely to add to the story. When you read back a quote to a subject, you're likely to get several more quotes that expound in greater detail on the topic.

In the Maumee River flood story, John Calderazzo recalls that he double-checked all the quotes and facts in the story in one way or another. "I never hesitate to call someone back a day or two later to ask the person to fill in things we didn't talk about at first, or just to double-check something important. In fact, sometimes, when I'm working on a story like that I'll just drive back over there to check things out again; maybe somebody I talked to previously had been having a bad day, and now he or she is ready to open up. It always adds to the story."

The result of that is a depth of quality and quantity in quotes that elevates the writing and earns the reader's trust. "One wrong fact or quote in a nonfiction story jeopardizes the veracity of the entire story," Calderazzo says, "so you have to get it accurate. I'm pretty much of a perfectionist in these things. You have to be."

Second, a follow-up adds to the story's quality and accuracy and also builds trust for future interviews. When you double-check quotes for accuracy, you're convincing interviewees that you can be trusted to get it right. As a result, not only will they be willing to talk to you the next time an interview comes up, but also they will be likely to spread the word that you can be trusted.

Finally, the writer who does follow-up interviews is the writer that editors learn to trust to get it right. And the most important trust you can build is the trust between yourself and your editor.

■ ■ ■

WILL CAROL MOSELEY BRAUN BE THE FIRST BLACK WOMAN SENATOR?

BY KARIMA A. HAYNES

The aroma of frying fish hangs in the evening air outside a meeting hall in Sherman, Ill., a tiny town about a stone's throw from Springfield, the state capital. A handful of local people are standing around chatting amiably about nothing in particular.

As the midnight blue Cadillac eases up the driveway and rolls to a stop at the building's entrance, all heads turn. Carol Moseley Braun, the newly elected Illinois Democratic Senate nominee, steps from the sedan and is blinded by TV camera floodlights and mobbed by well-wishers who have left their fish dinners in the hall to come outside for a glimpse of the rising political star.

In an instant, she is inside and up on the stage waving to the crowd that is chanting, "WE WANT CA-ROL! WE WANT CA-ROL."

"You want Carol?" she responds, paraphrasing Chicago's late mayor Harold Washington and flashing her megawatt smile. "You got Carol!" The hall erupts in applause.

She delivers a brief stump speech on opening up government to all people, greets Black and White supporters and then heads off to yet another campaign stop

where she will pump more hands and deliver her message of hope.

This has been Braun's routine since March when she shook American politics to its foundations by becoming the first Black woman nominated to the U.S. Senate by a major political party. If she wins the general election in November, she will become the first Black woman, and only the fourth Black American, to serve in the Senate.

"This nomination is history making," Braun says with the same quiet self-assurance that helped her overcome great political odds. "But history is a fluid situation. The real test is what kind of human being you are and what kind of mark you make."

Weighing her words carefully, Braun continues. "To the extent that there will be other women and Black people who will see the possibilities because of my candidacy, then I think that being nominated is a contribution that I can be proud of."

Although Braun may be modest about her political breakthrough, her upset victory has lifted the hopes of inner-city Blacks seeking a political voice, Whites fed up with incumbents and women still irked by the Senate's handling of the sexual harassment case involving then-Supreme Court nominee Judge Clarence Thomas and University of Oklahoma law professor Anita Hill.

Braun was among millions of television viewers who tuned into the hearings and saw, what she calls, "an elitist club made up of mostly White male millionaires over 50."

"To be honest, I couldn't bring myself to watch the hearings full-time," Braun says, a residue of anger still lingering in her voice. "The whole thing was an embarrassment. I mean, it was an embarrassment from the very beginning and by the time it got to the sexual harassment issue, it was beyond embarrassing, it was mortifying."

The anger felt by many Illinoisans after Democratic Sen. Alan Dixon voted to confirm Thomas fueled a movement to draft Braun to run for the Senate. "People were writing and calling me saying, 'You should run for the Senate. Our senator votes like a Republican. Our senator isn't really a Democrat,'" Braun recalls. "By the time I got a letter from a White man in a Republican county urging me to run, I knew there was something up and I really ought to consider this seriously."

So with no money ("You really know who your friends are when times are tough"), no organization and no political backing, Braun launched her old-fashioned grassroots campaign. Her announcement that she would give up her low-profile office as Cook County Recorder of Deeds to run

for the Senate barely made the six o'clock news.

Although Braun grew up on Chicago's South Side, attended city schools, the University of Illinois, the University of Chicago Law School and served as an assistant U.S. attorney and a state legislator for 10 years, she was virtually a political unknown. The political establishment snubbed her. Powerful women's groups listened to her stump speech and then politely showed her the door. Political pundits said she was out of her mind to go up against the congenial, good ol' boy two-term incumbent known as "Al the Pal" and the other challenger, Albert Hofeld, a personal injury lawyer with $5 million to burn on a campaign that included a carefully crafted media blitz.

Braun ignored the naysayers and hit the campaign trail. She wooed voters with a simple message spoken in her down-to-earth style: We can do better. Potential constituents, particularly White males in rural counties, looked beyond color and gender to bask in this woman's glow.

It was clear the connection had been made when election night vote totals showed she'd pulled off an unprecedented upset, helped in part by a three-way race. As she took the stage for her victory speech, Braun smiled broadly, pranced to "Ain't No Stopping Us Now," and waved to a throng of supporters carrying signs that read: "Make Herstory" and "Go Girl."

"One of the things that made the difference was that so many people wanted this to happen," Braun says in explaining her win. "A lot of the organization and work that happened out in the precincts happened because people did it as volunteers. So the commitment and the dedication overcame the dollars."

To the pollsters who said she didn't have the numbers to win, she says, "I've been in elections since before there were election polls and before there were instantaneous results. As a candidate you have a sense of how it is going, that is if you're paying attention."

Since her primary victory, Braun has been the toast of Washington politicos. She's been chatting with senators, doing lunch with leaders of national women's groups and charming crowds pushing to get up-close and personal with the candidate. She is philosophical about those who wouldn't give her the time of day last fall. "The political old-fashioned wisdom is: You don't get too excited when you're moving up, because you never know when circumstances will change and you have to move down. I want and welcome all the help I can get from any quarter."

Braun's winning style and infectious optimism have made her a media darling as well. Her historic victory was reported on Italian television and in London's International Herald Tribune. She takes it all in stride, however, calling her new found fame "pretty bizarre."

But she is not letting the adulation go to her head. In fact, she wants to make it clear that her campaign is not a Cinderella story. "This candidacy is not a fairy tale," she says with a cool force. "In the first place, I am qualified for this job. I am more qualified for this job than any of my opponents," including Richard S. Williamson, the White male lawyer and former adviser to presidents Reagan and Bush whom she will face in the fall.

And this is the point she really wants to get across. "Now, it is a great leap from recording deeds to the United States Senate," she concedes. "But in light of the fact that women and minorities are not generally put on the track to access the higher level positions in government, or anything else for that matter, the only way that you can move into these circles is to go for it."

It is that same steely resolve to overcome obstacles that helps Braun cope with childhood difficulties, specifically being beaten by her father with ropes and having to care for her siblings when her mother could no longer tolerate her husband's abusive behavior. Both are painful memories she doesn't like to discuss.

But her faith has kept her strong. It is the same faith she displayed when she thanked the Lord on election night for her victory. "My faith is as much a part of me as my name," she says. "I wouldn't be who I am without it. I would have cracked up years ago or given up years ago."

She called on that same gritty determination to continue after her 16-year marriage to Michael Braun, a White lawyer, ended in divorce about six years ago. This 44-year-old single mother's face lights up, however, when she talks about their son, Matthew, 14. "He's a sweet kid. A down-to-earth kid," she says. "It is important to me that he remember always that he has to make a contribution in his own right. And that my contributions, my celebrity and my achievements really don't have anything to do with the responsibility that he faces."

Taking on responsibility is at the core of her candidacy. "I've always felt that my obligation—my calling—is to use my talents on behalf of the public interest," she says. "Elected officials have to be very clear that they are not leaders, but servants of the people."

It is this attitude of service Braun hopes to impart to voters as she criss-crosses the state trying to garner enough support to win the November election. In order to do this, she must hold on to her core constituency of Chicago Blacks and liberal Whites as well as win over a sufficient number of Downstate Whites who have traditionally voted conservatively. Whatever the outcome, her nomination has raised hopes and opened the doors of opportunity.

■ ■ ■

This article first appeared in the June 1992 issue of Ebony *magazine. In November 1992, Carol Moseley Braun was elected to the U.S. Senate. Karima A. Haynes is associate editor at* Ebony *magazine in Chicago, Illinois.*

■   ■   ■

"YOU WANNA DIE WITH ME?"

BY ADRIAN NICOLE LeBLANC

A lanky girl descends from a yellow school bus. She walks the path leading to her white, clean home surrounded by green fields and mountains. Her older sister washes the car. The girls begin to argue and the younger girl slaps her sister across the face. In her bedroom, the young girl sits and cries. She takes off her baseball hat, pulling her ponytail through the opening above the adjustable band. She picks up a framed picture of her parents. She remembers the time her mother said she didn't love her. She takes her father's rifle out of a closet. As the camera pulls away from the bedroom window, the gun cracks.

The projector clicks off. From the darkened high school auditorium come claps and whistles. Several students mockingly sob and console one another. Others wriggle, their laughter careless, inattentive. Many bite their fingernails and stare indifferently ahead, caught in the numb monotone of a second-period assembly.

"Will those of you who haven't made airplanes out of the HELP cards please put them in your pockets?" asks today's Samaritan, stepping forward. A HELP plane sails past her. Students laugh. The assistant principal beckons for help from the teachers lining the perimeter of the gym. They arch their backs, coming off the wall slowly, and ease around the rough room. "Hey, *you!*" a teacher yells, pointing to a boy in the bleachers. "*NOW!*" The boy smirks and bounces down the rows. The teacher pushes him toward the exit.

Imagine you are a student here, at Leominster High. It's the fourth time this year you've had to listen to people talking about depression and death. The white-haired ladies speaking soothingly onstage—representatives of the Samaritans, a suicide-prevention group sent in from Framingham to help you—have already given you their pamphlets. You remain unresponsive to their pleas.

"This is a tough scene, and it's tough to cope," says the Samaritan onstage now, her passé language causing you to roll your eyes. Your neighbor picks lint off his jeans; another stretches and yawns. "Oh, Christ," a student behind you mutters, "here we go again." There's hissing. One girl writes a note to her friend. "You must be mad that you live in Leominster," the Samaritan continues, "because it's only known for one thing these days. Suicide."

Leominster is a largely working-class city of thirty-four thousand, forty miles west of Boston, with a strong French Canadian and Italian heritage. Its usual claim to notoriety is the group of factories that produced the first plastics in the nation. Lately it has had a more somber reputation. Between February 1984 and March 1986, ten Leominster teenagers died sudden, violent deaths, and eight of those committed suicide. This morning's assembly aims to avoid number nine.

"It's always a mistake to kill yourself," says the Samaritan. One boy sleeps through the presentation. A group of "trade rats" from the vocational high school jumps down from the bleachers en masse. The Samaritan tries to continue. "There's *got* to be *someone* you can talk to," she says.

"Listen to her," says the assistant principal, his voice rising.

"Listen to each other," says the Samaritan, her face strained and weary. Shoving and hustling one another, students pour down from their seats.

"Pay attention to the signals, keep your eyes open," the Samaritan yells. "Listen!"

"Talk to someone!" screams the assistant principal, lost among a crowd of heads and denim. "And go to your fourth-period class!"

■ ■ ■

About five weeks before her death, fifteen-year-old Melissa Poirier was beaten up twice in one day. That morning in school she had been jumped in the bathroom. Melissa and the two girls who attacked her were suspended, so Melissa went home. Soon after, one of her assailants went to her house, offering a truce. She asked Melissa to join her and the third girl so they could talk and work out the differences they were having over a boy. Melissa accompanied the girl to Pheasant Run, a derelict ski trail behind the high school where kids often drink and get stoned. The third girl waited beyond the trail. When Melissa arrived, the two girls assaulted her again. One held her down while the other pounded, and then the two traded positions. Half an hour later, Melissa managed to escape to a nearby garage, where she crouched behind a car for over an hour. She then made her way back home, carefully, through the woods.

Melissa was an extremely pretty young girl with thick, long hair, a button nose, shining eyes, and a neat, budding figure. When her classmates finished with her that day, her nose was fractured and both of her eyes were black. The blood vessels on her forehead had broken from repeated blows. Her face was swollen and her ribs were bruised.

"Melissa was tiny, five feet tall, and wicked cute," says one close girlfriend. "The girls never liked her because the guys did. Mel was hassled all the time."

The fight left Melissa despondent. Her mother, who noticed that she was afraid to go outside, encouraged her to see a therapist, but after three sessions, Melissa refused to return.

Andrea Paquette had been Melissa's best friend since fourth grade. The girls had started to grow apart (Andrea became involved with student government, and Melissa with drugs), but the two kept up their morning ritual of a walk before homeroom.

"She cried every day when the bell rang," says Andrea. "She never wanted to go in. Melissa hated school more than anything."

On the average morning at Leominster High, what Melissa Poirier wanted to avoid goes something like this: you might come in on time, drop your books off (if you took any home) but keep your coat on (to look as if you'd just entered the building, without books). You'd head straight for the girls' bathroom. You'd inhale the smoke and shiver; the bathroom is always cold. Graffiti covers the chipped gray paint on the windows and the doorless stalls: "Just because Im no slut doesnt mean I should become a fuckin nun Im no slob like most girls in this fuckin school!" You'd have fifteen minutes to get ready before the heads, the local drug population, took over the washroom. You'd comb your hair and watch your friends comb theirs and lean on a radiator half-covered with hardened wads of gum. You'd try to find your reflection between the black letters of the spray-painted SUCK on a mirror fogged with hair spray. You'd talk and look and tuck in your shirt. You'd put on a little more makeup, comb back your feathered hair one more time, then leave.

In the main corridor, dented light-brown lockers line the cinderblock hallways. Gray paint covers the old graffiti, and new graffiti covers the gray—"Helter Skelter, AC/DC, Led Zeppelin, DIE!" Boys, lined up by now outside the bathroom, shuffle and laugh, arms folded across their chests. Most wear denim jackets and high-tops or leather jackets and work boots. All collars are up.

The boys would tease you those early mornings, especially if they'd been smoking or drinking. You would try to get by untouched but very noticed. Some students kept bottles in their lockers and drank in the locker-room shower stalls. Some had gone to McDonald's for breakfast and had dumped out half their Cokes and refilled the cups with booze, usually vodka. Some students didn't drink, of course, but certainly no one thought it strange if someone skipped classes, went to an empty house with a friend, and drank away the afternoon. So you'd lean against the lockers with friends, eyeing everyone but the person you were talking to, trying to see who was out by who was in school that day, and wait for the tardy bell. And then, maybe, you'd go to homeroom. Otherwise, you'd leave.

"And that's if you were one of

the good kids," Melissa Poirier's mother says, a year after her daughter's death. "You just try and imagine what it was like to be one of the kids on the other side of the fence, one of the ones inside those detention halls, getting suspended, getting yelled at and punched at and hauled out two times a week. One of the kids called stupid by your teachers and, when you did go to class, one of those who was asked, 'Why did you bother to come?'"

Psychologists say the most dangerous time for a suicidal person is after emerging from depression or crisis. In fact, after planning a suicide, adolescents often look and feel better because a decision has been made, the burden lifted.

"It's like looking through a tunnel," says Susan Warner-Roy, who founded SPACE (Suicide Prevention Awareness Community Education) in 1980. Warner-Roy's own husband, Neil, hanged himself four years ago. "The darkness in the tunnel is the depression, and at the end of the tunnel is the light, the end of pain. To the suicidal kid, the light at the end of the tunnel is death." A couple of days before her death, Melissa's mood began to pick up. For the first time in months, Melissa seemed happy, upbeat.

"I thought to myself, 'Melissa's finally happy,'" says her friend, Andrea. "Her problems are finally over." But despite Melissa's abrupt mood swing, the suicidal symptoms

were still apparent: Melissa gave Andrea some brand-new clothes she hadn't worn yet. Melissa wouldn't make plans with Andrea for that afternoon. Melissa had written this poem to Andrea just one week before:

Andrea Happy Andrea,
  Joyful Andrea,
  I Love Andrea,
  I shall miss her,
She will hurt but will heal,
  Andrea is strong
  Andrea is brave
Andrea has helped a great deal
  She will pull through
She always knew this would
    be the way
  The end of the day!
  My end.

So Melissa Poirier may have been in an especially dangerous frame of mind when she and another friend, Melody Maillet, left Leominster High School early on November 1, 1984. Pushing out the bright yellow doors of a side entrance, Melissa and Melody turned left on Exchange Street and walked the potholed road scattered with Coke cans and trash. The girls probably strolled downtown, past the variety stores and barbershops and tenements, past the pale houses of the plain Leominster streets. They walked past Monument Square, newly renovated and green. They may have walked by the Vietnamese and Cambodian apartments near Red's Variety and the Elbow Lounge. The girls then returned to

Melissa's home with a bottle of cheap champagne they'd bought along the way, put on a Pink Floyd album, and began to drink.

The Wall, a series of songs depicting the progressive alienation of a rock star on the downswing, ranked high on the girls' list of revered albums. Each song, metaphorically "another brick in the wall," denotes the social forces propelling the rocker's snowballing anomie—parents, school, his wife—and the failure of the star's struggle to be understood. "Comfortably Numb," Melissa's favorite Pink Floyd song, expresses the rocker's peaking detachment. Melissa doodled the lyrics in her notebooks and in letters to friends:

> Hello,/Is there anybody in there . . . I hear you're feeling down . . . Can you show me where it hurts/ . . . I can't explain you would not understand/This is not how I am/I have become comfortably numb . . . /The child is grown/The dream is gone/And I have become/Comfortably numb.

The final song of the album Melissa quotes verbatim, in one of the five suicide notes the girls left behind:

> "Life sucks and then you DIE! *Goodbye cruel world I'm leaving you now and thiers nothin you can Say To make me change my mind!* YES SA! I Love to Die I'd be happier I know it! So Please Let me Go. No hard feelings. Don't Be Sad ReJoyce Its my new beginning! It Didn't hurt I'm free and happy.

Melissa Poirier's mother, Mariette, came home for lunch on that November day and found her daughter and Melody on the floor of the upstairs bedroom, with the Poirier family's 12-gauge shotgun beside them. The medical examiner found high levels of alcohol in the blood of both girls. Exactly how Melissa and Melody committed double suicide remains uncon-firmed. Friends believe that Melissa bent forward and leaned on the gun, which was pointed at her stomach, and that Melody climbed on her back. Mariette Poirier says she believes each girl shot herself.

Winnifred Maillet, Melody's mother, suspects foul play. (Susan Warner-Roy's husband, Neil, whose own suicide preceded Melody's by four years, was Winnifred's brother. And Winnifred's son, Bobby, had drowned in 1980.) Since Melody's death more than two years ago, Winnifred has worked to prove that the handwriting in Melody's own suicide note was not her daughter's. The graphology has become an obsessive project. When Winnifred says her daughter was not suicidal, there is an urgent determination in her voice: "We never saw her without the pretty smiling eyes. Always smiling like the dickens. She was always happy."

"She went out. She was happy," says Melody's father, Albert, who works in quality control for Digital Equipment Corporation. "She didn't have any problems at all. She had a few problems at school, and was always upset about being put on suspension once in a while, for maybe being tardy or not coming to school, but nothing out of the ordinary."

But Melody's friends feel certain that she was suicidal. One girlfriend says Melody had been asking people to commit suicide with her for a while, sometimes seriously, sometimes as a joke: "You wanna die with me?" Melody would say. "Melissa was the first one to say yes," says the friend. The two girls were known as partying buddies who shared a mutual love for acid rock.

"They dropped acid before an' shit, but they were really getting into it toward the end," says a close girlfriend of Melissa's. "We were losin' them."

Although adamant about Melody's emotional stability, Winnifred Maillet spoke of Melody's devotion to a print still hanging in her daughter's old bedroom among a collection of her things—Van Halen posters, a purple metallic electric guitar, and a black leather jacket she had bought. It shows a young girl who looks startlingly like Melody, a five-foot-eight Canadian beauty with jet black hair, olive skin, and huge, emerald eyes. The girl in the picture is tall and dark, but her eyes are detached, expressionless, complacent, while Melody's were warm. The girl's head is encircled by a lavender halo and she holds lavender feathers and a fan. The girl's skin is death-white.

"She loved the purple halo," said it was her purple haze," Melody's mother explains. Winnifred has since surrounded Melody's grave—a small pillar with Melody's picture in a crystal ball on top, leaning on a porcelain unicorn—with purple flowers. Acid rocker Jimi Hendrix popularized Purple Haze in his song about that form of LSD. And Melody referred to the purple haze, and to four of her classmates who died before her, in one of her suicide notes:

> Good Bye 'I did cuz I had to' I have to live among the Purple Haze! Tell Cecilia I love her very much! Im took advantage of you without realizing it! But now I will be happy with Jeff Mike David + Scott. 'Mom and Dad I love you' even though I've never tobl you, Im sorry It has to be this way I don't want to hurt anyone I love the Rest of the family very much. . . .

Leominster is not alone. Teen suicides nationwide have more than doubled since 1960. It's the second most common cause of death among youngsters between the ages of fifteen and twenty-four, and the number two killer among college students. One adolescent commits suicide every two hours. Cluster suicides, as in Leominster, have also continued to climb since the first documented case in Berkeley, California, in 1966. In Plano, Texas, seven occurred in one year. Three teenagers ended their lives in five days in Omaha, Nebraska. In New York's Putnam and Westchester counties, there were five in one month.

But why has Leominster joined this select and tragic group? For one thing, it has a very low residential turnover rate. Many kids in town will go to work in the factories after graduating from high school. It's impossible to know how youngsters interpret these circumstances, of course. But whatever Leominster's particular source of pain, its teenage suicide rate right now is ten times the national average.

Jeffrey Bernier was Leominster's first. On February 22, 1984, Jeff and his friends gathered in the Bernier family's second-story tenement, in the heart of Leominster's French Hill, which was built in the mid-nineteenth century to house Canadian laborers. School had let out early. Jeffrey took a .357 Colt revolver from his father's gun collection and began playing Russian roulette. Ignoring pleas from his friends to stop, Jeffrey placed the muzzle to his throat and pulled the trigger. The bullet passed through his skull and lodged in the ceiling. Jeffrey was fourteen. A teacher described him as a normal boy and an average student who "liked machine shop very much." Jeffrey's father said he had warned his son never to point a gun, at anyone.

Two weeks later, on March 7, 1984, Michael J. Bresnahan, also a freshman at the Trade High School's auto body shop, cut classes with a group of friends.

They went to the apartment of Matt Fallon, who wasn't home. There, Alan Arsenault picked up a .30-caliber rifle and shot Michael in the chest. A close friend said they were all very stoned, that it was an accident. Bresnahan's mother described her son as "a good little boy" who was looking forward to his sixteenth birthday and a job that awaited him at a local gas station. "It's a waste of life," she said.

Two months later, on May 11, 1984, the first double suicide struck Leominster. Trade school seniors Scott Nichols and David Dombrowick drove into the concrete loading dock of the RVJ trucking company at what police called "a very high rate of speed." A friend who had been with Scott and David earlier said that they had been driving around, planning their graduation parties (only a few weeks away) and getting high. They had shared seven joints between them in under an hour.

Scott Nichols had been depressed for a long time and had talked about killing himself for over a year. He had recently lost his job, and his girlfriend had split with him. His friends said he also had problems at home.

"After it happened," says Todd Holman, a 1984 graduate who knew both boys from the trade school, "Scott seemed like the person it would have happened to." Both Scott and David had reputations as "serious partiers." Says Holman, "Better life to them just meant better drugs—better mescaline, better pot." But like many of the people who knew him, Holman believes David Dombrowick never intended to kill himself. "People don't like to do things alone in life," Holman says. "Adults don't want to live alone. Kids don't like to be alone, either. Scott just didn't want to die by himself."

The Poirier-Maillet suicides followed, bringing the total number of deaths to six. The year after the girls' double suicide was particularly difficult for the high school, says Assistant Principal Peter S. Michaels. Some students made bizarre claims that they were approached by six men in hooded black capes, carrying swords, with the number six scrawled on their foreheads in blood. For weeks after the supposed visit of the hooded men, students unscrewed number nines from the building and turned them upside down. Some students removed numbers from the classroom doors, exempting six. Others drew sixes on their notebooks and papers. They wrote notes to their dead friends on what is sometimes referred to as The Wall, a long cinder-block corridor in the basement of the main school: "Why did you guys leave us?" "We miss you!" "Melissa and Melody live on!"

Nine months passed before Leominster witnessed its seventh teenage death, suicide number five. (Jeffrey Bernier's death in the game of Russian roulette was officially ruled an accident, while Alan Arsenault, who shot Michael Bresnahan, has been convicted of manslaughter.) On August 14, 1985, Randy Cleremont and three friends sat on the railroad tracks behind Nashua Street, drinking. A train approached and they moved. Randy jumped back onto the tracks as the train sped nearer. Thrown twenty-nine feet, he struck a utility pole and slid down a dirt embankment. His friends said he was not drunk. They said he had heard their screams. They said that Randy saw the train, and that he did not want to move.

Two months later, on October 23, 1985, John P. Finn, fifteen, and a friend who remains unidentified walked out of their third-period trade class. Leaving the school by a side entrance, they turned right and traced the battered picket fence circling the wide arch of road leading downtown. They took a left at the first variety store they came upon, passed the recently closed Carter Junior High School, and soon arrived at the home of a friend named Billy Lovetro. John Finn started to tease his friend with a .38-caliber revolver. Feeling uncomfortable, the boy went out on the porch. He heard a shot and told a neighbor to call an ambulance immediately, then ran to school to get help. Finn was Leominster's eighth death in twenty months, suicide number six.

John Finn had been living with the Lovetro family because he had been having problems at home.

The local newspaper mentioned John's lingering trademark—"an incredible smile."

On December 31, 1985, Billy Lovetro followed his best friend's lead—he drove into a concrete wall. Earlier, Billy is said to have taken a girlfriend to the spot on Adams Street where the wall stood and had told her, "This is where I'm going to do it." Leominster's superintendent of schools told a reporter, "I just don't know what to do anymore."

The school had handled the first death like any other—a moment of silence in the morning, a planned yearbook dedication, the morning announcement about calling hours. With the second, officials mandated the same procedure and prayed it would be the last. When Melody and Melissa died, the school established a Sudden Death Protocol. The steps, according to guidance counselor Patricia Pothier, were simple: "Don't call school off. Don't lower the flag. Play it low key without being callous. No glamour."

■ ■ ■

Dr. Pamela Cantor of Newton, Massachusetts, is former president of the American Association of Suicidology. Cantor says there is a contagion effect in these situations. "They must not treat the kid as a hero," she says. "The school must explain the event not as an act of intelligence or coherence but as a tragedy that was the result of stupidity." Calling school off,

dedicating the yearbook—such actions, Cantor believes, only heighten the effect of making the dead kid popular. "If you take a kid who is very troubled, with no stature or identity in school," she says, "he sees how the suicides are the center of attention. Other kids might get carried away in the emotion of it all. Their fragility in their depression allows them to see suicide as a model."

In the high school corridors, at hangouts around town, and on the street, the suicides are clearly on the minds of Leominster's teenagers. And they want to talk about it. "Subconsciously, in everyone's mind now, suicide is an option," says Diana DeSantis, a 1986 graduate of Leominster High who was vice-president of her class for four years. "You're upset. You say, 'I'm depressed.' You tell your mother, and it doesn't help. You tell your teacher, maybe, and it doesn't help. So you tell a friend, maybe even a professional—the same. Suicide might be next on the list. It's just higher up on your list of options in Leominster than anywhere else."

"How can you ever get used to it?" asks Matt Mazzaferro, another 1986 graduate, now attending Brandeis. "We were shocked every time. Each one was a whole different person." Mazzaferro modifies the assertion that his peers were looking for glamour. "They were just looking not to be another face in the crowd," he said. "That was their way to make noise." Often, the methods of their deaths are more accurately remembered than any aspect of their lives: people ask, "Was that the one who . . .?"

"It was my birthday when that last freshman killed himself," says a junior. "At first I was kinda pissed off, you know, 'cause I wanted to have a wicked great day, but afta homeroom it didn't really matter, I didn't give a shit, really. 'Cause it wasn't like it was new or anything, like the first ones. It didn't wreck my day or nothing."

"After the first few the atmosphere was real gloomy around here," says one secretary at the high school. "But by the third or fourth they got numb to it. It isn't such a big deal to them anymore." As one counselor puts it, "The kids are all suicided out." A student says, "I mean, afta *seven*, what difference does one or two make? Christ, you sit in homeroom and they say we haveta have this moment of silence, and you're like, 'Fuck, not again,' but it doesn't *surprise* you. I mean, it's not like some shock or somethin' when you hear it all the time."

■ ■ ■

Leominster has tried and is still trying. Parents have started support groups; the community has sponsored lectures. The Leominster Youth Committee was formed to look at the problems facing the kids—and then, on March 26, 1986, freshman George Henderson came home from track practice and shot himself in the head, the first suicide in three months.

Henderson's suicide vitiated the by-then usual explanations. The kids who killed themselves had been tough kids—some fought, most drank, most did drugs. They had reputations. Academically, some had special needs. Many of them had problems at home. Diana DeSantis says that, with the exception of George Henderson, all the students who had killed themselves had "the attitude": "They would be the kind of kids who would say, 'Life sucks. Adults suck. The high school sucks. Everything sucks. I just want to party.'"

But George Henderson didn't seem like the other nine at all. He never cut school. He didn't drink or smoke. He was on the honor roll. He was only fourteen and, according to a neighbor, came from a family that "did everything together," from mountain climbing to canoeing. His death seemed to be the one that bothered Leominster's adults most, because George was the first one they really could not understand.

"I don't know why people are so afraid to say it," says one sophomore. "He was the first kid who they didn't think was a real loser."

But the students of Leominster High weren't puzzled by George's suicide. To his peers, he wasn't a model boy—he was a freshman brain who had failed a Spanish quiz, maybe a nice kid, but a nerd, a wimp. His peer category may have been different from that of the students who died before him—he wasn't a burnout, or a head—but in a school that perceives jocks as the in crowd and druggies as cool, George had lost both ways. Being a brain was his marker among the crowd, and faltering grades may have threatened his identity at a time when peer acceptance was acute. "I wouldn't have gotten all upset about getting a warning card or nothing," says a sophomore. "But I can kind of understand how something like that could have really depressed *him*."

"With someone like that you can understand," says a freshman. "School was wicked important and stuff to him."

According to guidance counselors at Leominster High, the deaths have sparked dialogue. They say the students are more willing to talk about their problems, are more alert and more sensitive. "It's brought us closer," says one senior. "All the hugging and crying has made us tighter." But among the students, opinion diverges: "'How are you, are you feeling suicidal today?'" asks a junior sweetly, mocking a counselor. "'I haven't seen you in two years and even though you're flunking all your classes you are doing just fine. Things will be just fine, now, won't they? *Won't* they?'"

Some students harbor anger. They resent the reputation their city has acquired and feel betrayed by the friends who have left them. "Suicide is the ultimate act in selfishness," says a sophomore. "Why bother crying about a selfish brat?" One counselor shares her

favorite explanation: "It's the ultimate temper tantrum," she says. "Kids who can't have their lives the way they want them don't want life at all."

Outside the community, too, the response can be just as cold. Leominster and nearby Fitchburg have one of the oldest high school football rivalries in the nation, and school spirit runs deep. Leominster won the game last year, but Fitchburg got its licks in. KILL LEOMINSTER, read the inscription on the Fitchburg rooters' T-shirts, BEFORE THEY KILL THEMSELVES.

■ ■ ■

The dominating ambience of bewilderment and exhaustion makes Leominster's grief difficult to detect. Many adults refuse to discuss the tragedies at all. One student wrote a letter to the editor of the local newspaper after the death of John Finn, asking the community to confront the dangers rather than run away: "I've never felt such a sense of deep loss, pain or fear as during these three years at Leominster High," the letter read. "It's sad to think that some day our children are going to ask us what high school is like. What will we say? I spent most of my high school years mourning the loss of my friends. . . . Somebody must do something. We need help."

Donald Freed, an English teacher, was so concerned about the section he teaches on existentialism that he has recently modified the course. "Camus and Sartre[1] believe the choice to live is the most profound decision one can make, and you're telling kids that these great thinkers believed the choice must be made every day. That you must get up in the morning and decide whether you're going to go through with it or end it right then and there. That it's up to the individual *alone* to decide. In the context of these tragedies I've become slightly paranoid. How will the students take it? How seriously? How literally? What about the real bright ones? What about the ones who are down?"

Teachers, friends, and parents have substantial cause to worry about overlooking the symptoms. The teenagers who took their lives left plenty of clues first, as 80 percent of all suicides do. But "the problem is," says Patricia Pothier, the guidance counselor, "how do you tell the difference between symptoms of suicidal feelings and the normal business of being a teenager in the eighties?" Although preventive and educational measures are being taken, few Leominster residents feel their little city has witnessed its last teenage

suicide; those most actively involved in the aftermath still anticipate the next one. "I think it'll slow down," says one graduate who enrolled at the University of Massachusetts this fall. "Maybe at the rate of just one or two a year."

On the morning of a recent Samaritan assembly, a pair of sophomores held a homeroom period of their own in the woods, smoking. But then they reentered the building to hear what the Samaritans had to say. "They just said the usual stuff about suicide like they did last time," says a girl named Celeste in the corridor afterward. "It was dumb," her friend Carol adds.

It is time to go. The two girls start walking down the corridor. Carol turns her head when they are halfway down the hall.

"*You* can leave this school anytime you want," she yells. Then she begins to spin. "An-y-ti-me!" she yells, her voice waving louder and softer with her turns. She spins faster, sending her pocketbook flying, then jerks to a halt. The strap wraps tightly around her thin, young waist.

[1]Albert Camus (1913–1960), French philosopher, dramatist, and novelist, won the Nobel Prize in 1957; Jean-Paul Sartre (1905–1980), the French existentialist philosopher, won the Nobel Prize for literature in 1964.

■ ■ ■

This article appeared in New England Monthly, *December 1986. Adrian Nicole LeBlanc is a 1982 graduate of Leominster High School and received degrees from Smith College and Oxford University. LeBlanc wrote this article while an undergraduate at Smith.*

■ ■ ■

RANDY TRAVIS: ON THE OTHER HAND

BY MICHAEL BANE

It is raining in Cuba. Not sprinkles, not showers, but great gusts of tropical rain, sending the banana rats scurrying for the cover of the palm trees and the iguanas back to the shelter of the rocky shoreline. On stage, the water splatters against the sheets of plastic covering the equipment, runs in rivers across the base of the forlorn microphone stand. The last of a dejected contingent of garbage-bag-covered fans, Marines stationed here at Guantanamo Naval Base, file out, grumbling.

"It never rains!" one Marine yells. "It never goddam rains in Cuba!"

But it is raining in Cuba, and inside the cool, hastily assembled but posh dressing room—a spare room in a huge airplane hanger— Lib Hatcher is reminiscing.

"Remember the bread truck, Michael," she says, watching Randy Traywick/Ray/Travis, finish a taped interview for the Guantanamo base television station. "Remember we were so proud of that old bread truck, driving to gigs in that thing."

And I do remember, standing out behind some honky tonk north of Nashville, with Randy practically jumping up and down with excitement.

"Isn't it great?" he kept saying. "A bread truck! Carries all the equipment to the show! It's almost a bus!"

"Remember," Lib says, the rain pouring down outside, postponing the USO show until the next morning. "Remember, we were so broke. I'd sit there at the kitchen table, gather up all the bills and lay them out in front of me. Then we'd figure who got $5 this month. Five dollars here. Five dollars there."

Lib and I huddle in a corner of the dressing room. I have seen the pictures of the house in Maui, which is progressing; have talked about the latest upcoming appearance on *The Tonight Show;* marveled over the sales of the latest album. But, somehow, with the rain pounding down, hard lights shining on a deserted stage, the old times seem a lot closer, as if the saga of Randy Travis and Lib Hatcher were nothing more than a dream, less real than the lightning flashing to the north, towards America.

"You remember it, too, don't you?" Lib is saying. "I can't decide whether it seems a long time ago or yesterday."

The rain pours on.

■ ■ ■

"See," Elizabeth Grant is saying, "to really understand Guantanamo, you've got to understand those red and green sprinkles you put on Christmas cookies . . ."

Elizabeth Grant is married to a Marine who's across the floor of this concrete block honky tonk, the Lateral Hazzard, as it were, tossing darts. She is swaying slightly, as if in response to a whisper of a breeze. I am also swaying, I suspect in response to the local drink of choice, a "fireball," which proves to be cinnamon schnapps mixed with some hellfire-hot Jamaican hot sauce.

"See, when they've got the green sprinkles, they don't have the red sprinkles," Elizabeth Grant continues. "When they finally get the red sprinkles, they'll be out of the green sprinkles. So you never get cookies with red sprinkles and green sprinkles, because one or the other is always 'on the barge.' It's always on the barge . . ."

We have arrived at the Lateral Hazzard, next to the only golf course in the world that requires you to carry, in addition to your clubs, your own sod in the form of a square of Astroturf, because we are celebrities. Well, spin-off celebrities. Randy Travis—who is, wisely it would seem, back in officers' quarters asleep—is the biggest thing to hit the island of Cuba since the bearded man to the north made his big move. The Navy and the Marines are buying big time, and the Travis entourage is holding their own. More or less. Maybe less than more.

With war brewing half a world away, the USO has asked Randy Travis to spend Thanksgiving weekend in Cuba, entertaining the 2,500 troops and 5,000 support personnel stationed there. A USO trip is exactly the opposite of a normal concert tour, where the artist is insulated, for the most part, from the crowds. Part of doing a USO trip is mingling as much as possible. We've only been in the country a few hours, and we've been through two, maybe three parties, a chicken dinner and assorted introductions.

Randy is loving it. He has signed about a million CD and cassette covers, had his picture taken with an endless string of uniformed people and civilians and received more than his share of hugs and kisses. "You mean," says one young female admirer, "he's just standing there? I can go right over there and maul him?"

■ ■ ■

"You know," Lib Hatcher is saying, "sometimes he doesn't seem to have noticed that everything's changed. He still does the same things he always did. In fact, on some things, I think he's getting worse."

The rain continues unabated. Dripping roadies come in, grab a cup of coffee and head back out, getting the equipment under shelter.

"Remember, he was always one to sign autographs," she said. "He'd sign autographs for days unless we made him stop. Now, he can't even be satisfied with that.

He's got to interview the people who ask for an autograph. See if they've got the same cousin or something."

Sure enough, as if on cue, Randy looks up from across the small room, where he's engrossed in conversation with a family who's brought him a CD to sign.

"You know," Randy is saying when he looks up and catches our eye, "my people are from pretty close to there. . . ."

"Hopeless," says Lib, with an exaggerated sigh.

■ ■ ■

"Big night last night?" Randy asks, laughing. I have no comment. We are where you always seem to end up on trips with Randy Travis, at the gym. It is 7 A.M., and we are trying to pump iron to a continuous barrage of Randy Travis songs from the radio. I mean, I like "He Walked on Water" as much as the next guy, but it makes it a little tough to concentrate on biceps. Finally, even Randy, doing seated dumbbell curls, cracks up in helpless laughter.

"I can't get a pump with this music on," he says, laughing.

Maybe, someone else suggests, we can phone in a request for AC/DC.

Despite the orgy of Randy Travis ballads, we suffer through a couple of hours of iron, 'til the shoulders ache and the elbows glow from the exertion. The gym is Randy's salvation, home away from home. The weights don't care

much whether you're a star or not. They don't read Billboard or the National Enquirer.

For people whose weekly workout consists of hoisting a couple of brews on Saturday night, it's hard to explain the appeal of something as simple as lifting weights. Think, though—no crowds, no charts, no producers, no entourage, no excuses. The world may be going crazy around you, but within the confines of the gym, you're in control. Push hard, and see the results; slack off, and lose it.

There is, I think, a strange balance between Randy Travis the performer and Randy Travis the athlete (although Randy Travis scoffs at the notion he's a real athlete—"I just work out," he says). No matter what happens in the outside world, the world of tours and recording sessions, record deals and television shows, there's always the iron waiting. He lifts with quiet intensity, concentrating on correct form, broken only by brief spells of showing us what he's been learning from Chuck Norris.

"Basic kicks and punches, mostly," he says, demonstrating. "Lots of stretches." Chuck, we think, has his work cut out for him. Did you talk to Chuck about movies, I ask.

"Oh," he says, "Lib did. Lib don't miss a chance."

Simple statement, gospel truth. Lib Hatcher has guided—and still guides—Randy Travis' career through the treacherous shoals of Music City. She is part and parcel of the mythology of Randy Travis, the older "Svengali" who may or may not have orchestrated his rise to fame. There are people in Nashville who don't speak all that kindly of Lib Hatcher—she's hard, she's cold, she's tough. Interestingly enough, all these adjectives would be compliments if they were applied to men.

■ ■ ■

Randy Travis wasn't the first of country's "new traditionalists." Before Randy, there were The Judds. Before The Judds, there was George Strait. Before George Strait, Ricky Skaggs. But Randy was the first to really capture the audience's—and the media's—imagination. Not that there was anything wrong with country music in the early 1980's. The pendulum had swung from "outlaw" back to "pop." Willie Nelson played golf. There were still good songs and good singers. But what was missing was a voice, a new George Jones, a new Merle Haggard, a *standard-bearer*.

With "On the Other Hand" and "1982," Randy Travis became that standard-bearer, your basic lightning rod. With his successes, the floodgates opened, and, as it always has, country music changed, evolved. Within a few years, the business belonged to the "men with hats," traditional male vocalists.

But the music business is notoriously fickle. With all the "new" new traditionalists, what was there to say about the "old" new traditionalists? Especially, the one who had hit it big. *The Tonight Show*, network interviews, magazine covers, million-sellers, *Sesame Street* for heaven's sake! Randy Travis had gone from being a "fast train from Carolina" to the very top.

There must, then, be something wrong with him. And the supermarket tabloids will stop at nothing to find out what it is. Their coverage has Lib and Randy a little bit on edge.

"We don't talk about it," says Lib. "When people ask, we change the subject."

This is the same Lib Hatcher who, according to the supermarket tabloids, was tossed into the streets by a vengeful Randy Travis.

"Do I look like I've been tossed into the streets?" she says.

This is also the same Lib Hatcher who went to a costume party dressed in dozens of issues of the *National Enquirer*. She looked great.

"Ask Randy about it," she says. "It's up to him whether he wants to talk about it."

I do corner him and broach the subject, and he doesn't laugh it off.

"In a way," he says, "I try not to ever think about it. I try to ignore them—it's such a farce. I've never been in restaurants these newspapers said I was in; certainly never had a fight in them. A fight in a restaurant! You've known me a long time. How many fights in restaurants have I had?"

He smiles about the articles, but it's not a happy smile.

"I tell you this, Michael," he says. "If the person who wrote those things was with us right now, it would be hard for me not to remark about it."

So reporters call the office, see, and ask for Lib Hatcher.

"I take the calls," she says, "and then they don't have anything to say. I guess they're surprised I'm not off tossed in the street somewhere."

"Basically, you have some success," says Randy, "and people start looking for the bad as well as the good."

He does laugh, though, at the introduction of an authorized version of his life, *Randy Travis: The King of New Country Traditionalists.*

The writer, Don Cusic, stages an uninvited visit to Randy's family home in North Carolina, where Harold Traywick, Randy's dad, gives him the unceremonious boot.

"It is obvious that this is not a man to reason with," Cusic writes. "There is a violence about him you can feel in his presence. I turn, and as I head toward my car, I listen for a click, hoping he has left his gun inside the house. . . ."

Randy laughs.

"Daddy did run him off," he says. "And said several choice words. But that book kind of made me mad. We didn't cooperate with the guy one bit. Wouldn't talk to him."

We talk for a while about singing, about technique. His singing strength has improved since he was diagnosed as having an allergy to a number of common foods, including dairy products. The result is a very strict, low cholesterol, no-sweets diet that is, by his own admission, tough to stick to on the road.

"Like for Thanksgiving, I ate whatever I wanted," he says, "and I felt really, really bad. But, you know, after two years on the diet, it's getting easier and easier to sing. When I started singing, I thought you just *sang*, you know, like you talked. Boy, forget that! Technique, practice, learn more technique."

In the meantime, life's pretty good on the Randy front. Randy's got a couple of good cutting horses at the farm in Tennessee, and he'd like to spend a little more time there, riding.

We work out. We shoot pool—I lose, with amazing regularity. We worry about sneakers for running—he favors Brooks; I'm a Nike guy. We discuss custom gunsmiths and Randy's maybe movie career—"a western, of course." We compare karate moves. We laugh about our cattle drive together in Montana, filmed for The Nashville Network—"the worst horse I've ever ridden"; his friendship with Roy Rogers—"you know, he's just like I expected him to be"—and how I talked Lib and public relations wiz Evelyn Shriver into riding horses with me—"don't ever do it again." After six years caught in the gears of the star-making machinery, Randy Travis is the same Randy Travis I met in a honky tonk in Chattanooga, singing old Hank songs in front of a disco house band. We have traveled to Cuba, Grand Cayman and a place in Canada where the air was so polluted that the white birch trees were black (this is true), and, strangely enough, we've always had a great time.

"I swear," says an exasperated Lib Hatcher. "Sometimes I think he's oblivious to it all."

"You got to come to Nashville," Randy Travis is saying, "and spend some time. I've got this cutting horse that would be perfect for you. I mean, I'll teach you how to *really* ride."

I think I'll take him up on it.

It's hot in Cuba, blistering hot, the iguanas seeking whatever meager shade the cactuses and rocks offer. Across the bay, the mountains, where Fidel and the mysterious and romantic Che Guevara once plotted revolution, are lost in heat haze. On a stage in a huge aircraft hanger, Randy Travis is singing "An American Trilogy." In the audience, a woman in camouflage fatigues wipes her eyes, but quickly, lest anyone notice.

When he finishes, the ovation goes on for a long time.

■ ■ ■

This article first appeared in Country Music *magazine. Michael Bane is a full-time freelancer in Tampa, Florida.*

PUT IT INTO PRACTICE

Discussion

1. Two of the most common problems in interviewing come from subjects who won't open up at all and those who are quite the opposite, talking incessantly. It is difficult to get very much in the way of productive quotes from the first sort, and all too easy to get a lot of information, most of it useless, from the second.

   Discuss with the other writers in your class or writers' club how you would handle each kind of subject. Try to come up with helpful hints that utilize your communications skills to make for a productive interview.

   Assign someone to play the role of a reticent subject, and practice getting the person to open up. Try out some of the techniques mentioned in chapter one.

   Assign someone to play the role of an overly talkative subject, and practice getting under control the information the person offers. Again, try out some of the techniques mentioned in chapter one.

2. Some media critics might reasonably question the statement made in chapter one that interviewing "is very much a matter of manipulation. You are trying to get the subject to say things that are useful and important to you in the story you are about to write."

   Discuss the idea of controlling and/or manipulating the interview. Is that kind of manipulation unfair or unwise? Will you miss out on something by forcing the interview in a certain direction?

   What are the benefits of controlling the interview? What are the drawbacks?

Exercises

1. You have been given an assignment to do a magazine story on author Tony Hillerman. You have one week to prepare.
   a. Prepare a one-page background biography of Hillerman, including a bibliography.
   b. One week gives you time to read at least one of his novels, and probably two. Summarize in one page each what you have learned about the author by reading those novels. List a few questions that have come from your reading.
   c. List the people you will call for information about Hillerman.

2. Hillerman has agreed to spend several hours with you. Describe the kind of interview setup you will ask for, and tell why you would like that particular format.

3. Describe the kinds of sights and sounds that you will look for with Hillerman. Be as specific as you can about those sensory images, and then tell why they are particularly relevant to your story.

SEARCH TERMS:
RESEARCH FOR MAGAZINES

NARROW THE FOCUS

THE PAPER TRAIL

DETECTIVE WORK

Writer Joe Bargmann sat in his small apartment in St. Louis and watched on the evening news as a videotape shot by a bystander showed Los Angeles police officers arresting and beating suspect Rodney King.

The images of what seemed to be an abusive police department were strong ones, and Bargmann, a writer who specializes in investigative magazine pieces, saw a possible connection between the Los Angeles violence and recent local instances when the St. Louis Police Department had been accused of using violence to coerce confessions.

Bargmann talked it over with his editor at *St. Louis* magazine. As he recalls, "We had been interested for a while in doing a piece on police abuse, and the impact of the Rodney King case, I knew, made the story that much more viable. The L.A. incident was violence wrought for a different purpose, of course. But, basically, it seemed that police activity was coming under more scrutiny than ever before."

The editor agreed, so Bargmann decided "to do a story on how often this occurs, a big-picture kind of piece. I thought I'd talk to a bunch of lawyers, cops, judges, and victims of alleged brutality to get a good, broad perspective."

It all seemed pretty straightforward at that point. But Bargmann was soon to find out that his research would lead him in quite another direction, toward an even more powerful story.

In New York, recent Hofstra University graduate Sandra Donnelly left her editor's office at *Working Woman* magazine with her latest assignments, one of them to find out what part of the engineering field held the most job opportunities for women. Her story would be in the magazine's annual listing of the twenty-five hottest careers for women.

Donnelly was tempted to go with electrical engineering, a good field for women engineers and a story that had worked for the magazine before. But Donnelly's research soon sent her off in a different direction.

"I started my research by calling some engineering schools to find out where the student interest was and what new programs they were developing," she recalls. Those calls didn't seem to point toward any one field, but several of them did point toward the same good source.

As Donnelly remembers, "Several of the engineering schools mentioned Tim Brown at the American Society of Civil Engineers, so I talked to him several times. He was the one who led me toward environmental engineering as a subcategory of civil engineering. It was so new it didn't have its own discipline yet."

NARROW THE FOCUS

As writers, both Bargmann and Donnelly knew that the first step in doing research is finding out the broad background of the topic. During that process, they knew, they would begin to narrow things down, perhaps finding a particular aspect of the story—or even a whole new angle that began with such broad research—that would result in a tight, informative story.

Bargmann, for instance, discovered as he did his research that one specific example of injustice kept cropping up. He recalls that it began when "One of the lawyers I happened to speak to had this particular case of the guy who was wrongly imprisoned for two years."

The case sounded interesting, and seemed to focus Bargmann's general interest in the misuse of power by the police. Better still, his research showed a lot of information was available on this specific example of abuse. As Bargmann remembers, "There was pending civil litigation in this case, and you're lucky, as a reporter, when you have a pending case and a cooperative lawyer, because a lot of the documentation is right there. I had depositions, police reports, and, of course, I did my usual newspaper search."

What happened for Bargmann, then, was that what had begun as a broad story on police abuse began to narrow down to a major story on one specific case. As Bargmann worked his way into the research, he began to feel confident that his focus was on a suspect accused, and convicted, of a crime he didn't commit. The resulting story is on page 49.

In a different way, Donnelly's research, too, led her to a more narrow focus. In one sense, Donnelly started farther along the research trail than Bargmann had. As she explains, "I had been in engineering when I was first in college, so I didn't have to do as much background work as I sometimes do just to get to know the jargon and the field."

What she still did have to do, however, was discover which area within engineering seemed best for her story. To do that, she talked "to ten or fifteen people and slowly narrowed that down to Brown and a few others who told me about environmental engineering."

Like Bargmann, Donnelly used her background research—and in her case her own expertise—to narrow down her focus and pick a particular, strong element to follow. From there the story was able to blossom. "Part of what I found out in talking to Brown," she recalls, "was that, first of all, environmental engineering was fairly new, so that meant women could jump in there very easily. Also, there were growing environmental concerns about the problems in Eastern Europe and the cleanup that had to be done there, which meant a lot of jobs."

It wound up being just the sort of job opportunity she wanted to present to the magazine's readers. This story and several others like it that Donnelly has done for *Working Woman* begin on page 67.

As you will see in chapter twelve, by the way, getting a chance to write these short little pieces for *Working Woman* was a major step forward for Donnelly in her career, as she moved from the copyediting duties of a fact-checker to actually writing for the magazine.

Both of these writers routinely go through the hard work of in-depth research, knowing that it will pay off not only in a high-quality story but also in the writing process. Veteran writers know that a wealth of solid research makes writing the story much easier.

Just like in the interviewing process, writers who have done more research than they can really use are paid back during the writing process when a supportive fact is needed and the material—the exactly right material, not just a fact or figure that comes close or might be squeezed into the story—is right at hand.

Think of this part of the research process in the shape of an hourglass, in which a broad topic idea narrows down to one particular focus and then widens again below that as your research brings in more and more information about that focused theme.

THE PAPER TRAIL

Once you've narrowed things down and know just which story line to follow, the next step in researching is to gather as much detailed information as possible on the specific idea. That kind of investigation frequently begins with clips.

Bargmann, who is now senior editor at *Seventeen* magazine, started all of his research at a private library that he paid to belong to when he worked in the Midwest: the library contains the complete files of the *St. Louis Globe Democrat*, a major daily newspaper that went out of business in 1986 after a century of publication.

On the false-arrest story, Bargmann recalls, "There were dozens of clips from the *Globe* files. What I always do is photocopy all the stories in the files and then go through with a highlight pen and highlight every name in the story. Then I make an attempt to contact every one of those people."

In effect, Bargmann accumulates *documentation* and a *source list* for the story at the same time. That kind of research is time-consuming, he admits, but it leaves him with a thick file folder full of facts for each story, as well as a typical basic source list of somewhere around 65 or 70 names. On some stories, that list has increased to more than 125 names. Bargmann tries to call them all.

You will want to do something similar for your stories, putting the effort into a wealth of documentation and a lengthy source list that will not only help you tremendously in your later writing but also help your editor when it comes time to do the necessary fact checking for your story. For beginning writers, a story full of supportive documentation that comes with a source list (and phone numbers) impresses editors—it helps build that critical trust that you want your editor to have in you.

Donnelly's approach is similar, but for her clips she usually starts with NEXIS, a computer network database that *Working Woman* subscribes to. One of the great advantages of such databases is that a writer can simply start the research with a search term ("environmental engineer," for instance, for this particular story), and the computer search reports on all of the magazine and newspaper articles—from a database of thousands

B O X   2 . 1

WALKING THROUGH NEXIS

BY RANDY MILLER

Before an upcoming fun weekend trip, you're trying to finish an article about higher education funding, struggling to remember this wonderful quote you heard last month on a public radio newscast. Suddenly, three editors call with assignments: an essay on North American press freedom geared toward a controversial court case in Canada, a business story on the toy industry, and a personality profile on musician Tim Hauser of the Manhattan Transfer.

Your freelance career is ready to take off with a sonic boom.

In the days of yore, researching such stories would be a killer of your time. You would have:

- Worn out your eyes reading legal indexes.
- Begged your newspaper pals to let you use their electronic library for news clippings.
- Called your sole Canadian contact only to learn the person is vacationing in the States.
- Spent a day scouring microfiche for Manhattan Transfer reviews.
- Spent hours looking at musicians' biographical indexes.
- Called National Public Radio (NPR) to see if by way of a small miracle, someone had kept that story on tape.

And you hadn't even thought about the toy industry story yet. Better cancel that weekend trip.

Fortunately, today you have access to news database services like NEXIS. You may not solve every problem, but it can handle these research needs in an hour or so.

NEXIS is accessed through Mead Data Central's Meadnet. The software includes response prompts and will even help correct some basic errors in response formats. Libraries, universities, large corporations, and law firms are more likely than individuals to use the service, which can be expensive.

First, you should decide which categories—called libraries and files by NEXIS—to explore. The service lists some basic libraries: news, business, company, industry, people, political, international, legal, medical, and patent. Within those are numerous files—specific databases—of information.

For example, in the basic news library (also called NEXIS), your choices include major papers, newspapers, magazines, newsletters, wires, transcripts, Midwestern newspapers, Northeastern newspapers, Southeastern newspapers, and Western newspapers. In the international listing, you may choose among categories of most continents as well as Canada and the Middle East. Under politics, you can find listings for the three branches of government as well as transcripts of politically oriented newscasts.

In fact, the amount of information is almost too large to describe. After you choose a library and file, the NEXIS program asks you to enter a phrase, presumably the subject you're researching.

Because of the vastness of the NEXIS database, it cuts off searches that result in more than 1,000 responses. And users pay for each search. Therefore, good database search strategy becomes important—especially if your library doesn't have its own search consultant. NEXIS, like many databases, offers several options to searchers.

- You may link phrases through the use of "AND," "OR," or "W/" (Amtrak AND Alabama; Doctor OR Physician; Hallmark W/ Christmas). These more narrowly define your topic.
- You may use a universal character such as ! on the NEXIS system. "Transport!" would give you stories with not only the word "transport," but also the words "transporting," "transportation," and "transported."
- You may specify a search by date. On NEXIS, such searches may be ordered by a specific date, month, and/or year as well as before or after a specific date.
- You may also run a segment search, which looks for phrases in headlines, in bylines, and in text.

NEXIS reports its hits in full text, when possible, or in citations. A search for advertising guru and humorist Stan Freberg would highlight his name in the text as well as provide a publication and date.

In the example that began this discussion, an afternoon on

Continued

Continued

NEXIS replaces the days of searching. Searches under business and company give you a financial picture of leading toy manufacturers or a general idea to build on.

Your press freedom essay can start by examining Canadian news about the controversial news ban concerning the Paul Teale–Karla Homolka trial and can gain strength by studying the latest U.S. legal opinions in press law by searching the legal categories, which include several weekly law publications.

A quick search of the Allbio (biography) file in the people library shows a fairly detailed history of the Manhattan Transfer as well as several interviews that quote Hauser. You learn his voice changed somewhat when he quit smoking recently and that he drove a cab in New York before the group formed. You have good icebreaker topics that will make you seem as if you had seriously delved into his career.

That pesky NPR quote? You found it with a date search in NPR transcripts in the political library. It turns out it was part of a lengthy interview with the secretary of education that helped fill out your story wonderfully.

And you had a great time on that weekend trip.

---

of such publications—that used that term. Research that once took days is therefore accomplished in a few minutes.

Donnelly says that in her job as editorial assistant at *Working Woman,* "I use NEXIS four or five times a week, sometimes in my own research and sometimes for other editors who are looking for information.

"With NEXIS I can go do a search when I'm doing a profile, for instance, and just see what comes up. Not only do you get facts and information; it helps you later when you talk to someone. You can say, 'Oh, I read in that article in that magazine that you said this and that,' and it gets them talking on the subject."

Like Bargmann, Donnelly follows up that first step in her research with a source list, accumulating names and phone numbers of people she can contact to get quotes and other supportive documentation.

To construct that list, she and Bargmann both begin with names from the clips or from other sources (such as universities, government bodies, businesses, or whatever seems relevant) and then start making phone calls. Frequently, one phone call leads to several more as the experts they contact mention other experts who might provide information or quotes.

That technique of using each basic source as the starting point for a continual branching out of further sources is one you will want to practice. It will give you far more research than you can possibly use, and that, as you already know, is all to the good because it gives you more options in your later writing.

DETECTIVE WORK

[handwritten note: ✗ ask who else to talk to at end of interview]

There's likely to be more to research than just clips and phone calls, of course. Sometimes the reporter really has to dig for information. Bargmann's story, which follows court cases that involved arrest of a murder suspect, is a good example of one that required solid detective work.

"In this story," Bargmann says, "the lawyer had given me a bunch of files, everything contained in the court file. That's all strictly public record, so I could have gone down to the federal courthouse and gotten it, but it was just easier to have a friendly lawyer.

"This was a really rich case file. The great thing about when a case goes into this kind of further litigation, beyond the actual criminal stage, is that much of the evidence used in trial ends up becoming part of the public record through the process of discovery between the lawyers."

That meant Bargmann had stacks of evidence to wade through. He points out, "There were also police reports, various depositions and that sort of thing; it was a lot of stuff."

The story that resulted from all this was, Bargmann says, "really a classic sort of investigative piece, because it combined a lot of legwork with some knowledge and some ability to obtain and use documents."

With all that material to use, Bargmann says the writer's job is "something like what a lawyer would do when preparing for a trial: you sift through anything you have, sift through different accounts of the crime, and then you piece together a narrative of how it all went."

For Bargmann, "Where the various accounts start to diverge, that's where you have to concentrate your reporting. So, that's what I did."

Bargmann explains to his readers how he did his research. Notice how he points out where he gathered the information he presents. This not only adds to the readability of the story by giving it the kind of specific details that bring it alive, but also builds trust between the reader and the writer. We tend to believe what Joe Bargmann tells us, because he backs it up with proof. Look at this example:

> In a sworn statement on file in St. Louis Circuit Court, Ferndo says he was "beat up" by Cummings in the interrogation room. In interviews for this story, Ferndo has offered specifics. Cummings says he did not hit Ferndo.

The use of mention of a sworn statement effectively convinces the reader that Bargmann is to be trusted. Similarly, throughout this piece Bargmann uses a series of attributing qualifiers such as "According to Cummings' police report" (page 50), "In a lawsuit filed last year in United States District Court" (page 51), and others. In fact, in one stretch of the story, he refers to Cummings' report at least four times, hammering home for the reader that the evidence the writer is presenting is valid.

Donnelly says she enjoys the detective work involved in ferreting out details. In fact, she has a reputation for that at *Working Woman* magazine.

"I'm a tracker," she says. "If they need something tracked down at the magazine, they give it to me. That kind of hunting for the story, being on the go with it, really appeals to me. It's the kind of in-depth thing that magazines do best."

Sometimes the research goes well, and the details flow in. At other times writers find that even the smallest of details can prove hard to come by. Donnelly recalls the time the magazine ran a beauty article about base makeup. Her editor thought she recalled that presidential candidate Richard Nixon had worn such makeup during the Kennedy-Nixon presidential debate of 1960.

"They had me calling all over the country to find out what kind of makeup Kennedy and Nixon were wearing," she says. "I started with the Nixon Library, and they just laughed at me and hung up. So then I called Max Factor, thinking they might have it, but they didn't. Then I called the TV station where the debate was held, and the makeup guy who did them was still around but he couldn't remember. Finally, I ended up talking to the Kennedy Library, and the librarian there thought it was a challenge and found a very small reference for me that cleared it up."

Donnelly is convinced that fact-checking work is useful for a beginning writer. Not only does it give you a wealth of firsthand practice in research methods, Donnelly points out, but "It also really hones your interview skills. Sometimes the people you interview are annoyed. They feel they've talked to someone about this already, and you have to diplomatically get them to confirm the information without getting them all hyper about being misquoted or something."

Donnelly adds, "I've had people yell at me and ask to see the manuscript" (a request she has politely refused, by the way). Basically, as she puts it, "You just have to let them know that you're not out to get them and you just want to confirm the facts."

Since her days as a fact checker for *Working Woman*, Donnelly has moved on to an editorial position at Ziff-Net Publishing. Her fact-checking background, she says not only looked good on her résumé but also helped prepare her for that editing career.

■   ■   ■

THE WRONG MAN

BY JOE BARGMANN

In the early evening of March 24, 1986, Steve Ferndo was trailing three friends out of an apartment on South Grand Boulevard when Detective Don Cummings and his partner, Jackie Hendricks, pulled up in an unmarked car.

When his friends recognized the cops and warned Ferndo, he ducked back inside, reached in his pocket and gobbled ten tabs of Valium he had there.

At the car, Ferndo has said in several interviews, Cummings shoved him and said, "Where's my gun?"

"What? I don't have your gun," Ferndo recalls saying.

Ferndo says Cummings pulled out a pistol, cocked it and foisted the barrel in Ferndo's face, saying, "Here it is."

Ferndo remembers hearing a *click.*

On the way to the station, Ferndo asked: "What did I do?"

"You know what you did," Ferndo remembers Cummings saying. "You killed that fag."

A month earlier, the detective had questioned Ferndo about the murder of Robert Oxenhandler, who was found stabbed to death in his home on January 30, 1986. Police had discovered a nude

picture of Ferndo at the scene, but he denied everything.

This time, Ferndo says, he was seated and cuffed to a table in an interrogation room at the St. Louis Police Department. Ferndo says Detective Hendricks left the room. Cummings paced, back and forth, back and forth.

In a sworn statement on file in St. Louis Circuit Court, Ferndo says he was "beat up" by Cummings in the interrogation room. In interviews for this story, Ferndo has offered specifics. Cummings says he did not hit Ferndo.

Ferndo says Cummings stopped suddenly and swung up from the waist, backhanding him across the face.

"What did I do?" Ferndo says he asked, tears filling his eyes.

"C'mon," Ferndo recalls Cummings saying, "you know what you did. Just confess to it."

"I didn't do nothing."

Cummings backhanded him again, Ferndo says. He walked behind Ferndo, shoved his head toward the table. Then, Ferndo says, Cummings left.

When he returned, Ferndo says, he carried in several boxes. Big envelopes marked EVIDENCE. An umbrella. He lined up a few

Polaroids on the table, face down.

"Did you pose nude?" Cummings asked.

"No," Ferndo said. "No one takes pictures of me naked."

"You didn't let Robert Oxenhandler take nude pictures of you?"

"No."

Ferndo says Cummings turned the photos face up.

"He paid me," Ferndo said. "I needed the money."

Cummings read from his reports, confronted Ferndo with statements from several people who said they had heard Ferndo brag about stabbing a gay man.

Ferndo laughed. He denied telling anyone about any stabbing, said whoever said anything like that must be lying.

Ferndo says Cummings picked up the umbrella, asked whether Ferndo had told someone about stabbing Oxenhandler with it. "I never said anything about stabbing nobody with an umbrella," Ferndo remembers replying.

Ferndo says Hendricks then clipped a sample of Ferndo's hair for evidence, and left the room.

"Man, you are [screwing] up," Ferndo recalls Cummings saying. Ferndo says the detective raised his hand again. Ferndo flinched. "You're going to prison for the rest of your life. That is if you don't end up on Death Row. Big guys in there are going to be [raping] you. You're gonna be a little punk."

"What am I supposed to say? I didn't do anything."

"All you have to say is 'I did it,'" Ferndo remembers Cummings saying. "We can clean this thing up."

"But I didn't do anything," Ferndo said.

Cummings unshackled Ferndo and led him down a hall, toward the Prisoner Processing window. Hendricks walked ahead of them, disappeared into an office near the window.

Before they reached the booking window, Ferndo says in his sworn statement, Cummings slapped Ferndo in the face and said: "Do you want to go to prison for the rest of your life?"

"What am I supposed to say?" Ferndo recalls asking.

"When the other detective comes out, you just say you killed [Oxenhandler], that you just can't keep it inside anymore."

Cummings and Ferndo stepped closer to the window. Hendricks stepped out of the office.

"He's got something to say," Ferndo recalls Cummings saying to Hendricks. The detectives looked at Ferndo.

According to Cummings' police report, Ferndo said: "I killed him. I stabbed him. I killed Oxenhandler. I can't keep this inside of me anymore."

■　■　■

About two hours later, at 11 P.M., Ferndo sat in front of a video camera in a room at the St. Louis Police Academy, next door to headquarters at Clark and Tucker. His cheeks were red and puffy.

A single microphone stood on the small table in front of him. Ferndo barely looked all of his eighteen years. Not a big person to begin with, he shrank between the detectives.

Cummings placed a legal pad on the table in front of himself and Ferndo. And as the detective checked off details of the crime, contained in a list on the legal pad, Ferndo glanced over from time to time, apparently following the detective's lead, and gave a detailed confession to the crime.

Ferndo spoke haltingly and without emotion. When he offered a statement inconsistent with the physical evidence—for instance, that he delivered the final, fatal stabs in the bedroom—Cummings reminded him that the body was found in the living room, and said to Ferndo: "In an earlier statement, you told us. . . ." Having stated the facts, Cummings then asked Ferndo, "Is that correct?"

Ferndo replied emphatically, "Yes. Yessir. That's right."

■ ■ ■

St. Louis Assistant Circuit Attorney Dee Hayes had the taped confession, four witnesses prepared to testify that Ferndo had bragged about stabbing someone, and blood and hair samples linking Ferndo to the crime scene.

Assistant Public Defender Retta-Rae Randall, Ferndo's attorney, had her client's version of

how he had been forced into admitting something he had nothing to do with. (In a pretrial hearing to determine whether the videotaped confession would be allowed as evidence before a jury, Cummings testified that the confession was not coerced.) Randall also had discrepancies between Ferndo's confession and the physical evidence, as well as new tests refuting the initial evaluations of the blood and hair samples.

The lawyers cut a deal.

Ferndo would enter an Alford plea to a reduced charge of second-degree murder, conceding not that he killed Oxenhandler, but that the evidence was strong enough for a jury to find him guilty. In exchange, Ferndo would be sentenced to twenty years in prison—a far cry from the possibility of execution, or life without parole, if he had chanced going to trial on a first-degree murder charge.

On June 25, 1987, after more than a year in custody, Ferndo rode with a busload of other inmates into the prison compound at Moberly, Missouri.

On February 25, 1988, a 23-year-old man named Douglas Weems confessed to killing Robert Oxenhandler. Four days later, Ferndo was released from prison.

■ ■ ■

In a lawsuit filed last year in United States District Court, Ferndo claims Don Cummings "assaulted, beat and threatened to cause [Ferndo's] death" after instructing him exactly what it was he was supposed to confess to. The suit also names as a defendant Donna Bell, a police department crime lab employee, who allegedly "prepared a false report that blood samples from the scene of the crime were consistent with [Ferndo's] blood."

Cummings refused to be interviewed at length for this story, but in a brief telephone conversation in May, he denied any wrongdoing, and said he still believes Ferndo committed the murder. Bell also denied any wrongdoing.

Still, five and a half years after Robert Oxenhandler was stabbed to death, questions persist. Why did he have nude photos of Ferndo? What prompted Ferndo to brag to friends that he'd "stabbed a fag"? And if he was innocent, why would Ferndo enter an Alford plea?

Finally, what forces—in the police department, in the judicial system, in Ferndo's own twisted past—conspired to lock him in a Kafkaesque nightmare that, even today, more than three years after his release from prison, shows little sign of abating?

■ ■ ■

Steve Ferndo was born November 19, 1967, the son of a father who drank heavily and gambled, and a mother who married four times and divorced three. As a boy, he attended at least four St. Louis schools, moving from institution to institution, as he, his mother and sister moved from apartment to apartment on the south side.

Before he reached the eighth grade, he was smoking marijuana. After less than a year at Roosevelt High School, Ferndo dropped out and began spending much of his time in the streets. He started using heavier drugs, cocaine now and then, sometimes Valium.

About the time of his fourteenth birthday, Ferndo turned to prostitution to pay for his increasingly bad drug habit. Mostly, he worked the streets near Tower Grove Park.

At fifteen, he was married at City Hall to a woman eleven years his senior. The marriage was based on a shared addiction. Both were mainlining drugs: downers, cocaine, Preludin.

It was about this time that Ferndo met David Mutrux. The friendship was cemented quickly; drugs provided the bond.

In the mid-1980s, in the seedy culture of male prostitution and drug abuse around Tower Grove Park, Mutrux says he was a sort of guardian of the young street-walkers. A police report notes that Mutrux was known to some as "The Queen of the Fags." Ferndo became Mutrux's sometimes lover.

The police were aware of Ferndo's prostitution, and they knew he and Mutrux were heavily into drugs. But Ferndo and Mutrux also acted as informants for at least two St. Louis vice detectives and, in turn, escaped arrest.

In the summer of 1985, Ferndo was seventeen, not smart but streetwise, a junkie and hustler well known to the police. That's when he met Robert Oxenhandler.

Oxenhandler was born November 13, 1952, in St. Louis, one of three sons of Clayton real estate magnate Zale Oxenhandler. A family member who requested anonymity says Robert "was very bright, but impatient." Before reaching his teens, Robert had amassed a "huge" collection of 45s. He ran up big phone bills on the family line, calling disc jockeys around the country. At sixteen, he dropped out of Ladue High School to pursue a career in radio.

By the time he reached his early twenties, Oxenhandler had adopted an alias, Bobby Hattrick, and he was showing promise as a radio programmer. In the early '70s, he became music director of KSLQ radio in St. Louis. He was fired in 1976 and moved to Minneapolis, Minnesota, where he worked for a Doubleday broadcasting station. In 1977, he returned to St. Louis and took over as station manager of KWK, then in competition with KSHE for honors as the top rock 'n' roll radio station in town.

"In 1980, Bobby peaked," says Joel Denver, a columnist with *Radio and Records* magazine. Oxenhandler was appointed national program director of the Doubleday network, and his radio research earned him a national reputation. In 1981, Oxenhandler left Doubleday to start his own consulting firm.

Oxenhandler often worked more than twelve hours a day, and he was at it seven days a week. His personal life was another story.

"Bobby could read people very well," says a former friend and coworker who requested anonymity. "He knew that his sexual preferences would not, could not be accepted by the [radio] industry. He arranged his life so he could have both. This meant secrecy, deceit and cynicism."

Ed Walter, a longtime friend, says Oxenhandler began an unabashed tour of the underground in 1984, soon after moving to a rehabbed old house on Shenandoah Avenue, near Tower Grove Park. Oxenhandler, whom friends described as a "health nut" and "vitamin freak," bought Valiums by the thousands, cooked cocaine so he could smoke it, bought the finest marijuana.

Walter says Oxenhandler also "started getting promiscuous." He preferred young men, even boys. Driving a jet black Corvette, he picked up male prostitutes on Grand Boulevard, near Tower Grove Park, and took them back to his house, where he had sex with them, got high with them and sometimes photographed or videotaped them. He set up a telephone message service to take calls exclusively from hustlers.

"It was easy for Bob," Walter says. "He was very charismatic.

He could talk a blue streak. He knew music and had all this expensive stereo equipment. The boys were impressed.

"At first I think it was fun for him," Walter says. "He talked to me about it. Then, I think, things changed. He didn't tell me any more. I think it got a little out of hand."

■ ■ ■

The firefighters found Oxenhandler's body, riddled with more than 150 stab wounds. He had died on the living room floor, on his back, the broken neck of a bottle five inches from his head, wearing nothing but a pair of white socks and a long-sleeved shirt, unbuttoned and saturated with blood.

The fire at 4526 Shenandoah was reported just after 5 P.M., January 30, 1986. About an hour later, Don Cummings arrived at the scene.

Bloodstains started in the bedroom, trailed through another small room and ended in the living room, at the front door. Furniture was toppled, papers and record albums were strewn about. A bloody sock was draped over a doorknob. Many of the stab wounds were in pairs. Oxenhandler had been stabbed in the neck, chest, face, belly and back.

Outside, beneath a broken stained-glass window, shards of a bottle littered the sidewalk, and the smell of gasoline was strong. A Molotov cocktail, made by someone who knew how. Its broken neck still held the wick: cloth neatly rolled around a cotton strand, folded in half, the ends shoved inside the bottle.

Inside the back door, a room with a computer was charred. A broken 7-Up bottle was found on the floor, pieces of the glass bearing the scent of gasoline, and the neck was found with a burned wick inside. Molotov cocktail number two.

On the sidewalk in front of the house, Cummings interviewed friends of Oxenhandler's who had seen the televised news report. In his official report, Cummings notes, "It was learned that the victim was a homosexual who often picked up various sexual partners. He often brought them back to his apartment."

A house-to-house canvass of the neighborhood turned up only one person, identified as Secret Witness #1 in Cummings' report, who had seen or heard anything useful to the investigation. The witness was taking off her roller skates on the front steps of her house, in the 4500 block of Tower Grove Place, when she heard a loud "boom." She saw a man running from the back yard of Oxenhandler's house and through her yard. She described the man as white, in his twenties or early thirties, approximately six feet tall, of medium build, black or dark-brown hair with a tail down the back, moustache.

The next day, Detective Sergeant Steve Jacobsmeyer, two

other investigators and Officer Timothy Zoll went to Oxenhandler's home to gather more evidence. From the living room, they took the overturned chrome stool that had been at the computer stand, beneath the stained-glass window. There were two bloody, partial handprints on either side of the seat.

In the room between the bedroom and the living room, beneath a pile of papers, Zoll discovered a pair of scissors, one of the blades snapped off about three inches from the point.

On February 6, Cummings learned from a department fingerprint specialist that the prints on the stool had been smeared intentionally. The same day, lab results came back showing that human hairs recovered from the scene—most notably those stuck to Oxenhandler's fingers by dried blood—did not match the victim's hair, were chemically treated and were "of a blond or reddish tint." Also that day, an arson detective confirmed that the liquid used to set the fire was gasoline.

The physical evidence was coming together nicely. Now Cummings needed to work on a suspect. Murder victims almost always know their killers, so a logical place to start was a group of photographs of young men seized at Oxenhandler's house.

Cummings had shown the pictures to vice detectives Julie Rensing and Steve Strehl, who identified a young, blond man in one of the photos as Steve Ferndo. The detectives told Cummings, according to his report, that Ferndo was "capable of the murder," heavily into drugs and, when high, volatile.

Cummings also heard Ferndo's name from a fellow detective, Gary Poelling. Poelling's snitch, David Mutrux, had called Poelling when he heard about the Oxenhandler murder. He gave the detective the names of young men who hustled in Tower Grove Park, some of whom had been to Oxenhandler's house. Ferndo's name was among them.

On February 19, Cummings questioned Ferndo, who said he had nothing to do with the killing and agreed to take a lie detector test.

On February 25, the day after Ferndo passed the lie detector test, Cummings and Hendricks questioned Paul Perry, another hustler from Tower Grove Park.

According to Cummings' report, Perry said he had learned of the killing from David Mutrux. Perry said another Tower Grove hustler, nineteen-year-old Mike Cooper, had said Ferndo was bragging: "Any fag that [messes] with me is going to get stabbed. I'm tired of [messing] with these fags."

It was the first time Cummings heard reports of Ferndo talking about stabbing "fags." In the next few weeks, he would hear more detailed and more damning accounts of the same boasts.

According to Cummings' report, the detective later interviewed three South St. Louisans, who said they had enlisted Ferndo's aid in buying marijuana one night in January. One of them claimed Ferndo had announced to the group that he had "stabbed two fags and robbed them." Another told Cummings that Ferndo had said, "I just stabbed a fag in the stomach." And Michael Cooper, according to Cummings' report, told the detective that he had overheard Ferndo brag at a party that "I killed that guy. I cut him to pieces."

Finally, one of the trio who went looking for drugs with Ferndo remembers him saying he had stabbed his victim with an umbrella, as well as a knife.

The umbrella was a new and curious detail. Detectives had found no umbrella at the scene.

Cummings called Oxenhandler's friend, Ed Walter, who had helped clean up the apartment. Walter told Cummings he had found an umbrella in the foyer. Cummings picked up the umbrella at Walter's apartment. It had a pointed end, but no bloodstains. Lab tests turned up no trace of blood, no fingerprints.

Nevertheless, Cummings checked with Michael Graham, who had performed the autopsy, to see if any of the wounds could have been made with the tip of an umbrella. "Graham reviewed the morgue photos," Cummings says in his report, "and stated that about five or six of the wounds could in fact have been caused by that kind of instrument."

Cummings had heard enough. On March 24, he arrested Ferndo.

■ ■ ■

When in late June 1987, Ferndo was bused into the prison compound in Moberly, Missouri, the veterans of the prison system greeted the new arrivals with enthusiasm.

"Ooooh, yeah," Ferndo heard them say. "We got us [a new boy] here."

The next day, an inmate grabbed Ferndo by the arm in the prison yard. Another inmate hooked Ferndo's other arm. "This is my [boy]," he said.

While Ferndo was in prison, Dave Mutrux, feeling guilty that he had helped to implicate Ferndo in the Oxenhandler killing, sent his friend $50 a week.

■ ■ ■

Detective Gary Poelling was working the night watch on October 19, 1987, sitting in the homicide office downtown, when he got a call from Third District Officer Leonard Deschler. Deschler had just spoken with an assault victim, a young woman from South St. Louis, who said her ex-boyfriend had once confessed a murder to her.

"I'm calling about an old case," Deschler said. "You have a

case down there with a victim Oxensomething, Oxenberger, Oxensomething-or-other."

"Did the murder happen over near Tower Grove Park?"

"Yeah, yeah. That's it."

"Well, there was an arrest on that."

"I thought there was, I just thought I'd call anyway."

Poelling sensed he was about to hang up. "Wait a second," Poelling said. "What is this gal saying?"

"She says she knows who did it."

"Who does she say did it?" Poelling asked.

"Doug Weems."

At the Third District station, a block from the steaming Anheuser-Busch brewery, Deschler told Poelling that the woman, Robin Vonderhaar, had called police after her ex-boyfriend, Doug Weems, bloodied her nose and smashed her windshield.

Poelling called Vonderhaar, who told him that, about a year ago, Weems had told her about killing a man, stabbing him, and in the struggle, getting himself cut on the face.

■ ■ ■

Three weeks later, Poelling spoke with Assistant District Attorney Dee Hayes, who had prosecuted Ferndo, in her office in the Municipal Courts building. He told the prosecutor about his conversation with Vonderhaar.

Hayes said she already knew about the woman, and about Doug Weems.

It seems that when Vonderhaar was applying for assault warrants against Weems, she had told another assistant circuit attorney about Weems' involvement in the Oxenhandler murder. Vonderhaar's allegations quickly made their way to Hayes.

Hayes told Poelling other disquieting information. First, new lab results showed that the hair and blood taken from the scene of the crime were not Ferndo's. Second, there were important inconsistencies between Ferndo's confession and the physical evidence. (The bloody shoeprints did not match the sneakers Ferndo had said he was wearing the night of the killing, and while Ferndo had confessed to torching Oxenhandler's house immediately after the murder, the medical examiner said Oxenhandler had been dead at least twelve hours before firefighters discovered his body.)

Confronted with Vonderhaar's story, then, why didn't Hayes do more than suggest that the woman ought to tell homicide detectives the story about Weems? Because Ferndo had confessed. Because his picture was found at the scene. Because he had apparently bragged to at least four people that he'd stabbed someone. And because Hayes knew that a victim of an assault often seeks revenge by fabricating a story that implicates the attacker in another crime.

As far as Poelling was concerned, though, Oxenhandler's murder was far from being solved.

■ ■ ■

On November 9, Poelling interviewed Vonderhaar at 2623 Iowa, where she lived with her boyfriend. According to Poelling's report and several interviews with the detective, he learned the following:

Vonderhaar and Weems were good friends. About a year earlier, in the fall of 1986, Weems had been acting in a way she had never seen before. He spent nearly all his time inside his apartment at 4204 Shenandoah.

One day that fall, Vonderhaar and Weems were talking in his living room. According to Poelling's report, "Weems asked: 'Have you ever done anything you were ashamed of?'"

Vonderhaar confessed she had once broken out the windshield of a boyfriend's car. Weems said he had done something far worse. He asked her to promise she would never tell a soul.

It happened in the winter, late January 1986. Weems was at a south side bar, Baron's, on Morganford. There, he met a guy who joined him in the parking lot to smoke a joint. Later, the man asked Weems whether he would like to come back to his apartment, where he had some Valium.

The man lived on Shenandoah,

west of the Missouri Botanical Garden. Evidently he was rich. The apartment was big, loaded with the latest stereo and video equipment.

Weems was in a room with lots of video equipment. "Wait right here," the man said. "I'll be right back."

Minutes later, the man jumped into the room, naked from the waist down. Weems told him, "I'm not a queer."

The man jumped on Weems, pinned him down. Weems struggled, grabbed a pair of scissors off a night table. Vonderhaar told Poelling that Weems started to cry as he told this part of the story.

When he composed himself again, he said: "You might see movies where they stab people but they don't die. . . . I must have stabbed him two hundred times. I stabbed him all over his body, everywhere, but he wouldn't die.

"Don't look at me like I'm a freak," Weems told Vonderhaar.

"I don't want to know this," Vonderhaar said.

"Please don't leave. Stay here. I have to tell someone this."

"Did you kill him?" Vonderhaar asked.

"He was lying there, cold. He was dead, dead as a doornail."

"Why? Why did you kill him?"

"I had to do it."

He told her he had found a sock and, while the man lay motionless on the floor, wiped everything in the house he thought he might have touched, then left through the back door.

He told her he had driven around for some time, in a panic, replaying the scene in his head. Had he missed a fingerprint? Had he left something behind?

Weems told her he drove back to the man's house, went inside and—hoping to make it look like the man was killed while interrupting a burglary—took two VCRs. The man, Weems told her, "was lying in a pool of blood."

He said he later set the house on fire, hoping to cover the evidence. Vonderhaar could not recall for Poelling precisely how Weems said he had started the fire, but she seemed to recall something about gasoline in a bottle. Weems told her a cut he had on his face was caused during the struggle with the man.

Weems showed Vonderhaar the newspaper articles he had clipped about the killings. That's why he had been staying inside, Vonderhaar told Poelling. He was afraid he'd be arrested.

In fact, Weems told Vonderhaar, he could not believe police had arrested someone else, much less that this person had confessed.

■ ■ ■

The next day, Poelling returned to the prosecutor's office and told Hayes what he had learned. "We'd better go to Peach with this," Poelling remembers Hayes saying.

Poelling outlined the new evidence, told Circuit Attorney George Peach where the case Cummings put together against Ferndo might have been lacking.

In a letter dated December 8 to Captain Charles McCrary, then head of the homicide division, Peach said a reinvestigation of the Oxenhandler murder "must proceed cautiously but thoroughly." Peach outlined which details he wanted Poelling to nail down: Could it be confirmed that VCRs were stolen? To whom were they sold? Did Weems confess his deed to anyone else?

Peach closed the letter: "Please keep me posted personally."

■ ■ ■

Within three weeks, Poelling had found four people who said Vonderhaar had told them the same story about Doug Weems' confession. But Poelling needed physical evidence to back up the story. He found three major clues just by examining photographs of the crime scene and the body.

First, most of Oxenhandler's wounds appeared to be in pairs, which tended to confirm Weems' statement about using scissors. Second, a sock stained with blood was draped over the front door-knob; Vonderhaar said Weems had told her about trying to wipe up his fingerprints. And lastly, Weems told Vonderhaar he had stolen two VCRs to make it look like a burglary; the pattern of dust on the television in Oxenhandler's bedroom showed that something had been lifted from atop the TV.

Poelling found a twenty-year-old petty thief named Jimmy Stief in prison in Moberly. Stief confessed that, in early 1986, an acquaintance "had two VCRs for sale" that had been robbed from a "fag."

Two weeks into December, Poelling was in the homicide office, talking to an informant on the telephone. The informant told Poelling he had talked to Weems about the new investigation.

According to Poelling's report, Weems asked the informant, "How much do they know?"

■   ■   ■

In a confidential memo to Peach dated February 19, 1988, Poelling cited problems in Ferndo's confession:

Ferndo said a lock of hair was pulled from his head during the struggle with Oxenhandler, leaving a scar the size of a dime on Ferndo's crown. No evidence was found at the scene to support this claim.

Ferndo said he stabbed Oxenhandler with a knife. The main instrument in the assault was likely a pair of scissors.

Ferndo said Oxenhandler charged at him with his arms outstretched, hands open, palms facing front. The victim's wounds were on the backs of his hands.

Ferndo never mentioned stealing any VCRs, which were stolen from Oxenhandler's home.

Cummings did not know at the time that the VCRs had been stolen.

Ferndo said he tried to wipe up bloody footprints, as well as fingerprints. None of the bloody footprints were smudged.

Ferndo said that, immediately after the killing, he ran, covered in blood, to a gas station to make a firebomb. There was no attempt made to find a gas station attendant to verify this; the station Ferndo says he ran to is two miles from the scene of the crime; and the victim was dead for at least twelve hours before the fire was reported.

In his memo to Peach, Poelling says he asked Ferndo why he confessed. Poelling writes: "Ferndo stated Detective Cummings told him what he should say regarding this incident, and that it would be judged as self-defense. Ferndo stated Detective Cummings' only concern about the case was that it be 'cleaned up.'"

Peach says he doesn't believe that Ferndo was coached, or coerced, into confessing. "We believe," Peach says, "Ferndo knew about what happened because he was one of the group of kids who hung around Tower Grove Park, living off the homos that either paid them for sex or were ripped off by the kids. All the kids in this group knew about what happened to Oxenhandler. There were no secrets."

■   ■   ■

On February 17, 1988, Poelling located Secret Witness #1, the girl who had heard shattering glass and an explosion the early evening of January 30, 1986. Nine years old at the time, the girl had been sitting on the front steps of her home on Tower Grove Place, taking off her roller skates, when she heard the noise and saw a man running through the alley, away from Oxenhandler's house.

That night, after she had taken her bath, a detective, whom she would later learn was Don Cummings, came by the house. He showed her a group of pictures. All of the pictures were police department mug shots, except one, a Polaroid of a blond young man, Steve Ferndo.

According to Poelling's report, Cummings asked the girl to pick out a picture of the man she saw running from the house. She did not choose Ferndo's photo.

About two months later, Cummings returned. He showed the girl more pictures. She picked out another—again, not Fern-do's—and put her initials on the back. Cummings put the photos in a folder. He gave the girl his card and a St. Louis Police Department ballpoint and walked out of the house.

■ ■ ■

On February 25, Poelling drove to the Fenton trailer court where Weems lived with his girlfriend, Lisa Ruggeri. Poelling says she did not seem surprised to see the police at her door.

Poelling asked whether she knew anything about her boyfriend being involved in a killing two years ago.

"I don't know what you're talking about," Poelling recalls Ruggeri saying.

"Okay," Poelling said. "That's fine. But if he told you something about this, and you want to tell us about it, then you have to talk now. Otherwise, we're not going to listen to you anymore."

Poelling says she hesitated, then broke down. "Okay. He told me he did it. But it was self-defense."

"What else did he tell you?"

"He said this guy was trying to rape him."

Weems was waiting outside when Poelling and his partner pulled up in front of the concrete company where Weems worked.

In an interrogation room at the police department, Poelling said, "We understand that you had a cut on your face."

"Yeah," Poelling recalls Weems saying. "I had a cut on my face."

"Where did you get that?"

"At work."

"Do you remember when that was?"

"About two years ago."

"It was a pretty bad cut, wasn't it?"

"Yeah."

"Who else would have seen that cut on your face?"

Weems gave names of his friends.

"And it happened at work," Poelling said, "so the people at work are going to know about it."

"Yeah."

"Who's your boss? Who's your foreman?"

This game of cat and mouse went on for two hours. Poelling kept scribbling down names of people Weems mentioned.

Then Poelling made his move.

"Okay, here's what's going to happen next. This is a murder case. It is going to go to the grand jury, and we are going to subpoena all these people." He held up the pad of paper and dragged a pen down the list. "We are going to be asking them questions. And I hope that they are going to be telling us what you're telling us today, because, if they don't, man, you are out of luck."

There was a long silence. Weems looked at the floor.

"Is there anything you want to tell us?" Poelling asked.

"Yeah, I did it." Weems started to cry, and then he told a long story. It ended with Robert Oxenhandler lying dead on his living room floor.

At trial in June 1989, Weems was acquitted of second-degree murder, but found guilty of arson. Defense attorney Charles Shaw argued that Weems had killed Oxenhandler in self-defense. Shaw painted Oxenhandler as the villain, calling him a "wretched individual" who used the promise of drugs to lure young men to his apartment for sex.

Sentenced to five years in prison, Doug Weems is currently doing time at Fulton Diagnostic Center, a correctional facility in mid-Missouri.

■ ■ ■

On February 29, 1988, television crews and newspaper reporters crowded outside the courtroom of Judge Robert G. Dowd Jr., who would formalize Ferndo's release from prison.

With his mother stroking his arm, Ferndo told reporters he had confessed because of a death wish. "Drugs had ruined my life. I was down. I was a drug addict. I gave up on life.

"Now I don't even remember that life. Now I just want to go [out] in the world and put my life together. I want to be somebody. I don't want to be a drug addict.

"Prison life was hell. I am never going back to prison again. Never."

■ ■ ■

A rainy night in May 1991. Ferndo races into the parking lot of the 7-Eleven at Bates and Virginia, a few blocks from the apartment where he lives with his mother. He is driving a black Chevy Malibu, jacked up, chrome wheels. (Dave Mutrux takes care of Ferndo's car payments, insurance and maintenance.)

He's wearing a short-sleeved, button-down over a sleeveless T-shirt, his many tattoos showing. He has blond hair, spikes on top, a rat tail down the back.

He pulls himself from behind the wheel of his car, slams the door behind him. "I'm all depressed," Ferndo says in a monotone, leaning against a short concrete wall. "I've been laying in my bed with my gun. I almost blew my brains out. My life. . . . It's all screwed up."

It is a curious monologue, an answer to the simple question, "What's up?"

Ferndo says he wants me to meet a friend of his, and soon we are driving up Virginia Avenue. "I really don't feel so good," he says. "I'm hung over. I drank four cases of beer last night. No. Really. I did. I can really put away the beer.

"My life. I'm all depressed. I wish they would put me in some sort of treatment program."

After a stop at a south side convenience store, where Ferndo visits with a friend, we drive west, then turn off DeMun into a Clayton neighborhood with tree-lined streets. "I love that house," Ferndo says, pointing to a big Tudor. "I'll live in a house like that someday." He laughs. "In another life maybe.

"This is a nice neighborhood, ain't it? Some judges live in here."

In the darkness, we pull up in front of a big, ivy-covered stone house. Bearded iris are blooming in the yard. Dave Mutrux's parents live here.

"Wait here," Ferndo says.

He walks quickly to the door, bends at the knees, snatches an envelope from beneath the doormat. He peers in a window beside the door, rattles the doorknob. A woman opens the door and invites him inside.

A few minutes later, Ferndo climbs back in the car. "They give me an allowance," he says,

counting ten, twenty, thirty dollars in the envelope. "She was telling me to be careful, to stay out of trouble. And she says she's gonna pray for me. She always says that."

A mile away, we pull into the parking lot of the Parkmoor diner. His mother, Janie, a blonde, bespectacled woman in her late forties, is working the counter tonight. Ferndo takes a seat, orders a root beer float.

"I needed you last night," Ferndo says. "I drank too much."

"What did I tell you about that?" she says, scooping ice cream into a glass.

"It's the last time," Ferndo says.

"How many times have you told me that?" She sets the root beer float on the Formica. "He's a grown boy, but he'll always be my baby."

We drive to a pool hall in Affton, park the car in front. Conversation falls to the Oxen-handler killing, specifically to the question, Why did Ferndo tell peo-ple he had stabbed a "fag"?

"Because I did," Ferndo says. "Only it wasn't Oxenhandler."

Ferndo says that one night, about the time of the Oxenhandler killing, he had "tricked" with a man, a fairly regular customer. "He owed me more money, and he said he wasn't going to pay," Ferndo says. Ferndo and the man had completed the act inside the man's house, and they had an argument outside, at the man's car. Ferndo exploded in anger, slammed his boom box into the side of the man's car, denting it.

The man ran inside. Then, Ferndo says, two men came outside. One said, "C'mon, he's calling the police." Ferndo and the two men, whom Ferndo believed to be "fags," went inside. Ferndo says he thought the two men wanted to help him.

Ferndo sat in a chair in a small room, he says. The men sat in separate seats, in front of Ferndo and to either side. Each man pulled a knife, Ferndo says.

Ferndo says he kicked the knife from the hand of the man at his right, reached down, grabbed the knife and stabbed the man on his left in the gut.

As he tells this part of the story, Ferndo grabs an empty bottle from the floor of my car and swings it toward me, jabbing the neck of the bottle into my ribs.

"I'm sorry," Ferndo says. "I get wound up when I talk about this."

Though there is no way to corroborate it, this is not the first time Ferndo has told this story. It is contained in a November 1988 deposition taken by Weems' attorney, Charles Shaw, who called Ferndo as a witness at Weems' trial.

"I did stab a fag, and I thought I could have cut him bad enough to kill him," Ferndo says. "That's what I was talking about that night."

Why didn't he bring this up when he was brought in for questioning by Cummings and Hendricks?

"I did," Ferndo says. "Do you think they believed me?"

■   ■   ■

A week later, Ferndo is sitting in a back booth at the Parkmoor. It has been raining all day, but at twilight, the sun breaks through the clouds, and a shaft of sunlight streams through the big window, onto the side of Ferndo's face.

Since his release from prison, Ferndo has been arrested, but not charged, in more than a dozen cases, from assault to weapons violations to burglary. In January, Ferndo was shot five times by a former friend, who claimed he acted in self-defense after Ferndo pulled a knife. City prosecutors filed no charges. In early May, Ferndo was picked up and questioned about rapes he says he had nothing to do with. He has been tagged with more than a dozen traffic tickets.

Ferndo is not a reflective person. More often than not, he acts like a nervous child. A psychological exam after his arrest measured his IQ at 65, and he has been treated for "hyperactivity" as an outpatient at Malcolm Bliss State Mental Hospital.

But as the sunlight streams into the Parkmoor, Ferndo stops talking and fidgeting. He leans back in the booth, stares out the window at a park across the street.

"You know what I wanted to be when I was a kid? A cop—a detective or a cop."

Not anymore. "I guess [the lawsuit] makes the police department look like s - - -. But it should. You do something wrong, you have to pay.

"It's not just the money I want. I want the law to be done the right way."

■ ■ ■

Don Cummings, who was promoted to sergeant less than a year after arresting Ferndo, was cleared of wrongdoing in a St. Louis Police Department internal affairs investigation concluded in June 1991. "Everything he did was well within reason," says Lieutenant Harry Hegger of internal affairs. "If he had acted inappropriately, I would have charged him with employee misconduct."

It is not the first time Cummings' actions have come under official scrutiny. In October 1978, a federal grand jury indicted Cummings, accusing him of beating Tim Decker, an eighteen-year-old Affton man, on the steps of the St. Louis Police Department.

Witnesses for the government testified at trial that Cummings punched Decker in the face, grabbed his hair, banged his head against the concrete steps and kicked him. Decker was hospitalized after the incident.

Cummings testified that he struck Decker, who Cummings claimed had raised a hand against the officer, as a "preventative measure." Cummings was acquitted by a jury in November 1978.

In an internal affairs investi-gation stemming from Decker's beating, documents show, Cummings was cited for "violation of department procedures," and "rein-structed" on those procedures. The keeper of department records would specify neither which "procedures" Cummings violated, nor how he was "reinstructed."

After clearing Ferndo's name, the 41-year-old detective, Gary Poelling, became something of a pariah among his colleagues. "They were so convinced that I was wrong, and they had given me so much s - - - for going against them, that after it turned out I was right, they just ignored me," Poelling says.

In May 1991, Poelling entered early retirement.

■ ■ ■

Even when confronted with reports of another man confessing to the murder for which Steve Ferndo was imprisoned, the prosecutor, Dee Hayes, initially failed to insist that the killing be reinvestigated. Ferndo "said he did it," Hayes says, "and that was it, as far as I was concerned."

While stopping short of admitting she made a mistake, Hayes nonetheless says the experience has changed the way she approaches her job.

"Let's face it," she says, "he's not the first person who's gone to jail for something he didn't do.

"[But] I will always now be more skeptical . . . I will always be more concerned about a case wherein the only evidence is a confession.

"I will always remember Steve Ferndo."

This article appeared in the August 1991 issue of St. Louis *magazine. Joe Bargmann is now senior editor at* Seventeen *magazine.*

■ ■ ■

From 25 HOTTEST CAREERS FOR WOMEN

EXCERPTS BY SANDRA DONNELLY

Environmental Engineer

Meeting environmental regulations and addressing the concerns of communities faced with development is big business these days, and riding the crest of this new wave of eco-consciousness are environmental engineers. According to Timothy Brown of the American Society of Civil Engineers, the field is expected, over the next decade, to grow faster than the estimated 17.9 percent rate projected for civil engineering as a whole.

Environmental engineers are involved in everything from providing expert testimony in environmental litigation to working on site development, water purification and hazardous-waste assessment. They can work for private corporations or developers, government regulatory agencies, like the Environmental Protection Agency, or as consultants to law firms, private citizens or public-interest groups. In addition, the opening of Eastern Europe will provide new opportunities for American environmental engineers as they advise former Soviet bloc countries on the cleanup necessary after 50 years of largely unregulated industrial development. **Education:** A BA or BS in a relevant science major or engineering major is needed. Additionally, an advanced degree in environmental science or engineering is recommended. **Salary:** Entry-level jobs bring from $27,000 to $32,000. With experience, engineers earn from $55,000 to $70,000, topping out at $100,000.

Employment Attorney

Employees have become America's most litigious group, using the new federal, state and civil-rights legislation to make their cases. The passage of the 1991 Civil Rights Act, which now provides for compensatory and punitive damages to plaintiffs, will lead to even more litigation, and the EEOC predicts that the employment provision of the new Americans With Disabilities Act will alone generate 10,000 to 12,000 lawsuits annually.

Employment attorneys are hired to represent either management or employees in cases ranging from wrongful discrimination and termination to breach of contract and sexual harassment. "The increase in awareness of rights on the job has created more activity, which shows no signs of letting up," says Michael Lotito, employment-law specialist and managing partner at San Francisco's Jackson, Lewis, Schnitzler & Krupman.

Education: Standard legal training is sufficient, but a concentration in labor and employment law is desirable.

Salary: *Entry level:*
$55,000 to $72,000
Midlevel:
$75,000 to $130,000
Top level:
$90,000 to $500,000

Managed Health-Care Manager

With health-care costs predicted to skyrocket to $809 billion this year, traditional fee-for-service insurance is losing ground to managed-care outfits, such as health-maintenance organizations (HMOs), preferred-provider organizations (PPOs) and physician group practices, which offer discounted coverage to employers. Today, 59 percent of Americans belong to a managed health-care program, up from only 5 percent in 1981, and that figure will increase as affordable health care becomes a given in our country. As these programs continue developing, administrators, case managers and utilization-review specialists will be needed to help ensure that the highest-quality care is provided at the lowest cost. "Much of the demand in health-care reform is consumer-driven," says Thomas Dolan, president of the American College of Health-care Executives. "In a few years, every industry in the U.S. will be on some kind of managed-care program."

Education: An M.A. in health administration or public health is generally required.

Salary: *Entry level: $30,000*
Midlevel:
$40,000 to $50,000
Top level:
$60,000 to $200,000

■   ■   ■

The selections by Sandra Donnelly are excerpted from articles that appeared in the July 1991 and July 1992 issues of Working Woman *magazine. Donnelly is now associate editor at Ziff-Net Information Service.*

PUT IT INTO PRACTICE

Discussion

1. Most magazines these days are highly specialized. That means that the editor usually has an angle in mind when you get a story assignment. Do you think it's fair to have an editor assign you a story that begins with a certain outcome expected? If an environmental magazine, for instance, assigns you to research pollution in the Great Lakes and your research shows there isn't much, is it wrong for the magazine to not run your story?

2. Along the same lines, is it possible to "slant" your research to support a given point of view? Should you do that to make a story turn out the way your editor expects it to? How can you please the editor and still be fair in your research and its use?

Exercises

1. You have been given an assignment to write a story on current pollution problems in the Great Lakes. You have one week to get your research done.
   a. How do you go about tightening the focus of the story to cover only one or two major issues? Head to your nearest good library and use one or more of its databases to get a good hit list of current pollution issues. Type that list on one sheet of paper.
   b. Pick several topics from the list and do further database research to see how good each topic looks. Which ones strike you as particularly useful for this assignment? Write a two- or three-paragraph summary of each of those few top ideas.
2. Pick one of the topics and do further research.
   a. First, do a more extensive database search, including the full text of articles or complete articles from the periodical section of the library.
   b. Start your phone calls. Whom can you call to get quotes that expand upon, or perhaps dispute, the research you've uncovered? Do contacts mention others you should call? Remember to list the name and phone number of each person you contact.
   c. Finally, draw up a one- or two-page source list that gives a fact checker the information needed to verify your research.

THE BASICS

THE BASICS MATTER

GEMS IN THE SLUSH
Know Your Market
Look Professional

FORMATS AND SASEs

SPELLING, PUNCTUATION, AND GRAMMAR

PLAY CATCH-UP
Learn the Basics
Learn How, and Where, to Learn
Get Help for Your Current Stories
Read

Larry Heartbreak, senior editor of *Elvis Lives* magazine, sipped his morning coffee and stared at his stack of mail. There were, he counted, fifteen query letters and an even dozen manuscripts. It was 9:15 A.M., and he had to get through them all before his luncheon meeting. He set the queries aside for the moment (you can read about query letters and cover letters in more detail in chapter eight) and attacked the slush pile.

The first manuscript was sealed with special tape and nearly impossible to open, but Heartbreak finally managed, tearing open the other end of the envelope. Inside there was a fifteen-page manuscript, stapled together. Another staple fastened a handwritten cover letter to the manuscript. Disheartened by the tight seal on the envelope, concerned about

70

the staples, and worried about the handwritten cover letter, Heartbreak nevertheless began to read:

Amanda Jones, Editor
Elvis Lives Magazine
1234 Graceland Drive
Memphis, Te.

Dear Miss Jones,

I just know your going to love this story on Elvises early days that I have ritten about here for you.

This is a great story. You can reach me at 555-1212 if you want me to make any changes.

How much do you pay? I look forward to hearing from you in a few days.

Your Good Friend,

Rodney Writer

Heartbreak sighed and sipped again at his coffee. Would these writers never learn? There were all sorts of spelling and grammar problems in the cover letter, and it didn't tell him much at all about the story, either. That didn't bode well at all for the story itself.

In addition, the writer had stapled all this mess together instead of using the usual paper clips; Amanda Jones hadn't been editor of the magazine for almost three years already; and the tape job had made the envelope difficult to open—it was all just a mess, and very unprofessional.

Plus, there was no way in the world that Heartbreak had the time, or sufficient interest, to call writers unless he was going to buy their story. Finally—his sigh deepened—there was no self-addressed stamped envelope.

Most editors would give up at this point. The writer, after all, had emphatically presented himself as unprofessional. But Heartbreak had a soft streak, and besides, he needed a story for next March's issue. Maybe, just maybe, this would be it.

He folded the cover letter back and began to read the manuscript:

The National Six String
Rodney Writer

It was in 1955 that Elvis Aron Presly first laid eyes on his favrite guitar, a beutiful National sixstring that sits proudly in the window of MelBay's music store in Krikwood, Missouri, near Kansas City.

> Strumming a little tune in the store, the guitar was everything Elvis thought it would be, so he took a job pumping gas at a Sinclare station down the street for four hot summer weeks to save the money to buy the guitar.
>
> Finally, clutching $47.50 dollars in his hand, Evlis walks into Mel Bay's store, payed his money and got that guitar.
>
> The rest, like they say, is history.

Heartbreak laughed. He should have realized from the cover letter just how bad this story would be. He didn't bother to turn to page two of the manuscript. Instead, he placed it in a separate pile for those that arrived without SASE. Later, if he didn't toss it out with the trash, he might, if the mood struck him, return it.

THE BASICS MATTER

Beginning writers would do well to put themselves in the position of an editor like Heartbreak. On an average day, an editor may have to read a stack of unsolicited stories (called the slush pile), wade through another stack of unsolicited query letters, work with a writer under contract on a story that's planned for a future issue, make some decisions on content and design for the magazine's next issue, solve a few staff problems, worry about the magazine's financial status and its implications for his staff budget, and, when time permits, get a little editing done.

In short, a typical editor is far too busy to bother with unsolicited submissions that don't look promising.

"It better look professional, and it better look like the writer has read our magazine and knows our needs," says Murray Cox, senior editor of *Omni* magazine. "If it has misspellings, if it's sloppily typed, if it just doesn't look like the writer knows what he or she is doing, then it doesn't have much of a chance with us."

The basics matter. It's that simple.

The writer who isn't in full control of basic matters of presentation, grammar, and spelling; the writer who can't produce a manuscript that looks professional; and the writer who hasn't done enough homework to know the name of the editor he or she is trying to sell a story to and the length and thematic needs of the magazine is a writer unlikely to get into print, no matter how good the idea.

Not only does ungrammatical, sloppily written material look unprofessional and seem to announce that the writer can't be trusted, but it also frequently twists the meaning.

In the second paragraph of the Elvis story, for instance, the writer seems to be saying that the guitar strummed its own strings to play a little tune ("Strumming a little tune in the store, the guitar . . ."). This sort of mistake may give an editor a chuckle or two, but that's the last kind of reaction you want to your material.

See the problem from the perspective of editors like Cox or our mythical Larry Heartbreak. The editor isn't likely to place much trust in the reporting or writing of someone who wants to write about Elvis Presley but can't spell the singer's name correctly and who tries to have guitars play their own music.

And if our mythical Rodney Writer doesn't even know Heartbreak's space limitations—or Heartbreak's name for that matter—the editor can figure it is unlikely that Writer will produce a story that fits into the very particular needs of *Elvis Lives* magazine.

In fact, in all likelihood, Heartbreak wouldn't get much past the first paragraph or two of this submission before rejecting it. All of the work that this writer did to research, write, revise, and mail the story was wasted, because problems with the basics kept it from ever having much of a chance.

GEMS IN THE SLUSH

Editors call it the slush pile because it piles up on them the way that old, tired snow does on winter streets.

It's a tough part of the job, reading through the slush pile. Most of the stories, frankly, are not very good. But editors know that there are occasional gems in that pile, stories that will work for their magazine.

For you as a writer, the trick is to find a way to convince the editor that your story is just such a gem. To do that, you need to make sure you *know your market* and *look professional.*

Know Your Market

If you send a travel story to a sports magazine, you don't have much of a chance to sell it there. If you send a travel story to a travel magazine but the story is about Scotland and the magazine just ran a Scotland story a few months before, your odds are similarly dismal.

You simply must know your market. What kinds of stories does this magazine use? Has the magazine published a story similar to mine in the past few years? What are the magazine's length and style needs? You need the answers to those questions before you ever send a story out.

Writer Bill Smoot, an undergraduate enrolled in a magazine writing course, learned about a market when the editor of a regional magazine visited his class. Smoot found out that *Tampa Bay Life* magazine was interested in environmental pieces and also liked travel stories that told Tampa Bay area readers about other places in Florida they could visit.

That seemed to mesh well with Smoot's own interests, as well as with a particular idea he had for a story for the class.

"I pay a lot of attention to environmental issues," Smoot recalls, "and I had a story in mind that played off that strength. Plus, when the editor visited our magazine writing class, he talked about how he liked travel stories about odd and out-of-the-way places. I figured this was one of those kinds of stories, too."

Smoot submitted his story—a piece on a wilderness area in the Florida Everglades—to the editor a few weeks after that classroom visit, and the story came close enough that the editor asked for revisions and a resubmission. A few weeks later Smoot had his first sale. You can see the story on page 88.

Look Professional

A story that looks amateurish will be treated that way by the editor, who has very little time for amateurs. Beginning writers are not excused from the requirements of professionalism. Your work has to look every bit as professional as a veteran writer's work, even though it may be one of your first submissions.

"I knew that I had to make sure it looked polished," Smoot recalls. "The editor there told us how he sees a bunch of slush submissions every day. He told us that one way he weeds things down is just from appearances. Stories that don't look like the writer is a professional just don't have much of a chance with him."

It's not a difficult matter to look professional; it just requires that the beginning writer pay attention to some basic needs of the editor, who is looking for simplicity, clarity, and basic information.

FORMATS AND SASEs

A good basic presentation style for page one of a story is shown in Figure 3.1.

The second and all subsequent pages need some information, too. Remember that pages can become separated (accidentally, or occasionally on purpose, as particular passages are discussed) during the reading process; therefore information at the top of the page needs to be complete enough that the editor can put things back together. A good style for subsequent pages is depicted in Figure 3.2.

With this basic information at the top of the page, the editor can quickly see whose story it is, which story it is, what page he or she is reading, and whether or not the story is meant to end on that page. At the bottom of the final page of the story, put either -30- (an old newspaper code for a story's end) or -end- or even -bs- (your initials). Some writers also put their phone number on each page, for the editor's ease should it be necessary to discuss particular sections.

Remember that for payment purposes the magazine needs your Social Security number. Most writers put that on the cover letter page, but some include it on page one of the manuscript.

Finally, always remember to *include a self-addressed stamped envelope (SASE)* with adequate postage for the return of your story or query letter. Editors can't afford the time, or the expense, of addressing and stamping envelopes full of rejected stories.

If you don't include an SASE, it's quite possible you'll never get a response. And it will be your fault, not the editor's.

A current trend in SASEs, by the way, is to include only a legal-sized envelope, self-addressed, with first-class postage on it. This way, the editor can return a rejection letter, your cover letter, and perhaps the first page of your manuscript, saving you the postage (and expense of a large envelope) necessary to return the whole story. The ease with which computers can print out a copy of a story has made this technique increasingly attractive to writers—and to editors.

If you choose to use this technique, you need to mention on your cover letter, and perhaps on the first page of the story itself, that the story is a disposable manuscript. For instance, a typical last sentence on the cover letter might say, "Disposable manuscript. SASE enclosed for your

Bill Smoot   approx. 1,700 words
1234 Sailboat Drive
Sarasota, Fla. 12345
(813) 555-1212
ss#: 000-00-0000

The Fakahatchee Strand
by Bill Smoot

See

Self
addressed
stamped
envelope

Two weary, unshaven hikers trudge along an
unforgiving muddy path in the Fakahatchee Strand State
Preserve. A cool morning mist and overcast sky has given
way to the stifling humidity of an Everglades afternoon.
The cypress swamp stands silent and still, a butterfly flits
by in a burst of color, a bullfrog drones quietly.

The hikers push on through the ankle-deep mud. There
is a rustle in the bushes. The hikers stop. Look. A huge
black bear emerges from the ferns and brush and blocks
three-quarters of the path with his bristly bulk. The mad
scramble for the camera and binoculars begins. Hands
wave frantically, pleading with two lagging comrades to
drop and remain silent.

The large bear's black flanks gleam in the dappled, late
afternoon sun. He sniffs the damp ground below, unable to
see the human invaders with his poor eyesight.
Apparently satisfied, the rare resident of the swamps
takes one more long gaze around and ambles lazily off
into a thicket, never captured on film. The preserve has
suddenly proven it is one of the wildest spots in Florida.

- more -

FIGURE 3.1 *Page One of a Story*

Smoot/Fakahatchee Strand/pg 2

An extension of the Big Cypress Swamps above Everglades National Park, the Fakahatchee Strand is a place of diversity unsurpassed in the state. In this area of 75 thousand acres, there are more species of wild orchids than in all the rest of North America and 100 other types of plants are endangered. Its wildlife, flora and history make this one of the country's most special places.

The trails that wind through Fakahatchee are the primary points to observe wildlife. Deer graze on the tender shoots that sprout when the paths are cleared by rangers. Red-tailed hawks sit on the highest tree limbs, screaming at hikers that frighten their quarry. Countless tracks of bobcat, deer, raccoons and the elusive Florida panther tell secret stories of pursuit and ambush.

When the water in the swamp is especially high, alligators of all sizes emerge thrashing across the mud, their natural fear of humans intact from isolation. Unlike the alligators, the poisonous cottonmouths, or water moccasins, yield no ground. Poking the venomous serpents with a stick only elicits a deep hiss and menacing, gaping maw. It is best to recognize and avoid these snakes; the bite is excruciating and can be fatal and the ground is treacherous enough without someone to carry.

The night brings still more. The black water, stained by tannic acid released from the cypress trees, gurgles and splashes. Frogs chorus madly. Even shouting may not overcome the deafening din. Crayfish, hidden during the day, scurry away from flashlight beams in hordes, their

- more -

FIGURE 3.2 *The Second and Subsequent Pages of a Story*

response." (For more information on what else to include in a cover letter, see chapter eight.)

SPELLING, PUNCTUATION, AND GRAMMAR

Always remember that spelling and grammar are indicators for an editor. If your spelling is in trouble, so is your manuscript.

Nouns and verbs or nouns and pronouns that do not agree about what's singular and what's plural ("The team won their game," for instance, should be "The team won its game") represent good examples of problems that will hurt a story's chances to sell. Misplaced modifiers, dangling participles, half sentences—all of these kinds of basic errors hurt a story's chances.

A list of common errors is in Box 3.1, but don't count on their being all you need to know. If you have any doubts, look it up! And, as the following section explains, work hard to improve this basic skill.

PLAY CATCH-UP

If you don't have the basics of grammar and spelling well in hand but you want to sell stories to magazines, what can you do about it? Here's some advice on how to play catch-up: *learn the basics; learn how, and where, to learn; get help for your current stories;* and *read.*

Learn the Basics

Sorry, but there's no way around it. You simply have to get a good grip on the basics, both in terms of your writing skills and in terms of the appearance of your copy when it reaches the editor's desk.

Remember what Murray Cox of *Omni* has to say: "I'm afraid I just don't have much patience with unprofessional submissions. There are quite a lot of really good stories and story ideas that come across my desk almost every day. I don't need to wade through something unprofessional to find some gem. I have plenty of gems right in front of me that look professional and read cleanly."

B O X   3 . 1

COMMON MISTAKES

The following is a list of common mistakes made by beginning writers. The list is excerpted from *Working with Words: A Concise Handbook for Media Writers and Editors,* by Brian S. Brooks and James L. Pinson, 2nd ed. (St. Martin's Press, New York).

Of all the rules presented in this book, aside from spelling and wire-service style, the following are among those we've found violated the most in student and professional copy.

a/an: The article *a* is used before a word that begins with a consonant sound when pronounced; *an* is used before a word that begins with a vowel sound when pronounced. In case the following word is an abbreviation, the important thing to remember is that the choice is determined by the initial sound of the following word, not its appearance: *an (not a) FBI inquiry* because the initial sound is "ef"; many people also get confused by an *h* at the beginning of a word: *a (not an) historical event* because the initial sound is "hih."

adjective-adverb confusion: Many people confuse these two kinds of modifiers; in the sentence *Everything was running smoothly,* the word *smoothly,* an adverb, is correct; many would incorrectly say *smooth,* an adjective. Remember that adjectives modify nouns or pronouns, but adverbs modify verbs, adjectives, or other adverbs; in the example, the modifier describes the manner in which something was *running*—in other words, it modifies the verb. If the sentence had said *Everything was smooth, smooth* would be right because then *smooth* would be a predicate adjective modifying *Everything.*

adopt/pass: You *adopt* a resolution, but you *pass* an ordinance.

a lot: Commonly misspelled as *alot;* change to *many* or *much.*

alleged, allegedly: Avoid these words as modifiers, for they don't offer the legal protection many people incorrectly think. Instead of writing *Smith is an alleged rapist* or *Smith allegedly raped the woman,* say that a man raped the woman and that Smith was later charged with the crime.

among/between: Use *between* for two items, *among* for three or more.

Continued

Continued

as/like: As is a conjunction and should be used to introduce a clause; *like* is a preposition and should be used to introduce a word or phrase.

as, than: When either of these words is followed by a pronoun at the end of the sentence, the pronoun should be in nominative case because it's the subject of a clause in which the verb may be implied: *She's smarter than I (am).*

affect/effect: Affect is a verb meaning "to influence"; *effect* is a noun meaning "result" and a verb meaning "to cause."

blond/blonde, brunet/brunette: The forms without the final *e* are used as the adjective applying to either a man or a woman or as a noun applying to men only. The forms with the *e* on the end are used only as nouns applying to women, although many women would object to being reduced to a hair color. Many consider these distinctions blatantly sexist, but wire-service style maintains them.

centers around: Change to *centers on* or *revolves around* because the center is in the middle.

colons: Capitalize the first word after a colon if what follows the colon is a complete sentence; otherwise, the word after a colon is lowercase.

comma-splice sentences: A comma alone is not enough, ordinarily, to connect two independent clauses; add a conjunction such as *and* after the comma, or change the comma to a semicolon, or change the comma to a period and capitalize the next word.

compare to/compare with: Use *compare to* when similarities are emphasized; use *compare with* when differences are emphasized.

compose/comprise/constitute: The whole *is composed of* the parts or *comprises* the parts; the parts *constitute* the whole.

conditional mood: With something that is not now true but could be true under the right conditions, use *could* not *can, might* not *may, should* not *shall,* or *would* not *will.* This distinction comes up frequently in stories about government considering ordinances or laws; for example, don't write, *The bill will make gun owners register their automatic rifles* but *The bill would make gun owners register their automatic rifles (if passed into law).*

contact: Avoid as a verb; change to *call, write,* or *visit.*

convince/persuade: You're *convinced that* or *convinced of* something, but you're *persuaded to* do something.

dangling participles: A participle is a form of a verb, usually ending in *-ing,* used in place of an adjective. A participial phrase should always be placed next to the word it modifies; if it doesn't the resulting error is called a *dangling participle.* For example, in the sentence *Standing on her head, he watched the yoga teacher,* the participial phrase *Standing on her head* appears to modify *he,* the word it's next to—it sounds like *he's* standing on her head. The sentence needs to be rewritten as *He watched the yoga teacher standing on her head.*

debut: Use only as a noun, not as a verb; don't say a movie *will debut* but that it *will have its debut.*

different than: Change to *different from.*

exclamation marks: Avoid except in quotations because they make a statement sound gushy and introduce an emotional bias inappropriate for journalism.

farther/further: *Farther* is used for literal distance, such as *farther down a road; further* is used for figurative distance, such as *further into* a subject.

fewer/less: Use *less* to modify singular words, *fewer* to modify plural words. Remember that a word plural in form is sometimes singular in concept, as when *dollars* or *pounds* refer to a set amount as opposed to individual units. Use *fewer* with items that would take *many, less* with items that would take *much: He weighs less than 200 pounds* because 200 pounds is how *much* he weighs, not how *many.*

forbid/prohibit: You *forbid to* or *prohibit from.*

fragments: To be a sentence, a group of words has to have a subject and predicate, and express a complete thought. Although fragments are acceptable for certain effects, especially in advertising, be wary of them.

gerunds: Gerunds, which usually end in *-ing,* are forms of a verb and are used in place of a noun. If a pronoun directly precedes a gerund, the pronoun should be possessive: *They appreciated our* (not *us*) *staying to help.*

half-mast/half-staff: Flags are lowered, not raised, to *half-staff* on land, *half-mast* only on a ship or at a naval base.

hanged/hung: A condemned man was *hanged* by a rope; a picture was *hung* on the wall.

hike: Do not use in place of *increase,* according to wire-service stylebooks.

hopefully: Most editors insist that this word only be used to mean *in a hopeful manner,* not to avoid saying who's doing the hoping;

Continued

Continued

for example, rewrite *Hopefully, she'll be here soon* as *I hope she'll be here soon.*

host: Use only as a noun, not as a verb; don't say someone *will host* a party but that someone *will hold* a party or *be host* at a party.

if/whether: *If* is used for conditions, as in *if a, then b; whether* is used to introduce a choice, as in *I don't know whether to go* (notice the *or not* that some people add is redundant). Because many people misuse *if* when they mean *whether* but never the other way around, a handy test is to say the sentence with *whether*—if *whether* will work, it's the right word; if not, use *if.*

imply/infer: A speaker or writer *implies;* a listener or reader *infers.*

its/it's: *Its* is the possessive pronoun; *it's* is the contraction for *it is.*

lay/lie: *Lay* is a transitive verb meaning "to set something down"; its principal parts are *lay, laid, have laid, laying. Lie* is an intransitive verb meaning "to rest"; its principal parts are *lie, lay, have lain, lying.*

lead/led: *Lead* is the main present-tense form of the verb *to lead* and also the name of an element that used to be put in paint and gasoline; the past tense of the verb *lead* is *led,* not *lead.*

lend/loan: *Lend* is the verb; *loan* is the noun.

modifier placement: To avoid confusion, place modifiers as close as possible to what they modify. See also *dangling participles.*

murder: A *homicide* is not a *murder* until someone is convicted of the charge of murder—after all, it may prove to be a case of *manslaughter* or even a *killing* in self-defense. It is permissible to call the trial a *murder trial* before a conviction if murder is the charge the defendant faces, but the crime itself is not a murder until the suspect has been convicted of the charge.

myself: Use only in a sentence in which *I* has been used earlier: *I hurt myself,* or *I, myself, believe otherwise.* It should be used only when emphasis is essential.

none: The wire services make this word singular when it means, as it usually does, *no one* or *not one,* but make it plural only when it means *no two,* as in *None could agree.*

not only . . . but also: *Not only* must always be followed by *but also* later in the sentence.

premiere: Use only as a noun, not as a verb. Don't write that a play *will premiere* but that it *will have its premiere.*

prepositions at end of sentences: Most editors insist that you not end a sentence with a preposition; sometimes this means you should rewrite the sentence using *which,* as in changing *the re-public it stands for* to *the republic for which it stands,* or choose a different wording, where possible, as in changing *That's what I asked for* to *That's what I requested.*

presently: Means *soon,* not *now.*

prioritize: Change to *rank* or *order;* do not use to mean *make a priority.*

prior to: Change to *before.*

pronoun-antecedent agreement: A pronoun must agree in number, person, and gender with the word to which it refers.

pronoun case: Pronouns should use the form that agrees with their function as a part of the sentence. *Nominative case* should be used when the pronoun functions as a subject of a clause or as a predicate nominative; *objective case* should be used when a pronoun functions as any kind of object or as the subject of an infinitive; *possessive case* is used when the pronoun modifies a noun or gerund by showing possession.

proper nouns: Proper nouns should be capitalized, but two problems frequently arise: (1) Compounds such as *German shepherd* that seem to fall somewhere between a proper name such as *Fido* and a common noun such as *dog;* in these situations, capitalize only the part of the compound that would be a proper noun on its own. (2) The names of many trademark products, such as *Dumpster, Jell-O,* and *Styrofoam,* that have become so common that writers sometimes think they should be lower-cased as common nouns; to avoid legal action over trademark infringement, use the generic equivalent or capitalize the brand name.

quotation marks: At the end of a quotation, periods and commas always go inside quotation marks, colons and semicolons always go outside, and question marks and exclamation marks go inside if they're part of the quotation, outside if they're not. In front of a quotation, after a verb such as *said* attributing a quote, use a colon to introduce a quotation of more than one sentence, a comma for a quotation of less than one sentence, and no punctuation for a partial quotation (less than a sentence).

raise/rise: Raise is a transitive verb meaning "to lift something"; its principal parts are *raise, raised, have raised, raising. Rise* is an intransitive verb meaning "get up"; its principal parts are *rise, rose, have risen, rising.*

Continued

Continued

restrictive elements: Words, phrases, or clauses that modify something they follow are set off by commas if they are a parenthetical afterthought—otherwise, if they restrict (are essential to) the meaning of the sentence, they are not. For example, in the sentence *The director of "Chloe in the Afternoon," Eric Rohmer, also made the excellent film "Claire's Knee," Eric Rohmer* is set off in commas as a parenthetical afterthought (the sentence means the same without this detail), but *"Claire's Knee"* is not set off in commas because the meaning of the sentence depends on *what* excellent film this director also made.

robbery: For a crime to be a *robbery,* violence or the threat of violence must be involved. Someone who *burglarizes* a house while its occupants are away did not *rob* the house—instead, the crime should be called a *burglary* or a *theft.*

semicolons: A semicolon is used in place of a comma and conjunction to connect clauses that could stand alone as complete sentences. Sentences with independent clauses linked by a conjunctive adverb, such as *however,* must contain a semicolon. Semicolons are also used to connect items in a series that may not be complete sentences but have commas inside the items; in such a case, the word *and* at the end of the series should be preceded by a semicolon.

sexism and racism: It's not enough just to avoid sexist or racist *intent* in your writing—you also need to beware of language that is likely to be taken as sexist or racist in *effect,* no matter what you intended. In other words, you need to become more aware of how your audience is likely to *interpret* what you're saying.

set/sit: Set is a transitive verb meaning "to put something"; its principal parts are *set, set, have set, setting. Sit* is an intransitive verb meaning "to take a seat"; its principal parts are *sit, sat, have sat, sitting.*

split infinitives: Most editors insist that you not put an adverb between the *to* and the rest of the infinitive; instead of writing *to boldly go,* write *to go boldly.* It's a common misperception that verb phrases in general shouldn't be split—they may be.

subject-predicate agreement: The verb must agree in number with the subject of the sentence, but many common situations mislead our ear as to whether the subject is singular or plural or even what the subject is.

that: Omit *that* wherever doing so wouldn't change the meaning of a sentence. To avoid confusion, do not omit *that* when it follows a time element after the word *said: He said Monday that he would visit* because without the *that,* it's confusing whether he said this on Monday or would visit on Monday.

that/which: Use *that* to introduce restrictive (essential) clauses that do not require commas, *which* to introduce nonrestrictive (nonessential) clauses that do require commas.

that/who: Use *that* for inanimate objects and animals without names; use *who* for people and animals with names.

their: Remember that this pronoun is plural; do not use it in place of *his or her* when the context means either a single woman's or a single man's. *Their* is the best choice, however, from both a grammatical and nonsexist perspective when there does not need to be an emphasis on individuality and the entire sentence can be recast in the plural: *Teachers should do their best,* rather than *A teacher should do their best* (ungrammatical) or *A teacher should do his best* (sexist) or *A teacher should do his or her best* (unnecessarily awkward because a better choice is available here).

tightening: Use shorter, simpler, more common words wherever possible; cut any words that do not add to the meaning. Remember, however, not to change the meaning of the passage; the goal is not just to be *brief* but also to be *concise*—to be complete as briefly as possible.

under way/underway: The one-word spelling is used only as a modifier in front of something nautical, as in *the underway fleet.*

utilize: Change to *use.*

very: Always eliminate, except in quotations.

while: For clarity, use only to mean *simultaneously;* if contrast is meant, change to *although* at the beginning of a clause, *though* in the middle of one.

who/whom, whoever/whomever: *Who* and *whoever* are nominative-case pronouns; *whom* and *whomever* are objective-case pronouns. A handy way to make sure you use each pair correctly is to begin reading a sentence after the choice between *who/whom* or *whoever/whomever,* adding either *he* or *him* to complete the thought; if *he* works better, use *who* or *whoever;* if *him* works better, use *whom* or *whomever.*

who's/whose: *Who's* is the contraction for *who is; whose* is the possessive form of the pronoun *who.*

Learn How, and Where, to Learn

Too many writers count on friends and helpful editors to get them off the hook, and though that may work for a single story here and there, it won't work in the long run.

You need to actively want to learn the basics. Your friends and/or a helpful teacher will soon tire of giving you the same advice and rectifying the same mistakes time after time, and if you don't begin to improve at this most basic level, the odds are that you will never improve in other ways either. You must want to improve.

First, you need to acquire the basic grammatical and spelling skills you lack. There are several good sources. A few of them are:

The Elements of Style, by William Strunk Jr. and E. B. White (Macmillan Publishing, New York)

The Associated Press Stylebook and Libel Manual, edited by Norm Goldstein (The Associated Press, Reading, Massachusetts)

Working with Words, by Brian Brooks and James L. Pinson (St. Martin's Press, New York)

Accept the fact that you're going to have to learn these things, and get busy working at it. Then, while that process is under way, get started on the second phase.

Get Help for Your Current Stories

Once you've begun the task of relearning those things you've forgotten since elementary school or high school (or perhaps you never learned them), get some help for your current stories, and then learn from that advice. Go to that friend who's a writer, or that old professor or favorite teacher, or your parents, or that roommate who gets A's in English composition courses—and ask for some help.

The most important thing about that advice is that you have to learn from it. It won't help your career to have someone clean things up for you if you never get around to learning the skills on your own. Use as a learning exercise for your own writing each and every edit job that someone does for you.

Sometimes you'll find that those who edit for you are sure what's correct but can't quite say why. "It just looks right this way" is a common expression. And the odds are they are right. How, then, did they manage it? How did they know?

That leads us to the easiest way to learn those basic skills.

Read

Most professional writers are readers: of magazines, newspapers, books of all kinds, pamphlets, and even the backs and sides of cereal boxes—just about anything that has the printed word on it appeals to them.

Because they read so much and because most of what they read is written by people who know their basics, these writers have effortlessly learned the right habits on matters of spelling, grammar, style, and construction.

Frankly, if you ask them the rule that they applied in order to make that decision on which pronoun to use or whether the verb was singular or plural, they'll most likely just scratch their head and mumble something about how it just looks right.

In fact, one of the problems you'll encounter if you're forced to learn these basic rules as an adult is that learning the rules (say, for a test) and applying the rules (to stories you are writing) are two quite different things. Somehow, the rules have to become second nature to you, part of your basic writing skills, and not stumbling blocks that force you to halt every sentence or two while you figure out whether a "team" is an "it" or a "they." The best way to do this—to make the rules an effortless part of your writing—is to read, so that you can invoke the looks-right rule with some sense of accuracy.

The author has worked at several newspapers and magazines where the looks-right rule was in common use, and the vast majority of the time those editors who invoked it were correct. It looked right to them because it was right, and they knew it: From years of reading material that used the language correctly, they simply knew it.

You can acquire the same skill. The easiest way is to read often and well. In particular, spend time reading those magazines that you'd like to submit to. If you read them critically, that is, keeping an eye not only on the types of stories they like to publish but also on matters of spelling, grammar, style, and structure that pertain to that particular publication, you can't help improving your own skills while you are getting a better idea of what sort of material the magazine tends to use.

■ ■ ■

THE FAKAHATCHEE STRAND STATE PRESERVE

BY BILL SMOOT

Two weary, unshaven hikers trudge along an unforgiving muddy path in the Fakahatchee Strand State Preserve. A cool morning mist and overcast sky has given way to the stifling humidity of an Everglades afternoon. The cypress swamp stands silent and still, a butterfly flits by in a burst of color, a bullfrog drones quietly.

The hikers push on through the ankle-deep mud. There is a rustle in the bushes. The hikers stop. Look. A huge black bear emerges from the ferns and brush and blocks three-quarters of the path with his bristly bulk. The mad scramble for the camera and binoculars begins. Hands wave frantically, pleading with two lagging comrades to drop and remain silent.

The large bear's black flanks gleam in the dappled, late afternoon sun. He sniffs the damp ground below, unable to see the human invaders with his poor eyesight. Apparently satisfied, the rare resident of the swamps takes one more long gaze around and ambles lazily off into a thicket, never captured on film. The preserve had suddenly proven it is one of the wildest spots in Florida.

An extension of the Big Cypress Swamp above Everglades National Park, the Fakahatchee Strand is a place of diversity

unsurpassed in the state. In this area of 75 thousand acres, there are more species of wild orchids than in all the rest of North America and 100 other types of plants are endangered. Its wildlife, flora and history make this one of the country's most special places.

The trails that wind through Fakahatchee are the primary points to observe wildlife. Deer graze on the tender shoots that sprout when the paths are cleared by rangers. Red-tailed hawks sit in the highest tree limbs, screaming at hikers that frighten their quarry. Countless tracks of bobcat, deer, raccoons and the elusive Florida panther tell secret stories of pursuit and ambush.

When the water in the swamp is especially high, alligators of all sizes emerge thrashing across the mud, their natural fear of humans intact from isolation. Unlike the alligators, the poisonous cottonmouths, or water moccasins, yield no ground. Poking the venomous serpents with a stick only elicits a deep hiss and menacing, gaping maw. It is best to recognize and avoid these snakes; the bite is excruciating and can be fatal and the ground is treacherous enough without someone to carry.

The night brings still more. The black water, stained by tannic acid released from the cypress trees, gurgles and splashes. Frogs chorus madly. Even shouting may not overcome the deafening din. Crayfish, hidden during the day, scurry away from flashlight beams in hordes, their eyes reflecting like hundreds of scarlet stars.

A barred owl calls from a barely audible range; hooo, hoo-hoo-hoo. A return call from a camper brings it closer. The dialogue continues until the owl is perched above the hurricane lamp-lit campsite, silent and staring. After brief oohs and aahs from the adventurers, he lurches from the limb and arcs silently across the treetops to investigate another call.

Finally, the swarms of biting mosquitos cannot be forgotten. In the winter and early spring they are little more than a nuisance, the weather is cool and the water high and moving. At this time of year the water is stagnant, the mosquitos breed and repellent is a practically useless deterrent. May through November, with little exception, they will drive out the most intrepid explorer. An employee at the ranger station said they get so thick at times "you can literally wipe them off."

Plant life in the Fakahatchee is seldom sparse and makes some trails impassable. Trees festooned with bromeliads make a side trip from the paths disorienting. In the deepest reaches of the swamp are several secondary sloughs (natural drainage trenches) and a central slough of pop ash and pond apple where most of the orchids and sensitive plants grow. The canopy here is lower than in other places, forming a "cathedral" of over-hanging vegetation. A college instructor said a "wet walk" to one of these is an unforgettable experience.

The largest stand of native royal palms in Florida grows in the preserve. Some of the older palms tower over the shorter surrounding swamp trees, their fronds clearing the canopy by 20 feet or more. It is here that a peregrine falcon will patiently wait to launch itself at passing prey.

There are mixed communities of trees, cypress being very common. Most of the ancient giants are gone, victims of the axe and saw. Huge stumps, some big enough to lie on, are reminders of what used to be here.

From the confines of the swamp, the open expanse of Four Stake Prairie seems worlds, rather than footsteps, away. The 600-plus-acre stretch of brown grass is only broken occasionally by small islands of trees. The cypress swamp borders it like a natural 50-foot fence. There are no power lines and no buildings, only a sea of rustling waist-high grass and the open sky above. At night, unobscured by city lights far away, stars blanket the sky like a twinkling carpet.

Park rangers give a wealth of history and information about the Strand. Its condition, which seems so pristine now, has suffered heavily from human impacts. Most of the trails used to get around the preserve are remnants of roads and railroad tramways built by the logging industry to reach the giant bald cypress trees. The cutting didn't stop until the 1950s after all but a handful of the majestic trees were turned into lumber. A short boardwalk on the western side of the Strand just off of U.S. 41 is a great place to see what "was." The planks meander through an impressive stand of ancient cypress, some thousands of years old.

Old hunting shacks dot the swamp, most deserted when the preserve was created in 1974. Several are clearly unsafe to venture into, but a few are sturdy and many look lived in. Some still have washers and dryers, drawers full of neatly stacked silverware and the mildewed remnants of clothes hung out on washlines. The urge to examine further is overwhelming.

A pushed door creaks open to reveal a dusty, gloomy interior. Beds are made but caked in years of undisturbed dust. Deteriorating paintings hang from the shack's walls and a child's broken doll stares from a dingy corner.

The sound of a footstep from behind would stop every heart in the room. The only occupant, a startled leopard frog, nearly accomplishes just that, leaping from a stack of boards into the center of the floor.

A night spent near these collapsing skeletons is eerie, the feeling of isolation immense. Headlights from the road a mile and a half away leads to speculation of returning owners. The lights disappear quickly, but the uneasiness lingers until dawn drives away the shadows.

The ownership of the Strand is in itself, diverse. It is a checkerboard of state, county and privately owned properties. Much of the privately owned land was purchased in an old real estate scam. There is no running water, no electricity and no pest control. Ranger Charles Dutoit said many owners will come to see the property, then sell it to the state for little or nothing.

Maps, time and an inquisitive mind are invaluable assets to a good stay. The old tramway paths (trams for short), which range from grassy and muddy, to vine entangled, to underwater, are mostly self-guiding. A wet walk should include a ranger and requires the better part of a day. The Strand isn't heavily visited, so rangers are always ready to give tailor-made information for different individual and group interests.

Preparation is a must, but over-preparation should be avoided. Trail lengths do not take topography into account, so think light. The "Everglades mile" is unrelenting on the heavy packer.

Even the dry areas of the Strand can get wet and many places have permanently standing water. The whole preserve is basically a natural watershed that meanders southward to the Gulf of Mexico. Since all drinking water must be carried in, a jump in a canal along the trams every once in a while is sufficient for bathing.

The only thing that is likely to ruin a trip to the Strand is what other people leave behind. Factors that are poisoning the rest of the Everglades, such as high levels of mercury and pesticides, have had limited effects here. Poachers and litterers take up the slack.

Signs and roadside objects leading into the Strand are often full of bullet holes from guns that shouldn't even be there. The stench of a dead 7-foot alligator, killed illegally for the tail meat and hide, lingers for a half-mile through the still air. Rangers said many local people reject the idea that they can no longer hunt here and want to continue their ways. Ironically, if the preserve wasn't protected, development would take even more of their rights away.

Careless visitors make it impossible to get lost on Four Stake Prairie. An Evian bottle here or a Coke can there marks the path of civilization. Swamp buggies that occasionally sneak in leave narrow swaths of flattened vegetation.

Although unfortunate and preventable, these factors are easily forgotten. The challenge of navigating the trams and spotting wildlife can lead to discovery and adventure limited only by the hiker. Half the fun of the place is the collection of minor day-to-day struggles.

The Fakahatchee Strand State Preserve has all the wilderness and isolation a primitive camper could want. While the winter tourists gather en masse on beaches or at amusement parks, the Strand is a great place to go because so many stay away.

To get there, take I-75 to Alligator Alley and turn right at S.R. 29. Drive several miles and turn right onto W. J. Janes Memorial Scenic Drive, just outside of Copeland. The ranger station is an inconspicuous wooden building about 1/4 mile on the right. It is best to call or write before leaving to make arrangements for activities and find out mosquito and trail conditions. There are no bathroom facilities, no running water and campfires are discouraged, so plan accordingly. For further information call (813) 695–4593, or write Fakahatchee Strand State Preserve, P.O. Box 548, Copeland, FL 33926.

■　■　■

This article was accepted for publication in Tampa Bay Life *magazine. Smoot is a social worker in Brooksville, Florida, and a part-time freelancer.*

PUT IT INTO PRACTICE

Discussion

1. Put together a list of five favorite magazine articles you've read in the past few months. Compare and contrast that list to a similar one by a classmate or other beginning writer. Bring in two or three of the articles and try to dissect the writing. Look for errors in grammar or spelling, especially errors that are from your own list of five problem areas (from exercise 3, following). Do the same with your classmate's articles.

2. Discuss mentoring as a tool for beginning writers. Is it fair to ask a successful writer or editor to take the time to work with you? Is it fair to ask a professor for help when you are no longer in that professor's class? Get your professor involved in the discussion. Is he or she willing to look at your material next semester? next year?

Exercises

1. Assume you are the editor of a regional travel magazine aimed at readers in your part of the country. Have all of the members of your class or writers' group submit the first two pages of their travel story to you (or have them write just the first two pages of a new story). Pick the one or two of these submissions that you find best and want to publish in your magazine.

    Tell why you rejected others. Were there problems with format? Were the rejected stories inappropriate to your needs? Were there troublesome grammar problems?

    To add a taste of realism to the exercise, put a strict time limit of five minutes per story on your reading of them. Does (Do) the same story (stories) still stand out?

2. Put together a list of 25 words that you have trouble spelling correctly. Purposefully misspell some (but not all) of the words, then trade your list with a classmate's or other beginning writer's, and see how the two of you do with each other's list.

3. Try to identify five major problem areas you have in matters of grammar. Is one of them noun/pronoun agreement? noun/verb agreement? dangling participles?

    On one sheet of paper, list those five major problem areas along with two good examples of each. Compare your list with the lists of others in your class or writers' group. Are there common areas of trouble? What can you do to avoid those problems?

    Save the list, posting it near your word processor.

CHAPTER 4

SET THE HOOK

EXPECTATIONS

SET THE HOOK

Draw the reader into the story!

Robin Smith walks over to the baby's room and listens by the door. Wonderful, Samantha is sound asleep with no fuss at all for a change.

It's been a long day. Robin was in meetings and on the phone straight through from 8 to 5. In her job as comptroller for a large engineering firm in Dallas, there are always problems to solve and egos to soothe. It's a high-stress job.

Now, with her husband off in the TV room watching the basketball game, with the baby asleep, and with the day's work problems behind her, Robin has an hour to herself. She smiles at that thought, sighs contentedly, and sits down on the living room couch to look over the magazines on the coffee table.

They've been piling up for days: *Ebony, Working Woman, Executive Female,* the *New Yorker, Texas Monthly, Omni, Islands,* and others. Robin is behind in her reading and would like to go through them all, but she can't. Instead, starting almost at random, she leans forward to pick up *Ebony,* flips it open, and glances at a story that starts right in the middle of the magazine:

Will Carol Moseley Braun Be the First Black Woman Senator?

BY KARIMA A. HAYNES

The aroma of frying fish hangs in the evening air outside a meeting hall in Sherman, Ill., a tiny town about a stone's throw from Springfield, the state capital. A handful of local people are standing around chatting amiably about nothing in particular.

As the midnight blue Cadillac eases up the driveway and rolls to a stop at the building's entrance, all heads turn. Carol Moseley Braun, the newly elected Illinois Democratic Senate nominee, steps from the sedan and is blinded by TV camera floodlights and mobbed by well-wishers who have left their fish dinners in the hall to come outside for a glimpse of the rising political star.

In an instant, she is inside and up on the stage waving to the crowd that is chanting, "WE WANT CA-ROL! WE WANT CA-ROL!"

"You want Carol?" she responds, paraphrasing Chicago's late mayor Harold Washington and flashing her megawatt smile. "You got Carol!" The hall erupts in applause.

Robin smiles. She's heard of Braun and her campaign successes, but this is the first piece she's seen to really tell her about the candidate. As a black woman herself, Robin is intrigued by Braun's success as the first black woman nominated to the U.S. Senate and she wants to know more about her.

The story seems to convey the excitement of Braun's campaign, and, Robin thinks, she may find out some useful information about Braun's stand on various issues in this piece as well. Hooked by that exciting lead and curious about what she'll learn from the story, Robin sits back on the couch, relaxes, and reads on.

EXPECTATIONS

Boil it all down, and the job of a magazine writer is to entertain and inform, and much of the time in the magazine business the priorities are in just that order. First you have to entertain the reader, then you can inform.

That's quite different from the task facing a newspaper reporter, whose job is primarily to inform. If a news reporter manages to write a piece that is emotionally moving as well, all the better. But the primary task for most newspaper reporters is to inform, and the writer and the reader both know that.

Consider the differences between the way that Robin, above, is reading her magazines and how she read her newspaper that morning.

In the morning, she rose about 6 A.M., showered, and if she was lucky had 15 or 20 minutes to glance through the newspaper before the baby woke up and she started getting herself, the baby, and her husband ready for the day.

To read that paper, she glanced at each headline, made a decision on whether or not to read the lead paragraph, and then made another decision on whether or not to go on with the story. Most often, of course, she chose not to continue. After all, the headline and the lead paragraph gave her the basic information. And, basically, she just didn't have the time to read more.

In fact, if Robin has a favorite comic strip or two, or if she's a sports fan and reads through the scores and standings, then the rest of the paper gets even less of her attention.

The result is that, like most newspaper readers, Robin skimmed the paper, got what she needed from it, and then got on with the day ahead.[1]

Because of this and the need for editors to be able to quickly cut a story to fit a given space, newspaper reporters have learned to write in the inverted pyramid style, with some variation of the five W's and an H in the lead paragraph, and the inverted pyramid style structuring the story underneath that lead so that the most important news is at the top, and the least important at the bottom. It's not always an entertaining style, but it does its main job well; that is, it gets the most important information to the reader as quickly as possible.

In the evening, with magazines, it's different.

Now Robin has more time and an entirely different set of expectations. Now she is ready to take a little more time, derive more enjoyment, and be more fully informed by what she is reading. As a result, the structure of the stories she reads in her magazines is rather different from the structure she finds in her daily newspaper.

Karima Haynes, writing for *Ebony* magazine, had a clear understanding of that difference fully in mind when she wrote the Carol Moseley Braun story for *Ebony*.

---

[1]There are some places in the modern newspaper where stories aren't skimmed quite so much, including the feature section and the sports section. And on Sundays, many readers traditionally approach the paper quite differently, taking their time with a leisurely read. But these are the exceptions to the general rule that newspaper readers are in a hurry and want a quick load of information, not a leisurely excursion through all the various angles of a story.

Knowing that Robin and other readers like her will make a time investment to read fully most stories that they get started with, Haynes, a newspaper journalist herself before she came to *Ebony*, approaches magazine writing quite differently from the way she did her job as a newspaper reporter.

"Well, we know that once we get people started in the story that they'll spend some time with it. That's different from newspaper stories. So my job in this story was to bring them into the story and then let them see what Braun is really like on the campaign trail," she says.

SET THE HOOK

It all starts with the hook. Though magazine stories are read differently from newspaper stories, writers know they still have to reach out and convince the reader that this story is worth spending some time with. There are a number of different kinds of hooks. Four of the most important for beginning writers are the *summary, startle, descriptive,* and *narrative* hooks.

Each of these has its place in certain kinds of stories.

The *summary hook* is a common technique for newspaper writing, and some variations on it are useful for newspaper feature writing and some kinds of news-oriented magazine writing. Most magazine writers, though, don't find it particularly useful, for it relies completely on the news value of the story to hook the reader, and it reads so much like a newspaper lead that readers may pass it by.

The *startle hook,* sometimes called the shocker, is also used for those stories whose news value is paramount. These hooks tend to be brief, to the point, and very powerful. See how writer Joe Bargmann handled this type of hook for an award-winning story he wrote for *St. Louis* magazine:

Twice a Victim

BY JOE BARGMANN

Kelly Brown Miller was held captive and raped for more than four hours. She collected evidence a detective ignored. She led police to the suspect. She even discovered a legal mistake prosecutors had made. And just when it appeared she had won her battle for a trial, the judge accepted the rapist's guilty plea, blaming the victim because she had offered him a ride.[2]

You can see that most of the power of this hook comes from the very compelling first sentence. Startle hooks are meant to shock the reader into continuing, and they can be very effective at that when the subject matter merits the form. A word of warning, though: the startle hook should be used rarely, because its impact declines quickly with overuse.

As Bargmann put it, "The strength of this story came from the horror of the rape and her courage. She wanted me to use her name, to make a point about prosecuting these crimes. I decided to just simply say it all in a few words and let the impact of the crime, and her courage, hit the reader."

The *descriptive hook* opens the story with a vivid piece of description of the person or place that is at the core of the story. For instance, John Calderazzo in his story "Come Spring and High Water" (see page 100) used this descriptive lead:

1) Startle/Shocker
2) Narrative

Come Spring and High Water *3) Descriptive*

BY JOHN CALDERAZZO *4) Summary*

When winter comes to Grand Rapids, the Maumee River doesn't just freeze. It waits. While its coat of ice grows thick and granite-hard, backing it-self up for miles behind the concrete spillway at Thurston State Park just above town, the pressure of its own freezing momentum also grows. Occasionally, the townsfolk can hear it—the muffled roar of cracks shooting deep through acres of ice as a million tons of stopped-up river rearranges it-self to relieve the pressure. Impatient for spring, the river growls in fitful hibernation.

Notice how Calderazzo describes how the river's ice is "thick and granite-hard" and how people can hear "the muffled roar of cracks." These kinds of descriptive hooks, when handled as well as Calderazzo handles them, grab readers by bringing them into a scene as if they were there.

The *narrative hook* adds action to that grab, dropping the reader right into the heart of that action. Karima Haynes, for instance, does it with a narrative lead that brings readers right into the middle of a fish fry.

[2] *St. Louis* magazine, June 1990. The name of the rape victim has been changed for publication in this text.

Her goal, she says, was "to take the reader where the reader can't otherwise go, right there in Sherman, Ill. I wanted to pick the reader up and put her in the place, right up front, right next to Braun, smelling the fish frying and hearing the cheers from the people, seeing who she is, seeing her flashing that smile, all of those things.

"That's the kind of thing that a reader can't necessarily get from a newspaper story. That's the kind of thing that adds so much to a story like this."

The narrative hook is one of the more popular techniques used by veteran magazine writers. When done well, it creates an emotional link between the reader and the story, setting a tone (see chapter six for more information on tone) that the reader can expect to enjoy for the remainder of the piece.

See how Texas writer John Morthland does this with the following story:

Fire Power

BY JOHN MORTHLAND

The first burn was the deepest. Chile entrepreneur Jeff Campbell had been waiting for months to sample one of his homegrown habanero chiles. A Stonewall farmer who eats chile peppers at every meal and snacks on whole jalapeños, Campbell had heard that the habanero was the hottest pepper known to man, but he had never tasted one. So when it came time to harvest his first habanero, he pulled a ripe one off the bush and bit into it as he would a jalapeño.

"That was a major mistake," he recalls. At first Campbell tasted only the chile's distinctive flavor, followed by a several-second lull, during which he wondered what all the fuss was about. There then blasted forth a hellacious afterburn, a chemical heat like nothing he had ever experienced. It spread across his tongue and through his mouth, pausing momentarily to regroup before continuing to surge for at least the next ten minutes.

What Morthland has done is set you down right next to farmer Jeff Campbell as he takes that first bite into a potent pepper. The result is lighthearted, but also informative. Morthland continues that pleasant mix of important information mixed with a light tone throughout the story. You can read the result at the end of this chapter, on page 130.

"I think of the lead, the hook, as something that not only needs to catch the reader, but something that also needs to set up what's going to come," says Morthland. "I wanted this story, for instance, to tell you a lot about habaneros, and about Jeff Campbell, but I wanted to make sure, too, that you knew just how hot these things are. And they're really *hot*."

Morthland has written books as well as magazine articles and now works in the new field of CD-ROM technology that may well dramatically change the magazine industry (see more about this new technology, and Morthland's work in it, in chapter thirteen). Like Karima Haynes, he is a veteran writer and knows that the hook is only the start. Once you have the reader involved in your story, you have to follow through with a tightly constructed piece that continues to balance entertainment with information.

Summary - News oriented

Startle/shocker - vivid, descriptive, traumatic, dramas, compel reader to continue reading.

descriptive - Story of somebody. A central figure to/an emotional link to the reader

descriptive -

■ ■ ■

COME SPRING AND HIGH WATER

BY JOHN CALDERAZZO

When winter comes to Grand Rapids, the Maumee River doesn't just freeze. It waits. While its coat of ice grows thick and granite-hard, backing itself up for miles behind the concrete spillway at Thurston State Park just above town, the pressure of its own freezing momentum also grows. Occasionally, the townsfolk can hear it—the muffled roar of cracks shooting deep through acres of ice as a million tons of stopped-up river rearranges itself to relieve the pressure. Impatient for spring, the river growls in fitful hibernation.

At times like these, the residents and shopkeepers of Grand Rapids, population nine hundred sixty, don't sleep so well themselves. Perhaps better than anyone else, they know what the Maumee can do, and so at winter's end they (and hordes of curious onlookers) come out and stand near the spillway or along the old canal towpaths and wait for the river to rupture and begin to surge toward Lake Erie.

It all starts maybe a day earlier, fifteen miles upriver in Napoleon, or sometimes even farther up, in Defiance. With a sound that's truly frightening—the bones of a huge animal breaking deep under the earth—floes as big as football fields tear slowly away from the main ice. They crawl downstream, crunching into one another like icebergs and, as the gray water rises and picks up speed, they smash into bridge pilings, snap or uproot trees, twist and tumble. Grinding themselves down to the size of boulders, they give off a steady roar that can be heard for miles. When they ram the spillway at Thurston Park, they buckle and heave themselves up into spectacular ice mountains twenty-five, fifty feet high, and then they move on.

Some of the larger floes plow partway up the more shallow river banks, as though trying to straighten the Maumee's curves. And this seems appropriate: Originally carved by a glacier, the ice-shattered river now looks like one—a glacier viewed with time-lapse photography. Its shearing power is phenomenal. It once peeled the planks off the historic Ludwig Grain Mill like so many wood shavings; in 1904 it shoved a steel railroad trestle off its pilings and pummeled it like a toy.

Usually, though, while the tourists and the television crews take pictures, the frozen wreckage just grinds harmlessly by. It's the water that jams up behind the ice, the melting snow draining from six thousand square miles of northwest Ohio farmland, that causes the real damage. Major floods have swept through the low-lying center of Grand Rapids five times in this century. Although the last four of these—in 1913, 1936, 1959 and 1982—have occurred at twenty-three-year intervals, the townsfolk take little solace from the Maumee's apparently clock-work decision to run rampant. They've lost too much property to minor flooding in the intervening years to relax their watch on the river. As Jim Carter, head of the Grand Rapids Historical Society, says, "Every year we live with it, from winter freeze to spring thaw."

Nick Weaver lives with it. Weaver runs a millwright business on Front Street in a neatly painted brick building that once housed a blacksmith shop. Small and worried-looking, Weaver stands at the edge of the old canal that runs behind his land, midway between Front and the river, and squints through the warm September sun upstream at the spillway, where a few fishermen wade hip deep in the gently purling water.

"Three times I've stood here and watched the river push over that dam like it was bulldozing boulders," he says. "It sounded like a million windshields being smashed. Then it came into my place, and there wasn't a thing anybody could do about it."

Weaver walks to the front of his building and stops before a drain in the street. "And here's where your water comes up first," he says, idly kicking the metal grate as though that might seal it. "Your water comes boiling out and then follows that curve down the street, crosses over and starts filling up them stores over there one by one."

The stores Weaver points to form the heart of the downtown: A cluster of red brick or wood-paneled antique and curio shops, most of them meticulously restored to evoke the flavor of turn-of-the-century, small-town Ohio. It's a perfect setting for crafts fairs or historical pageants, and in fact the annual apple-butter festival in October rolls both into one, with corn husk dolls, old-time farm machinery chugging away like Rube Goldberg contraptions and maybe a bowler-hatted bicyclist or two wobbling through the crowds.

But look hard enough past the facades that Walt Disney would be proud of and the stores also reveal the scars, human and otherwise, from the Maumee's worst splurges. In Don and Audrey Entenman's Olde Gilead Country Store, with its counterful of candy jars brimming with fireballs, giant jawbreakers and cream filberts, there is a notch on the wall marking the high-water mark of the 1913 flood. Audrey has to stand on her tiptoes to reach it.

Across the street at LaRoe's Restaurant & Bar, where every day during breakfast (early breakfast) the old-timers haggle over the prospects for next spring's deluge, they talk about the time the pike ran through Front Street, and how the receding waters of the '36 flood stranded ice chunks the size of refrigerators on the sidewalks. At the bar, a customer's knee might scrape the plaque commemorating the water level of the Big One of 1959.

Over at the Mid-American Bank, branch manager Jim Thomson explains the slightly odd bit of remodeling he ordered several years ago, raising the safety deposit boxes thirty inches above the floor. "Keeps those documents and what all dry," he says. "Not many people realize it, but water can eventually seep through a vault door, even when you grease it." He should know. He grew up around Grand Rapids.

But one afternoon last March, even Thomson's home-grown experience wasn't enough to save the bank's carpet or the wood molding in the lobby from the water that percolated up in front of Nick Weaver's place, slid down across the street and once again filled up all the stores in the business district, one by one.

That of course was the beginning of the flood of 1982, in some ways the most devastating ever to hit the village and the one then-Governor James Rhodes called the worst to hit northwest Ohio in half a century.

What happened in Grand Rapids during the flood (and soon after) is the story of how a proud and close-knit Ohio community, with help from its neighbors,

battled one of nature's most overwhelming forces and revealed the cheerful stoicism necessary to live year after year with the strong possibility of disaster.

Clearance Sale: Get Ready To Fish
—Sign in shop window,
Friday, March 12, 1982

■ ■ ■

Better to sell your goods cheap than watch them float out the door or simply rot underwater—that's what a lot of the downtown merchants were thinking. Looking ahead to their annual waiting game with the Maumee, most of them had been carefully reducing their inventories for months. Now that the breakup of the ice looked imminent (considering all the creaking and groaning coming from the river and the sightseers pouring in from Toledo and Bowling Green and wherever), it was time to speed up the process.

It was also time to Move Up. Up into second floors and attics and specially constructed lofts. Up the precious few feet that cinder blocks stacked under desks and other heavy furniture could provide. Up to the high, dry ground of barns in the country whose owners drove their pickups into town, unasked, to offer help. Sure, flood insurance was available to everyone, but those who owned a business or house at the lower end of Front Street didn't exactly get bargain rates, so a lot of folks preferred to take their chances and scramble.

The Man Who Measures the River was pretty busy, too. Joe Boyle runs the Rapids Pharmacy on Front Street. Like a lot of other couples in town, Joe and his wife came to Grand Rapids to escape the hectic pace of big-city life. An affable man, Joe takes great pleasure from the camaraderie of his neighbors and gives a little of himself back by keeping a close eye on the river. Once a week he checks the water level for the National Weather Service in Cleveland; lately he'd been checking it daily. On Friday he'd been at the river almost hourly. Flood level was fifteen feet. Normal was about five. By midafternoon the water was over ten feet and rising.

Late that night, acting Volunteer Fire Chief Steve Parsons put his men on round-the-clock ice watch, and back in the station the ladies' auxiliary plugged in their big coffee pot and started cranking out the sandwiches.

Nevertheless, many of the old-timers at LaRoe's were betting that the flood would not come. A lot of other villagers agreed.

Then, in the middle of the night, it rained.

Early Saturday morning Parsons received word that huge chunks of ice were crashing over the top of the Damascus bridge about twelve miles upriver. People up there were fleeing their homes, one couple reportedly tossing some clothes into

a canoe and paddling away from their front steps. Joe Boyle noted that the river was rising an inch every five minutes. The downtown sirens blared.

Still, many were slow to move. It just didn't seem like the kind of day for a flood. The sun bounced brightly off the ice. Some of the merchants got together and asked Jim Carter if he couldn't convince Mayor Harry Jeffers to put off the downtown evacuation for a little while. Weekends brought in the shoppers. To clear the streets prematurely would cost the village a lot of money.

So the Mayor took a look for himself. Harry Jeffers will cheerfully admit that formal education did a good job of eluding him after the seventh grade, but on matters of the river he is almost professorial. Whether he is holding forth from the tattered armchair in his bait shop or walking through his marine-supply store, all the while fiddling with the dials on his new boats, he gives the impression of truly knowing the river, its quirks, its moods.

"It's coming," Jeffers assured Jim Carter, "and it's coming *big*." The sirens were turned back on, and the fire department went through the streets with megaphones urging people to leave and helping them turn off their gas and other utilities.

To Allen and Marilyn Burns, moving as fast as they could in their brand-new Apple Tree antique shop, the wail of the sirens may have seemed ironic. That was one of the sounds of the frenetic urban life they thought they'd left behind in Toledo when they opened the Apple Tree the previous November. They had been attracted to Grand Rapids by its old charm, its people, its promise of peace and quiet, and now they were racing the river, frantically trying to cram their furniture into a loft that was just too small, while outside the sirens screamed.

In the middle of the afternoon, the frigid water slipped under their back door, forcing them to leave behind several good-sized cupboards. Standing on a nearby hill, Marilyn watched the water fill up the object of so much of her time, money and affection, turned to her husband and friends, and said, "Well, I wanted a new rug, anyway."

On the other side of the river, two boys from town were enjoying a much more exciting—and dangerous—view of things. Robert Kaposy, twelve, and Steve Rahmel, nine, had somehow worked their way over to the towpath, the thin strip of trees between the canal and the Maumee; and now they were watching gleaming ice chunks whiz past along with garbage bags, splintered trees and even a picnic table. They were so absorbed that they did not at first notice the water creeping up in the canal behind them, cutting them off from the mainland. Nor, at first, could they have fully comprehended their peril— darkness was dropping, no one

knew where they were. No one was even aware they were missing.

Meanwhile, help for other problems was coming in from neighboring communities. The Wood County Sheriff's Department in Bowling Green lent the fire department a portable communications system, which firemen set up in the station in three inches of water. Someone from Neapolis drove over with extra fish from a fish fry earlier that day.

At this point Grand Rapids was accepting whatever it could get. Although Steve Parsons had forty firemen on duty ("Make that eighty, with the wives"), checking for looters and keeping the roads clear of sightseers was an endless struggle. Some of the curious simply abandoned their cars and tried to slog around in the business district. "Don't those people know that manhole covers can *float?*" Parsons grumbled.

The water rose higher and higher. By dark it had topped out at 22.5 feet, 7.5 feet above flood stage and an all-time high. Marilyn Burns' cupboards were sitting in three feet of cold river.

At 7:30 P.M. Jeffers got word that Robert Kaposy and Steve Rahmel were missing. With the temperature steadily dropping and a wind kicking up, town leaders frantically, laboriously pieced together information that put the boys near the canal that afternoon. Fire department searchlights were dispatched to sweep the towpath area, now almost completely underwater, but the trucks could not get very close because the river had widened itself by several hundred yards, sending ragged pieces of ice flowing through a cow pasture.

At about eleven o'clock one of the spotlights found them. They were huddled in the notch of a tree, water swirling around the trunk. Steve, wearing only a light summer jacket, was cradled in t he older boy's arms. They had apparently been there for hours.

Speed was now more crucial than ever: Underdressed, unable to move, the boys could die of hypothermia. Jeffers and Parsons took two men each and went after them in boats, but they had to dodge ice floes and fight the treacherous, fifteen-mile-an-hour current, and then they had to climb out and push the flat-bottomed boats over ice patches. After that came something that even Harry Jeffers could not have expected—a barbed wire fence. Close enough to hear a faint voice, perhaps two voices, above the monster roar of the river, the men were forced to go back for wire cutters.

It was midnight before they pulled the boys from the tree. Both were suffering from exposure and Steve Rahmel was unconscious when fireman Dick Kiefer gave him mouth-to-mouth resuscitation in the boat, but his rescuers thought they had gotten to him in time— barely. When they rushed him onto the helicopter waiting on shore, the boy seemed to be coming around.

The river rose no higher that night. The villagers were fatigued but beginning to see the brighter side of things. Once again the Maumee had burst its banks and hit them with everything it had, and once again they had beat it back. During the next few weeks and months they could clean up their homes and stores. They would repair the battle-scarred dikes and replace the boats that Joe Boyle said had been "crinkled to hell and back again." They would prepare for next year's battle of wits with the river, although—who could say?—the next big one might not come for another twenty-three years. There was even talk among some of the townsfolk of ordering T-shirts that would say, *I Survived the Flood of '82.*

But then, towards morning, came the news Steve Rahmel had died from exposure.

Had the men in the boats really heard his voice along with Robert Kaposy's? Doctors told them that this was unlikely, if not impossible. The condition of the boy indicated that he had been unconscious for quite some time, although for how long no one could tell. For all those involved, this uncertainty only deepened the tragedy.

Sunday morning brought thousands of gawkers, a blitz from the news media and, finally, the National Guard. The roads around town were jammed for miles and the skies were thick with photographers. A single-engine plane circling over the swollen, now-muddy river narrowly missed a helicopter, prompting an observer to say that the scene looked like something from Vietnam. Governor Rhodes flew in at midmorning, declared a state of emergency, and called in the 612th Engineer Battalion. Within an hour they took over for the firemen, police and women in the auxiliary, many of whom had been working for forty-eight hours or more.

The river was dropping, but much more slowly than it had after other floods. Now there was little to do but wait. When a downtown grocer heard that food was running low for the emergency workers, he gave the key to his store to the National Guard and they went shopping in boats. Sometime Monday night, after seventy-two hours of continuous use, the ladies' auxiliary coffee pot sprang a leak.

It was Wednesday before Don and Audrey Entenman were able to return to the store they had been pouring their energies into for seven years, spearheading a resurgence of the once-neglected business district. The couple had first come to Grand Rapids for its sense of intimacy and ease. "I can take my coffee and walk down the street and talk to the postmistress. Where in a big city can you do that?" says Audrey, conducting a whirlwind tour of the shop. "Besides, it slows you down, and that's good for you."

But what Audrey and Don found when they opened their mud-encrusted doors dismayed them even more than they expected. It wasn't just the ninety antique chairs that would soon require four washings apiece, or all the other lovingly polished oak and maple and walnut and cherrywood surfaces, swollen and stained now to the point of who knew what amount of repair. It was the whole place. Packed wall-to-wall with dark, thick clay, the store looked like the bottom of the Maumee itself.

"Then in came all the firemen with their hoses," Audrey says. "I thought I'd have a heart attack. All those big men clomping through *my* store. But they were so careful, so gentle. They scrubbed the hardwood floors for four days. We'll never be able to thank them enough."

It was the same story everywhere else on Front Street. Many of the firemen and other volunteers took leave without pay from full-time jobs to scrape and push and hose the last of the river back down into the drains. Nick Weaver had a dozen men helping him dig out of the mud. People Jim Thomson had never seen before walked into the bank, offering to sweep out the water.

With a lot of hard work and more than a little help from its friends, the town was slowly returning to normal.

■ ■ ■

One hundred eighty days after the flood, Grand Rapids gave thanks.

Overhead fans twirled through the mid-September heat in the auditorium, from which you could see the Maumee flowing lazily by, its rocks bone-dry in the sun, the tree trunks along both banks still scraped raw from the ice. On the stage beneath the Apple Tree's yellow banner of tribute were a pile of oversized soap boxes, a few mops and a flat-bottomed boat. A bouquet of flowers sprouted from a fireman's boot on the refreshment table next to the stage.

Reminders, said emcee Jim Carter. Reminders of the hard work and loyalty of friends and neighbors who pulled together. Reminders of courage, of tragedy.

On behalf of the town, Village Administrator Chad Hoffman accepted a check for the first of the federal disaster money from State Representative Bob Brown. Applause. They'd eventually have to find more money, though, Hoffman pointed out. There was over $500,000 damage to business, village and personal property and in lost revenue, not counting the cost of repairing the dikes. Until they were fixed, the town would be more vulnerable than ever to flooding.

Nods. Newcomers such as Allen and Marilyn Burns were perhaps thinking about changes they had already made for their next stand against the Maumee. They had replaced the ruined wall paneling and insulation in the Apple Tree with sections of barn siding and batting that could be hauled out in a few hours' notice. Longtime residents were undoubtedly reminding themselves of something that Steve Parsons gave voice to later: Our determination to live here is equal to the force of that river.

And now it was time to show the video tapes that several television stations had donated to the town Historical Society. Nobody had had *time* to watch the newscasts during the flood itself. But first there'd be a word from the Man Who Measures the River.

"Checked it just this morning," shouted Joe Boyle. "Water level's at 1.95 feet, and falling."

Applause, much laughter. A technician played with some of the dials and everyone craned their necks for a view of the screen. Long before the distorted blue image untwisted itself, a familiar sound filled up the room. It was a roar, the deep steady animal roar of the river. Everyone stopped moving in their seats and grew very, very quiet.

■ ■ ■

This article first appeared in the March 1983 issue of Ohio *magazine. Calderazzo is an English professor at Colorado State University.*

■ ■ ■

TWICE A VICTIM

BY JOE BARGMANN

Kelly Brown Miller was held captive and raped for more than four hours. She collected evidence a detective ignored. She led police to the suspect. She even discovered a legal mistake prosecutors had made. And just when it appeared she had won her battle for a trial, the judge accepted the rapist's guilty plea, blaming the victim because she had offered him a ride.

Miller* never told her story to a jury, but she tells it here, in an explicit, disturbing account of rape and its aftermath.

Sitting at the dining room table of her South St. Louis apartment, Kelly Brown Miller starts to cry. She is a small woman with sandy-blond hair, blue eyes and delicate features. She breathes deeply, presses a hand to her chest, exhales slowly. "You have no idea how defeated I felt," she says. She has been telling her story for two hours. She hangs her head and waves her hand in front of her . . . . it's time for a break.

I return to the dining room minutes later and see the basement door ajar. Light shines from below. "I'm down here," Miller says. There is a rustling sound, then footsteps on the stairs. She appears in the doorway, hugging a large brown paper bag with the word EVIDENCE printed plainly across the front. "Here," she says, "I've wanted you to see this."

She sets the bag on the floor, opens the top. "Everybody was trying to get me on how I looked," she says. "During the deposition, there was a question about how high my heels were." She tosses a pair of shoes on the table. Tan, Bass lace-ups with flat rubber soles. "Provocative, aren't they?"

Her hands shake as she grabs a small manila envelope from the bag, tears open the envelope and spills the contents on the table. "These are buttons that were torn off my coat."

She pulls a gray woolen overcoat from the bag. "There was blood on it somewhere. Oh yeah, there," she says, pointing. "There was blood all over the place, but, you know, *he didn't hurt me at all, right?*

"This is the racy outfit that I was wearing that night." She unfolds a tan, print polyester shirt with a Peter Pan collar, now splattered with blood; a wool skirt that would hang mid-calf, now stained in the back by a large circle of blood; a

*Name changed for publication in this text.

gray lab coat, ruined by a four-inch circle of blood and a large tear where material was removed for analysis.

She holds up a beige bra . . . "Racy, sexy, huh?" . . . and white semi-opaque hose . . . "These were hot, too, let me tell you."

She drags a slip from the bag. "Ewww, the stink," she says, shuddering. That same rank smell of alcohol and body odor made it difficult for her then-fiance to comfort her with a hug soon after the rape. She closes her eyes and grimaces. She says, "I do not smell like that. . . ."

She shakes her head, then gazes into the empty bag, lost for a few moments.

"It hits hard to show you these," she says. "You know, I'm not perfect, and maybe I do feel com-passion a little too easily. Maybe I do think I have more power to deal in situations than I actually do. And maybe I get too intimidated, too easily. Believe me, I've thought about all that.

"But I am not sleazy. There was something done to me to cause this much blood. And I have lost many nights of sleep because of it."

■ ■ ■

The eldest of four children, Kelly Brown left home at the age of seventeen. She worked her way into and through Illinois State University in Normal, Illinois, waiting tables, tutoring math, working at the university coun-seling center. In 1985, she

entered a master's program at SIU-Edwardsville, and in 1987, she met Scott Miller, a painter and art student at the Meramec campus of St. Louis Community College.

The two dated that fall. She had just ended a relationship with another man. He was coping with the death of an uncle who'd been very close. "We kind of mutually helped one another," he says. "She was extremely caring. And she is really bright. She was able to help me, to understand, when I was feeling really bad."

Eight months after they met, the couple decided to share an apartment and eventually marry. Money was short. He was still in school, and the little income he received were checks from the Veterans Administration. She was working as a counselor and re-searching her master's thesis. At the time, an engagement ring was an unthinkable luxury. But at the end of November, after months of being shortchanged, he received a large check from the VA. He bought a simple ring with five small stones—three sapphires and two diamonds.

On the night of December 3, 1988, while she was at work, he sat in their living room and admired the ring. He wrapped it, then removed the paper to look at it again. He rewrapped it, then unwrapped it to look at it once more. Finally, he hid the ring under a cushion on the couch.

She arrived home upset. It was

the anniversary of her maternal grandmother's death. He persuaded her to sit down on the couch. He slid his hand beneath the cushion, pulled out the engagement ring and held it in front of her face.

■ ■ ■

On Saturday morning, December 17, 1988, Brown drove from the couple's South St. Louis apartment to the Washington University Medical Center on Kingshighway, where she was to counsel two children of alcoholic parents. As it turned out, she was unable to see either child that day. She made arrangements to see them at 7:30 the next morning.

Perturbed by the delay, she made her way through the halls of the hospital, taking a shortcut to her car. She came upon an elderly woman who was disoriented, mumbling, in need of help. Brown took her by the arm, found a wheelchair and wheeled her to the emergency room. The woman looked up at Brown and said, "Something good is going to happen to you."

But Sunday brought more frustration. When Brown arrived at the hospital, the nurse told her the children were still asleep. "Come back around 5:30 tonight," she said. "You can see them then."

Brown and Miller spent a lazy day together. They saw a matinee, *Dirty Rotten Scoundrels*, at Ronnie's 8 Cine and then shopped for Christmas presents. "We don't

often go out," Miller says. "That day was one of the best days we had had together."

Just after 5 p.m., he was dozing in bed as she slipped on her coat. They said goodbye with a hug, and she walked out into the cold.

When she arrived at the hospital, the children were still unavailable. Exasperated, she strode out to her Chevrolet Chevette, which was parked in a lot half a block away. It was a few minutes before 6 p.m., but the lot was almost deserted. The students were home for the holidays.

■ ■ ■

Brown unlocked the door, opened it. She began to step in when she was startled by a man's voice: "Hey!" She turned, looked over her shoulder. He was six feet away, just about as tall, wearing a heavy jumpsuit that zipped up the front. He stepped toward her, still talking. He closed in until she could smell him: alcohol, strong body odor.

"I need a ride," he said, his head hanging. His eyes were cloudy, his lids heavy. "I'm sick. I'm cold."

She felt trapped. He stood even with the end of the car door. No one else was around.

"I don't know . . . ," she said. Fear and sympathy crept in together.

"I work in maintenance," he said.

The jumpsuit. That makes sense.

"I stay a couple of blocks away," he said, gesturing. "Just a couple of blocks."

She sat down behind the wheel, reached over and unlocked the passenger door. She gathered papers from the passenger seat and set them in the back. The man climbed in. He was wearing a black ball cap with gold lettering: CADILLAC. His hair was a nappy Afro.

She strapped on her seat belt and asked him to do the same. He did, and she slid the T-shaped gear-shift into reverse. She pulled the T-stick into drive and took a right out of the parking lot, heading east on Scott Avenue. "You're going to have to tell me where to go here," she said.

"Right." His voice was barely audible.

She made the turn. She felt nervous. *Should I make conversation?* "Do you work indoors or outdoors?" *Easy question to answer: The jumpsuit looks heavy.*

"Outdoors."

"Have you worked long at the hospital?"

"No."

Single-word answers. No use. Why talk to a drunk, anyway?

As the car glided through an intersection, the man spoke up, louder this time. "That way!"

"Oh, s---," she said. Missed the turn. "You've got to clue me in before we get through the intersection, OK?"

"Next one, then."

She made a left. *Desolate old neighborhood. This does not look so great.*

"Do you live very far from here?"

"Just up the street." She drove another block. Then another.

"This block?"

"No. Go down more."

She drove further along Chouteau. Run-down, brick rowhouses lined the street. *I want this to be over. I am a minority in this neighborhood.*

"Here?" she asked, pointing to the buildings.

"No."

She noticed the street sign as they crossed Tower Grove Avenue. Out her window she saw in the distance the huge white cylindrical tank that squats beside Highway 40. "I stay here," he said. "Pull over."

She did, but not all the way to the curb, rather just out of the line of traffic. She stopped in front of a brick house. *Christmas lights in the window. At least he's got some Christmas in his house. It can't be such a bad place. Not a place he would starve or anything.*

"Well, take it easy," she said.

He took off his seat belt and leaned toward her, much too close. He said, "You know what I want."

"Hey." She recoiled, raised her hands.

He pressed closer. "Don't make it hard for me. Don't make me do you like this."

"Look," she said, "I gave you a ride, and I've been nice about it.

Now you need *to . . . get . . . out.*" She was deliberate, firm.

He pushed closer. "I want p----."

She pushed him away, opened her door with her left hand, unlatched her seat belt with the right. "Get the f--- out of my car!"

Suddenly violent, he grabbed her by the coat with both hands. He yanked her head forward and down, and she turned to avoid smashing her head on the gearshift.

She struggled. A group of teen-agers was walking down the sidewalk. She honked the horn, opened the door, stepped on the street with one foot, fought to stand until her mouth was about even with the roof. "Help me!" she yelled. "Help me get this man out of the car! Call the police!"

The kids, perhaps four of them, laughed and walked on.

He pulled her back inside by the coat, and with his left hand he gripped a hank of her hair at the back of her head. He clasped her upper arm with his right. She tried to calm herself, but he was pulling her this way, pushing her that way.

"Drive!" he shouted. "Up there, then left."

A bus lumbered toward them. She drove, and as she reached the intersection, she cut off the bus, slamming her foot on the brakes, the car into park. The man exploded in anger, cursing. His fingers now tangled in her hair, he slammed her head down onto the shift lever and held her down.

The bus swerved. She glanced up. The bus passed, a blur of light and passengers.

Now he grabbed her around the neck with both hands. She couldn't breathe. "Why you gonna make me do this?" he said. "I'm gonna kill you! Now turn!"

She turned left, nosing the Chevette into a light-industrial area with idle warehouses. *No one lives around here.*

He was still holding her, shaking her. It was hard for her to drive. She slowed the car. He reached down and rammed the gearshift to park. The car jerked to a halt. The man held her by the hair just above the nape of her neck. He screamed, "I'm gonna kill you, bitch!"

She believed him. She struggled, tried to open her door, managed to roll down the window and scream. He put his hand over her mouth, tossed her around by the hair. The struggle lasted five or ten minutes. His hands were still across her throat when he said, "Now drive."

Her headlights illuminated a sign—40 East—as she took a right on Papin Street. *Someone might see us. There might still be a chance to escape, if he doesn't kill me first.*

She pulled over in front of a church beside a large, vacant lot and a burned-out house. Traffic on Highway 40 buzzed so near. There was an entrance ramp just a few yards away. Twenty minutes, maybe a half hour, had passed since she left the security of the hospital, since the man had said innocently, "Just a couple of blocks." Now, he was all but strangling her.

Kelly Brown the counselor, Kelly Brown the quick-thinker began to negotiate with him, to appease him, to deceive him, to flatter him, whatever it would take to escape.

"I know you're drunk," she said. "I can get you some help."

He shook her again. "Shut up. Get in back."

"Look, maybe we can go someplace else. I don't want to do this here. Why don't we go to my house?"

"I was in jail. Do you know how long it's been? They said I killed somebody but I didn't."

"Oh, so I'm gonna get in back and you're going to kill me, right?"

"Get in back, or I *will* kill you. Now get in back."

"Look, I'm begging you. I'll do anything you want, but I just got engaged."

The man was quiet now. His silence caused her to panic—*survive, survive*—and the pleading streamed from her mouth, involuntarily. "I'm going to throw up. I'm on my period."

The headlights of a car approaching the highway entrance shone through the back window. She screamed "Help!", flung her keys in front of the car, pushed open her door, arms flailing outside. *They've got to see me.*

The man pulled her backward with what she thought was a death grip around her neck. She kicked her legs out the door. Cars passed. The man flew into a rage. He choked her still harder. "Get in back or I'll kill you."

She straightened. "OK, then kill me, if that's what you're gonna do."

"I won't kill you. Just shut up and get in back. Get the f--- in back!"

He began pushing her toward the back of the car. The back seat of the hatchback was folded down. As he pushed, she reached behind the passenger seat. Her hand came to rest on a tire iron. *Here is a chance. One swing and . . .* She didn't do it. It was so cramped in the car. And he was too quick, too alert—not like the man who minutes earlier had seemed so intoxicated, so sick. *If I miss, he'll use it on me. Kill me.*

She pushed the tire iron beneath a pile of crumpled papers and released her grip. The man pushed her toward the back and was crawling on top of her when her knee thrust up, into his testicles. It was not intentional. The man grunted in pain and tightened his grip on her neck. "Bitch."

Cars were driving by, so close. He hiked up her skirt, yelled at her to pull down her panty hose and underwear. He started to do it, pulled her hose part of the way down, but she was disgusted by his touch and did it herself.

He pulled on the string of her tampon. It hurt her. Days had passed since her period had ended, but she always wore a tampon for a while afterward. She hoped the tampon, the thought that she might be having her period, would disgust him. But it didn't. He ordered her to pull out the tampon herself.

The man unzipped his suit. He held her down with one hand. She struggled to get out from under him, but he grabbed her by the neck and slammed back her head. Then he hooked his arms under her legs and pushed them up over her head. Her feet were on the ceiling, her arms pinned beneath her.

She was shaking. The man could not get an erection. He made her perform oral sex, and then he pulled her back up and held her beneath him. He pushed his penis inside of her. She squeezed her eyes shut. *That's it. I've been raped. Now I must fight to stay alive.*

"Stop shaking," he said.

"I can't. You're going to kill me."

"No, I won't."

She struggled again, trying to free herself from beneath him.

"Cut the s---," he said angrily, and he grabbed her again and slammed her down. "Or I will kill you, bitch. Cut you up. Drop you in a can."

Brown stopped struggling.

"Now tell me it feels good," he said.

"No. I won't."

"C'mon, tell me it feels good."

A silent pause.

"Whose p---- is this?"

Another silent pause.

"I'm supposed to say, yours!" she screamed. *But I won't say it. If I'm going to die, I'm going to die with dignity.*

"Say, 'I want you to d--- me to death.'" he ordered.

"I'm not going to say that. If I do, you're going to kill me."

"Well, you're just going to have to," he said.

She didn't.

"Have you ever been f----- before?" he asked.

"Once, and I hated it," she snapped.

"Well, you're young, a little girl."

"Yeah."

"What are you, twenty?"

"Yeah," she lied. She was twenty-seven.

"Young p----," he said, over and over. And he continued to rape her.

Nearly an hour passed. Cars still drove by, rolling onto the Highway 40 entrance ramp.

Kelly prayed. *Lord, grant me the serenity to accept the things I cannot change; the courage to change the things I can; and the wisdom to know the difference. Five more minutes, Lord. Let me make it through five more minutes. Please let me see Scott again. Please let me live to see my family again.*

"Look, it's so small back here," she said. "We've gotta get out of here." A car passed. *I'll try to make him paranoid.* "People can see us. They know what you're doing."

He stopped raping her. "I think you're fine," he said. "You liked it, didn't you?"

"No."

"I know you did."

"No, I did not. Look. Just let me go. You did this. Now just let me go home. I'm not going to tell anybody, I swear."

"What about your people?"

"I don't know anybody here except my boyfriend, and if I told him he'd kill me. I'm from Chicago, and my people are from there. They won't bother you. Please let me go. I don't even know where I am."

There was a brief silence.

"OK, but we'll do this again," he said.

Sure, sure, anything you say. But just let me out of here alive.

■ ■ ■

Once she had put on her shoes and was climbing toward the front of the car, Brown thought for a moment that she might be able to leave. But the man held her hard by the arm and pulled her from the passenger side of the car. "Just let me stay here," she pleaded. "I don't even have my keys."

"No," the man said. "I'm going to have you walk me down here, behind the church, then I'll let you go."

He led her along the side of the abandoned church, beside a vacant lot, and to a shed behind a house. He pulled her inside the shed, tried to convince her that she liked what had happened in the car. He kissed her. The kisses felt like spiders on her cheeks. "I love you," he said.

"If you love me, you won't make me do this," she said.

"Really, we'll get together some other time."

"Just a second," he said. He freed her from his grip, walked to the front of the shed and peered at the back of the house.

She dashed toward the front of the shed. He turned and grabbed her. He held her more tightly than ever, his arm around her head, his hand across her mouth. He dragged her out of the shed, toward the back of the house.

He pulled her up a couple of stairs and knocked on a door. He turned to her and said through clenched teeth: "Be quiet, or I will kill you. This is where my people stay. I have brothers. If you make any noise, they'll do you, too. Then they'll kill you."

The man yanked her up another step, still holding his hand over her mouth. The door opened, and another man stood in the doorway.

The man who had raped her dragged her inside, and the other man disappeared into the house, shutting the bedroom door behind him. There were three beds. The rapist turned off the lights and turned on the television. She smelled urine.

He walked to the bedroom door, checked that it was shut, and Brown started for the door to the back yard. He rushed toward her, grabbed her, said: "Cut that s--- out, or I'll kill you. Now take off your clothes."

"No. No. Please. No more."

"Take 'em off, or I will," the man said, touching her blouse.

Brown recoiled. "I'll let you go home in a little while."

"I *won't* take off my clothes," she said.

He reached for her again, but she backed away. Defeated, she started to undress. *Lovers take off one another's clothes. I will not let him undress me.*

Once she was naked, the man dragged her down on the middle bed. He raped her again. *Help me make it through five more minutes, Lord. Please let me see Scott again.*

She focused on the television: "The regularly scheduled episode of *Murder, She Wrote,* will not be seen tonight so that we may bring you *The Brady Bunch Christmas Special.*" She thought of watching *The Brady Bunch* when she was a child and wondered if she would see her family again.

At one point, while Brown lay stiff on the bed, he gnashed his teeth around her face and parts of her body. He barked and growled like a dog. He licked parts of her body. *Rape is supposed to be fast. This has taken hours. This is more like torture.*

She sobbed loudly. She lost her breath she cried so much. She screamed, and a voice on the other side of the bedroom door yelled, "Turn up the television, turn it up!"

Brown started to scream again, but stopped herself by biting down on a blanket. The blanket was wet: she realized it was urine-soaked.

The man knelt behind her, raping her, holding her by the neck and pulling back, choking her. He was talking now. He said he wouldn't let her go until she had an orgasm. "You're going to stay here. You love me . . . You're my girlfriend . . . You are my p---- . . . I'm going to kill your boyfriend. . . ."

The bedroom door opened, and the man who had stood in the doorway when she arrived at the house stepped inside. He leaned against the wall for a few minutes, watching. He left without a word.

■ ■ ■

After two hours, he stopped raping her. He had not ejaculated. Again he said he would let her go. But there were conditions. First, she must walk through the house to be introduced to the many people who were there. She must smile and tell everyone she was his girlfriend. Then, she must speak into a tape recorder, giving her name and address and saying: "He didn't take my p----, I gave it to him."

He made her rehearse what she would say on the tape. Then he said, "I want the ring," grabbing her hand, holding it up, smiling as he eyed the sapphires and diamonds.

"No way. It's my engagement ring," she said, pulling away her hand. He kept grabbing at her hand, but she resisted. "NO!"

"Give it to me or I'll do you again," he threatened.

She thought for a moment, then

flopped back on the bed. *When you've been raped for this long, what's one more time? This ring has kept me alive tonight. Scott and my marriage to him, my connection to him, are the most important things in the world. This man can rape me, but he can't take that away from me. He can't have my ring.*

He laughed while she lay on the bed. "You must want that ring pretty bad," he said. He pulled her to her feet again, snatching her by the wrist. He started licking her fingers, laughing throatily. He licked the ring, drooled on her fingers. Then he pulled off the ring and pocketed it.

She began to cry. He rifled her coat pockets, saying he needed change for cigarettes. In her pockets were four cents, a stick of lip gloss and a pack of Wrigley's Spearmint gum. He took everything.

He offered her a stick of gum, which she refused. He smeared the lip gloss on his lips, grabbed her hard by the hair on the back of her head, smudged her lips and pressed his lips on hers.

He opened the bedroom door and paraded her from room to room. There were at least eight people in the house. The man stopped and bummed a cigarette from a young man. Two young women were there, late teens, early twenties. There was a man in his mid-thirties and a boy, perhaps ten years old. The faces flashed before her, and she feared she

would scream out. She recalled what the man had said on the back steps. His brothers. They would get her, too. Then they would kill her. Kill Scott. Kill her family.

It did not seem out of the question. Here was the man who had entered the room to watch her being raped. Another person at the house had simply asked that the rapist turn up the volume on the television. What would stop them from hurting her more?

The man led her downstairs, where two young couples were cooking hamburgers. The man introduced her by name. "Ain't she pretty?" he said. He held up the engagement ring proudly on the first knuckle of his pinky. "She's engaged," he said, smiling.

The man pulled her into another basement room—dark, dirty, foul-smelling—where a man and a woman were watching television. There was a very young child in the room, too. She thought she might lose control and scream. The rapist handed her a piece of paper and a pen. "Write down your name and phone number," he said.

She held the paper against the wall and prepared to write, but the child caught her eye, and she looked up. The toddler was reaching for a mouse trap. She reached for the child's hand to stop it from triggering the trap, and the woman said, "What's she doin'?" Brown tried to explain about the mouse trap, but she stopped mid-sentence.

Her mind raced as she prepared to write. *Do I give him my real number?* She had told him the correct number in the bedroom. She couldn't think of anything but the numbers of her friends then, and she wouldn't give him those. What if he were to remember the number she had given him before? "C'mon," the man said, staring. Finally, she wrote down the correct number.

"Don't do those sevens like that," said the man, unable to read them because she had crossed them. She wrote the phone number again, with plain sevens. "Let's go, OK?" she said.

He led her back into theother basement room, where the young couples were cooking hamburgers.

"Do you want one?" one kid asked.

She shook her head.

"I'll have two," the man said. "I'll be back soon."

The man led Brown back upstairs and through the bedroom, where two boys sat watching television on the edge of the bed, which was stained with the blood of the rape. The man walked her to her car. He called her his girlfriend in one sentence, and in the next, threatened to kill her.

"Get in the car," he ordered. He walked to the middle of the road, where she had tossed her keys. He returned to the car, motioned for her to roll down the window and handed her the keys.

Then he grabbed her by the back of the head and kissed her.

"That's Highway 40," he said calmly, pointing to the entrance ramp, reminding her of the conditions of her freedom. "No police. I give you fifteen minutes to get home, then I call. If you don't answer, I come after you. And if you tell anybody about this, I kill your family. Every one of them."

She started her car and drove away from the curb, steering toward the ramp. Behind her, the man yelled, "Turn on your lights!"

■ ■ ■

Scott Miller was sitting on the living room couch, watching television, when she arrived. He had been wrapping Christmas presents that night, and he answered the door holding some in his hands. "Don't answer the phone," she said. "He's going to call. He'll kill you!"

He moved toward her. "Don't touch me!" she screamed, and she ran past him, into the bathroom. He followed, but before he could reach her, she slammed the bathroom door behind her and locked it. A foul odor lingered in the hallway.

He could hear her crying. "He's got our number," she said, sitting in a corner, hugging her knees. "He's going to call."

"Who's going to call?" he asked.

"I can't tell you," she said. "You'll leave if you find out."

"Please, Kelly, what's going on?"

"If I tell, he's going to kill us. He'll kill you if you find out."

Brown cried and wailed. She hugged the toilet bowl, nauseous, but unable to vomit.

"Please come out," he pleaded. "Please tell me what happened."

Finally, she said, "I've been attacked and raped."

She opened the door to the bathroom, and he embraced her. It was a tentative embrace. She was shaking, crying, trying to talk. And the smell of the rapist clung to her.

He telephoned a close friend of Brown's and the friend met them at St. Mary's Health Center.

Brown lay on the examination table, her legs in stirrups. "This might hurt," said the doctor, and Brown, who had been sobbing and whimpering, broke into hysterical laughter. "I don't feel a thing," she said.

They went about collecting the evidence. An intern tried to clip Brown's fingernails, to collect any of the rapist's skin that might be lodged beneath them. But the intern was shaking too much to do it. Brown took the clippers and did it herself.

Detective Edward Prenavo interviewed Brown at the hospital. She was "confused and upset," according to a police report. Still, Prenavo heard enough to inform Brown: "It doesn't sound like you have much of a case." The rapist had been clever, the detective said. By leading Brown through the house and introducing her as his girlfriend, he had made it difficult to pin a charge on him. And Prenavo was troubled by one question: Why did she let him into the car?

When the detective left the hospital, he neglected to take with him key evidence, most notably Brown's soiled clothing.

Later, on the way home, Miller leaned toward her and asked: "Are you bleeding?"

"Everywhere," she said.

■ ■ ■

The next day, Brown telephoned St. Louis City Police Detective Ray Ghrist. On December 20, Ghrist picked up Brown at home. She gave him the rest of the evidence, and the two drove to the parking lot where she had been accosted. She drove the route with Ghrist, recounting the events of that night, and she pointed out the house.

Ghrist dropped off Brown at home and returned to the run-down, red-brick home at 919 Talmage St. A man fitting the description of the rapist answered the door.

Elvis Williams led the detective to the back room. "You are a suspect in a rape case," Ghrist told him. "Do you know what I'm talking about?"

"Yeah," Williams said, "but I didn't have no gun or knife to force her to do anything."

Williams handed over his green coveralls, which were stained with blood at the base of the zipper, near the crotch. Written on a scrap of paper in the pocket were KELLY and 771-8849, once with the sevens crossed, once without.

Before driving Williams to the station, Ghrist went next door, where he found a young woman, a friend or maybe a sister of Williams', wearing Brown's engagement ring.

■ ■ ■

Elvis Williams was born August 6, 1961, the oldest of eight children. Records conflict as to his place of birth, but it was either St. Louis or Beulah, Mississippi.

Williams was raised in poverty. His father, a heavy drinker, was working at Midland Color, a St. Louis ink manufacturer, at the time of Elvis' arrest for rape.

Williams dropped out of Soldan High School in 1978, having completed the ninth grade. His overall grade point average was .375 out of 4.0. He took a building maintenance job in 1979 and worked for the same company, off and on, until 1986. He never made more than $5 an hour.

In the early 1980s, Williams met Annette Lawson, who would bear three children by Williams. They eventually married. Like his father, Williams drank heavily. When he drank, he became quarrelsome, though Lawson never knew him to be violent.

In 1985, Williams had his first run-in with the law as an adult—a traffic violation that he never showed up in court to address. Over the years, his brushes with police became more serious— drunk driving, stealing, indecent exposure, marijuana possession. Most of the times he got into trouble with the law, he was drunk. After he separated from Lawson in 1987, he began to drink more heavily.

He also became more violent. On July 21, 1987, according to police, Williams got into a shouting match with a fifty-five-year-old man, pulled a knife on him and threatened to slice him up. Minutes later, police arrived to find Williams still holding the knife.

The felony charge of "flourishing" the knife was reduced to third-degree assault, a misdemeanor, and Williams was sentenced to six months' probation. Two subsequent arrests for third-degree assault—one in September 1987, another in May of 1988— landed Williams in the workhouse.

At the time of his arrest for raping Brown, he was wanted by St. Louis County authorities for burglary.

A court-ordered investigation concluded: "Williams is a young man without sophistication and without education and training. His assets are few. His liabilities are severe and include violent and aggressive acts against others."

■ ■ ■

In the weeks following the rape, Brown told her story no fewer than ten times, reliving it each time. One place Brown told her story was on the witness stand before the grand jury, which returned six felony counts against Williams: one second-degree robbery, one kidnapping, two rape and two sodomy.

The case would be handled by Assistant Prosecutor Mike Quinley, who had six years' experience as a prosecutor and a trial record of forty-nine wins and three losses.

His support seemed unequivocal. In the warrant office at the city courthouse, Brown asked him: "Is this going to be plea-bargained?"

"No," Quinley replied. He told her that the prosecutor's office has "a strong policy of not reducing charges.

"You are a good witness," he told her. "You can remember details and articulate points that another witness simply couldn't."

"People were supportive," she recalls. "They told me it wasn't my fault, that I didn't do anything wrong. I went to counseling, and I forced myself to keep up my routine. I went back to work."

On May 20, she was married and became Kelly Miller. One of the guests at the wedding was Detective Ray Ghrist.

The couple wasn't sure that she hadn't been infected with the AIDS virus, so they practiced safe sex. She was treated for gonorrhea and spent thousands of dollars on medical treatment and counseling. No matter how difficult, she was determined to deal with her problems head-on, as she had so often counseled others.

■ ■ ■

A deposition of Kelly Miller was scheduled for July 19. It was a routine preparation for trial, which had been set for July 24.

A week earlier, however, the prosecutor's office had decided to cut a deal with the rapist and his lawyer. On July 13, at a regularly scheduled Thursday meeting, Sam Bertolet and four other assistant prosecutors gathered at The Olive Tree Cafe on South Grand Boulevard. Bertolet is chief trial attorney to St. Louis Circuit Attorney George Peach. The other four lawyers were the assistant prosecutors with the most trial experience. Each week, they gather to consider upcoming prosecutions. Is a case strong enough to take to trial? Should it be plea-bargained? If so, what sentence will the prosecution settle for?

Quinley submitted a single page of handwritten notes to the committee, listing the weaknesses of the case. The list began, "The victim makes a very poor witness," offering no further explanation. Quinley went on to note that the rapist had entered the victim's car on the Barnes' Hospital lot, that she had accompanied the rapist to his house, where she was introduced to his family and friends as the rapist's "girlfriend."

(He did not mention that the rapist had paraded her around the house after more than four hours of holding her hostage and assaulting her.) Quinley also wrote that Brown "gave" Williams her engagement ring and wrote down her correct phone number for him.

The committee decided the case was too risky to take to trial, and that the state would recommend a five-year sentence. Of the six original charges, the rape and robbery charges would stand, but the rest would be dropped.

Bertolet says the prosecutors opted for the minimal sentence because it was a virtual guarantee that Williams would plead guilty and have the rape on his record. If Williams were ever to be convicted of rape again, he would face a mandatory sentence of thirty years without parole, but only if prosecutors were to exercise their discretion and charge him as a "persistent offender."

At 10:30 a.m., on July 19th, she arrived at the courthouse, ready for the deposition. She didn't know about any deals. She didn't know about the prosecutors' meeting. She didn't know about Quinley's list. "I told her what the recommendation was," Quinley recalls. "I was upset with it, but I didn't push it." Quinley admitted to her that he made a mistake by "selling it too cheaply—I thought it was worth fifteen, not five."

"You told me we were going to trial," she recalls saying to Quinley that morning. "You told me it was because I was a good witness."

Quinley told her that there had been problems with the case from the start. He said she had impressed the grand jury as "too rational." (Quinley says now, "It's better sometimes to acknowledge some uncertainty rather than having a ready answer. Too much rational explanation doesn't ring well.")

"But you never tell a witness they are a bad witness," he told her, "because you might have to use them at trial."

She asked Quinley what she could do to protest the plea. Quinley told her she could ask Peach to intervene on her behalf and that she could write to the judge. Quinley warned her, however, that judges rarely set aside plea agreements.

■ ■ ■

After speaking with Quinley, Miller sought refuge in the office of Kim Norman, a staff member of the Victim Service Council, which operates under the aegis of circuit attorney Peach. "You got screwed over," Miller recalls Norman saying. (Norman declined to comment for this story.)

During the next few hours, she counseled with Norman and went to see her friend, Detective Ghrist. She was upset the case would be plea-bargained. She was even more upset at the recommended sentence of five years.

Five years is the minimum possible sentence for rape and for robbery, and, as Miller had discovered since the rape, state law requires that sentences for such charges run consecutively, not concurrently. If both charges stood, it would be contrary to law to offer a total sentence of five years.

She found the statute in the law library of the Victim Service Council, then settled in to wait for Peach. At about 3 p.m., he appeared at the door of Norman's office, where, as he recalls, he spent "the better part of an hour with (Miller)."

"I don't think you know, but I was misled about the plea bargain," she recalls telling Peach. She remembers the conversation this way:

Miller: "I think something is wrong here. I was told over and over that I was a good witness, that there would be a trial, and now I find out none of that is true, and the recommended sentence is five years."

Peach: "I think this is the best you're going to get. You did let the guy into your car. What did you expect?"

"Not to be raped."

"It was the middle of the day. (Williams had accosted her at about 6 p.m., after dark.) There were a lot of people around."

"Well, I'm sorry, but you're wrong on that count, too."

"I don't know what you want me to do."

"I want you to intervene."

"I can't do it."

"I don't see how there can be all these charges and the recommendation ends up being five years." She pointed out the law.

"You might be right about this. I'll see what I can do."

(Peach says now: "I knew nothing about her case until she explained it to me [that day]. We then highlighted six or seven factors that we would have to overcome in a trial, not just her letting him in the car. Since I have the power to intervene, I don't know why I would have said I wouldn't!")

■ ■ ■

Later that afternoon, Peach called Miller at home. "It was determined that the offer was going to be ten years," Peach says, recalling that she responded: " 'That's wonderful. That makes a world of difference to me. Now I feel that he will be in there long enough to get help for his problem.'

"I was a little surprised," Peach says, "because maybe there isn't a big difference between ten and five, but to her, it seemed as though there was. I thought, 'Well, that's the end of that.' "

Miller: "I said I was grateful . . . , that I thought ten years was better than five. But I told him I still thought there was something wrong here. I didn't know at this time that all the wrong information had been given to the committee.

"If Peach tries to say I approved of the plea arrangement, he's wrong," Miller says. "He's dead wrong."

■ ■ ■

On the morning of July 24, Kelly and Scott Miller sat in the court-room of Judge Jack Koehr. Moments before Elvis Williams was going to take the stand and plead guilty, Williams' lawyer, Assistant Public Defender David Ferman, talked with Quinley in the judge's chambers.

"I don't think he'll plead if she's in the courtroom," Ferman said.

"What are you trying to say?" Quinley asked.

"He is going to plead. But I'm not sure he'll say, 'I did it,' if she's in the courtroom. Could you ask the victim to step outside?"

"Hell no," Quinley replied.

"Well, then can you at least let her know what I said?" Ferman said.

Quinley joined the Millers in the front row of spectators' seats. "I think you might have to leave the courtroom," Kelly Miller recalls Quinley saying. "The defense attorney says he doesn't think Mr. Williams will plead if you're here. I think it might be best if you left."

"Why?" she asked.

"If you stay in the courtroom, we might end up going to trial," Quinley said.

"That would be fine with me," she said.

"If I have to take this case to trial today, there's a good chance (Williams) might walk," Quinley said.

Kelly Miller reluctantly left the courtroom. Standing outside in the hall, she peered through the small window in the courtroom door. She couldn't hear his voice, but Elvis Williams admitted his crimes.

■ ■ ■

Back at Quinley's office after the plea, Miller asked Quinley what had been conveyed to the prosecutors' committee before it recommended the five-year sentence to begin with. "You're not gonna like me when you read this," she recalls Quinley telling her as he handed her the list.

■ ■ ■

That night, as she was drifting off to sleep, scenes from the rape and the courtroom flashed in her mind. She climbed out of bed, fighting back tears. She threw on a dress, darted from the bedroom, down the stairs, slammed the front door behind her and ran out into the night, shoeless.

Shaking and crying, she gripped the wheel of her car. The images played over and over in her head. She drove to the house where the rape took place and sat in her car. *Had it all really happened? Or was it some twisted dream? Was it my fault somehow? What could I have done to stop it?*

Then she drove to the court-house. *I was powerless here, too. I did everything I possibly could, but it didn't matter. What will it take for them to see how serious this is for me? Do they want a corpse? Then*

I'll give it to them. I'll drive full speed into the side of the court-house.

No, I'll just wait until Quinley or Peach comes around, and I'll just go off on them. I'm not a good witness because I'm too rational, too much in control? I wish they could see me now.

She opened the door and bolted from the car. Moments later, she realized she was alone on the deserted streets. She panicked. She saw light spilling through the glass doors of the police station.

She rushed inside. Police officers milled about. Suspects were led in and out. She stood there, lost. One suspect looked her over and made a lewd comment. She broke into tears. She walked to the glass doors, peered down the street. Several men stood near her car. *Now what do I do?*

Finally, a man in blue noticed her distress and approached. She began to tell him what had shaken her from her sleep, how she felt she had been wronged in the courts, how she had ended up at the police department that night. "I've done everything that I can. I've done everything that they told me to do. But it doesn't matter. I want someone to help me."

The officer calmed her down, explaining that no one at the department could help her that night. "I'm afraid to walk back to my car alone. Would you please walk me there?" she asked.

"Do you promise to go home?" he asked.

"Yes. I just want to go home."

■ ■ ■

Miller: "You know, so much of my life and what I do for a living is about helping people to avoid becoming victims and to take action. What happened in court that day undermined everything I believe in.

"I had no hope anymore. It was over. And it was over because, in my opinion, people chose to hide behind things, to ignore things. They chose to make a decision based on who I was as a person and to blame it on me. It was personalities before principles. It was politics. And I was so disgusted.

"After I left the police station, I went home, and I made a decision. There was no way I was going to sit there and take it. I was going to go to Mike Quinley's supervisor and tell her about all the mistakes in his letter to the prosecutors' committee. I was going to send a letter to all the committee members, to George Peach and to the judge.

"I am a rational person. I am in control. That was one of the things that kept me alive. For me, to drive around hysterical at night, I mean. . . . After the rape, I didn't even do anything like that. It was my absolute bottom. But I decided I was going to fight."

■ ■ ■

Soon thereafter, what *Post-Dispatch* columnist Bill McClellan would later call Miller's "letter-writing campaign" began in earnest, and she hired a lawyer, Clayton attorney Bob Adler, to ensure that her best interest would be protected in court.

In single-spaced, typewritten letters to the people she had promised to write, she laid out in detail the mistakes she saw in the handling of her case.

"I plan to continue to make my desire for a trial or a lengthier sentence known," she wrote to Peach in a letter dated August 11. "I feel much harm has been done, but it's not too late to remedy this. I would like you to look into this matter, perhaps to tell the judge of the misinformation on the case."

Miller also wrote to Paula LeGrand, of the Missouri Board of Probation and Parole, who was responsible for conducting the pre-sentence investigation of Elvis Williams. In explaining the initial confrontation with Williams, Miller wrote: "He was obviously intoxicated and claimed he was sick and cold—too sick and cold to make it home a couple of blocks away. He also said he worked in maintenance and wore the green jumpsuit that some of the workers wear. I believed him and tried to help him. [But] he was not as intoxicated as I had thought, nor was he physically ill. I made a mistake."

Those last four words would come back to haunt her.

■ ■ ■

On September 1, Williams was to be sentenced in Judge Koehr's court.

After sometimes-heated questioning and testimony about Miller's involvement in the case—or lack thereof—Judge Koehr finally said: "Let the record reflect that I think the input of a victim goes beyond just the cold black-and-white contained in the alleged victim's right to testify or make a statement. This particular victim does not feel—at least at this point in time—that she has been treated fairly by the system and is not happy with the results of the system. I think this is a fine opportunity to afford society as a whole the knowledge that this system stresses and tries to be fair to all participants, whether it be a defendant or a victim or the State of Missouri.

"And further, because the victim was not allowed to make a statement or was not informed that she could make a statement prior to this defendant entering a plea of guilty the court now rejects the plea bargain and the plea of guilty heretofore entered."

Miller appeared on the ten o'clock news that night. Not only was it highly unusual that a judge had thrown out a plea bargain, but it was extraordinary that a rape victim would agree to go before the cameras.

"I know you'd had some doubts about how the system worked," one newsman said to Miller. "What's your feeling now?"

"My feeling now is that it's not over yet," she said.

■ ■ ■

It appeared in the ensuing weeks that the case would indeed go to trial. Miller once again recounted the details of her rape during a deposition by assistant public defender Ferman on October 19, and the trial was set for October 30 in the court of St. Louis Circuit Judge Daniel Tillman. On the morning of the 30th, however, Quinley and Ferman were called into Tillman's chambers.

"Is this going to be a trial or a plea?" the judge asked the attorneys.

"My client wants to plead guilty," Ferman said.

Tillman turned to Quinley. "Well, what's the state's offer?" the judge asked.

"It's still five for rape and five for robbery, for a total of ten years," Quinley said.

"I hope the offer's still open," Ferman said. "Is it?"

"Yeah," Quinley said.

■ ■ ■

On the witness stand that afternoon, Miller tried to tell Tillman of her injuries, what a horror the rape had been. Judge Tillman informed her that he had read copies of the letters she had written in the weeks after the July 24 hearing in Judge Koehr's court. Then the judge tried to educate Miller on a process she had come to know all too well.

"Now, before I was a judge, I was a prosecutor, too," Tillman said. "And before I was a prosecutor, I was a defense lawyer, and I lived in the community before that. And I have to consider the totality of the circumstances. And I think you summed it up quite well in your statement when you said, 'I made a mistake.' Do you remember in your letter you said you had made a mistake by letting him in your car?"

"And I've paid for that mistake," Miller said.

"Indeed you have," Tillman said. "But that in itself diminishes the nature of . . . That was something that the circuit attorney had to consider."

"So if you try to help somebody and you get raped, it's different?"

"No, no," Tillman said. "I'm saying you put yourself in a predicament where it would diminish the value of the case."

"Oh, so . . . ," Miller began, but Tillman cut her off.

"So if you see somebody, you call the cops," Tillman said. "If somebody needs help, you call. You're a young lady by yourself at night. I'm not attempting to make you feel bad. I'm attempting to tell you why things happen the way they happen. Do you understand this?

"See," the judge continued, "I've got a daughter about your age, and I have a wife much older than you, and they are told don't ever let nobody in the car, and if they get in the front of the car, run them over, because you have to protect yourself."

Elvis Williams was sentenced to ten years in prison. Given credit for the time he had served before the sentencing, he would be eligible for parole in two and a half years. (His first review for possible parole is scheduled for December 1990.)

As he was led from the courtroom by a sheriff's deputy, Williams turned to his family and friends, smiled and flashed a thumbs'-up sign.

A newspaper story three days later questioned whether Miller actually had objected to the sentence Williams ultimately received. Despite Miller's repeated statements to Peach indicating that she was dissatisfied — in the August 11 letter, in person and by telephone — Peach was quoted as saying: "At the time, ten years was okay with Kelly."

■ ■ ■

"I'm quite sure that the assistants in the office read the articles about it very closely," Peach says. "We didn't call a meeting or reinstruct anyone. But I'm sure that the assistants who deal day to day with victims have said, 'I don't want this to happen to me, I'm going to communicate better with my victims.'"

One point Peach will not concede, however, is that the Miller case might have been a good one to put before a jury. "In the old days, rapes just weren't

tried," Peach says. "But we like to try them now, we really do."

The "old days" for Peach were the first years he was in office. In 1978, thirteen rape and sexual-assault cases were tried by Peach's assistants; seven resulted in acquittals. In 1979, only eighteen cases went to trial; five ended with not-guilty verdicts.

In 1988, his office brought thirty-three sex-crime cases to trial and lost nine of them. In 1989, the year the case against Williams would have been tried, the number fell back to nineteen, two of which resulted in not-guilty verdicts.

Quinley says the case has stuck with him, too. "Kelly has certainly encouraged me to include the victim, if at all possible, before I seek a recommendation on a case."

Quinley also says it's not likely he'll ever ask a victim to leave the courtroom while a defendant pleads guilty, a mistake he admits he made with Miller. "If he's not willing to plead in front of the victim, then the plea is not worth much."

■ ■ ■

"I am tired of being scared," Kelly Miller says. "I am tired of bad memories flooding back when I touch my husband intimately. I'm tired of jumping ten feet when I hear a loud noise. Do you understand? There is not one day that I don't live in fear."

Today, she is coping with that fear in the same way she has from the beginning—by trying to maintain her daily routine and put the rape as far behind her as possible. She has not resumed the research she was in the midst of when the rape occurred, but she is working as a counselor, sometimes with families of alcoholics and drug abusers.

As for Scott Miller, he is attending art classes and working at Maryville College, though he says that since the rape, "My colors have changed." His palette used to be filled with bright greens, yellows, teals and blues. After the rape, he favored black, dark blue and red.

And there are other funda-mental changes. "Our sex life is, more often than not, a very harsh experience," Scott says. "It's hard to get through sex without the rape coming up, without her shuddering at some time, without my saying something that triggers a bad memory for her." He says he also has trouble with inti-macy.

"I don't know when to expect it to get better," he says, tears coming to his eyes. "And that scares me. But I uhhh . . . dammit. My trust in everyone is gone."

The rape has deeply affected Kelly Miller's relationships with her siblings, too. Her younger brother, Kevin Brown, tells of a late-night conversation in December 1989, when the two were in Florida, visiting their mother.

Kelly and Kevin conversed in urgent whispers, trying to hold down their voices, but the dis-cussion became heated, more and more intense. Finally, fearing that the talk might wake their mother, Kevin reached back and swung the door shut.

His sister straightened, then squared off defensively.

"No man will ever lock me in a room again," she said.

"C'mon, Kelly. I'm your *brother*."

■ ■ ■

Now Miller has finished showing me the clothes she was wearing the night of the rape. As she repacks the big bag marked EVIDENCE, she pauses as she holds up the overcoat. "Nice, isn't it? I saved up to get it. It was my favorite coat. I deserve to have a coat that I like, don't I?" She flashes a smile, then stuffs the coat in the bag.

"Part of my recovery, someday, is going to be to wear these clothes," she says. "Maybe not the entire outfit at once. But I'll wear these clothes."

■ ■ ■

This article first appeared in the June 1990 issue of St. Louis *magazine. Joe Bargmann is now senior editor at* Seventeen *magazine.*

■ ■ ■

FIRE POWER

BY JOHN MORTHLAND

The first burn was the deepest. Chile entrepreneur Jeff Campbell had been waiting for months to sample one of his homegrown habanero chiles. A Stonewall farmer who eats chile peppers at every meal and snacks on whole jalapeños, Campbell had heard that the habanero was the hottest pepper known to man, but he had never tasted one. So when it came time to harvest his first habanero, he pulled a ripe one off the bush and bit into it as he would a jalapeño.

"That was a major mistake," he recalls. At first Campbell tasted only the chile's distinctive flavor, followed by a several-second lull, during which he wondered what all the fuss was about. There then blasted forth a hellacious afterburn, a chemical heat like nothing he had ever experienced. It spread across his tongue and through his mouth, pausing momentarily to regroup before continuing to surge for at least the next ten minutes. "I spit it out," Campbell says, "and drove as fast as I could to the bar. Actually, I'm being a smart aleck when I say that; I got water somewhere to wash it down, and then I came to the bar and drank a cold beer." After regaining the feeling in his mouth, he drank some more beer, just to be safe. And

Campbell, a man who heretofore had feared no chile, has not bitten into a whole habanero since.

The habanero is the chile of the moment. But Campbell's ten-acre spread in Central Texas is one of only two farms in the nation—the other is in California—that grows habaneros commercially. If the fad continues to grow, however, other farms will undoubtedly sprout up in the next few years.

At the Third National Fiery Foods Show last February in Albuquerque, 10 percent of the one-hundred-plus booths featured habanero-based products such as sauces and jerk mixes—Jamaican dry spice rubs for meats. In Texas fresh, dried, or ground habaneros have turned up in the produce section at supermarket chains like H.E.B. as well as at farmers' markets and specialty spice shops like Pendery's in Fort Worth. Habanero sauces are also becoming fairly common—labels to look for include El Yucateco, La Anita, and Loltun from Mexico and Melinda's from Belize.

What is it about habaneros that tantalizes people? Some say it's the aroma and the flavor. They do give off a wonderful fruity fragrance, somewhere between an orange and an apricot, and the flavor is equally rich. But the real fascination is the habanero's firepower. Habaneros check in at 200,000 to 300,000 Scoville Units, which is the measure of capsaicin, the chemical that gives peppers their burn. That means habaneros can be more than a hundred times hotter than jalapeños, which measure a wimpy 2,500 to 6,000 Scoville Units. We are not likely to see habanero-eating contests in the near future—although in the Yucatán and the Caribbean, where most of the world's supply is grown, some people apparently do munch them raw.

Because this chile is so new here, little is known about it. "Habanero" means "Havana-like" or "from Havana," which indicates that the chile probably originated in Cuba. In 1722 Dominican priest Francisco Ximénez, in a natural history of Guatemala, mentioned a chile from Havana so hot that one pod was enough to make "a bull unable to eat." Researchers think he was referring to the habanero; it is the only pepper in the Yucatán that doesn't have a Mayan name, which suggests that it was imported. The habanero is a variety of *Capsicum chinense* (most peppers belong to *Capsicum annuum*). Until recently, it was believed that the habanero could not be grown outside the Yucatán and the Caribbean.

But that was before Jeff Campbell decided to try it. When the burly, bearded Alabaman first arrived in Stonewall in 1984, he

raised tomatoes, onions, and various chiles. He learned of habaneros from a magazine a year or two later, and at the next Terlingua Chili Cookoff, a friend gave him habanero seeds from Belize. Campbell and his partner, Lester Betts, planted half an acre of habaneros and took a sackful of pods to the First National Fiery Foods Show in El Paso. Nobody knew what they were, but they were a hit.

Considering his novice status, Campbell has had relatively few problems raising habaneros. The hard part is processing them. To grind jalapeños, for example, he wears surgical gloves and a dust mask, and he works in a back room at his Stonewall Chili Pepper Company shop. But when he grinds habaneros, he must close the shop so that customers won't breathe the chile dust. He wears a long-sleeved shirt buttoned at the top and a bandanna around his neck. A respirator with an air tank replaces the dust mask, and he leaves his gloves on to wash out pots. "You get that habanero on your hand and it *hurts*. I have gone to sleep at night with my hand in a bucket of ice water because of it," Campbell says.

Still, he's not about to stop working with habaneros. Last spring Campbell and Betts planted four acres, and they will easily sell their whole crop after they harvest it this month. At his shop on U.S. 290 in Stonewall, Campbell sells his devastating Salsa Habanero (which he recommends using only as a flavoring in soups or stews), a more manageable Salsa del Diablo to eat with chips, and such novelties as habanero-flavored suckers and ketchup. He also has powdered habanero and fresh or dried habaneros. Heat enthusiasts regularly make the pilgrimage to Campbell's store to buy the peppers; one customer flies down from Alaska annually and buys half a pound to a pound, enough to make chili con carne every week for a year. Campbell also ships fresh habaneros to a gourmet shop outside Chicago and to an Oregon restaurant run by an El Paso native.

Working with habaneros has given Campbell some insight into the strange ways of human nature. "People always do want it hotter; that's the reason habaneros caught on," he says. "I don't know if there's anything like developing a tolerance or not, but I know I like it hotter than I did ten years ago." Back then, Campbell ate only in bars when he went up north, because he knew that a place that made Bloody Marys would at least have Tabasco sauce. Nowadays chiles are so pervasive, he doesn't need to pack his own bottle of Tabasco when he travels. As Dave DeWitt, the editor of Albuquerque-based *Chile Pepper* magazine, says, "The fiery-foods market is continuing to grow, and the mystique of being the hottest chile pepper is definitely helping the habanero. It's one of those things you either like or don't like."

But for Jeff Campbell and his fellow heat lovers, it's the only way to go.

■   ■   ■

This article first appeared in the September 1991 issue of Texas Monthly. *Morthland is a full-time freelance writer in Austin, Texas.*

PUT IT INTO PRACTICE

Discussion

1. What do you think of the statement, early in this chapter, that a newspaper reporter's job "is primarily to inform. If a news reporter manages to write a piece that is emotionally moving as well, all the better. But the primary task for most newspaper reporters is to inform, and the writer and the reader both know that."

    Discuss modern newspaper writing in the light of that statement. Do most newspaper reporters write to inform, knowing that most readers won't get past the first few paragraphs, or are they writing stylish, entertaining stories that are meant to be read in their entirety? Are the two types of writing mutually exclusive?

2. Discuss the hooks from recent stories that you find in the feature section of your daily newspaper with those found in magazines. How are they different? How are they the same?

3. Discuss the expectations that readers hold for newspaper writing, and then contrast those expectations with those that readers hold for magazine writing. How are they different? How are they the same?

Exercises

1. You're a freelance magazine writer living in Texas, and you have an assignment to do a story on the new rage in Texas cuisine: the habanero chile. You do your background research, interview several people (including farmer Jeff Campbell), and then sit down to write the story. Using the "Fire Power" story found in this chapter as your information source, write the following:

    a. A one-paragraph summary hook, focusing on the most newsworthy elements of the story.

    b. A one-paragraph startle hook, focusing on the most dramatic elements of the story.

    c. A two- or three-paragraph descriptive hook, focusing on the best sensory images available in the story.

    d. A two- or three-paragraph narrative hook, which attempts to draw the reader into the heart of the story. Focus on that element of the story that offers the most impact but is appropriate to the story's overall tone.

    Now share your hooks with another writer in your class or writers' group. Which one of the hooks written by your classmate works best? Why? What does the classmate think of your hooks? Why?

Finally, revise each other's hooks, trying to sharpen them for impact. Then repeat the analysis process, handing the hooks back to the original writer and assessing the editing improvements. See chapter seven for advice on editing and revising.

2. Use the notes belonging to one of your stories for class that you haven't written yet or perhaps have only roughed out, and try writing each of the four kinds of hooks covered in the chapter. Which works best for what you have in mind for the story? Why? Again, just as you did with the Campbell story, trade these hooks with a classmate for assessment, editing them and trading them back. Repeat the analysis process.

3. Go to several other stories reprinted in this book and analyze their hooks, listing what kind of hook is used and why. How does the hook, in each case, reflect the needs of the magazine in which it was published?

    Are there hooks in any of the articles reprinted in this text other than the four kinds of hooks studied? In many cases, the four kinds mentioned here are blended. See if you can find those blends and list them.

4. Finally, take a major story from page one of today's newspaper and rewrite the hook for a magazine story. Make sure you keep in mind a particular magazine that you'd be likely to find the story in.

Body Building

▼

BACKGROUND AND KEY FACTS

QUOTES

DESCRIPTION

ANECDOTES

TRANSITIONS

THE END

◄

Magazine writers quickly learn that there is no easy, set formula to follow when it's time to build up the body of a story. There are just too many variations in the material, characters, scenery, information, interviews, and anecdotes that form the tools at a writer's disposal when it comes to writing nonfiction.

There are, however, certain basic elements that writers probably want to have in their story, including some solid *background and key facts*, relevant *quotes*, a certain amount of *description*, and *anecdotes*. And writers want to weave all of these elements together with *transitions* before coming to a solid, purposeful *end*.

BACKGROUND AND KEY FACTS

Remember that the reader needs a context to understand what the story is all about. Some *background* material is almost always necessary. Think of this as the history of the story.

In Karima Haynes's story on Carol Moseley Braun, for instance, the background comes from passages like this:

> Although Braun grew up on Chicago's South Side, attended city schools, the University of Illinois, the University of Chicago Law School and served as an assistant U.S. attorney and a state legislator for 10 years, she was virtually a political unknown. The political establishment snubbed her. Powerful women's groups listened to her stump speech and then politely showed her the door: Political pundits said she was out of her mind to go up against the congenial, good ol' boy two-term incumbent known as "Al the Pal" and the other challenger, Albert Hofeld, a personal injury lawyer with $5 million to burn on a campaign that included a carefully crafted media blitz.

This background information appears just before a section in the story that outlines Braun's political successes in the Illinois primary, and it achieves two things: First, it establishes for the reader that despite her relative anonymity, Braun does have strong, legitimate credentials. Second, the quick contrast between those humble beginnings and her later success makes the upset primary win all the more impressive to the reader.

John Morthland does something similar in his habanero story:

> Because this chile is so new here, little is known about it. "Habanero" means "Havana-like" or "from Havana," which indicates that the chile probably originated in Cuba. In 1722 Dominican priest Francisco Ximénez, in a natural history of Guatemala, mentioned a chile from Havana so hot that one pod was enough to make "a bull unable to eat." Researchers think he was referring to the habanero; it is the only pepper in the Yucatán that doesn't have a Mayan name, which suggests that it was imported. The habanero is a variety of *Capsicum chinense* (most peppers belong to *Capsicum annuum*). Until recently, it was believed that the habanero could not be grown outside the Yucatán and the Caribbean.

In this case, not only does the background give a brief history of the pepper; it also raises for the reader the importance of farmer Jeff Campbell's success by noting that until he grew them, the habanero peppers were thought to be limited to the Caribbean basin.

"My thinking in these kinds of stories," explains Morthland, "is that if the reader doesn't have a background in the topic or person, then he or she can't really appreciate the significance of the story, or at least not the whole significance."

Haynes feels the same way. "I spent weeks getting the background on Braun, just so I could ask the right questions. For readers to understand Braun's responses to some of those questions, they need to know a little bit, at least, about what I found out. It establishes a context for the quotes."

Like background information, *key facts* build confidence. When you can ground your story in factual support for what you are saying as the writer (and for what your subjects are saying in their quotes) then you have taken a strong step in the direction of believability and validity.

Without these facts your story will seem facile, light, all opinion with no proof. With supportive facts, the story takes on a core of believability that will convince the reader to trust you as the writer.

Sometimes these facts can be woven into the story in a critical sentence here and there. At other times, an entire paragraph seems necessary to establish the story's credentials for the reader. Frequently, it is a blend, in which factual support appears in the second half of a paragraph that begins with opinion.

In Morthland's story, for example, there is a paragraph that shows how factual support can lend legitimacy to opinion.

> What is it about habaneros that tantalizes people? Some say it's the aroma and the flavor. They do give off a wonderful fruity fragrance, somewhere between an orange and an apricot, and the flavor is equally rich. But the real fascination is the habanero's firepower. Habaneros check in at 200,000 to 300,000 Scoville Units, which is the measure of capsaicin, the chemical that gives peppers their burn. That means habaneros can be more than a hundred times hotter than jalapeños, which measure a wimpy 2,500 to 6,000 Scoville Units. We are not likely to see habanero-eating contests in the near future— although in the Yucatán and the Caribbean, where most of the world's supply is grown, some people apparently do munch them raw.

The hard facts about Scoville Units convert a paragraph that begins with the writer's unprovable opinions ("wonderful fruity fragrance" and "the flavor is equally rich") into a paragraph of undeniable fact (the Scoville measurements). For the reader, that unquestionable factual evidence, given in the back half of the paragraph, lends credence to the writer's opinion at the beginning. Readers will trust the subjective opinions of a writer who is able to show such factual proof when it is needed.

Omni magazine Senior Editor Murray Cox thought of the use of such factual support as grounding the story.

"I always ask writers for those concrete details," Cox said. "I don't think writers do enough of it. I need something to bring the story down to earth and give the reader a moment of hard reality."

A word of caution: Such factual supports can also be roadblocks to smooth reading if they are not handled well. They can break up the story's smooth flow, and overuse of key facts can overwhelm a reader.

Even Murray Cox, who often asked writers for more factual information in a story, would add, "Sometimes the reader is given too much information at one time. There's an overload, and you need to go back and break it up, perhaps with some examples of what you are saying."

The important thing is to use your factual support judiciously, just often enough to establish the story's validity. If you've done enough research (see chapter two), then you have plenty of factual support to work with. Pick those facts that are the most relevant—those that are just right for the support you need at that point in the story—and the reader will trust you. You don't have to use all your research, just a small portion—but the correct small portion—of it.

QUOTES

Quotes, of course, are essential to most magazine stories. The key (see chapter one) to getting good quotes, of course, is to have high-quality interviews. But remember that how you use the quote in structuring the body of the story is also critical to your success.

Good quote usage should illuminate the subject for the reader. Not only should the quote convey some information; it should also give a feel for the more human, emotional aspects of the subject.

For instance, in Karima Haynes's story on Carol Moseley Braun, the candidate tells the readers (through Haynes's story), "This nomination is history making. . . . But history is a fluid situation. The real test is what kind of human being you are and what kind of mark you make."

Braun's words both give readers factual confirmation and support of Haynes's previous paragraph about the importance of the election and also tell something about the candidate. There is a certain humility in those words. While the reader gets a feel for the candidate's quiet acceptance of the significance of her effort, Braun's statement about what "the real test is" gives the reader a feeling that Braun sees herself as part of something larger.

In the next paragraph, Haynes lets Braun expand on that idea: "To the extent that there will be other women and Black people who will see the possibilities because of my candidacy, then I think that being nominated is a contribution that I can be proud of."

Haynes used those quotes quite purposefully as she constructed this story. "I felt like she was a very impressive figure," Haynes says, "and I wanted to bring that out in the story. She was an outsider, although she's very politically savvy, and she clearly had an idea of just what her candidacy meant. It made sense to me to have her say that to the reader."

In a similar fashion, Morthland lets Jeff Campbell speak for himself about the potency of the habanero chile. In a paragraph late in the story, about the difficulties of processing the peppers into powder, Campbell says, "You get that habanero on your hand and it *hurts*. I have gone to sleep at night with my hand in a bucket of ice water because of it."

That's a short quote at the end of a long paragraph, but it is effective because it emphasizes, in the subject's own words, what the writer has been describing.

"You don't need to use a lot of quotes in a story," Morthland explains. "But every quote you use has to be a good one — one that not only moves the story along but says something important. I thought this one made clear that there's some real danger in working with habaneros, but that Campbell pretty much knew what he was doing with them."

To build quotes into a story you need to anchor them with a setup in the preceding paragraph of the story. Occasionally, you can alter structure by dropping the anchor in after the quote.

Notice in Haynes's story that the preceding paragraph introduces Braun's words smoothly by bringing out the information that if she wins "she will become the first Black woman, and only the fourth Black American, to serve in the Senate." This way, Braun's quote about her awareness of the part she is playing in the larger picture of black America's participation in politics has more impact. It looks like this:

> This has been Braun's routine since March when she shook American politics to its foundations by becoming the first Black woman nominated to the U.S. Senate by a major political party. If she wins the general election in November, she will become the first Black woman, and only the fourth Black American, to serve in the Senate.
>
> "This nomination is history making," Braun says with the same quiet self-assurance that helped her overcome great political odds. "But history is a fluid situation. The real test is what kind of human being you are and what kind of mark you make."

It is important to note that Haynes and Morthland both avoid a common fault of quote use, redundant quotes.

Beginners, in trying to introduce a quote they like, all too often introduce the quote with a paraphrase that offers the same information. Readers don't need to see it twice. Were Haynes a less polished professional, she might have introduced Braun's quote with a setup that read, "Braun knows that her nomination is history making" and then followed that with the actual quote: " 'This nomination is history making,' Braun says."

The redundancy is obvious. Not only does the quote serve no useful purpose at this point (since the statement has already been made), but the specific facts that Haynes offers (first black woman in the Senate) are lost in the generalities.

In fact, this particular passage illustrates one good way to structure quote use. The setup and its quote should move either from the general to the specific or from the specific to the general.

In this case, the facts moved from specific (first black woman) to the general (history making). If Braun's quote had included the details of her being the first black woman, then Haynes could easily have reversed the process, and set up the quote with the general statement about being history making. The overall key, then, is to bear in mind that the quote should be useful to the story, should move things along, and should not be dropped in thoughtlessly. For more information on how to use quotes, see the section on Transitions in this chapter.

DESCRIPTION

It is easy to overdo description. Even beginners know that they need description in their work to draw for the reader a picture of the person or thing being discussed.

What the professionals have learned is that the quality and the specific detail of a description matter more than the quantity. Each bit of description should contribute something to the story, should describe it in such a way as to help the reader better understand what is going on.

In Morthland's story, for instance, this bit of description says a lot:

> The hard part is processing them. To grind jalapeños, for example, he wears surgical gloves and a dust mask, and he works in a back room at his Stonewall Chili Pepper Company shop. But when he grinds habaneros, he must close the shop so that the customers won't breathe the chile dust. He wears a long-sleeved shirt buttoned at the top and a bandanna around his neck. A respirator with an air tank replaces the dust mask, and he leaves his gloves on to wash out pots.

Morthland spent several days with Campbell, and he gathered a note-book full of description. Yet this is the only descriptive passage of this sort in the entire story. Was all that reporting wasted?

Not at all. In this one scene the potency of the habaneros—which is at the core of the story—is clearly conveyed by the description of the processing involved.

"It was the best kind of interview, one where he said, 'OK, why don't you just come hang out with me, and we'll talk during the course of the day,'" says Morthland. "That meant a lot of good questions, and page after page of description.

"I always take a lot of description notes, not because I plan to use all that much of it, but because you don't know going in just which one you might use."

For Morthland, the single passage "really displayed how careful he has to be, wearing a long-sleeved shirt, and breathing through the respirator and all. I thought that really showed it."

There are stories in which description is more important than in others. Indeed, at times the description is at the heart of the story, as in John Calderazzo's piece on the Maumee River floods in Grand Rapids, Ohio. In these kinds of stories there may be considerably more description, much of it a kind of sensual writing that goes beyond just visual description, as in Calderazzo's opening paragraph, in which he hooks the reader with lines such as "the muffled roar of cracks shooting deep through acres of ice as a million tons of stopped-up river rearranges itself."

But even in that story (reprinted on page 100), Calderazzo chooses his spots wisely.

"I knew I wanted to start with that description of the ice," he says. "I rewrote that maybe ten or fifteen times, tightening it and trying to get it right because it was setting up what was to come later.

"You have to be careful with description," he adds, "because it's easy to overdo. And if you use too much of it, then the description that really matters—the material that conveys important information about the story—gets lost in the mass of other stuff."

You can read more about John Calderazzo's thoughts on descriptive writing for certain high-style stories in chapter six.

In most magazine stories, description is important, but rarely is it meant to dominate. It must be woven into the structure of a story so that it blends evenly with the other elements, giving the reader a seamless whole that entertains and informs without calling undue attention to any one element. It's a technique that takes practice, both in the reporting (knowing what details to notice and learning how to notice them) and in the writing (selecting just the right ones to include in the story).

B O X   5 . 1

DROP YOURSELF A LINE

One of the major problems faced by beginning writers is focus. Especially in longer pieces, it is all too easy both to wander away from the story you really meant to write and to get lost in some of the structural elements you find engrossing and worth writing about, though they don't really pertain to the story.

Those kinds of wanderings are something you want to avoid, and veteran writers know they must not give in to the temptation that, for example, even a great anecdote can offer.

In John Calderazzo's story on the Maumee River flooding, for instance, it would have been easy to spend considerably more time on anecdotal information about Nick Weaver, much of it not directly connected to the story, but all of it interesting on its own merits.

And Adrian Nicole LeBlanc recalls that early drafts of her story on teen suicide contained many pages of statistics on teen suicides nationally. The numbers were arresting, but eventually LeBlanc came to realize that using them took the reader away from the real story she was telling.

Every well-reported story offers writers a wealth of information they would love to include. For Karima A. Haynes, the temptation was to give the reader a lot more description about downstate Illinois and its people. For John Morthland, it was to include even more factual detail about the habanero chile.

But all of these writers had learned, as you must, that you can't include everything and that what you do include must stay tightly tied to your story's *theme*.

Theme is what the story is about in its deepest sense. You'll need to learn to recognize that what you've really written about in that story on a cancer victim, for instance, concerns courage in the face of tragedy. And what the piece on hang gliding is really about is the fascination some people find in facing danger.

Sometimes a writer discovers the theme during the writing of the piece. You may think your story is about a local politician who has risen to national prominence, but as you do your reporting and writing, you begin to realize that it's really about opportunity, about hope for the disenfranchised. In this sense, theme ties in closely with subtext (see pages 149–150). What is your story really talking about? When you can answer that question in one short phrase, you have your theme.

Every story has a theme. In fact, a typical nonfiction magazine story may have not only a major theme but also one or more minor themes that revolve around the major one. It is your job as the writer to keep your story focused on that major theme, whether the theme is nature's inescapable power, the frighteningly potent emotions of teenagers, the hopes that a politician can raise for her people, or the danger of our public servants' abusing their power.

For purposes of structure, think of the theme—the main focus of the story—as a fishing line that drops straight down from the hook right to the story's end. All the story elements that are discussed in this chapter have to pertain to that theme or the story starts to wander. You can certainly go off in digressions, especially in a longer piece, but the digression had better have some relevance to the theme.

You might visualize it this way:

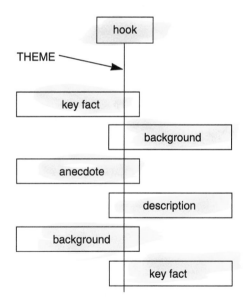

As you can see, all the elements have to touch base with the theme line that runs through the whole piece. Therefore, each element that you use to construct the story should be as directly relevant to your theme as you can possibly make it. If you've done enough good reporting, this isn't at all difficult to do. If you have plenty of anecdotes and a wealth of interview material, descriptive

Continued

Continued

notes, key facts, and background, then all you have to do is to include the material that usefully illustrates the theme and to avoid
the material that may be entertaining and informative but is not
supportive enough of the theme.

It will help you if you jot down the theme at the top of the
first draft when you print it out, or you can even type it in capital
letters at the top of your computer screen, just to serve as a reminder.

ANECDOTES

The author of this book recalls being fresh out of college some years ago
and having the chance to write a story on baseball star Bob Gibson for
Sport magazine. After a few weeks of research, interviewing, and writing,
the story was ready—and it seemed to have it all: the hook was a real
grabber, the description was vivid, the information was accurate, the
background complete.

But the story was rejected by the editor, who sent it back in its SASE
with the comment, "There are a lot of words here, but they don't say
much. There's not an anecdote in the whole piece, no real people doing
real things. Sorry."

And thereby a lesson was learned. Anecdotes, good ones, add measur-
ably to a story, giving life to otherwise dry information and unattached
description.

Readers want to read about real people, not just about things. And
anecdotes, those crucial little stories within the story, bring characters
alive.

Like all the other elements involved in the structure of a story, anecdotes have to be used with restraint. Sometimes one good one will do for
a whole story. The key is that *the anecdote has to illustrate the thematic
point of the story,* bringing it alive by putting real people into the piece
and involving the reader with those people.

John Morthland does exactly that with his anecdotal hook in the "Fire
Power" story. When Morthland describes how Jeff Campbell, "when it
came time to harvest his first habanero, pulled a ripe one off the bush and
bit into it as he would a jalapeño," we are there with Campbell for the re-

sult. The theme of this story is that the habanero chile is potent, indeed, and becoming a hot new product. Morthland's choice of anecdote illustrates that point exactly.

And Karima A. Haynes uses the same technique for her anecdotal hook in the Carol Moseley Braun story, mentioning that she is visiting a small town in downstate Illinois and then showing us how Braun "steps from the sedan and is blinded by TV camera floodlights and mobbed by well-wishers who have left their fish dinners in the hall to come outside for a glimpse of the rising political star."

In both of these cases, a single, strong anecdote tells us important things about the story and its central character. Morthland's anecdote tells us that Campbell has had successes with growing the habaneros on his first try (an important fact that is discussed later in the story), that he is a novice when it comes to their firepower (biting into a raw one and then paying for it), and that they are indeed very, very hot.

Haynes's anecdote, similarly, clues the reader in that Braun is very popular (the TV floodlights and being "mobbed by well-wishers"), that she is a "rising political star," and that she has appeal beyond her big-city Chicago constituency.

There are times, of course, when the opportunity for multiple anecdotes is there. If they all contribute to the story, that's fine. In John Calderazzo's Maumee River story, for instance, there are several, including an extended anecdote about two boys who were trapped by the rapidly rising river. One of the boys died as a result.

"The anecdote about the two boys really deepens the story, I think," says Calderazzo. "The idea that something like this could change so quickly for those kids seemed compelling and terribly sad. It said a lot about how nature can turn on you, which is at the heart of the story."

Several of the other anecdotes that Calderazzo uses accomplish much the same thing, illuminating the story's main theme in a human, poignant way. One, appearing early in the story, discusses how a local millwright watched the floodwaters rise. Another, toward the end of the story, describes a couple's facing the damages that the floodwaters brought to their business.

In both cases, you can see how the anecdotes give us a personal glimpse of what otherwise might be dry, unemotional facts or description.

Also remember that good description benefits from having people involved in it. A descriptive passage that has real people in it doing real things connects better with typical readers than can the same passage with no humanity at all.

What anecdotes do, then, is help make a story more accessible to the reader, bringing the reader more deeply into a level of emotional contact with the story.

It's crucial, of course, that you look for anecdotes when doing your reporting. Search for hints of them in your research, and be looking for them when doing your interviewing and taking your notes for description. If you can learn to find the right anecdotes and use them well, they will help you sell your stories to those jaded editors who have, sometimes literally, seen it all in their field.

This author can vouch for that. Without being asked for a revision, he nonetheless rewrote the Bob Gibson story, added several of the anecdotes he had in his notes, and resubmitted the piece to *Sport*.

The editor bought the rewrite.

TRANSITIONS

The good magazine writer must learn to blend all these various elements of the structure together into a seamless whole, a story that flows from the hook right to the end, with no jarring roadblocks that stop the reader. The writing of this seamless whole requires the deft use of *transitions*, some of them just a word or two long, others a sentence or more.

As you shift from one element to another while writing a story, you must make sure the flow is logical, that the new thought you're bringing up follows coherently from the previous one.

Smart writers learn to begin their transition toward the end of the previous paragraph and then to follow through smoothly at the start of the next. This avoids the clumsiness that can come from transitional paragraphs (usually one sentence long) that are often redundant and almost always useful for no other purpose than the transition itself.

Remember: Everything in the story's structure should be aimed toward the story's thematic purpose—whatever it is you're trying to say. A clumsy transition, in calling attention to itself, detracts from that purpose.

A transition such as the following italicized one, for instance, glares at the reader:

> So with no money ("You really know who your friends are when times are tough"), no organization and no political backing, Braun launched her old-fashioned grassroots campaign. Her announcement that she would give up her low-profile office as Cook County Recorder of Deeds to run for the Senate barely made the six o'clock news.
>
> *That lack of attention came even though Braun does have a lengthy list of credentials.*

> Braun grew up on Chicago's South Side, attended city schools, the University of Illinois, the University of Chicago Law School and served as an assistant U.S. attorney and a state legislator for 10 years.

The clumsy middle paragraph in the example above does, indeed, make the transition from a discussion about the start of Braun's campaign to the background information about her credentials. But notice how deleting that short paragraph, inserting the word "although" in front of the credentials, and then finishing the listing of the credentials with a phrase that takes the reader back into the campaign accomplishes the transition much more successfully.

> So with no money ("You really know who your friends are when times are tough"), no organization and no political backing, Braun launched her old-fashioned grassroots campaign. Her announcement that she would give up her low-profile office as Cook County Recorder of Deeds to run for the Senate barely made the six o'clock news.
>
> Although Braun grew up on Chicago's South Side, attended city schools, the University of Illinois, the University of Chicago Law School and served as an assistant U.S. attorney and a state legislator for 10 years, she was virtually a political unknown.

Now—without the italicized paragraph—the story moves smoothly from one idea (the humble beginnings of the campaign), through a quick recitation of Braun's credentials, and back to her being a "political unknown." The reader has been informed about her background without having the flow of the story disrupted.

As Haynes explains it, "I certainly wanted to get in the information about just how much background and expertise she had for the job, but that wasn't the major point. The point was she was an unknown at the start of the campaign, despite those credentials, so fitting them into the middle of that section made sense to me."

And it makes sense for the reader, too.

To effectively make those transitions, then, try to begin the process toward the end of the previous element and lead smoothly into the next element with just a word or two.

Conjunctive adverbs frequently handle this transition work. Typical conjunctive adverbs are *accordingly, although, at the same time, besides, consequently, for example, furthermore, however, in addition, instead, meanwhile, namely, nevertheless, on the other hand, second (third, fourth . . .), still, therefore,* and *thus.*

Correlative conjunctions also are frequently used as transitions. Typical correlative conjunctions are *as . . . as, both . . . and, either . . . or, neither . . . nor, not only . . . but also,* and *whether . . . or.*

Coordinating conjunctions, such as *and* and *but,* also serve as good transitional words, connecting equal words, phrases, or clauses.

Remember that many times you won't need even one word to make a smooth transition. If the elements flow smoothly and logically, then don't bother with a transitional word or phrase.

But when a transition *is* necessary, keep it as simple and unobtrusive as you can.

THE END

Good newspaper reporters try to write stories that have a solid tag at the end, something that wraps up the piece for the reader. But all too often, the pressure of deadlines and the restrictions of tight space mean that many newspaper stories simply end where they may.

The same constraints that force the newspaper reporter into writing in some form of the inverted pyramid mean that the least important part of the story is at the end, and so the final paragraph or two frequently contribute very little to the story.

Newspaper feature writers, columnists, and sportswriters sometimes have it better and can plan on tying things up neatly at the end of a story. But even those writers suffer from the way newspapers are read. Most readers, frankly, don't make it to the end of most stories. Studies consistently show that very few readers finish front-page stories that are complete on the page, and even fewer follow stories that jump inside.

Thus, even those reporters who carefully construct a story to make sure it is a complete whole, with an end that serves a useful purpose, may sometimes feel that their effort is wasted.

For magazine writers, the situation is quite different. As we've seen, magazine readers settle back and read an entire story. For magazine readers, the ending does matter; therefore the writer needs to be aware of that and must craft an ending that is a significant part of the story's structure.

There are several ways to do this. One is called the *circular end*, which refers back to the opening. John Morthland does that in his end to the habanero story, with a simple sentence that refers to Jeff Campbell "and his fellow heat lovers." That thought reflects the first two sentences of the story, which referred to "The first burn" and Campbell's entrepreneurial efforts.

Another kind of ending is one that is *summary,* that is, it summarizes the story and draws a final conclusion. This technique is most useful for opinion pieces.

For many stories, the best ending is one that *makes the point* about what the story really concerns.

Most stories have a subtext—some meaning or theme to the story that lies below the surface. In Karima A. Haynes's story on Carol Moseley Braun, for instance, the subtext is one of hope for more opportunity for blacks and women in politics. Although the piece's principal story line follows the Braun political campaign, that message of hope and opportunity is clearly there, just below the surface.

One thing a good ending can do for a magazine story is to clarify that subtext for the reader by bringing it up from below the surface and showing it to the reader.

It's almost as if the writer says, "And the moral of this story is . . ."

See how Haynes does this in her final paragraph:

> It is this attitude of service Braun hopes to impart to voters as she criss-crosses the state trying to garner enough support to win the November election. In order to do this, she must hold on to her core constituency of Chicago Blacks and liberal Whites as well as win over a sufficient number of Downstate Whites who have traditionally voted conservatively. Whatever the outcome, her nomination has raised hopes and opened the doors of opportunity.

The final sentence sums up the real point of the story, the thought that lies at the heart of the piece, that Braun's effort has "raised hopes and opened the doors of opportunity." If readers haven't quite understood that point yet, Haynes doesn't want to allow them to miss it here, so she states it quite baldly.

In short fiction, a writer may choose not to raise up the subtext and display it so blatantly at the end for the reader. Like the background music of a film, the subtext should add some emotional impact to the story, but not call attention to itself in the process. Making it so obvious at the end may seem heavy-handed to a short-story writer.

But readers of short stories usually expect that sort of subtlety; readers of nonfiction do not. In a nonfiction magazine piece, readers expect the writer to clearly and concisely make the point for them. The idea, after all, is to inform as well as to entertain.

If the subtext is critical to a full understanding of the story, then there is a clear need to bring it out at the end and make it crystal clear. The benefit of this is that the reader gets a real sense of closure, of finality, from the story when that final point is made. Now I know what the story is really all about, thinks the reader. And that adds significantly to the story's impact.

In the Braun story, for instance, the final thought at the end makes it clear that this campaign is about much, much more than one woman's effort to get elected to the U.S. Senate.

For more on the idea of subtext and how to handle it, see Box 5.1.

PUT IT INTO PRACTICE

Discussion

1. Have each member of your class or writers' group analyze a story from this book. Do a rough outline of the story's structural elements (see exercise 1, following), and then, as a group, discuss how the stories have handled weaving these elements together. In what ways are the stories similar? In what ways are they different?
2. Have each member of your class or writers' group analyze a story of choice from a local daily newspaper, and then discuss how those stories compare to the magazine articles reprinted in this book, in terms of structure. Are there marked differences? Are they surprisingly similar? Focus on news stories, then on feature stories. Again, are there differences? similarities?
3. Choose one story reprinted in this book, have each member of your class or writers' group read it, and write down a one-sentence summation of the story's theme. Discuss how close the group came to unanimity in describing the theme. Then have each member of the group try to find those areas in the story in which the elements may have wandered away from the theme or in which the writer clearly chose a particular element because it tied in so nicely to the theme.

Exercises

1. Choose one of your own recent magazine articles and choose an article from this book that has a similar theme and tone. First, for the reprint from this book, analyze the piece for its use of background and key facts, quotes, description, and anecdotes. Do a rough outline, numbering each paragraph and listing it by element, thus:
    1. description
    2. key fact
    3. quote
    4. background
    5. quote
    6. quote
    7. description

    and so on.

    Analyze how the story from the book uses the elements this chapter discusses. How many are there of each element? In what pattern do they seem to typically occur (or perhaps there is no pattern)?

    Now take your own story and repeat the process, analyzing it for the same elements of structure. Compare your story with the one you've chosen from the book. How do the patterns compare? Does your story have a preponderance of quotes? of description? of background and key facts?

Write a two-page summary of the comparison.

2. Now go through the same process, using the same two stories, for an analysis of transitions. Reread the chapter's discussion of transitions, and ask yourself how the book's reprint handles its transitions. How does your story handle them?

    See whether you can edit the transitions in the reprint to make them tighter and smoother. Then do the same for your story.

    Write a two-page summary of the comparison, citing specific examples.

3. Now repeat the same process for endings. Write a one-page summary of your comparison of the endings based on their effectiveness.

4. Finally, repeat the same process one last time for theme. Write a one-page summary of your analysis

STYLISH WRITING

CHARACTER AND SETTING
Physical Description
Describing Activity
Emotions

PLOT AND CONFLICT

VOICE AND TONE

MARKETS FOR STYLE

All it takes is a little courage and a lot of hard work to write nonfiction with as much style as the best short fiction. Oh, and a little ignorance can help, too.

Writer John Calderazzo recalls that he wasn't afraid to take the techniques he'd learned in writing short fiction and apply them to nonfiction because "I didn't have the barriers that said I couldn't do that. No one had ever told me you aren't supposed to think of characters or setting or plot when you write nonfiction, so I naturally used them."

It's reasonably common now to think of nonfiction as using the techniques discussed in this chapter, but it hasn't always been that way. Calderazzo, who teaches at Colorado State University, adds that, in fact, "I still find it now with some students. They have these self-imposed barriers. They're genre freaks in that old 1950s way; this is what fiction does, this is what it's about, and this is what nonfiction does and what it's about. They're afraid to cross over."

Well, don't be afraid. Take the chance, because once you've mastered the basics of structuring a story and have learned how to weave the quotes, anecdotes, description, background, and key facts together into an entertaining and informative whole, you should be ready to take that next step—the move toward writing with real style.

It's a step many writers never take. For some, the techniques simply prove too difficult to master. For others, the effort doesn't seem worthwhile. After all, a freelancer can sell stories to certain magazines just by using the kinds of basic structure covered by the information in chapter five. Many magazine editors, frankly, are quite happy to work with writers who can produce clean, dependable—if not terribly stylish—copy on deadline.

And the truth of the matter is that there are risks associated with trying to write with a sense of style. You may find it's all too easy to make mistakes when you leave the basic formats and structures you've come to depend on.

Once you're aware of the demands of character and setting, of plot and conflict, and of voice and tone, you may discover to your dismay that those elements, if handled poorly, can ruin an otherwise acceptable magazine piece. The story can begin to sound pretentious, stilted, and just plain wordy. You may find that the effort to raise your story to a new level ruins what effectiveness the story already has.

For certain editors and writers, though, this is a risk worth taking. They have found there are readers out there who want more from a magazine story than a simple transmittal of information. Such readers find the basic story too one-dimensional. It doesn't offer them anything they can't find in their daily newspaper, and that's not good enough. Such readers look for something more personal, skillful, and artistic from you as a writer. They want to hear your voice in the story, and they want to trust your understanding, your interpretation, of the story at hand. They expect you to be in control of the emotional context of the story and to lead them to an honest sharing of the deeper values of the story as well as its basic information.

For such readers, you need to be able to write a piece that is factual and accurate, of course, but one that also brings real depth of understanding about the people, places, and things involved in the story, and does so in a way that holds the reader's interest from start to finish.

Think of it this way: The typical basic newspaper story, limited by time and space, might offer a tiny sliver of the total reality of the story you're writing (i.e., all of the information available about the story) (Fig. 6.1a).

A basic magazine story, unfettered by some of the limitations of daily

a. newspaper story

b. basic magazine story

c. high-style magazine story

d. nonfiction book

FIGURE 6.1   *A Comparison: How Much Information Does a Story Convey?*

Because they are subject to fewer limitations of time and space, high-style magazine stories are able to flesh out structure, add depth, and show multiple aspects of character and setting.

newspaper publication, can do better, offering much more of that total reality (Fig. 6.1b).

But the high-style magazine story with a clear writer's voice gives valid interpretations of events and people as well as emotional values, multiple characteristics of character and setting, and even a kind of nonfiction plot that develops and resolves a conflict. All these elements flesh out the structure, adding to it. They make the main characters, facts, and story line more complete and more real for the reader, so that a much larger portion of that total reality can be enjoyed by the reader. This kind of magazine writing has several names, including *literary journalism,* *high-style writing,* and *"faction"* (factual writing done in the style of fiction).

When it's handled well, this kind of story can do much better than the other types in transmitting that reality, the elemental truth that readers have a right to expect from your writing. The model might look more like Figure 6.1c. A book-length treatment of the topic would, of course, provide an even more complete picture, as Figure 6.1d shows.

CHARACTER AND SETTING

Here's the opening hook of a high-style story by writer John Calderazzo:

Eulogy in a Churchyard

BY JOHN CALDERAZZO

They were a boisterous bunch, the Bridinger kids, one girl and four large boys who would grow to the size of NFL tackles. They lived with their parents, Chalmer and Madeline, in an old clapboard farmhouse, courtesy of Tiffin's Greenlawn Cemetery, whose gentle slopes started just across the street from their front porch. And now and then, on the days when the boys were being boys and their nonsense had exhausted their parents' patience and imprecations, their father—all 6′4″ and 170 pounds of him—might have to deliver the Ultimate Threat.

"You damn kids don't behave, you ain't gonna ride in any more funerals!"

Calderazzo's story, reprinted at the end of this chapter on page 168, reads as if it is the beginning of an interesting short story—one that uses funeral and cemetery metaphors to good effect, you might expect—but it is very much nonfiction, a personality piece on a grave digger who has followed in his father's footsteps.

By means of this hook, the reader is introduced to the family, is shown the setting in which the whole story takes place, and is given the elemental sense of good-natured, if dark, humor that helps make this an entertaining and effective story. Compare that hook with a more conventional lead paragraph—one you might find in a newspaper feature story or a less ambitious magazine piece:

Like many a dutiful son, Tom Bridinger has followed in his father's foot-steps, taking over the family business when his father died.

For the Bridingers, that death was an integral part of the change in own-ership. His father was a grave digger, and his son's first act as the new owner of the business was to dig his father's grave.

This lead works well enough. It summarizes the story's theme, intro-duces the main character and his father, and generally gives the reader enough information about the story to be able to decide whether or not to go on reading it.

But this hook relies completely on the basic facts for its interest level. It doesn't offer any setting (and think about how important the setting is to this story), it doesn't get very far into the theme of strong family ties that the story contains, and it certainly doesn't give the reader any real emotional feel for Tom or for his father.

In Calderazzo's version, notice how phrases like "They were a boister-ous bunch, the Bridinger kids," and ". . . when the boys were being boys and their nonsense had exhausted their parents' patience" give the reader both a sense of family for the Bridingers (which is at the core of the story's theme) and a feel for the personality of both the "boisterous" Tom Bridinger and his father.

In his hook, Calderazzo has also done a fine job of establishing the setting for the entire piece by telling us the family lives in "an old clap-board farmhouse, courtesy of Tiffin's Greenlawn Cemetery, whose gentle slopes started just across the street from their front porch."

It is both the placement of this family into this setting and the subtle inclusion of personality traits in the scene that help to make this hook, and indeed the entire story, such a fine example of accessible high-style magazine writing. For Calderazzo, character and setting are the basic ele-ments around which any story revolves.

"Certainly it all begins with characterization," he says. "What I try to do is get into the main characters involved in the story as quickly as I can, and place them in an appropriate setting right away, so the reader can begin to know them. After that, the real action of the story begins."

Robert Plunket, a magazine writer who writes novels also, agrees with that idea of building character and setting first. For his story on an arrest involving Paul Reubens (aka Pee-wee Herman), Plunket knew "The first thing I had to do was make Paul and his family human beings. That was the sort of thing that was missing from the newspaper coverage of the story. Who were these people? Who was Paul?"

Plunket does this by providing information about the Reubens fam-ily in the first few paragraphs of the story. By the sixth paragraph, he is building the Reubens character for the story with passages like this:

And if I thought he was fading into a relic, his moment of glory over, his family and friends certainly did not. They felt he had still-unmined depths of talent. He had never intended to spend his whole life being Pee-wee, they insisted. "Don't you think he feels a little silly, a grown man dressing up in that suit?" Judy once said to me. For years she had been saying that he felt trapped, that he wanted to move. "He loved Pee-wee," said his friend Stephanie Moss. "But he wanted out."

Notice how Plunket includes his own thoughts on Reubens ("I thought he was fading into a relic") and then allows others close to Reubens to dispute that thought with their own ideas of his future ("unmined depths of talent" and "he wanted out"). The result is several different viewpoints on Reubens—all of them expert and honest opinions—that combine to give the reader a candid perspective on just this one small factor in the story's development. Plunket's story, "Pee-wee, Paul, and Sarasota," is reprinted on page 174.

As a writer, in an effort to build real characters for the reader, you'll find it necessary first to do a good job of understanding and reporting on the characters yourself. Remember that you need to report on them *physically, actively,* and *emotionally.*

Physical Description

You need to give the reader some physical description and in as relevant a way as you can. In the Bridinger story, for instance, Calderazzo says that the four boys "would grow to be the size of NFL tackles" and that "At 6′2″ and 200 pounds—down thirty from a few months back—Tom could pass for a heavyweight boxer, or the honorable-mention all-Ohio defensive back he once was at Tiffin's Calvert Catholic High School."

Not only has Calderazzo built a physical picture of Tom Bridinger for the reader, but he uses comparisons to do so that relate directly to the story. Bridinger's physical size figures into the story in several ways, including his appetite, his grave-digging skills, and his football-playing past.

Plunket, in similar fashion, describes Paul Reubens physically this way: "Out of his Pee-wee garb, with the beard and long hair that he would grow whenever on hiatus, Paul was virtually unrecognizable. He could go anywhere and not be noticed, except as a tall, thin man with a blank and passive face. . . . The entire world knew who Pee-wee Herman was, but virtually no one knew who Paul Reubens was."

Plunket has given us the physical description ("beard and long hair," and "tall, thin man with a blank and passive face") and connected it up directly to the story, with his final sentence on how no one knew who he was.

Describing Activity

You need to put your character into motion. What does the character *do* in this story? What actions are taken? Again, these actions need to be directly relevant to the story at hand.

In Calderazzo's piece, Tom Bridinger is first seen as a child who "would get to ride along and lead the parade." Later, the reader sees Bridinger locating grave sites, digging graves (and Calderazzo wisely gives the reader considerable detail about that), and interacting with his mother. All of these are directly connected to the reader's understanding of Bridinger as a person.

In Plunket's piece, the reader sees Reubens incognito in a post office, in a convenience store, and at his high school reunion, as well as in several gay bars. All of the activity is directly related to the story's main theme, and each activity the reader sees contributes to a fuller understanding of the Reubens character.

Emotions

Emotions are the most difficult aspect of character building for you to handle in nonfiction, because fairness factors in. You need to be willing to show the reader the emotional values of the characters you are working with; those values are often hidden, however, masked by characters who are reluctant to share something so personal as their emotions. You owe it to your readers to find those emotional values, but you have an equal debt to the person you are writing about to be absolutely fair, and accurate, in your presentation of them.

Calderazzo gets around the inherent difficulties of the task in his grave digger story by letting Bridinger's quotes do much of the emotional character building. Quotes such as "Sometimes I need a map to find where to dig. . . . But Dad, he'd take you right to 'em. He knew everybody in the place and became friends with a lot of their families, too, as they'd drop by to visit," do much to convey Bridinger's love and admiration for his father without there being any question of Calderazzo's fairness in finding just the right words to express it.

Plunket, on the other hand, had no quotes from his principal character to fall back on, so he was forced to deal in other ways with the tricky aspects of the emotional context. He managed with quotes and informa-

TIME AND SPACE

Time and space are the enemies of newspaper reporters. The pressures of daily deadlines (or weekly deadlines for the lucky feature writer) and the constraints of tight space mean that most reporters most of the time are forced to make frequent compromises in the quality of their stories.

Heavy revising, for instance, is something that newspaper reporters rarely have time for. And for the typical reporter with a busy daily paper, there often isn't any time for that extra interview or any space to include many good quotes that aren't otherwise absolutely necessary for the story to make sense.

For magazine writers, though, time and space are usually allies. Most of the time you will be operating under deadlines that are many days, even weeks away, so there's plenty of time to finish that first draft and then work hard on the second, third, and fourth drafts afterward.

In addition, the relatively longer length of many magazine pieces means that the information that fleshes out a story can be included, even though such information may not be crucial to the piece. It is, however, that nonessential information that often gives a story the extra emotional impact that adds to its appeal to readers.

For freelancers, in particular, time and space are equalizers. Most freelancers don't have the resources that are available to magazine staffers and newspaper reporters, such as free use of a telephone, inexpensive computer access to databases as well as word processing, free mail privileges, and expense accounts for car travel, plane flights, and hotel stays.

But the freelancer has time and space: the time to do multiple interviews with a subject over a long time span, the time to interview a variety of other people who know something about the subject, the time to spend days writing a story and many more days revising it, and the space to use the best of all of that material—not just the portion that fits.

In short, the freelancer has the time to get the job done right. The wise freelancer takes full advantage of that available time as follows:

- If you're writing the whole story before ever sending it out for sale, take all the time you need in order to get all the reporting done that the story needs, all the time you need to write, and all the time you need to revise. Don't shortchange yourself by imposing artificial deadlines.

- If you're working from an idea, and sending out query letters (chapter fourteen), get the bulk of your reporting done before you ever send out the query, so that an acceptance leaves you with a story already at least half done.

- Once you've agreed to write a story for an editor, try to set a comfortable deadline and an adequate length—things you know you can meet with high-quality work. Don't do a rush job unless the editor absolutely needs one, and in that case make sure the editor understands that you've been forced to hurry the piece.

- Remember to take the time at the end of your writing to set the story aside for a day or two; then come back to it fresh, for another look. Don't be afraid to edit or revise one more time.

- And then remember: whatever deadline you've agreed to, meet it. That builds trust for you with the editor. A high-quality job, done on time, will get you more work from that editor. Sloppy work, or late work, probably won't.

---

tion from other sources (all of them directly relevant and knowledgeable, of course) and with his own expert interpretation of the facts at hand.

Sentences such as the following give the reader Plunket's interpretation of how Reubens felt: "The picture that finally emerges of the Paul Reubens who returned to Sarasota in the summer of 1991, on the eve of his third arrest, is that of a serious, enormously successful artist who led a series of highly compartmentalized lives. The rigid split between Paul and Pee-wee was just the beginning."

Plunket, as you can read in the story, defends that interpretation with judicious use of the facts at hand. The result is a powerful, effective look at a complex character.

A final thought on characters: Remember that you must do a good job of reporting before you can use these techniques for building characters in your magazine articles. During the interviewing and fact-finding process, you must bear these end results in mind. Doing so will help you take the kind of notes, and find the kind of facts, that will help make high-style writing possible later.

PLOT AND CONFLICT

Both Calderazzo and Plunket know that while any cleanly written magazine story can pass along a certain amount of information to the reader, writers who want to create a story with real style want to do more. Such writers want to create real characters and then follow through with actions that show conflict, rise to a dramatic moment, and keep the reader interested and involved, moving quickly through the story right to the end.

In short, a good magazine writer likes to discover a plot in the story and move the characters through it, just as a fiction writer might.

Fiction writers can do this through invention, taking make-believe characters and putting them through a make-believe conflict that finally reaches resolution. Nonfiction writers have to do it with reality, with what's really there in the story. But this isn't as difficult as you might think.

After all, what most fiction tries to do is seem real. Fiction writers work very hard to make characters real and a plot seem reasonable and plausible.

As a nonfiction writer, you are lucky in that the characters and the plot are out there already, just waiting to be discovered. Your task is to work hard enough and be perceptive enough both to find the real conflicts that real characters run into and then to set to work presenting that story to the reader.

Robert Plunket says that, for him, "All my magazine writing is non-fiction short stories; it's the only way I can look at it. If you do write fiction, as I do," Plunket adds, "then you're always looking for that moment when everything explodes, and this was certainly one of those moments."

When it came to the story on Paul Reubens, Plunket knew he had the potential for a great plot. The story had everything a writer could ask for, including an interesting, complex main character and a plot that included sex, scandal, and a conflict between what Plunket saw as an intrusive sheriff's department and a children's media star.

"Conflict" is the most important word to remember when it comes to nonfiction plot. Almost all stories of this type have it, either out in the open or in the subtext. In most cases, several conflicts are involved.

In Plunket's piece on Paul Reubens there is conflict between the sheriff's department and Reubens, as well as conflict that Plunket sees between the city officials and sheriff's department and the citizenry of the town. See how this passage defines that conflict:

But what people found even more disturbing was the behavior of the Sheriff's Department. Spending hours in an adult theater seemed a poor use of police time. Sheriff Geoff Monge claimed that the South Trail Cinema was targeted only once every three or four months, a remark that startled employees of the theater. One employee estimates that a more realistic estimate would be twice a month; that the police (in groups of three to six) would spend up to six hours at a stretch in the theater; and that they would sometimes sit in the theater while it was completely empty, for up to an hour, waiting for people.

When Pee-wee supporters rallied in New York City, County Commissioner David Mills declared that Sarasota stood behind the police and wouldn't tolerate behavior like Paul's. But letters to the local paper told a different story. Writer after writer expressed support for Paul and advised the police to "keep their pants on" and concentrate on serious crimes. Community leaders, such as Ed Foster, assistant principal at Sarasota High and advisor to Paul's senior class in 1970, spoke out for Paul, describing him as "very talented" and "very humble." Said Foster, "There's nobody in that entire class, I'll bet you, that disowns him for anything."

What this conflict between the official reaction to the incident and the apparent reaction of the people of Sarasota does is create tension in the story. The reader, aware of the disagreement between the sheriff's department and many of the people in the town, reads along hoping to see that conflict resolved. Plunket, a talented writer, knows that he can use that tension to hold reader interest until the very end, when there is some resolution to the conflict.

The conflict in Calderazzo's piece on the Bridinger kids is more subtle, but it's still there. Think of the classic conflict implied in this story between the son's dreams for his own life and the responsibilities of taking over the father's business. Think of the conflict between the business the way it was in his father's day and the way it is today and how that has affected his mother: ". . . for a long time now, the cemetery business has been changing, it's much more a money game, and that makes her sad. She's been kind of eased out as superintendent by new ownership."

Finally, think of overall thematic conflict in this story. The main character, Tom Bridinger, is clearly in love with life and yet also seems to truly enjoy his work as a grave digger. This quote near the end expresses that internal conflict well:

> "Now, this is my best friend when I was a kid. He died in a cycle accident. I dug his grave. This one, she's a former teacher of mine, a nun. Here's an old man who said he didn't want to go on living without his wife. He was gone in a couple of months. Here's a girl who was a dancer, blonde—God, she was beautiful. She died of cancer at twenty-two."

The resolution in this piece comes from our final appreciation, at the end of the story, of how Bridinger resolves this internal conflict. Calderazzo doesn't give us an easy answer. Sometimes a plot's resolution is in the form of the admittance of continuing tension, as in this final scene:

> At this moment, Hollywood might well freeze this frame, leaving you with the image of a man—tall and muscular and bristling with energy—caught midway between earth and air, a man frozen between worlds.

Bridinger's internal conflict, the reader is made to understand, isn't one that is easily, cleanly resolved in one direction or another. Instead, it is a conflict he has learned to live with. Perhaps Calderazzo means to leave us all with a message in that final thought.

A final thought on plot and conflict: Remember that in working to find a plot in your story, you will need to discover the conflict, tension, and resolution inherent in almost any interesting drama, whether it's fact or fiction. Just as with the reporting for characterization, you must keep these elements in mind when you are doing the reporting for your story. If your notes reflect the conflict you have uncovered, as well as the tension in the story, then you'll have an easy enough time bringing it all to a resolution that works for you, as well as for your editor and the magazine's readership.

VOICE AND TONE

Voice is that element of writing that tells the reader something about you as the writer. It is, in many respects, how you sound to the reader. Either your voice can be very loud, in the sense that you are very much in the story, or it can be very quiet, in the sense that you disappear. The more intrusive you are in your writing, the louder your voice.

Tone is the manner in which your voice speaks to the reader. It can be sarcastic, sardonic, academic, informal, conversational, or any of dozens more.

The important thing to remember is that the story *will* have voice and tone in it; the two are unavoidable. It is your job to learn to recognize and control these two elements. You can't begin to write really stylish work until you can manipulate these elements to suit the needs of your story.

In newspaper writing, most journalists try to speak in a neutral voice and a flat tone. In effect, they want the writer to disappear so that the news itself carries the full weight of the story. There is little or no sense of personal interpretation or opinion from the writer.

That's an admirable concept—for newspapers, wherein a certain neutrality is a good idea. But modern magazines are rarely neutral, and many editors expect to hear your voice in the story.

"We're always looking for different writers to bring something to us, a point of view, a voice," says Joan Tapper, editor of *Islands* magazine, a slick travel magazine that publishes writers from Paul Theroux to relative unknowns.

"Really," Tapper says, "what we're looking for in a writer is insight and literary style. I like to tell a writer when I send one on assignment that what I like best is a mix of place and the author's personality. I think it's important that the best travel writers are subjective." For Tapper, travel writing is more believable, more trustworthy, when the reader "knows somebody is there, with prejudices and preconceptions, and not afraid to have an opinion."

John Calderazzo explains it this way: "Newspapers, and some magazines, tend to have an institutional voice, where all the stories sound the same. I like to think that a lot of magazines, though, really search for writers who have an individual, or idiosyncratic, voice." In other words, the writer is very much present in the story. The reader recognizes the writer's narration and gets more from the story for that voice having been there.

Listen to the voice in this passage from Tapper's own story in *Islands* (the complete story is reprinted on page 261):

> Over the next few days I came to recognize the rhythm of that daily bustle, which rose in the morning and evening and slowed in the torpor of midday. My explorations took me up and down the narrow streets of Lipari's old town—into passages barely an arm's length wide—where islanders gesticulated in intense conversations that turned mundane exchanges into little street dramas.

Tapper's voice is that of a curious traveler, one seeing a place for the first time. She sounds perceptive to the reader (recognizing "the rhythm of that daily bustle"), and curious as well—eager to learn about the locals and the place where they live. Her voice is one that a reader can trust in a travel story. She can be expected to do a good job of seeing the people and things that make these islands special. Her tone, related to that voice, is almost romantic, caught up in the visual splendor and long history of the Aeolians.

Compare that to this passage from John Calderazzo's piece on grave digging:

> Tom always digs a grave in three layers, like a cake, carefully removing all the "crumbs," or loose soil, before moving down a level. Halfway through layer two on this dark Saturday morning, the gloom thickens. "A lot of people think a cemetery is dead and cold, but to me, it's alive and warm. It's a transitional place. The only time I saw Dad cry was when it was a small child. Look around, this place is full of people; every headstone is like a book about somebody's life. Death is life—or the next life, anyway."
>
> Far off in town, the bells of a church begin to chime. "Lunch!" says Tom. He carefully gathers his tools. "You'd be surprised what people'll steal. They'll even switch around the plastic flowers."

Calderazzo's approach is very different from Tapper's. He doesn't use first person in this piece, so there is no "I" making the voice clear to the reader. And Calderazzo stays out of this story entirely, at least on the most obvious level. But as this passage shows, Calderazzo is definitely there, noticing the close details on how Tom digs the graves, taking notes on how the church bells chime. The writer's voice, in this case, is attentive and authoritative. The tone is warm and supportive. Calderazzo clearly likes his subject, and that feeling comes through in the writing, as it should.

Because of the voice of authority that tells the reader the story of Tom Bridinger and because of the warm tone in which the story is told, the reader is more willing to believe the information that is read and to share the emotional context of the story. And that's effective, high-style writing.

A final thought on voice and tone: In the same way as character and plot do, voice and tone require the up-front reporting work that allows you to make the proper decisions for your writing. If you have really done the job you need to do in your reporting, you'll be comfortable with an authoritative voice, for instance. If you haven't done enough reporting, your voice will show it.

And as for tone, be wary, because it is all too easy to adopt a tone that excludes the reader. If you try first-person narration, for instance, you may well find yourself writing in a condescending tone that talks down to the reader and that almost never succeeds. Remember to be inclusive in your tone, reach out to the reader, and make the reader welcome in the story.

MARKETS FOR STYLE

Like many of the best magazine writers, Calderazzo, Plunket, Tapper, and most of the other writers and editors interviewed for this book know that good writing is good writing, and for many of them the techniques of fiction writing offer ample opportunity for a nonfiction writer to produce stories that have emotional impact while they entertain and inform the reader.

One of the keys, of course, is to find those magazines that give writers the kinds of opportunities we're talking about. Many magazines do not, or cannot.

On the national level, there are several general magazines that are famous for in-depth, high-style stories, including (but certainly not limited to) *The Atlantic,* the *New Yorker, Esquire, Playboy,* and *Harper's.*

Travel writing is justifiably famous for encouraging this kind of writing, and a magazine such as Joan Tapper's *Islands* represents one fine example. Top sports magazines, too, like *Sport* and *Sports Illustrated* find these techniques useful in their personality pieces on sports figures.

But as a beginning writer, you should know that there are magazines accessible to you locally or regionally that are quite willing, indeed, to publish this kind of work. Many of the city magazines, many of the so-called "alternative" tabloids, and a healthy list of regional magazines all use these kinds of stories.

John Calderazzo recalls finding one market for them this way: "I discovered *Ohio* magazine when I was teaching in the state. I'd never really looked at the magazine before and as I did, I realized that the magazine lent itself to literary journalism—the editors let you go as long as you wanted; you could do scenes, you could do a slow, subjective setup. It was terrific to find out that they were open to that.

"I like a human story, and it was good to find a magazine there in Ohio that was interested in that. I'd written short stories before, and that experience with fiction writing was tremendously helpful to me. The idea is that it's the story that counts and there are many ways to tell that story."

In other words, there are plenty of magazines that are open to high-style stories—pieces that present fact in a way that resembles the best of short fiction. You just have to search for them.

If you enjoy producing interesting, informative, emotional, personal work that displays your talents as both a reporter and a writer, then you'll find that a search worth making.

■ ■ ■
EULOGY IN A CHURCHYARD

BY JOHN CALDERAZZO

They were a boisterous bunch, the Bridinger kids, one girl and four large boys who would grow to the size of NFL tackles. They lived with their parents, Chalmer and Madeline, in an old clapboard farmhouse, courtesy of Tiffin's Greenlawn Cemetery, whose gentle slopes started just across the street from their front porch. And now and then, on the days when the boys were being boys and their nonsense had exhausted their parents' patience and imprecations, their father—all 6'4" and 170 pounds of him— might have to deliver the Ultimate Threat.

"You damn kids don't behave, you ain't gonna ride in any more funerals!"

That would do it, especially for young Tom. Tom *lived* for funerals. They were the most important and exciting events he could imagine, and once, twice, three times a week, rain or shine or blizzard, they took place literally right under his nose.

Out from town along the country road they would come— long lines of shiny cars filled with adults in their Sunday best, even on weekdays. And at the head of it all, lights flashing impressively like the Indy 500 pace car, was the lead car that had stopped traffic for miles and drawn the stares of downtown shoppers and even, if he was lucky, Tom's schoolmates. In that car sat Tom's father, Chalmer—cemetery superintendent, chief grounds-keeper, gravedigger *nonpareil*— the man one of his employees called "The Mayor of Marble City."

And if Tom was very lucky indeed, he would get to ride along and lead the parade, help his dad help all those people who had come to bury their dead. More important, he would be helping the dead themselves.

"After all," says Tom, "digging a grave is the last special thing you can do for someone."

■ ■ ■

Saturday morning. Hollywood could not have created more perfect weather for gravedigging: bone-chilly, a wet sheen covering the roads like sealskin, ragged clots of fog standing in the fields, blurring the point where a herd of sheep ends and the fog begins. You wouldn't be surprised to see a druid standing behind a tree, or a hunchback—named Igor, probably—limping along the shoulder of the road.

"God, Dad loved it out here," says Tom, loading three shovels, a pick, an ax and assorted metal rods into the bed of a dilapidated dump truck. "He knew every tree in the cemetery and said there were as many kinds as there were counties in Ohio—eighty-eight. He tried factory work in town once. After a year he said, 'That's history,' and never worked indoors again." Tom wrenches open the truck door and cranks up the engine with an unmuffled roar.

"Funerals were family affairs for us. For years my granddad was foreman of the cemetery. He taught the business to Dad, and after Dad died, Ma took over as superintendent. Over the years Dad had all us kids out here, mowing, trimming around the monuments with a sickle, watering flowers, laying foundations for the head-stones. Of course, as we got older, he taught us to dig."

Tom pulls out of the driveway of the house that he still lives in with his mother and one brother, Mike, who sells tombstones across town and coaches football at Tiffin University. In a few seconds he has rumbled through Greenlawn's tall front gates and is curving past tombstone-covered slopes. Even on a gray morning, it's obvious that it's a pretty place, 100 rolling acres nestled among thick woods, a park and cornfields—a few of them owned by the cemetery, Tom says, "for future development."

Today he'll be digging the long-postponed second half of the double grave. After years of widowhood in the warm South, an elderly Tiffin woman has returned to lie beside her husband—a typical story in marble cities all over the North. In the end, no

matter how far they've strayed, native sons and daughters often move back to the serene, silent suburbs of the livelier towns they grew up in.

"Sometimes I need a map to find where to dig," says Tom, as the cemetery road winds between glistening, rain-black buckeyes and maples. "But Dad, he'd take you right to 'em. He knew everybody in the place and became friends with a lot of their families, too, as they'd drop by to visit. You'd be surprised how many old ladies around town left him things in their wills, a favorite chair, whatever." At age sixty-one, when Chalmer was himself buried at Greenlawn, he had worked here more than half a century. Tom, who's now thirty-four, apprenticed as a gravedigger to the master when he was thirteen.

Tom finds his spot, carefully backs up the truck and jumps out. He's wearing his gravedigging regs—work boots, orange sweat pants, a red sweat shirt with a towel curled around his neck. At 6'2" and 200 pounds—down thirty from a few months back—Tom could pass for a heavyweight boxer, or the honorable-mention all-Ohio defensive back he once was at Tiffin's Calvert Catholic High School. Football earned him a scholarship to Temple University, where he toiled unhappily as an interior lineman and fantasized for a while about becoming "a fancy Philadelphia lawyer." But that was before he caught the teaching bug. Now he teaches English at Calvert and PE at the junior high, and coaches junior varsity basketball at Heidelberg College. Sometimes, on the day after he's been up late digging a grave, his high school students notice his red eyes and say, "Did'ja get another one last night? Did'ja?"

He teaches at the cemetery, too. "A grave should be seven feet ten inches by three feet two inches. I used to have to measure, but Dad taught me to eyeball it, and now I can pretty much step it off. You hear all that stuff about six feet under, but graves actually aren't much more than four feet deep. Hell, if I went down much farther, I couldn't get out. I'd be digging my own grave."

But before he stakes out the corners, he pushes a thin metal rod into the earth. A couple of feet down it stops with a thud—the sound of metal against concrete. He tries again a few inches over and presses the rod smoothly in. Here's where he'll dig.

Normally he slices the sod into strips with a special shovel and rolls them cleanly back, like carpets, to be unrolled and tamped back down after the burial. But today, because of the muck and the sparseness of the grass, he just digs right in with a spade. "Hey, not too bad! No frost, not even next to the headstone, where you always get it first. This won't take more than three, three and a half hours. The drainage is bad in this part of the cemetery, though. Once I hit water at the bottom of a grave at five below zero."

Since death does not keep

banker's hours, Tom has worked under every condition imaginable: by car headlights or lanterns in the middle of the night, a stereo headset clamped to his head; swinging the pick for nine hours at clay baked hard as stone; filling a hole with water, like a private swimming pool, so he wouldn't pass out from the heat; digging and bailing in downpours; chipping at frost 3 feet deep— ground so tough he finally called in an old crony of his dad's, seventy-four-year-old Leonard Graham, who went at it with an air hammer.

Tom has seen one graveside mourner punch another who said that, frankly, he'd never much cared for the deceased. He's seen a motorcycle gang serenade a fallen comrade by revving up their Harleys and lifting their front wheels as the coffin was being lowered. One time a man leaned over an open coffin and slipped a hundred-dollar bill into the suit pocket of the dead man. "A hundred bucks!" says Tom. "I felt like exchanging it later for a blank check."

Tom peels down to a Kansas City Chiefs sweat shirt and drapes his old one over the headstone. He switches to a 16" spade and starts tearing through roots, prying out long, smooth sections of soil and tossing them into the truck bed.

"Dad was from the old school. He'd have a fit if he saw the dump truck out here. It had to be a *wheelbarrow*. And he dug entirely by hand because he thought that was the only way to do it right—

no fancy backhoe for him. He could read the grain in the wood handle of a shovel like you and I read a baseball bat.

"The cemetery was his whole life, but it's only part of mine. About a month ago I met a gal from Texas. Boy, does she love to dance! After a couple of dates, she said, 'Hon, you don't *really* dig graves, do you? That's not what you wanna do the rest of your life, is it?' I don't know . . . sometimes I think about moving away—Texas might be nice. Sometimes I think I'd like to stay here and dig forever, at least part time."

A breeze comes up and riffles the faded American flags that the Legion has put on the graves of veterans. "I mean, I can't think of anything negative about it. It's great exercise, plus it relaxes me, helps me straighten out my thoughts. I can hear Dad talking to me when I dig, saying, 'Do it right, Dummy!' or telling me to suck it up or whatever and keep going. I'm also practicing an art that's been passed down through my family—carving something out of the earth for somebody who needs it. When I'm about to take that last shovelful of dirt, I always think of a sculptor getting ready to take the final chip off a statue—you know, the hammer poised over the tip of the nose or the chin."

Tom leans forward on his shovel. "Not that it's all serious business. Once, a doctor who was treating Dad's heart condition asked him what he did for a living. He said, 'Well, Doc, I cover up your mistakes.' They didn't get on too well after that."

Tom always digs a grave in three layers, like a cake, carefully removing all the "crumbs," or loose soil, before moving down a level. Halfway through layer two on this dark Saturday morning, the gloom thickens. "A lot of people think a cemetery is dead and cold, but to me, it's alive and warm. It's a transitional place. The only time I saw Dad cry was when it was a small child. Look around, this place is full of people; every headstone is like a book about somebody's life. Death *is* life—or the next life, anyway."

Far off in town, the bells of a church begin to chime. "Lunch!" says Tom. He carefully gathers his tools. "You'd be surprised what people'll steal. They'll even switch around the plastic flowers."

■ ■ ■

"I didn't lose thirty pounds eating like this," Tom says, gazing happily at his mother's kitchen table with its steaming bowls of bratwurst, mashed potatoes and homemade sauerkraut, plus huge servings of fruit salad, cheese, ice cream and bread. Then he attacks. "When we were kids," he says between mouthfuls, "Dad told folks, 'The little bastards sit at one end of the table with their mouths open, and I just *tip* it.'"

Madeline Bridinger, leaning against the stove, puffs a cigarette and watches the food disappear. "You know, it's amazing, Tommy gets more for digging one grave these days than Chal used to make for a whole week, and we brought up five kids. Why, Denny, he's the oldest and a high school principal, he could polish off a loaf of bread, a head of lettuce and a gallon of milk at a sitting. He got up to two hundred ninety-five and once made the final cut with the Cleveland Browns."

She gazes over Tom's head at the refrigerator, where a sticker on the door says KEEP SMILING. "How'd we make do on so little money? We stuck together as a *family*. And this was a great place to raise one—plenty of work for the kids in the cemetery, them woods to play in and the park for sports.

"You know that old barn down the hill? There were horses boarded there, and in the winter we'd hook 'em to one of those old-fashioned sleighs, and all of us ride through the cemetery and then down the back roads. Every year Chal would shinny up a pine and chop the top off for a Christmas tree. Shoot, you didn't need money to have fun."

She plunks a tin of coffeecake on the table. "Full yet?"

■ ■ ■

Driving back through the cemetery, Tom says, "Ma's a real peach, huh? And *tough*. One day during a football game I got absolutely crunched near the sideline, and when I looked up she was leaning right over me, hissing, 'You PUSS, get back in there!' Neither she or Dad ever had new clothes when

we were growing up, but they always made sure we had the best football, the best baseball glove.

"But for a long time now, the cemetery business has been changing; it's much more a money game, and that makes her sad. She's been kind of eased out as superintendent by new ownership. It's a good thing Mike and I bought the house from the cemetery a few years back.

"And of course, she misses Dad terribly. He had a spot picked out near the house, but when he died she said, 'Get him out of there. I don't want to look out the window every day and see him.'"

Tom drives a few hundred yards past the half-finished grave, then gets out. He saunters up a slight rise, moving from tombstone to tombstone in a way that suggests a nature guide pointing out flowers. Or books.

"Now, this is my best friend when I was a kid. He died in a cycle accident. I dug his grave. This one, she's a former teacher of mine, a nun. Here's an old man who said he didn't want to go on living without his wife. He was gone in a couple of months. Here's a girl who was a dancer, blonde—God, she was beautiful. She died of cancer at twenty-two." Her epitaph reads: "And when the earth shall claim your limbs, then shall you truly dance."

Near the top of the rise, Tom stops. He slowly folds his arms. "And here's Dad. He picked the stone himself, naturally." It's an ordinary-looking stone with one exception—no dates. "Dad always said, 'It's nobody's business, plus I'll never really die, anyway. I'll always be with you.' And he didn't want an open coffin. He said, 'If the sons of bitches didn't wanna see me when I was alive, I don't want 'em looking at me now.'

"Of course, hard as it was, I carved his grave. My sister came and helped—she was real close to him, too—and some friends. It was snowing. The ground was hard, and there were lots of roots to tear through, and I could hear him laughing at how long it was taking. I could hear him saying things like 'Get the hell off the crumbs!' or 'Get out of that hole and pay attention to the way I do it!'"

Tom stares at the ground as though the grave were still open. "This one's my masterpiece. My Picasso, my Pieta."

Tom works on the third and final layer, sparks shooting up as he grazes a rock while squaring a corner. He's got his rhythm now, and he digs hard, sensing the end. "I'd like to get my jog in before nightfall," he says. The mist has lifted, but the air still feels as wet as the clay that squishes around his ankles.

"These people that buy twelve thousand dollar copper vaults while there are kids starving all over the world—I can't see it. We're gonna go back to dust anyway. Me, I'll be cremated. I'll have them put my ashes right next to Dad. Or right on top."

He's near the bottom now. The heavy clay makes sucking noises whenever he tries to lift a boot. Tom looks down for a moment, then reaches for a cup of water he's propped in the vaseholder of the headstone. It's a long way from dancing in Texas.

Tom measures the depth of the grave with his shovel, scoops out a little more mud, and says, "That's it." He places an arm firmly on the edge of the hole. "Here's how you get out—Dad could do it one-handed even in his late fifties." He kicks up his inside leg and jumps, but the muck at the bottom clings hard to his other leg.

At this moment, Hollywood might well freeze this frame, leaving you with the image of a man—tall and muscular and bristling with energy—caught midway between earth and air, a man frozen between worlds. But this isn't the movies, it's reality. As the clay lets go with a loud suck, Tom Bridinger, son of the mayor of Marble City, rises up, up and *out*.

■ ■ ■

This article first appeared in the May 1986 issue of Ohio *magazine. Calderazzo is an English professor at Colorado State University.*

■ ■ ■

PEE-WEE, PAUL, AND SARASOTA

BY ROBERT PLUNKET

You would think that for a gossip columnist like me, being in the middle of a major sex scandal would be a career highlight. And it was. Unfortunately, it was also many other things. An immensely talented artist's career was ruined, the town's eye was blackened by the world press and many, many people were hurt. It was the saddest week I've ever spent in Sarasota.

When I first heard the news, I was watching TV in a motel near the Miami airport. I remember sitting bolt upright in bed and thinking, "Oh, my God, I was afraid this was going to happen."

Only two days before I had bumped into Paul Reubens' mother, Judy Rubenfeld, in Morton's Market. I had known her for years. At first our relationship was business: I was Mr. Chatterbox, the town's gossip columnist; she was the mother of our most famous celebrity. She gave me news, I gave her son (or rather, Pee-wee Herman) publicity. But over the years a real friendship had developed, and nowadays we were more likely to discuss her other kids, whom I found at least as interesting as Paul.

There was Abby, an attorney specializing in gay-rights issues. She had been legal director of the Lambda Legal Defense and Education Fund, but now she was moving from New York to Nashville and Judy was worried that it might not be a good town for a lesbian activist. And Luke, the youngest, was having trouble finding himself. He had recently opened a lawn statuary store on the South Trail, and I had dutifully done a story at Judy's request. During the interview he told me that he and his famous brother were planning a Pee-wee Herman lawn statue; it would have a special weird feature, something like water dribbling out of Pee-wee's nose into a large seashell he would be holding.

But today things were a little awkward. I was in a hurry and Pee-wee Herman wasn't such big news anymore. We chatted for a while, mostly about how busy we had been lately; and after we said our good-byes and I moved away, I realized that was the first conversation we had ever had where Paul's name hadn't come up.

If it had, I would have learned that he was right here in Sarasota.

And if I thought he was fading into a relic, his moment of glory over, his family and friends certainly did not. They felt he had still-unmined depths of talent. He had never intended to spend his whole life being Pee-wee, they insisted. "Don't you think he feels a little silly, a grown man dressing up in that suit?" Judy once said to me. For years she had been saying that he felt trapped, that he wanted to move on. "He loved Pee-wee," said his friend Stephanie Moss. "But he wanted out."

The time had finally come. Earlier this year, he had declined to sign a new contract for his TV show. He hadn't worked since April. He was on an extended vacation—other trips to Nantucket and Europe were in the works— using his time to relax and try to figure out what to do next. He was considering anything and everything—acting, writing, producing. What *did* he want to do? I asked Judy later. "He really didn't know," she said, and seemed to mean it. Once she had told me how, back in the old days, just as he was becoming famous, he would sometimes stop in Sarasota on his way to appear on the David Letterman show. When he left she would find his room littered with little notes he had written to himself, things he might try on the show.

The success of Pee-wee Herman had astonished everyone, even Paul. It started with the appearances with an underground comedy troupe in L.A. in the late '70s, then went on to the nightclub act that HBO picked up as "The Pee-wee Herman Show" in 1982. Then came two movies, *Pee-wee's*

Big Adventure and *Big-Top Pee-wee,* "Pee-wee's Playhouse" with its 16 Emmies, the cover of *Life* and *Rolling Stone,* even the keynote speech at the Republican National Convention, in which Michael Dukakis was compared to *him.* Football players did the Pee-wee dance after scoring a touchdown. By the end of the '80s, an incredible 96 percent of all Americans recognized Pee-wee's name.

And the children—millions of them idolized and imitated him. It always struck me as one of the more bizarre progressions of modern culture that a strange midnight comedy act full of sexual ambiguity and subversiveness—in the original act Pee-wee had mirrors on his shoes so he could look up girls' skirts—would have evolved into the most important children's TV show since "Sesame Street." Paul was known to be at ease with children, but he never pretended that they were his mission in life. Being a kiddie role model was not a position that he aspired to; he was an actor, an entertainer, an artist. His mother told me how he dreaded those encounters with terminally ill children whose last wish was to meet Pee-wee Herman. He couldn't say no, but seeing them remained a sad and painful ordeal for him.

■ ■ ■

It was only natural that he would come to Sarasota to think and relax. It was, after all, his hometown, the place he grew up in and the place his parents still lived. He came surprisingly often, sometimes for extended stays. Though his parents' home on Siesta Key is right across an unpaved road from the beach, in a rustic, expensive, and slightly arty neighborhood—their nearest neighbor is painter Syd Solomon—Paul usually stayed at a hotel. He was, after all, a 38-year-old bachelor. This trip he was at the Resort at Longboat Key, still often referred to by its old name, The Inn on the Beach. It's hard to say whether it or the Colony can claim title to "Sarasota's fanciest hotel," but there is no doubt that the Resort is the more secluded of the two, hidden behind the gates of the Longboat Key Club. Paul had a "club suite" for which he was paying $150 a night, the going summer rate. Judy Rubenfeld would show up regularly, carrying a bag of groceries.

Paul and his manager Michael McLean had made a very conscious "creative decision" early on: There was no Paul Reubens, there was only Pee-wee Herman. No interviews with Paul were allowed, no photos of him were available, no allusions to him were permitted. The "home-town-boy-makes-good" story I kept wanting to do was always squashed, and with what I considered a very heavy hand. We were even told that if we persisted we would not be allowed to publish *any* pictures,

including ones of Pee-wee. But if McLean's tactics suggested that you were dealing with a paranoid control freak, you also had to admit they were very successful.

And the creative decision turned out to have an unexpected bonus. Out of his Pee-wee garb, with the beard and long hair that he would grow whenever on hiatus, Paul was virtually unrecognizable. He could go anywhere and not be noticed, except as a tall, thin man with a blank and passive face. He was probably the only major TV star who enjoyed such anonymity. The entire world knew who Pee-wee Herman was, but virtually no one knew who Paul Reubens was.

No one except Sarasota, that is. It's impossible to hide from your hometown, and Paul didn't try very hard. Though I have never met him, I have run into him twice, once in the post office and once at the Short Stop convenience store downtown. Each time, there was that double take. "Gee, that man looks familiar—oh, my God, it's Pee-wee Herman." In 1990 he had attended his high school reunion at the Hyatt—as Paul—and had made a moving little speech about the importance of old friendships that was the high point of the evening. Occasionally you would hear about an indiscretion on his part. He had been sighted in the town's gay bars on several occasions, though I should point out that in a town like

Sarasota, the gay bars are the only nightspots that can even remotely be described as "hip." All sorts of people turn up there—Ringling art students, Lucie Arnaz, when she was in town for a performance, even former society columnist Helen Griffith, at the time well into her 80s. Still, for someone in Paul's position, it seemed like a slightly dangerous thing to do.

What I found much more worrisome was his arrest. Only a handful of people knew about it, but for those of us who did, it was a scary secret. Back in 1983, just as he was starting to become famous, he had been arrested during the Christmas holidays at the adult bookstore on the South Trail. Nobody knew exactly what had happened, but his name and address—actually his parents' address, as he was by that time living in California—had been printed in the paper. I kept my mouth shut out of loyalty to his mother, but still, it worried me. His manager must be nuts to treat the press the way he did with something like that lurking in the background. What if it got out? It was the sort of thing that could ruin Paul's career. . . .

■ ■ ■

Sarasota is not at its best in the summer. Each day is a carbon copy of the last: The temperature hovers in the low 90s, in a haze of white heat and wet, muggy air. Lightning is a major public safety problem. Many people, especially the newcomers, hardly ever go outdoors all summer. It's just too uncomfortable.

And then there's the red tide. An algae that periodically "blooms" in the Gulf, it poisons fish and causes asthma-like attacks in humans. By Friday, July 26, Sarasota's worst red tide attack in five years was already fermenting in the lukewarm waters offshore.

But the biggest problem may well be boredom. The snowbirds have fled north and the social season has ground to a halt. There is little going on to keep one amused, although the antics of the vice cops were titillating the town. It wasn't the first time. In the past year or two, local cops had arrested beachgoers for wearing too-revealing bathing suits. Then they busted a clerk at Specs—he turned out to be a black honor student, active in church work—for selling a 2 Live Crew tape. Both cases made national headlines.

This time it sounded like they had really gone too far. A cop had actually taken off all his clothes while busting a prostitute, and she had touched him "in an orally sexual manner"—*then* he pulled his badge. They had it all on videotape, or maybe they didn't, depending who you talked to. The whole town was debating both the ethics of the case and what exactly "in an orally sexual manner" meant. As an old '60s liberal, I was delighted to see that when the paper's "Inquiring Photographer" asked people at the mall what they thought about the case, all six of them said the police had gone too far.

Over at the Asolo Theatre Company, preparations were already underway for the fall season opening of an elaborate new musical called "Svengali," based on the famous story about an opera star controlled by her evil manager. There were plans to try and take the show to Broadway. That the Asolo would be routinely involved in such a scheme shows how far it had come. The almost brand-new building was another indication of the Asolo's success. The enormous structure contains a 503-seat professional repertory theater, an acting conservatory, and a film and television school. It had been dedicated only a year and a half before in an elaborate ceremony attended by Burt Reynolds, only fitting since Reynolds personally donated $1 million of the $15 million needed to complete the project.

Since it was a Friday and not much was happening, Vic Meyrich, the theater's production coordinator, decided to show the staff an old documentary he had recently come across in a store room. It dealt with the "old Asolo" days—the late '60s and early '70s—so he put out the call that former members of the company were welcome. Among those who showed up was Paul Reubens.

Sarasota is full of people who grew up with Paul Reubens and were his friends. There's mayor Fredd Atkins, who was a classmate at Sarasota High. There's the girl who's always introduced at parties as the *real* inventor of the Pee-wee dance; there is an Episcopal priest at St Boniface of Siesta Key; there is Cynthia Porter, who married the town's leading black minister and now helps run his "Love Campaign." But the people who worked at the Asolo in the late '60s, many of them still involved with the theater, are probably Paul's closest Sarasota friends. Paul sat in the back; most people in the audience had no idea he was there.

The film brought back powerful memories. As with most things that had turned into institutions, there is a great deal of nostalgia for the Old Asolo, when the place was less professional, perhaps, but more a part of the community. Afterward, a group of the old timers hung around for a while to reminisce. Then Paul drove over to Vic's house; Vic and his wife Stephanie Moss are good friends from the old Asolo days. When he had called them a week or so ago to check in and say hello, he had spoken with their son Hart, aged six. The boy had been thrilled to be talking to Pee-wee Herman, his parents' famous friend but someone he had never met. Paul, who is conscientious about such things, promised he would come over to say hello.

"He was in great spirits,"

Stephanie recalls. He was rested and relaxed and tanned. This wasn't the way she had found him on his last visit, about a year ago, when the TV show was still in production. That time he had been exhausted. The strain of making "Pee-wee's Playhouse" was clearly burning him out. Most TV stars only have to act; Paul controlled every aspect of the show, from its concepts to its writing to its direction and production. His perfectionism and obsession with the smallest details were legendary and had won him enormous respect in the business. He even oversaw every aspect of all the Pee-wee merchandising spin-offs; he had reportedly sent one Pee-wee doll back for revisions eight times before he was satisfied. He literally worked from the moment he got up until the moment he went back to sleep. "He didn't have a life," Stephanie says. "It was the most exhausting thing."

They chatted for the rest of the afternoon, mostly about old friends and Paul's life in California. Then Paul spent some time with Hart, who was a little puzzled by this person with long hair and goatee who looked and acted so unlike the Pee-wee he knew from television. Never did Paul suddenly break into Pee-wee; and although he quoted a few Pee-wee catchphrases, he was low-key, soft-spoken, low-energy.

Stephanie begged Paul to stay for dinner, but he declined. After an autograph for Hart and a snap-shot of the two of them together, Paul drove off in his rented Mazda. He didn't tell them what his plans were for the evening. Perhaps he didn't even know himself. But it turned out that he would get his picture taken again that night.

■ ■ ■

The South Trail Cinema is Sarasota's only adult movie theater. It is owned by a friend of mine named David Warner, a 42-year-old writer/videomaker, whom I first met at Liar's Club, that famous Friday lunch gathering of local writers. David has a rough-hewn Southern edge to him, but after a while I began to suspect there was something unusual about his background.

I found out what it was when I went with David once to visit his family in Tuscaloosa. His father is Jack Warner, an enormously wealthy Alabama paper manufacturer. We flew up on the Warners' private jet. David had told me his father collected art, but nothing prepared me for the astonishing paintings that covered the walls of the company headquarters, several historic homes downtown, and the Warner mansion at the Northfield Yacht Club. It may well be one of the most important collections of American art still in private hands. There are Sargents, Churches, Bierstadts, Winslow Homers, and a whole roomful of Georgia O'Keeffes. But the thing that impressed me most was the snapshot I saw framed and hung on the wall of the laundry room. It was of Lord Mountbatten, a family friend, taken when he dropped by Tuscaloosa to visit the Warners.

David is one of those enviable young men who can afford expensive toys, and the one thing he had always wanted—other than a redneck bar, which he also bought—was his own movie theater. He started out with the most altruistic of motives: He would show classics and foreign films. But in 1981, when he took over, there wasn't much of a market for that sort of thing in Sarasota. After several dismal months of trying to make a go of it, he discovered what there *was* a market for: adult movies. The theater has been in the black ever since.

There have been some problems over the years. The building was firebombed (case still unsolved by the Sarasota police) forcing it to close for six months. And though it seems almost too good to be true, the theater was actually struck by lightning during one showing, frying the projector and forcing another shutdown. But the biggest problem has been the video revolution. People can now watch adult movies at home, and most of them do. To help offset this, David started a video rental club. He asked me to help him pick out the tapes; we spent hours poring through the catalogs, deciding what to order. Ed Baatz, who manages the theater for David, once invited me to the employees'

Christmas party and I leapt at the invitation. I was a little nonplussed to find several families having hot dogs out by the pool, with a lot of dogs and kids running around.

But if David's audience was deserting him, a certain hard-core element remained. They included: 1) Older men who had been attending such theaters regularly for years and weren't going to change now. 2) Those couples one sees now and then in adult theaters and finds impossible to figure out. 3) Homosexuals, some cruising, some not. 4) "Traveling sales-men"—men who are stuck alone in Sarasota and are interested in some action but not quite sure how to find it. And 5) The Sarasota County Sheriff's Department.

That July night there were four deputies inside the theater. They were dressed as usual for a sting operation of this sort, in T-shirts and cut-off jeans. Ed Baatz had always been annoyed at how scruffy the deputies looked; they certainly stood out from the rest of his clientele, whom he describes as having more of a "country club" look. The cops had arrived around five. They would stay 5 ½ hours. In that time, they would arrest four men. If Paul had arrived a few minutes earlier, he would have seen one of the arrests. The brother of one of Sarasota's most prominent businessmen had been charged with masturbating while watching the movie. He was a married man in his 50s, with a history of health and alcohol-related problems.

Paul parked his car and entered the theater. The ticket seller did not mention the cops. He had been forbidden to do so by the officers; as they flashed their badges for admittance, they told him that if he warned anyone of their presence, *he* would be arrested for obstruction of justice.

After Paul paid his admission ($8) he entered the theater itself. It's a rather grand space that appears larger than its 120-seat capacity. Red sound curtains line the walls, and there is a strong smell of disinfectant. Six ceiling fans kick up a breeze; combined with the air-conditioning—which comes on with a roar that makes everybody flinch—it could easily have been the coolest place in town.

The theater was not full. Although it was Friday, the day the movies change (*Catalina Five-O Tiger Shark, Turn Up the Heat* and *Nurse Nancy* made up the new triple-bill), if 20 people are there at any given time, it's a crowd. Paul chose a seat in the third row from the rear, toward the end farthest from the entrance. According to deputies, he masturbated twice, once at 8:25, then again 10 minutes later when a new movie appeared on the screen. The police report gets quite specific; it is this attention to detail, perhaps, that makes you feel when you read it that someone is being spied on in a private act.

How long Paul remained in the theater after being observed by the deputies is unclear; one report says five minutes, another over an hour. At any rate, as he was leaving he was stopped in the lobby by Officers Walters and Tuggle, who identified themselves and told him he was being placed under arrest. Then they escorted Paul out to the parking lot.

"This is embarrassing," Paul told the policemen, according to the report. "Can I show you some I.D.?" Though the dialogue sounds awkward, it is not hard to imagine the growing panic he must have been feeling. He explained that his wallet was in the trunk of his car, and the two cops escorted him to the Mazda. There was some confusion; he had concealed it under the carpeting and Sgt. Tuggle lifted it up for him. Paul retrieved his wallet, but before the policeman got a good look at the name on the license, he blurted out, "I'm Pee-wee Herman." According to the deputies, he then made a suggestion: Maybe he could do a charity benefit for the Sheriff's office. The officers didn't say no, but told him he would have to be arrested anyway. The report says that Paul told them he knew people got in trouble fooling around with each other in the theater, but he thought it was OK if you were "by yourself."

The police explained Paul's "court options," but his mind was elsewhere. "How can I handle this with the least amount of publicity?" he asked. The detectives didn't have a satisfactory answer to that. They placed Paul in a marked police car and drove to the Sarasota County Jail.

There he was fingerprinted and photographed. He was charged with Exposure of Sexual Organs. The bail was $219; he was $40 short. Police Lt. Joan Verizzo, officially on maternity leave, happened to be at the jail. She has been one of his sister Abby's closest friends for years and was a member of the women's rap group in high school in which Abby had first publicly confronted her homosexuality. She lent Paul the extra money.

It is against official Sheriff's Department policy for an employee to pay the bail of anyone other than a family member. Though Joan—and Judy Rubenfeld— insisted she was like family, Joan was suspended from the force for a day.

■ ■ ■

Back in the early days it was Judy Rubenfeld who called *me,* always drumming up publicity for her son's career. She would call any reporter in town if it meant a story; and she did not hesitate to complain about the lack of coverage he was getting, particularly from the *Sarasota Herald-Tribune.* But as Pee-wee's fame grew to such astonishing proportions, it was I who started making the begging phone calls. Could I interview Paul? Could I get a picture of the ring Zsa Zsa

Gabor had given her the last time she visited Paul in Hollywood? Could she talk Paul into appearing at our AIDS benefit?

She always tried to help out. But after Paul got a new manager, Michael McLean, there was little she could do. The policy that hid Paul Reubens from the public extended to his family. Earlier there had been a half-hearted attempt to turn them into Pee-wee's parents, a couple named Honey and Herman Herman, but this was wisely abandoned. And while they could on special occasions appear in public—the whole family flew out to Los Angeles for the unveiling of Pee-wee's star on Hollywood Boulevard—they were expected to keep quiet and not talk to the press. When the *New York Times* did a story about Abby and her work on gay legal issues, it never once mentioned that she was Pee-wee's sister. Judy told me once how she would have loved to appear on talk shows when they did "celebrity mothers" (she was asked all the time) but the manager just wouldn't let her.

Which is a shame, because she would have been great. A funny, outspoken woman who likes to talk, she speaks with a comedian's timing, jumping from punchline to punchline. Occasionally, a mild profanity— very mild—is used, but always for comic effect. In a town whose matrons tend to be Midwestern and whitebread, she is a character.

When I heard about Paul's arrest, I made a decision: I would not write about it. The Rubenfelds had enough troubles at the moment. But human nature being what it is, within 24 hours I had reversed myself. The event was seizing the country's attention; nobody could "get to the family"; but they might—just *might*—talk to me.

So I called Judy. I got the answering machine, arranged in such a way that it was impossible to leave a message. So I scribbled a note asking her to get in touch with me, and sent it Federal Express.

She called the next morning. She didn't identify herself, and it took a couple of seconds to realize who it was. I was dreading having to deal with a weepy, emotional woman; to my relief she seemed in good spirits, if slightly frantic. A long monologue poured out—she was angry, she was fighting mad, in fact—but still, everything was couched in the wisecracks she is famous for. She described the pain of what they were going through—Abby seemed to be taking it the hardest—and the hysteria and paranoia that had taken over Paul's managers, lawyers and publicists. She stuck up for Paul's local attorney Dan Dannheiser, even though he had tried to make a deal with the *Sarasota Herald-Tribune* (again, offering them a benefit if they wouldn't break the story) and then had told a reporter that Paul's career was ruined. "He

thought he was talking off the record," Judy insisted. She was upset at the way the *Herald-Tribune* was handling the story; they jumped on every sordid detail, she said, and had yet to say—or even report—a sympathetic word.

I saw my opening. "That's what I want to do. Tell Paul's side." She paused for a moment. "Does that mean I'll get my subscription on time?"

An operator broke in. "I have an emergency call from Dale in New Jersey," she announced.

"I'll call you back," Judy said. I stood motionless by the phone until it rang again, three minutes later.

"Well, I'm sure you can guess who that was," Judy began, sounding drained. I got the feeling Paul had yelled at her when he found out who she was talking to. The jokes stopped; she seemed distracted and uncertain. She told me she would get back to me within 24 hours.

Like everybody else close to Paul, she stuck by him completely. Never for a second did she suggest that he might have an emotional problem or need professional help. All she knew was that a terrible hurt had been dealt her child.

■   ■   ■

Judy once told me how fascinated Paul had been when he discovered that he and Mel Gibson had both been born in Peekskill, New York, within six months of each other. The families didn't know each other, though. The Gibsons moved to Australia shortly thereafter, and eight years later the Rubenfelds were gone, too, off to Florida. Though they had owned a profitable Lincoln-Mercury dealership there, none of them seemed to miss the place. Peekskill was the site of the famous '50s Peekskill Riot, when the police stood by and did nothing as the Klan broke up a Paul Robeson concert. It was perhaps not the best place for a liberal Jewish family.

Their new home, Sarasota, was very much a small town back in those days, but it already sported a reputation as a sophisticated place, conservative but socially concerned and a genuine arts colony. It also had a unique and colorful history—it was the home of the circus. It was also the home of the circus *stars*, people like Sylvana Zacchini, the first woman shot out of a cannon, and Franz Unus, who can—or could, anyway—stand on one finger. There were former Munchkins galore, and all the great clowns, like Lou Jacobs, the creator of scores of classic gags, including the one where all the clowns pile out of the tiny car. The most famous clown of all, Emmett Kelly, lived only a few blocks from the Rubenfeld home, an eccentric and fondly remembered place near McClellan Park. Judy and Milton bought the Lamplighter Shop (they've since sold it); the family's lifestyle was solidly upper middle class, but with a slightly Bohemian bent.

The most remarkable thing about Paul's childhood was how early his talent showed and how eager he was, even then, for success. Judy remembered his audition for "A Thousand Clowns" at The Players when he was in sixth grade: "His father didn't want him to try out. He said, 'If he gets the part, he's really going to have the bug,' 'cause that was a big part for a kid. I said, 'I think we should let him try out 'cause he won't get the part. There are far better kids, and it will nip it in the bud.' Of course, he got the part."

By the time he reached Sarasota High, his life was absorbed by the theater. He acted in the school plays—most memorably as Colonel Pickering in "My Fair Lady"—and was voted "Best Actor." And he was hanging out at the Asolo constantly, an accepted member of the family. He was in awe of the real actors but quickly made friends with them; for their part, they liked this bright young kid enormously and were glad to teach him their craft.

"He was incredibly hard-working," recalls Isa Thomas, who played his mother in "Life With Father." "And *bright*." Everyone mentions his self-discipline, his eagerness to learn, his astonishing self-confidence. "Paul was not a high-school kid," says Tim McKenna, a fellow apprentice who shared an apartment with Paul in 1970. "He was popular and well-respected at school, but there was no hanging out.

Academically, he did very well, but that was like an afterthought. His life revolved around the Asolo. He was driven. He had a strong sense of where he was going."

He was considered serious and thoughtful, anything but the clown. He was shy unless he knew you well; then his sarcastic wit would bloom. "We used to sit in my dressing room and hoot and howl," recalls Stephanie Moss, who is nine years his senior. "He was the sharpest and wittiest kid I ever met. He wasn't loud, but he had a startling satirical edge. These little diamonds were always slipping out of the side of his mouth."

His goal was to become a serious actor. No one doubted he would make it. "I always thought he would end up a respected actor in rep," says one friend. Isa Thomas recalls being impressed with the way he took to Shakespeare without any training.

Paul also fell in with the so-called "Andy Warhol Set," a group of arty teen-agers. They were the exception in Sarasota in those days, recalls McKenna; often city bus drivers wouldn't let them board because of their long hair. "They were a little piece of New York City in this extremely conservative Republican town," Stephanie Moss recalls. "A breath of fresh air."

It was the late '60s, a time of artistic excitement and sexual experimentation. It was also a time of marijuana. When Paul was 18 he was busted for possession of pot. Stephanie can't remember the details, but she does know that it was because of Paul's carelessness. "He left some joints on the seat of his car, or something like that. I said, 'Paul, how can you have been so stupid?'"

■ ■ ■

The picture that finally emerges of the Paul Reubens who returned to Sarasota in the summer of 1991, on the eve of his third arrest, is that of a serious, enormously successful artist who led a series of highly compartmentalized lives. The rigid split between Paul and Pee-wee was just the beginning.

First, and most important to him, there was his career. Here he was shrewd, disciplined, tireless and brilliant. Though he had made millions, everyone agreed that money was not the motivating force. (After he had become a star he was still driving the car he had inherited from his grandmother.) The general public knew him as a clown, a freakish comedian, but in the entertainment business he was considered something of a genius. Many serious critics classify him as a performance artist, perhaps the first one who has crossed over to mainstream popularity. No one who knows him feels his success was a lucky fluke; it was accomplished by his drive and his uncanny ability to take huge risks and make them pay off.

Then there was his personal life, consisting of family and friends who can only be described as loving and supportive. Isa Thomas mentioned that he told her recently that he didn't like many of the people he had come across in California. But among his old friends, he inspires remarkable loyalty and protectiveness. The reason that so little about "the real Paul" appeared in the papers after his arrest was that his friends were furious at the press; rather than provide information and insights that would make him come alive, they instead begged reporters not to print *anything*—or, more often, just hung up. And those who did talk, while they made it quite clear that Paul was not a drooling sex maniac or a coke-head, seemed uneasy. You got the sense that there were secrets within secrets, and that the situation was infinitely more complicated than it seemed.

And finally, since it prompted the whole thing, there is his sex life. I had a conversation with someone who claimed a sexual encounter with Paul, and while I found the account convincing, what I remember most are not the titillating details—they were, in fact, rather banal—but the depressing resemblance the scene described had to the sex lives of so many unmarried, middle-aged men.

■ ■ ■

The week that Pee-wee was on the front pages, the red tide hit Sarasota full force. The beaches were covered with dead fish, and the resulting stink was a perfect counterpoint for the mood of the town.

First of all, the place was getting lousy publicity. In a town so image-conscious, where millions of dollars are made selling a sophisticated, cultural "lifestyle" to affluent newcomers, bad publicity is a big problem.

Over at the *Herald-Tribune* they were collecting columns about the incident from papers all over the country, and the word on Sarasota was not good. The police were coming across as very foolish and the city was becoming identified with some appalling images: porno theaters, lewd beachgoers, tough prostitutes—an atmosphere of heavily charged but vaguely comic sexual tensions.

But what people found even more disturbing was the behavior of the Sheriff's Department. Spending hours in an adult theater seemed a poor use of police time. Sheriff Geoff Monge claimed that the South Trail Cinema was targeted only once every three or four months, a remark that startled employees of the theater. One employee estimates that a more realistic estimate would be twice a month; that the police (in groups of three to six) would spend up to six hours at a stretch in the theater; and that they would sometimes sit in the theater while it was completely empty, for up to an hour, waiting for people.

When Pee-wee supporters rallied in New York City, County

Commissioner David Mills declared that Sarasota stood behind the police and wouldn't tolerate behavior like Paul's. But letters to the local paper told a different story. Writer after writer expressed support for Paul and advised the police to "keep their pants on" and concentrate on serious crimes. Community leaders, such as Ed Foster, assistant principal at Sarasota High and advisor to Paul's senior class in 1970, spoke out for Paul, describing him as "very talented" and "very humble." Said Foster, "There's nobody in that entire class, I'll bet you, that disowns him for anything."

A small town operates on its own social contract. People are much gentler with each other than in a big city. Certain things that everybody knows are never said in public. And while it's OK to embarrass someone if a lucrative political office is at stake, you are never allowed to be cruel. And the Sarasota police had become cruel.

At first their sting operations involving victimless crimes were rather funny. The big T-back scandal, in which several beach-goers were arrested for wearing those backless bathing suits, had even ended up on "Donahue." But when the police began trolling the porno theater and the men's room out at the beach, the strangest thing happened—instead of uncovering the dregs of society, they were uncovering its pillars.

Ministers, bank vice presidents, social leaders—lives and families were being ruined, and people didn't feel right about it. It's taken the disaster of Pee-wee Herman to make many realize they don't want that kind of police force.

Judy and I spoke twice a day, so often that she and my father, who was taking my messages, began what she called a "phone affair." She was sad and angry, but always on. "I hear 'Prime Time' is in town," I told her. "'Prime Time'? Which one is that?" "Diane Sawyer." "She's been calling me! Oh, God, how can I lose 20 pounds fast?" But when asked if Paul had any sense of humor about what happened, she was silent. "No," she said quietly. "He is devastated." Finally she called to give me the final decision—Paul was planning to plead innocent; the lawyers and managers and publicists would not allow her to talk to anyone. She was sorry. "I was hoping Hedy Lamarr would knock us off the front pages," she said, just before we hung up. The day before the 78-year-old former star had been arrested in nearby Altamonte Springs for allegedly shoplifting $20 worth of laxatives. "They're being much nicer to her," Judy said. "Not that I have anything against Hedy Lamarr," she added quickly.

There is something so awful and complete about the Pee-wee disaster. The biggest children's star in the country arrested for

masturbating in a porno theater—
it has already entered American
myth. People will talk about it for
years to come; it will affect public
attitudes about sex, the police,
privacy, and the media.

For Sarasota it is a profoundly
unhappy event. People realize that
more than one reputation was
shattered that hot Friday night.
"Look what happened to Arcadia,"
they shudder.

Perhaps the only good thing
about a disaster is that it allows the
survivors to start over with a clean
slate. Pee-wee Herman may be
dead, but Paul Reubens isn't. His
friends say it would take more than
this to destroy his drive and
creative force.

"He will turn this around," they
insist.

Sarasota may have a harder
time.

■ ■ ■

This article first appeared in the October 1991 issue of Sarasota *magazine. Plunket, author of two novels, is a full-time writer in Sarasota, Florida.*

PUT IT INTO PRACTICE

Discussion

1. Discuss the differences between short fiction and high-style nonfiction. A short story is reprinted on page 395 of this text. Discuss how that story can be rewritten as a piece of high-style nonfiction. Discuss how the Calderazzo and Plunket stories reprinted at the end of this chapter, and the story "Twice a Victim" from chapter four, could be rewritten as fiction.

2. Discuss the limitations of high-style nonfiction writing. Is it always appropriate for a given topic? Is it always appropriate for a given magazine?

3. Consider the following statement: The writing of short fiction is the process whereby a writer tells a series of untruths in an effort to arrive at a final, significant great truth. The writing of literary nonfiction is the process whereby a writer uses a series of small truths to arrive at a final, significant great truth.

   In your class or writers' group, do most agree with the statement? Disagree? Why?

   What are the implications of the statement for writers of high-style nonfiction?

Exercises

1. You have an assignment from a top regional magazine to do a story on a Hollywood star who comes from your state. The star will be in that hometown for several days, and you have arranged for as much interview time as you need. In a paragraph or two for each, list what you might be looking for in terms of character, setting, plot, and conflict. Next, in a paragraph or two, list what kind of voice you might use to write the piece and what kind of tone you'll take.

2. Take a story from somewhere in this text that you think is not particularly stylish, and give a two-page explanation of how you would go about rewriting it for high style. What other kinds of reporting would you need? How would you change the writing? Take a few paragraphs from the story and rewrite them for high style. Follow that with a one-page explanation of how your rewrite turns the story into a high-style piece.

3. Reread the story "Twice a Victim" at the end of chapter four, and ask yourself how this piece works structurally as a fictional short story.

What does it offer in terms of plot? Conflict? Characterization? Write a two-page summary of the story's plot, its characters, and its subtext.

4. Take any three stories from this text and give a one-paragraph assessment of each one's subtext. Then take one of your assessment paragraphs and find at least one more story from the text that has the same subtext.

CHAPTER 7

EDITING AND REVISING

—▼—

LAYERS OF REVISION

WORKING WITH EDITORS
The Writer-Editor Relationship
Fact Checkers

WORK IN PROGRESS

—▲—

Deidre Sullivan was formerly creative director of a newsletter called *Nature of Realities* and is the author of several books. She is a polished, professional writer. On an assignment for *Omni* magazine, she spent weeks pulling together the research, doing her interviewing, and then writing and revising the story.

So when *Omni's* senior editor, the late Murray Cox, sent her a letter asking for a series of quite specific revisions on the story, she made the sort of response you might expect from a veteran writer who receives that sort of note from an editor.

She happily made the changes.

As Sullivan explains, a good writer should always be glad to work with a good editor. The common goal of the two, after all, is a great story, and, she says, "You just can't see everything, no matter how many times you edit and revise your own work."

In the case of "Portrait of a Prophet," Sullivan found that "Murray's comments were incredibly insightful. He's the kind of editor who takes a lot of care with words and takes a lot of care in working with writers."

Because of that care, and because of Sullivan's willingness to work with Cox on polishing the story, both the magazine and the writer benefited. The result appears at the end of this chapter.

A successful relationship like this one between a writer and an editor provides another benefit for the writer as well. Shortly after this piece was published, Cox gave Sullivan another assignment. He knew she was talented, hardworking, able to meet her deadlines, and willing to revise. In short, he knew he could work with her, and that's important.

Sullivan's experience with Cox at *Omni* is one you need to be familiar with as you begin your writing career. Editing and revising are two of the most important aspects of the craft of writing, and freelancers who don't realize that are unlikely to find much success. You need to be able to edit and revise your own work, certainly, and you also need to be able to work with an editor to meet the needs of the magazine.

LAYERS OF REVISION

The revision process starts with your attitude. There is a certain mind-set to writing—one in which you get lost in the creative process, in which the subconscious seems to take over, and from which the words emerge. It's a stimulating, exciting mental exercise, writing that solid first draft of a story.

But as most writers learn, that pleasant creative state of mind is only the beginning of a sequence of necessary steps the writer must take to get the story into print.

The second step is your editing of the story, and there's quite another mind-set involved in doing that. The revision process requires that you be cold-blooded and sharp-eyed, willing to change or get rid of a word, a phrase, or an entire passage that sounded terrific when it first came to you but now, as you edit, seems overblown, unnecessary, out of place, or just plain wrong.

Every one of the dozens of writers and editors interviewed for this book referred to his or her own editing and revision process as the necessary hard work that turns a good idea into a polished story. Joe Bargmann of *St. Louis* magazine, whose work you've seen in several chapters, says, "It's a rare bird who doesn't do a lot of revision these days. Frankly, I welcome it. I don't consider myself a good first-draft writer. I think that the first draft for me is more of a blocking out of scenes to see where the structure is. Then, in the revising, I get into the real polish, the wording of the story."

B O X 7 . 1

EMBRACE REJECTION

It's hard to think of rejection in anything but negative terms when you get a form letter in the mail telling you, "Your story just doesn't meet our needs at this time."

It's painful having your stories rejected. You've spent a lot of time and effort writing them; you've put a lot of yourself into them. Especially for beginning writers, there is a heavy emotional investment in a finished story, and so it's natural that you feel it personally when the story doesn't sell.

But despite the pain, rejection is something you have to learn to like, for it means several good things are happening to your writing career. In fact, you must learn to embrace rejection, in the sense that it is a necessary part of your career, and the only way to avoid it is to avoid writing.

When you have a bad day in the mail, with a favorite story's being returned, consider this:

1. *If you're getting rejections, that means you are writing and submitting.* This is no small thing. There are many thousands of would-be writers out there who never get rejected because they never actually submit. They may talk a lot about writing, but talk is pretty much all they do. They aren't willing to risk rejection. You, on the other hand, have the courage necessary to make it as a writer.

    Remember, when you start to succeed and your stories are selling regularly, others will still be only talking about writing.

2. *If you're getting rejections, your work is out there and perhaps beginning to have an impact.* No editor is ever going to psychically pick up the vibrations that you have a story and then give you a call out of the blue asking to see it. You have to take the initiative and send it in. Then, even if it's rejected, it has been read, an editor has seen what you can do, and you may have begun to build a reputation, no matter how small, that will stand you in good stead for the next submission.

    When you begin to get personal rejections that talk about liking your work but being unable to use it this time around, you'll know that these small steps to reputation building are worth taking.

Continued

Then, when you sell, you'll think that every small step, every painful rejection, was well worth the pain.

3. *If you're getting rejections, you are learning.* Every time you send a story out, you've learned a little more about writing. Every time you get a rejection, you learn a little more about the whole process of getting your stories into print. Every time you open up that returned SASE, you are finding out something about yourself, about your writing, and about your ability to stick to it, keep learning, and persevere until you sell.

It isn't easy, no question about that. But it is possible. Remember: There are many, many would-be writers who drop out along the way. Frequently, the writers who make it are the ones who grow and learn through the rejection process and who emerge from it stronger, better, harder-working professional writers.

And that, ultimately, is what you want to be: part-time, full-time, staff, or freelance—a professional writer.

And John Calderazzo, too, whose work you've also encountered in several chapters, admits, "I'm a fanatical rewriter, which is why I've never really been a newspaper writer and why this kind of writing suits me better." Calderazzo spends most of his revision time on his opening. He feels he has to "work and rework and rework the opening sequence, in particular, of any story."

"I might write and rewrite that thing five, ten, or fifteen times," he says, "and each time I'm rewriting it in a way that will set up what's going to come later." Calderazzo says he spends half of the total time it takes him to write a story just in writing the hook and then rewriting it again and again. After that, for him, the story seems to move along more quickly.

Writers follow various paths when it comes to revising and editing their own work. Some write a complete rough draft, then come back to it and edit carefully before coming up with a second draft. Others—Calderazzo is one of them—revise as they go. "I'd like to write one draft all the way through," he says, "but I don't seem to be able to do it. I get maybe halfway and then I rework things. By the time I get to the last twenty-five percent of the story, it's pretty much writing itself, and that gives me a really solid first draft."

On the other hand, fiction and nonfiction writer Scott Russell Sanders, whose work is found in chapter eleven, gets a complete first draft done first and then comes back to revise and edit for "the polishing of language. The structure usually, for me, doesn't change very much after I do the whole draft. I feel my way through the form, and by the time I've finished that full draft, the form is usually set."

Although the techniques of editing differ from writer to writer (and editor to editor), basically three kinds of work take place. So it may be useful for you to think of editing and revising as a three-stop process that goes something like this:

1. **The copyedit procedure,** when you come back to the draft of a story and do a line-by-line edit for typos, misspellings, and grammar problems: As mentioned in chapter three, if you make mistakes here that get into the final draft, you're unlikely to be very successful at selling your stories.

2. **The structural edit procedure,** when you take a look at how the story is put together: As discussed in chapter five, you need to make sure that your structure holds up logically and thematically and that it flows cleanly from one element to another in the story.

3. **The style edit procedure,** when you work on the story in order to improve it stylistically: As explained in chapter six, not all stories lend themselves to this kind of writing, but those that do can be real gems if the writing is in control and the stylistic efforts are relevant and useful to the story. It's your job when you're editing to make sure that is the case.

Take a look at this first draft by writer Deidre Sullivan:

It's nine a.m. in Tokyo. The chairman of large Japanese trading company has called a board meeting and instructs the members to take their seats on one side of the highly polished board table. Sitting across from them is an impeccably dressed American businessman and his translator. The chairman explains to the executives he has invited someone new to visit the company, a consultant who has never studied their book or their operations before. He says that the gentleman sitting at the table is a has come from the Center for Applied Intuition (CAI) an organization in Fairfax, California, and that he's available to answer any questions that they might have about their company and work.

That's a pretty solid hook, but there are a few typos (the "a" is missing after "chairman of" in the second sentence, and four lines from the end there is the phrase "is a has come from," where Sullivan obviously changed her mind midsentence but didn't quite clean up the change) and a phrase or two that could be tightened.

When she came back to this paragraph later, Sullivan made the changes, and the second draft looked like this:

> It's nine a.m. in Tokyo. The chairman of a large Japanese trading company has called a board meeting and, as the executives enter, he tells them to take their seats on one side of a highly polished table. Sitting across from them are two impeccably dressed American businessmen. The foreigners have never studied the corporation's books. They do not know how the company operates. In fact, they had never stepped foot in headquarters of this corporation until minutes before the scheduled board meeting.
>
> The older of the two, Bill Kautz, briefly introduces himself as a scientist and founder of the Center for Applied Intuition (CAI), an organization based out of Fairfax, California. He then sits quietly. The other, Charles Nunn, explains that he works with CAI as an "expert intuitive" and that he will answer any questions the executives might have about their company.

The changes incorporated into this second draft range from the small to the large, from cleaning up the typographical errors of the first draft to a major restructuring of the passage about CAI so as to include the names of the two principals involved.

It's important to note that revising and editing your story do not necessarily imply tightening, or shortening, the piece. Sullivan's story became much longer in the revision process and thus did an improved job of informing and entertaining the reader.

"By the time I'm into the second draft," she explains, "I usually know what's needed to make the story complete and keep it focused, what parts to flesh out and where to cut back."

And, Sullivan knows, there is frequently more editing to come after that second draft, as the writer and editor work together to polish the piece and get it ready for publication.

WORKING WITH EDITORS

As Sullivan made clear at the start of this chapter, professional writers welcome an editor's input into their story.

Sullivan's editor at *Omni*, Murray Cox, did several edits of each story he planned to run in the magazine. He was looking, of course, for typographical errors, the occasional grammatical mistake or misspelling (though there shouldn't be many at this level of the business), and the rough phrase here and there that could be smoothed out.

But that sort of editing, while useful, wasn't where Cox spent most of his energy. Cox said his real work was to "keep the tone straight for the writer and then help the writer get the reader from A to Z in the story. I like to try and look at the overall piece in terms of structure. Every story, especially in science writing, has a valley," he explained. "How do you get the reader through those valleys and keep the reader going? I want to see where my interest flags, where I get bored, where I start to yawn."

In Sullivan's story, Cox found, "Her structure, for the most part, was fine, though I did in the final draft make some changes, pull up some things." It wasn't always that easy for Cox: "A lot of times I find something in the back of the story that's pertinent and needs to be brought up."

To help himself see what kind of revisions might be necessary for an article that he'd bought, Cox frequently outlined the article before putting together the revisions. For instance, he felt, "Deidre's first draft for me was a little too ethereal. I didn't have a strong enough idea, at the end, of what the point of the article was." To clarify the point, Cox began to put together an outline. As he did, he began to feel that Sullivan "really needed to ground the piece. My suggestions were very specific on how to do this."

In this letter, portions of which are reprinted in Box 7.2 on page 198, Cox reminded Sullivan, "the article needs to be grounded with as many concrete examples as possible," and then he moved on into specific requests. Among those requests were:

To give details about how the main character, Bill Kautz, works. What are his methods? Cox asks. He also asks Sullivan for more examples of the phenomenon—in short, more specific details.

To get some reaction from other scientists about Kautz and his work. (Did they consider him "really weird"? Cox asks.)

To add supportive quotes from other clients of Kautz.

To better define several terms found in the story.

To "ground" the story in general, with as many concrete details and examples as possible.

Cox's advice is good generally for any writer (you might want to consider your own stories and how they would benefit from the aforementioned five points), and the advice was certainly useful for Sullivan. Her

AN EDITOR'S ADVICE

The following is excerpted from the letter Senior Editor Murray Cox of *Omni* magazine sent to writer Deidre Sullivan about her story "Portrait of a Prophet."

Deidre,

Overall, in the final draft I think the article needs to be grounded with as many concrete examples as possible. As you can see, I've pencil-edited the article, tightening, cutting a bit, and asking questions. Don't freak out. This is my style. I throw all my questions out to writers, but you don't necessarily have to answer them all. I just want you to see where things can be clarified or added to.

Specific requests:

1. Before you go into Kautz's background, you need a couple of graphs on applied intuition via Kautz, details on how Kautz works, his methods, how rigorous are they? How does one acquire "the gift"? Can anyone acquire it?
2. How many American companies used him? How much does he cost? If he won't give that to you, would he give you a ballpark figure?
3. Can you get a quote from a peer of Kautz's at SRI?
4. You need some quotes from CAI clients, some anecdotes showing how intuition has solved problems or done whatever it's supposed to do.
5. The earthquake thing and the Middle East peace option are wonderful, wonderful, but need to be filled in a bit. What does his study on earthquakes show?
6. The kicker: The last quote is nice, but I think you can make the ending even stronger. Can he give you anything brand new from one of his research projects or his four books?

Finally, remember, none of this is cast in stone, so, look over my marginal notes, think about what I've thrown at you, and then talk to me.

story was a good one as it stood, yet, Cox thought it could be an even better one with some improvements.

Cox's advice on revising the story took up two and a half pages, single-spaced. Cox included praise with his advice, at one point noting that a section is "wonderful, wonderful but definitely needs to be filled in a bit," and that other sections worked fine.

Finally, he closed with: "None of this is in stone, so, look over my marginal notes, think about what I've thrown at you, and then talk to me." And he even offered to reschedule the story if the revisions would take too much time. That's a thoughtful, helpful editor.

Sullivan's response was simple. She got busy making the revisions. After all, she says, "Murray had a great sense of the overall structure of a story and how it should work." As she puts it, "Working with Murray, frankly, helped me get better."

In turn, Cox felt that her response to his advice was helpful, indeed. "The second revision with Deidre turned out very nicely," Cox recalled, "and that's the way it should be. My experience has taught me that after the first rewrite, you shouldn't still be doing structural things; the writer should have everything that's needed at that point. Even if it's not in the story, it should be in the notes."

Note that Cox, unlike some editors, wasn't comfortable doing his own revising on the story. He wanted the writer to do the actual revising, with the editor along as a sort of adviser or writing coach.

"I feel very strongly that I shouldn't insert my own words in an article," he explained. "I may do it when I'm up against a deadline wall and something has to be done and the writer is unavailable, but that's it. And I certainly never put my words into a piece without at least checking."

The Writer-Editor Relationship

You should know that complaining about editors and their editing is common among writers, and occasionally there are editors who have dramatically altered a story without permission from the writer.

But those instances are rare, and the word about such editors does get around.

Cox said, "I've worked with rewrite editors who can be very cavalier, turn articles upside down so that, well . . . writers have a very legitimate gripe with those kinds of editors. I have seen articles go into print where you could look through and identify maybe ten sentences that were really the writer's. Something's wrong there.

"It's a philosophical, vocational decision, as far as I'm concerned. If you do that, you're a rewrite editor and you'll get that reputation among the writers."

Cox felt that the best relationship is one in which "the editor serves as a handmaiden to the writer, releases the writer's energy."

At *St. Louis* magazine, Joe Bargmann felt that his editor there served that function. "When we worked together on a piece it was a pretty organic process. There was always a lot of discussion, a lot of debate about the stories, and to me that was ideal, in terms of learning and developing professionally."

Now, as senior editor at *Seventeen* magazine, Bargmann gets to return the favor. "And I always find that the best writers are the ones who want to work to improve their stories," he says. "Even for longtime professionals—but especially for beginners—working with an editor gives you a chance to grow."

That is something you'll want to be concerned with, as well—learning and developing professionally. If you see the editor as an enemy, you won't be allowing yourself much room to grow. If you can learn to see the editor as a coach, someone working with you to make the story all it can be, you'll improve not only the story at hand but also your future writing by paying close attention to how the editor has improved the story.

Fact Checkers

Finally, when working with editors and their magazines, you'll find yourself dealing with *fact checkers*. Fact checkers are editorial assistants whose job it is to double-check all the facts, quotes, and names in your story. Once the story has been through whatever revision the editor asks for, and the final draft is in and accepted, fact checkers start making phone calls.

Sandra Donnelly worked as a fact checker (in many places the job title is editorial assistant) at *Working Woman* magazine. She explains in chapter twelve that fact checkers know it's a foot in the door in terms of their career, and they take the job seriously.

The fact checkers for Deidre Sullivan's story found a few items on various pages of her manuscript and noted them for Sullivan to fix.

Typically, most of the issues caught by fact checkers are small. Most often, they simply ask for clarification or slight modification of quotes or facts. Occasionally, of course, the problems are more serious.

A list of fact checker items for Sullivan's story is in Box 7.3.

A professional writer like Sullivan includes relevant phone numbers and sources at the end of the manuscript for the fact checkers' use.

BOX 7.3

FACT CHECKERS' RESPONSE

The following is excerpted from the fact checkers' work on Deidre Sullivan's story "Portrait of a Prophet."

Page 1. No corrections
Page 2. Nunn says one (not two) board members were found to be working for a foreign government.
Page 3. No corrections
Page 4. Brendan O'Regan calls himself vice president for (sted ("of") research.
Page 7. This year (sted month) CAI will begin offering services in Europe.
The French translator [xx] is running (sted going to run) CAI's operation in France.
Kautz's wife is a social worker (sted psychologist).
Page 8. New phrasing: When Kautz returned to the Bay area, he sought out other intuitives (sted trance channels).
Page 9. Rephrasing in the quotes from Oliver Markley: One group was doing futures (sted society-oriented) research. . . .
Page 10. Tal Brooke suggests we add something of his background for contextual purposes. Before converting to Christianity, he was for many years a top Western disciple of Indian guru Sai Baba. He is now the best-selling author of "When the World Will Be As One."

WORK IN PROGRESS

In terms of revising your work, perhaps it might be best for you to think of every story you write as a work in progress until the day you see it in print.[1]

First you come up with the idea, then you do the interviewing and research, then you write the first draft, then you revise and edit to polish a second or third or fourth draft, and then you send it out. In some cases, that's it. The editor buys the story, sends you a check, prints the story, and

---

[1]For some writers, even getting a story into print doesn't end the revision process. When they sell reprint rights, they revise the story again, not only to update it but also in the firm belief that you can always improve a piece.

sends you a copy of the issue. Frequently, though, the story travels a long path that keeps it in revision for months, or sometimes years.

Perhaps the story is rejected. In that case, if the rejection comes by way of a form letter, you won't gain any hints about whether the story needs improvement. After all, there are any number of reasons the piece can be rejected that have nothing at all to do with the quality of the story—perhaps the magazine ran something similar just a few months ago, or it is overstocked with that kind of story just now, or any one of a dozen other reasons for rejection.

But perhaps quality was a factor. You can't know. So you'll need to read the story closely and look for ways to improve it. In that case, some revision is likely.

The good thing about getting rejected is that it gives you the opportunity to see your story with fresh eyes. Mistakes both large and small can be hard to see when you've recently finished a piece. After all, you were the one to make the mistake, so it's not surprising that you have a hard time seeing it shortly thereafter. But when the story comes back weeks, or months, later, some of those mistakes will leap right off the page at you. Fix them. And then make sure that the corrections blend in smoothly with the story. And then send it back out again.

And if it comes back, then repeat the process. You're not only improving the story each time, but you're learning about writing and revising as you go.

Perhaps the rejection came with a note from the editor mentioning things that he or she saw wrong with the piece. Don't idly dismiss those remarks. Remember that editors see dozens, perhaps hundreds, of stories weekly or monthly and have a broad background of recognizing both good and bad writing as a result. It's quite likely that editors really do know what they are talking about when it comes to your story's weaknesses. So take those comments to heart and factor them into your revision.

And then send the story back out again. (But not to the same editor, unless a revision and resubmission were requested. Try someone new.)

It's worth noting, by the way, that editors can disagree on some aspects of a story. What pleases one editor may bother another, so don't automatically rewrite based on one editor's thoughts. Just include those thoughts as one factor in your thinking as you go through another revision on the story.

The author, for example, can recall rewriting the ending of a particular story to meet one editor's request for revisions and then having that rewrite rejected. The next editor to see the story liked it fine, except for the ending, which he asked the author to revise. With a sigh, the author rewrote the ending again, back into what was similar to the original, and resubmitted. That time the story sold.

Finally, it may happen that an editor likes your story generally but not quite enough to buy it as is and asks you to revise and resubmit on speculation. There are no guarantees based on such a request, but the editor is indicating the desire to see it again after you've worked on it.

My best advice in this case is to give it the revision the editor wants, unless you have strong disagreements. Then resubmit, noting in a cover letter (see chapter eight) where you have revised to suit the editor's needs and where you have disagreed.

If you do a good job on the revision, you'll have a sale, and the odds are that the editor's comments will improve the story in any event, so if it doesn't sell to this editor, it may well sell to the next.

Remember: the key is to think of the revision process as never being over until you see the story in print.

■ ■ ■

PORTRAIT OF A PROPHET

BY DEIDRE SULLIVAN

A Scientist Reveals the Secrets of the Super Conscious Mind

It's 9:00 a.m. in Tokyo. The chairman of a large Japanese trading company has called a board meeting, and as the executives enter, he tells them to take seats on one side of a highly polished table. Sitting across from the VIPs are two impeccably dressed American businessmen who had never stepped foot in the headquarters of the corporation until minutes before the scheduled board meeting. They have never studied the corporation's books. They do not know how the company operates.

The older of the two, Bill Kautz, briefly introduces himself as a scientist and founder of the Center for Applied Intuition (CAI), an organization based out of Fairfax, California. He then sits quietly. The other, Charles Nunn, explains that he works with CAI as an "expert intuitive" and that he will answer any questions the executives might have about their company.

Taking the lead, the chairman poses a question about the relocation of a manufacturing plant. Nunn provides information on possible sites and offers his suggestions. The VIPs, stunned at Nunn's responses, begin to question him. Who is the best person for the director of sales? Is it wise to establish a relationship with a particular London-based firm? How can the Okinawa office be made more profitable? Nunn answers each question in detail while Kautz, the more grandfatherly of the duo, looks on. Kautz is pleased.

After the meeting, Nunn asks the chairman to call him at his hotel *from a pay phone*. When they speak later that evening, the chairman is shocked by Nunn's revelations: One board member is working for a foreign government; the office phones are tapped. Within days, an investigation proved Nunn's hunches—his intuitive responses—had been correct.

For Kautz and Nunn, the morning board meeting's been, well, just business as usual. CAI provides individual counseling "sessions" and intuitive consulting services for major Japanese corporations, including financial services companies, retail organizations, and food-processing concerns. As director, Kautz organizes sessions both in the U.S. and abroad, serving as a liaison between his staff of expert intuitives—Nunn's in popular demand—and the outside world.

Kautz is part wise man, part scholar, part hand holder, though he spends a lot of his time as interpreter. Inevitably, Kautz gets linked to the New Age movement and he is constantly asked to differentiate between CAI and, say, the standard fare of San Francisco Bay Area psychism. According to Kautz—he's a man uncomfortable with much of the pop jargon and emotional excess which seems to take root and blossom on the West Coast—CAI's in a completely different league.

New Agers would certainly call Nunn's work "psychic." After all, Nunn and the highly intuitive CAI staff seem to have access to extrasensory knowledge, often gained through trance channeling. To Kautz, however, the term *psychic* is misused and misunderstood. His CAI staff are not psychics, he says; they're "expert intuitives." Similarly, Kautz doesn't use the word *reading* when he describes what Nunn does. Instead, he prefers *session*. Even the concept "extrasensory" is problematic. "What has traditionally been labeled as extrasensory or as paranormal is a universal human capacity which most people haven't chosen to exercise or develop," he says.

There are a number of differences between hiring a psychic and working with CAI, Kautz claims. "Many psychics don't understand the processes they are dealing with," he says. "They are neither skilled nor responsible." And few psychics, he asserts, see their work in the context of broad social concerns and problems. "At CAI, we are professionals, committed to studying and analyzing the intuitive process."

Like many New Age ideas, intuition seems easy to define—at least at first. In actuality, however, pinning down the concept is like tackling a greased pig. Slithering in and out of the pursuer's grasp, the animal defies capture, wriggling free from every headlock. "Intuition is that inner knowing process by which we acquire knowledge," Kautz says, trying to grab the evasive "creature." He cautions not to get hung up on the method from which it flows. "It might come in a dream, from a gut feeling, as an insight or a hunch. It might come through what some people call channeling. A specific mode doesn't make the information any less valid or credible."

Asked for examples of the intuitive process, Kautz says intuition manifests itself nonverbally to artists and composers through sounds and symbols. "When doctors or people in the helping professions just seem to *know* where the problem is and then go *there* and apply their rational skills, that's intuition at work. I'm more concerned about the nature of the information than about *how* it gets here," Kautz reiterates.

For Brendan O'Regan, vice president for research at the Institute of Noetic Sciences in Sausalito, California, intuition is "a welling up into awareness of data that doesn't appear to derive in a linear fashion from normally perceived data." An intuitive person, he says, pays attention to nonrational aspects of thoughts and feelings about complex problems. O'Regan maintains, however, that the word *intuition* has become a cover term for what in the seventies used to be psychic research. "I simply don't consider trance channeling and clairvoyant activity intuition."

It is no secret, of course, that psychics claim they can predict the future, and many traditional psychics garishly market their abilities as such. CAI intuitives, Kautz says, do not predict the future *as such.* "Most people are afraid that their future is preset and psychics will reveal what's going to happen to them," Kautz says sympathetically, adding that he believes natural events can be predicted, but a human being's freedom of choice—the ability to decide—is inviolate. "We create our own world through the complex process of decision-making, both individually and collectively."

Whenever Kautz takes his intuitives into a corporate setting, the question, Can you predict the future? invariably comes up. "We're not people who predict,

although that may be a byproduct of what goes on," Kautz says. "Much of our work involves pointing out alternatives. We're more like Old Testament prophets or social engineers who see the way society is moving and identify the forces which are behind the movements. We recognize the critical role a person's choice plays in effecting what's going to happen in the future. We present options. That's the real nature of prophesy."

With his deep-set eyes and gray beard, Kautz looks like he'd be more comfortable in a classroom than in a sweat lodge. A graduate of MIT with degrees in electrical engineering and mathematics, he defies New Age stereotyping with his ultrascientific background and experience. Before he got involved in intuitive studies, Kautz was a staff scientist for over 35 years at the prestigious Stanford Research Institute (SRI) in Menlo Park, California, where he worked with a team of scientists to develop the first mainframe computer for the banking industry.

It's simple to see why Kautz and expert intuitives like Nunn work well together. Nunn is as non-New Age and pragmatic as Kautz. Before getting involved professionally in intuitive work—an area he had studied on the side for over a decade—Nunn had an equally "straight" career both as a corporate consultant to manufacturing companies and as the head of two start-up companies in the South. Semi-retired and in his mid fifties, Nunn now lives on a 10,000-acre ranch in northern California near the Oregon border where he rides motorcycles and raises cattle. Like Kautz, he has little regard for New Age jargon and social excess.

From corporate America's point of view, Nunn represents the respectable side of CAI. He accesses information and talks with ease about budgets and strategic plans. Not only does Nunn speak the language of business, but he dresses the part as well—details which are very important to business people in the Far East. "I wear a suit and carry a briefcase," Nunn says. "I don't use a crystal and I don't wear beads. I never use what might be considered New Age jargon. For most business executives, here and abroad, that kind of talk is a turnoff."

Other CAI expert intuitives, however, are trance channels who summon forth entities—reputedly from another dimension—with exotic names like Etherion, Hilarion, and Ecton. "No entity talks through me," Nunn says. "I don't channel. I simply take a few moments to become quiet and the information comes to me."

That Kautz, a former SRI scientist, utilizes trance channeling to access what he calls intuitive information upsets a host of individuals, from his less-open-minded fellow scientists to evangelical Christians who see trance channeling as a Trojan Horse for the demonic. How Kautz

defines intuition, how he gathers intuitive information, and what he represents—a scientist working in the realm of the nonrational—invariably seem to provoke curiosity, criticism, and, at times, derision.

But CAI hasn't suffered for clients. Hundreds of people—many of whom are Japanese—happily pay CAI intuitives to answer questions such as, Where should we allocate our research and development dollars? Prices for services vary. Private counseling sessions cost $200. Half-day corporate sessions cost $600. This year, CAI will begin to offer services in Europe. Co-written with Melanie Branon, Kautz's first book, *Channeling: The Intuitive Connection,* has been translated into French, German, and Italian. In fact, the French translator became so interested in Kautz's work that he's running CAI's operation in France.

Kautz's intuitive life began very innocently. In the early seventies while working at SRI, Kautz became increasingly interested in the ways human beings acquire knowledge. Where do ideas come from? How do people discover something new or find a solution to a vexing problem? These questions became increasingly important to him as a scientist working on complex computer-related problems. His wife, a social worker, steered him toward books and thinkers who over the centuries addressed the issue.

"I was surprised to find out that many bright ideas were not the result of a lot of rational thinking and that scientists who made great breakthroughs usually got their crucial ideas in a flash," Kautz says. "More importantly, they realized in retrospect that what came to them in a flash could not have been rationally deduced from knowledge they had before."

To illustrate, Kautz tells a story: German-born chemist Friedrich August Kekulé von Stradonitz was napping in front of a fireplace, and he dreamt that a snake was biting its own tail. From the dream image, he conceived the benzene ring and the basis of modern organic chemistry. Kautz, very gently, also likes to remind critics that Albert Einstein himself said, " I did not arrive at my understanding of the fundamental laws of the universe through my rational mind."

Eventually, Kautz's curiosity led him to the works of Jane Roberts, the woman who channeled the entity Seth. After reading the book *Seth Speaks*, Kautz flew to New York to meet Roberts and had a number of sessions with Seth. He was intrigued by the idea that Roberts tapped into knowledge through Seth about subjects that were unfamiliar to her. During his sessions with Seth, Kautz posed personal questions, scientific questions, and questions about issues most people have no direct knowledge about, such as the origin of language. Kautz was so impressed by the quality of Seth's answers that he attributes his experience with Seth/Roberts as "the log that broke the jam."

When Kautz returned to the Bay Area, he sought out other intuitives. Penney Pierce, a former art director who is a CAI expert intuitive, met Kautz at the now nearly defunct Gaia Institute, an organization in San Francisco dedicated to exploring issues in consciousness. "Bill Kautz was so refreshing," she says. "He was the typical absent-minded professor trying to learn, taking notes on little slips of paper. His whole approach to channeling was so methodical and grounded."

For seven or eight years, Kautz lived a double professional life. At SRI, his fellow scientists knew that he was investigating intuition and creativity, but most of them weren't all that interested. So Kautz quietly plodded along giving unto SRI what was for SRI and giving unto intuition whatever he discovered in his travels. But people did begin to talk. "At SRI, trance mediumship is one area of research which has a high giggle factor," says Oliver W. Markley, the former methodology director of a futures study at SRI. A comparable example, he cites, would be NASA scientists who are "closet UFO freaks."

Fortunately for Kautz, he wasn't the only SRI scientist to embrace the seemingly nonrational. During the mid seventies, SRI became a spawning ground for renegade scientists and engineers who were looking at nontraditional ways of gathering information and solving complex problems. One group was doing futures research, trying to determine what direction America might be taking 33 years into the future. One of their conclusions: Rational/analytical/linear thinking would have to be replaced by more intuitive methods of learning. Another group began a government-sponsored series of remote-viewing experiments in which people in one room would describe what was going on in another location.

Today, many SRI "graduates" and former "straight" scientists work in areas such as consciousness studies and futures research—just like Kautz. As professor of human sciences and studies of the future at the University of Houston in Clear Lake, Markley now runs the nation's only degree-granting program in futures work. Another former SRI scientist, Willis Harman, became a well-known author and president of the Institute for Noetic Sciences, founded by Edgar Mitchell, the Apollo astronaut who, when he saw the earth from space, had a profound spiritual experience. The Institute is one of the premier centers for consciousness studies in America. O'Regan, Noetic's VP for research, is also a former SRI staffer. Other SRI personnel from this period include Marshall Pease, executive director of the Foundation

for Mind/Being Research in Los Altos, and Hal Puthoff, a scientist at the Institute for Advanced Studies in Austin, Texas, an organization that pioneered zero-point energy and its applications and quantum fluctuations in empty space.

In 1977, while still a scientist at SRI, Kautz started the Center for Applied Intuition. His mandate: to apply intuitive principles in areas where intuition experts had rarely ventured—personal counseling, business consulting, and scientific inquiry. To assemble a staff of highly intuitive individuals, Kautz, in effect, held auditions. "I needed to find people who were responsible and who had a high degree of integrity. If they were into channeling for stock tips, forget it." During the interviews, Kautz says he discovered an important parapsychological principle: The inquirer must need the information from the channel. "Asking questions simply out of curiosity does not work," Kautz says. "That's why so much parapsychological research has failed over the past 150 years. Researchers ask questions which have no use to anyone, or they already know the answers to the questions they ask." According to Kautz, the need to know is a critical factor when working with channeled information.

The individuals Kautz ultimately asked to join CAI came from a variety of backgrounds ranging from computer programming and engineering to fine art and holistic healing. Nancy Sharpnack, for example, a mother and former statistician with the U.S. Forestry Service, channels a spirit. Hers is called Etherion. Other intuitives like Pierce and Nunn work in altered states (which more closely resemble normal consciousness than trances), offering what Pierce calls "heightened common sense." Kautz says he's never been able to find anything the intuitives have in common with each other except that they share a willingness to develop their intuitive abilities and they have a more spiritual outlook on life. "They've developed their natural intuitive abilities and learned to use their intuition in a deliberate, focused, and conscious way," Kautz says.

In 1985, Kautz left SRI to pursue his intuition-related interests full time. During the late eighties, Kautz's eclectic staff and his own scientific reputation attracted a diversity of clients such as Funei Research and Development based in Osaka. With over 1,200 clients, Funei is one of the largest consulting firms in Japan, and Kautz and Nunn worked with over 25 Funei clients. CAI also sponsored a number of sessions in the United States for a broad spectrum of individuals, from Japanese housewives to dentists and businessmen. The groups typically spend a week and a half in California attending CAI lectures and workshops which cover topics such as dream work, self-awareness, and consciousness.

During this period, Kautz plunged into a number of research projects and pioneered the method of inquiry known as "intuitive consensus," which involves posing independently the same set of carefully prepared questions to three to seven expert intuitives. Their responses are compiled, compared, and integrated into a report. One of Kautz's first studies focused on earthquakes. Choosing this phenomenon was a logical extension of Kautz's belief that natural events can be predicted where human decision-making factors aren't present. He also believed that by performing a consensus study, the intuitives might be able to generate a range of new hypotheses in the area of geophysics.

The CAI team's consensus: The components which cause most major earthquakes are, among other factors, low-frequency electromagnetic radiation from the interior of the earth, the release of fossil-generated gases to the earth's surface, and extremely dry weather patterns. Contrary to current ground-based theories, what triggers an earthquake, the team discovered, lies in the atmosphere—not in the ground. According to Kautz, two recent government-sponsored studies conducted at SRI and observational data from earthquake monitoring stations around the world have corroborated some of Kautz's findings, giving credibility to the team's revolutionary hypothesis.

No matter how rigorously Kautz approaches his intuition work, his methods—using trance channels to generate consensus or hiring out expert intuitives to access information—inevitably challenge the principles of a rational, mechanistic view of reality, particularly in the United States. "The farther you go in intuition studies, the spookier it gets for a lot of people," says Harman of Noetic Sciences. "If you push it to the extreme, you get into things like channeling." Harman thinks we're at a peculiar point in history. A generation ago, we wouldn't have thought about looking into areas such as intuition, levitation, or remote viewing. A generation from now, people will wonder what all the fuss was about. "Bill Kautz is an explorer, someone who charges out and plants a flag 'out there' in front of even the vanguard and then wonders why various missiles come his way."

Like many new-paradigm thinkers who embrace a more holistic view of the nature of reality, Kautz says that his work with intuition has dramatically changed the way he looks at life. "Science has been the source of authority in our modern world, and it's based on shaky assumptions— causality, opposition of subject and object, rigid distinctions be-

tween observer and observed," he says. "Science assumes that there is an objective world out there, obeying mathematical laws, and we can learn all about reality by breaking matter down into its simplest components and then observing and measuring it." Kautz no longer believes the prevailing view can explain the nature of reality. Neither does Harman. "All the old puzzles in science— falling bodies, frictionless planes, space/time continuum—have been framed so that the observer assumes separability first and then asks the appropriate questions. When you look at things from the assumption that everything is connected, the picture changes," Harman says.

Some of Kautz's harshest critics come from the evangelical Christian community—and again, it's a question of a world view or perspective on the nature of reality. Evangelicals acknowledge a spiritual realm where the forces of light and darkness are engaged in warfare. From their Biblical point of view, Kautz is tampering with evil. "The phenomenon of trance channeling can't be denied when people seem to manifest personalities," says Tal Brooke, president of the Berkeley-based Spiritual Counterfeits Project. "The question is, how do we interpret it?" Some say that there is nothing supernatural going on; it's simply psychological projection, says Brooke, who was for many years a top Western disciple of Indian guru Sai Baba before converting to Christianity. As a Biblical theist, however, he believes channeled entities could be real, "If they are, we know they can't be of God because mediumship is condemned by the Bible."

What about hunches, premonitions, and sudden bursts of knowledge? Where do these not-uncommon happenings fit into the Christian world view? "There are Christians who accept a neutral, latent psychic power in man, but I don't," says Brooke. He believes in intuition, but he doesn't think it's capable of revealing information apart from the five senses. When someone reveals supernatural knowledge that can be verified but which couldn't possibly have been known, "there has to be a spirit power involved, and it can only be one of two origins—God or the powers of darkness," Brooke says.

Does this mean that the spirits are seducing international business executives who enlist the services of CAI? Why the Japanese gravitate to Kautz has as much to do with economics and politesse as it does with spirituality and belief systems. The Japanese place a great deal of trust in all forms of intuitive communication. Even seemingly conservative businessmen accept the idea that certain people have special knowledge, unusual insight.

"Japanese businessmen rely a great deal on *haragei,* which means belly talk," says Margaret Haas, the president of Haas International, a New York–and Tokyo-based executive recruiting firm. "It's belly-to-belly, gut-to-gut information. They honor intuition." And, Haas says, Buddhist influences still permeate Japanese culture. It's not uncommon for a Japanese executive to refer to karma or fate when talking about a business deal or meeting.

Whether or not American businessmen and corporate executives come to embrace the work of CAI is yet to be seen. Although most of CAI's on-site corporate work has been in Japan, Nunn reports that he does consult for American companies—a behind-the-scenes kind of assignment. Typically, Nunn is hired by one individual, usually the CEO, to spend time at the company observing the day-to-day happenings. So as not to attract attention, Nunn's business card simply says "consultant."

The reluctance to openly invite expert intuitives into the American boardroom and workplace may be shifting. Sales of books about enlightened leadership and management trends are on the rise. Americans—across the spectrum— are expressing a longing and interest in understanding more about the spiritual realm. "More and more people are crossing over a threshold from one way of looking at the world to another," Kautz says. "If they are reaching and want to break through, then maybe our work at CAI can help them through the doorway. If they're not there, I can't do anything." For a long time Kautz thought there was only one way to acquire knowledge—the scientific, rational way. "Today, I know that there is another way to learn—through direct knowing, through intuition. My career has involved going from one camp to the other. The only thing I can do is to try to bring the two together."

This article first appeared in Omni *magazine. Sullivan is a full-time writer in Brooklyn, New York.*

PUT IT INTO PRACTICE

Discussion

1. How is it, do you think, that you can so easily find mistakes in the stories of others that are so difficult to find in your own, though they are there? Discuss an editor's mind-set and how it differs from the writer's mind-set. Some of the people in your class or writers' group are probably better at various kinds of editing than others. If someone has strong copyediting skills, get that person to talk about looking for mistakes. Is there someone who does an especially good job of finding structural problems? How does that person go about the job of editing? And is there someone in the group who has a good sense of style? How does that person go about revising stories?

2. Discuss the difficulties some writers have in accepting criticism from editors. Why are such writers so sensitive? Do editors need to be nicer somehow? Do the writers need to have a thicker skin? See if you can arrive at an appropriate tone for a conversation between an editor and a writer about revising a story. Is that tone deadly serious? more lighthearted? Does it depend on the relationship that the writer and the editor have? What if this is their first encounter?

3. Discuss what a typical day might be like for a senior editor at a major magazine. Where does the writer fit into that day? What is the likely response by an editor who has to work with a difficult writer during the revision process?

    If you're the writer, how do you build a productive relationship with an editor?

Exercises

1. You are the editor of a top national magazine, and in response to a query, you have assigned a beginning writer to do an interesting personality piece. Take that submitted final draft (in reality, a personality piece by someone else in your class or writers' group) and give it an edit.

    First, do a first-level copyedit on the story. Are there many mistakes? Talk to the writer about them.

    Then do a second-level, structural edit on the story. Are there areas where you would move paragraphs or sections around? Are there areas that do not seem to flow logically or thematically?

    Finally, do a third-level, style edit on the story. Are there areas where revision could bring out a better, more stylish final draft?

Discuss your editing with the person whose work you've been handling. Does the person agree with what you've done? Disagree? Why? Have your instructor take a look at the editing, especially at the areas where you and the writer disagree. What is the instructor's assessment of the job you've done as an editor? How could you improve that job?

2. Repeat the process involved in the first exercise, now taking the writer's perspective. You're a beginning writer and a top regional magazine has responded positively to a query of yours on a local personality. You've turned in your final draft but have received a phone call from the editor handling your story who mentions a number of editing changes.

    Has the editor found many copyediting errors? How has the editor dealt with your writing structure? Do you agree or disagree with any changes?

    How has the editor worked to make the story more stylish? Do you agree or disagree with any changes?

    Just as in the first exercise, show the story and its changes to your instructor and get feedback. Did the editing improve the piece?

    What have you learned from the work the editor did on the story? See if you can pinpoint some particular things you need to work on as a writer.

3. Go through the same process one more time, this time taking the role of the editor, but working with one of your own stories, as if it were submitted by a stranger.

    First, do a first-level copyedit on the story. Are there many mistakes? Are you surprised to find them?

    Then do a second-level, structural edit on the story. Are there areas where you would move paragraphs or sections around? Are there areas that do not seem to flow logically or thematically? Again, are you surprised to see these structural flaws?

    Finally, do a third-level, style edit on the story. Are there areas where revision could bring out a better, more stylish final draft? And again, are you surprised to see these things now, when you didn't see the possibilities as you wrote and polished the piece?

    As you've done before, have your instructor take a look at the editing. What is the instructor's assessment of the job you've done as an editor? Did you improve the story or not? What does that tell you about your strengths and weaknesses as a writer and as an editor?

QUERY LETTERS

—

—

Before writer Deidre Sullivan got very far into writing her story "Portrait of a Prophet," she wanted to make sure she had a commitment for the piece from a major magazine. A busy freelancer with her own consulting business, Sullivan doesn't have the time to write unsold stories and then send them out in the hopes they'll be published somewhere. For her, an early and essential part of the job is writing the query letter, that one- or two-page letter in which the writer asks the editor if he or she would be interested in seeing the story.

To write her query for this story, Sullivan first focused her own thoughts on the subject so that she knew exactly where the story was going. Then she did the necessary market research to find the best possible magazine for the piece. *Omni* magazine, with its focus on science but its willingness to explore topics outside the scientific mainstream, seemed like a good possibility as a market, so Sullivan wrote her query for the story on Kautz and the Center for Applied Intuition and sent it off to *Omni* Senior Editor Murray Cox. Her query opened like this:

Picture this: a group of senior executives sitting around a table asking a consultant questions about a strategic planning initiative. It sounds like an everyday occurrence—except for the fact that this particular consultant is a trance channel and has been hired for his intuitive abilities.

Is this the board meeting of the future?

While working on What Do We Mean When We Say God? (Doubleday, 1991) I had the opportunity to meet many provocative thinkers, one of whom is Bill Kautz, the director of the Center for Applied Intuition (CAI) in Fairfax, California.

I'd like to write a story about Kautz and his work at CAI.

Kautz, a graduate of MIT, was a research scientist with SRI International for over 25 years. During this time, he worked in a range of areas from mathematics to geophysics. In 1977, Kautz left SRI and founded CAI in order to conduct research on the intuitive process and to explore ways in which intuition can be applied in science, technology, the social sciences, and other fields.

Kautz's scientific background and approach to the question of intuition clearly separates his organization from the pack of trance channelers out there trying to sell themselves to the gullible public.

In these six short paragraphs, Sullivan accomplished several of the major things a good query letter must do:

She clearly stated her proposal, but kept the letter short.
She gave enough background to make clear she knew what she was talking about.
She made clear her own expertise and credentials as a writer and as someone with the background to handle this particular story.

You'll need to do the same if you want editors to respond favorably to your queries.

BE CONVINCING

The query letter is an essential part of the freelance process, especially for beginning writers. The key, especially for beginning writers, is to be convincing in two separate ways.

The well-written query needs to accomplish two major things: It convinces the editor that your idea is right for his or her magazine, and it convinces the editor that you are the right person to write the story.

To do that, you need to keep in mind those things that Sullivan's letter accomplished and make sure your letter does the same.

State Your Proposal Concisely

When you state your proposal, perhaps in the very first paragraph and certainly somewhere within the top few paragraphs, remember that clarity and brevity are important to your success.

"Keep it short" is Sullivan's advice. "Think about what the editors have to do, about how busy the editors are. They have deadlines to meet, they have an editorial mix to think about, they have to get things edited, get headlines done—there's a lot that goes into the whole process. Don't waste his time or her time. Get right to the point, tell what the story is and how you would do it."

If you take your time getting around to discussing exactly what you'd like to write about, the editor is likely to quit reading and return your query with a form rejection before ever getting to your idea. So get right to it. Notice in Sullivan's query that by the second sentence the editor knows the basic premise for the story.

Remember also that you need to have an angle, something special about your story that makes it unusual and worth publishing in the editor's magazine. For most editors, the angle you take is the single most important thing in selling the story.

"The angle is the funnel that directs everything, for me," says Cox. "It's what sells the piece."

In the query, you've got to make that special angle crystal clear. For Deidre Sullivan, her angle on the story was the way a respected mainstream scientist went into more nebulous sorts of research. You can read more about angles in Box 8.1 on page 220.

Give Background Information

When you give background information about the proposal, you're helping the editor make a quick decision in your favor. Not only does the background information you provide make clear to the editor that you have already done much of your research for the piece, but it also gives the editor a context in which to understand the story and its potential.

Notice how Sullivan's fifth paragraph gives background biographical information on Kautz. When Sullivan says Kautz "was a research scientist with SRI International for over 25 years. During this time, he worked in a range of areas from mathematics to geophysics," she is not only giving Cox some needed information about her proposal but also announcing to him that she has done her research and knows what she is talking about. You'll need to do the same.

Establish Your Credentials

Somewhere in your query letter you need to tell the editor enough about yourself that the editor can be comfortable with giving you the assignment—or at least asking to see your story on speculation. To accomplish that, you need to give your credentials. Sullivan does it with one phrase ("While working on *What Do We Mean When We Say God?*"), which makes clear she is a published author.

You may need a little more. If you have published other stories in magazines or newspapers, you might want to mention that in a separate, short paragraph. The more relevant those publications are to the story you're proposing, of course, the better. For instance, if you're proposing a personality piece on someone and you have published other personality pieces, such credentials will carry some weight.

If you're proposing a personality piece on someone and your writing has been limited to covering high school sports for the local newspaper, then your credentials might not have quite the same impact. Still, published is published. After all, a high school sports stringer for the local paper can at least claim to be able to write cleanly, concisely, accurately, and to deadline. And that matters to any editor.

And it's worth noting that college publications are, in most cases, very helpful, for they not only add to your credits but also provide you with clips to send along with the query. (Some magazines like to see clips; others don't. Check one of the writer's market guides to see what the editor wants.) And those clips prove your ability to write well.

Also, remember that there are other kinds of credentials as relevant to the story as your publication credits. If you have expertise or experience in a subject or if you have special access to someone who's newsworthy, those kinds of credentials matter to an editor. You need to mention them in your query letter. In Sullivan's case, she had not only the writing background but also the special access and the expertise. It's no wonder that Cox at *Omni* went for the idea.

"Well, I certainly wouldn't have been able to write this sort of story unless I'd written the *God* book," Sullivan says. "And it shows that your best chance to sell comes when you stay within your area."

THE MARKETPLACE

One of the most common mistakes for beginning magazine writers comes not in their research or writing but in their marketing. All too often, beginning writers send query letters or stories off to magazines where the idea has no chance at all of selling.

The same beginning writer who was willing to spend days or weeks on researching a piece, then many more days or weeks on writing it, seems to find it reasonable to take shortcuts in the marketing of the story.

Veteran writers certainly know that poor marketing of an idea is a mistake that you can't afford to make. There are three ways that beginners can go wrong. The first is *submitting an idea that has already been done* by a magazine. This happens with surprising frequency, and such queries and story submissions are a common complaint among editors. When you submit an idea for a story that's the same as or similar to a piece the magazine ran within the past year or two, you're admitting to the editor both that you are not a regular reader and that you don't know the editor's needs. That's not an admission you want to make. To avoid that, do a little research. Most magazines are indexed, and you can simply look it up to see if anything similar was done recently. If the publication isn't indexed, read through back issues at the library.

The second problem editors also complain about is that they receive *queries and submissions that are simply not the kinds of material that they use.* Again, this displays the writer's ignorance of the publication and is a waste of time and energy for the writer as well as the editor.

The third thing many writers forget is that *every story needs an angle,* something special about it that appeals to the magazine's readers. It may be that you are presenting a brand-new idea—one that hasn't been done before—and so the idea can stand alone. In that case, your angle is the idea you've come up with, and you can sell it that way. But in most cases it's not that simple. Popular music magazines and sports magazines, for instance, are flooded with queries about interviews with the field's top names. But without a special angle, most of those ideas just don't work because they've been done many, many times before.

Beginners, caught up in the excitement of having an interview with a rock star or famous athlete, sometimes lose sight of the fact that many other writers around the country may have had the opportunity to do the same interview. What can you offer the editor that is special about your personality piece?

It is often not enough to want to do a story on a topic or person of interest; you must also be able to offer something special—some specifically new and fresh approach—that the editor will like. In your query letter, you need to make clear what that fresh angle is that you're offering. Did you get to travel with the rock band from one city to another on the recent tour, instead of just having an hour's interview after the show? Perhaps that's a new approach for that magazine.

Do you have some special insight into the life of that baseball star? Perhaps you found out that a much-maligned star has a special charity that he or she gives to, and discussing this charity brings out a new side to the star's personality.

Those are the kinds of angles you need to look for if you want to sell to the magazines. Finding the angles, of course, is the trick.

Here is some advice for finding those fresh angles: (1) Keep an eye out for an angle or two during your research. Don't wait until you're in the interview stage or trying to write the first draft to figure out an angle. You should have one or two possibilities in mind before you start the interview process. (2) Think through that magazine's readership—the people you are writing for—and search for angles that might meet those readers' needs. Who reads the magazine? What age groups? What economic groups? What ethnic groups? Men or women? Put yourself in the place of those readers and ask yourself what your expectations are from the magazine. Then ask yourself if there might be an angle to the story that meets those expectations.

Finally, and most important, to accomplish both of the aforementioned points, what you want to do is to find the unusual and the unexpected, not only during your research but also during the interview.

If you've done enough background work about the markets that might buy the idea, you know what ideas have already been done. It's your job to look for aspects of the story that you know, the moment you encounter them, have *not* been done. If you've done your reading and know the marketplace, those aspects will be obvious.

BREAKING IN

Sullivan thinks that expertise is especially important for beginning writers. "When you're trying to get started, you need to try and sell something that you know. If you're a top-ranked squash player, or if you play rugby in a rugby club, it would be logical that you could sell something about rugby."

As far as Sullivan is concerned, "The best way, I think, to sell a first story is to sell it on particular knowledge; that kind of knowledge can open the door.

"If you're a landscaper, you have a ton of particular knowledge, you know about evergreens or perennials, and not a lot of people know about this stuff but a lot of people want to learn. So, if you can just go in and see the editor with a really good query letter there's a possibility she might take a shot on you."

Consider student writer Bill Smoot, whose work appears in chapter three. Smoot had a deep interest in environmental writing and was doing a good job in his magazine writing class. With no previous credentials, he turned that combination into a sale to a respected regional magazine.

Larry Marscheck, who was editor of *Tampa Bay Life* magazine when it bought Smoot's story, points out that queries are especially important for beginning writers.

"If you're just getting started it's difficult to call up an editor and sell a story. I'll just have to ask for you to send some clips and a résumé anyway.

"But a really good query gets around some of that by outlining the story you're interested in doing and also listing some of your credentials."

Marscheck adds that "The query needs to show me that you're familiar with the magazine, what kind of stories we're looking for, and basically how we want a story done."

Importantly, Marscheck emphasizes that the query needs to show that you "either have a fresh idea or a fresh angle on an old idea."

Marscheck reminds beginners: "It's up to you to come up with that fresh idea or that fresh angle, and with something that will last for a month or two, too, after it's published, some idea with a little staying power."

Marscheck, like Sullivan, knows that queries require their own special kind of writing.

"They're almost like writing a story, really, but in miniature," he says. "A query needs to entice me. One of the best ones I had was one that gave me pretty much the lead of the story. It really caught my attention, and the writer explained that this was the lead of the story on such-and-such, and then followed that with an outline. After that came a paragraph on the writer's credentials. That worked for me."

As Marscheck put it: "Remember it's a persuasive letter; you're trying to persuade an editor that your story the way you're going to tell it is perfect for his or her publication."

Some editors might not agree, but Marscheck advises to close the query letter with a promise to call in a week or two to see if the editor is interested. Other editors might advise against that (they don't want a flood of phone calls). All would agree that a self-addressed stamped envelope for their response is a must. Queries without SASEs often never do get a response.

As you write more and more queries, you may find that certain techniques begin to work for you. Deidre Sullivan, for instance, likes to close her query letters with a list of questions. For her, the technique works because the questions "give the editor some room to explore your idea. In a way, it's like headlining what you're doing. I think rather than explaining all the answers that it's best to put up the questions. It gives you a lot of freedom to show that this is really an interesting issue and here are some of the questions you should be thinking about in regard to this."

She is careful to limit the questions, of course, to those that really matter to the story. "Basically," she says, "I ask the W's and an H that you will answer in the course of the story." (The five W's and an H, of course, are who, what, when, where, why, and how.)

You can see Sullivan's query letter in its entirety in Figure 8.1.

The question technique may or may not work for you. The important thing is to find out what techniques *do* work and then use them to sound convincing.

QUERY FORMAT

Any good business letter format will work for a query letter. The key is that the letter must look and sound professional. What you must do is offer your idea in a clear, concise manner that includes all the information from the piece that will help sell the idea to the editor.

Some writers and editors these days use variant names for query letters, referring to them as *proposals* or *memos* rather than queries. And there are some differences in format behind the new terminology. A proposal or memo often includes the first paragraph or two of the actual story, the idea being to offer the editor a handy example of the writer's skill. It is even possible to send along a brief outline of how the story is structured.

QUERY: CENTER FOR APPLIED INTUITION

Picture this: a group of senior executives sitting around a table asking a consultant questions about a strategic planning initiative. It sounds like an everyday occurrence—except for the fact that this particular consultant is a trance channel and has been hired for his intuitive abilities.

Is this the board meeting of the future?

While working on What Do We Mean When We Say God? (Doubleday, 1991), I had the opportunity to meet many provocative thinkers, one of whom is Bill Kautz, the director of the Center for Applied Intuition (CAI) in Fairfax, California.

I'd like to write a story about Kautz and his work at CAI.

Kautz, a graduate of MIT, was a research scientist with SRI International for over 25 years. During this time, he worked in a range of areas from mathematics to geophysics. In 1977, Kautz left SRI and founded CAI in order to conduct research on the intuitive process and to explore ways in which intuition can be applied in science, technology, the social sciences, and other fields.

Kautz's scientific background and approach to the question of intuition clearly separates his organization from the pack of trance channelers out there trying to sell themselves to the gullible public.

Kautz works with a select number of "expert intuitives," people who have extraordinary abilities and are able to access information not available by ordinary means. As part of their work at CAI, these expert intuitives serve as consultants to a number of major Japanese corporations including Matsui, the largest department store chain in Tokyo.

CAI never evaluates a client's problems or prepares an analysis—like other consulting firms. The expert intuitive simply visits the client's office or headquarters and an-

FIGURE 8.1   *Deidre Sullivan's Query Letter*

swers any questions that the president or the board of directors might have.

This may sound "way out" but it seems to work. Typical questions include, "Should we relocate our manufacturing facilities?" "Who is the best person for this job?" "How can we increase productivity?" "What is the best timing for this product launch?" and so on. The expert intuitive has no prior knowledge of the company's activities, but is able to offer distinct information and guidance. Last year, in fact, one of the CAI intuitives unexpectedly pinpointed an embezzler.

My story will examine the work that CAI is doing in the field of intuition and intuitive consulting. What has Bill Kautz learned about intuition? How does his research differ from what people like writer and therapist Frances Vaughn are coming up with? Is there a way to measure the results of intuition? How does the average person learn more about his or her own intuitive abilities? Why is CAI so well-received in Japan? Is it because the Japanese give more credibility to inner processes? What are some of the obstacles to acceptance CAI is encountering in the United States? Is consulting CAI-style going to be more acceptable in the future or is CAI another New Age aberration?

This sort of query operates along the lines of the book publishing business, in which it is common to send in sample chapters and an outline to sell a book to an editor.

However you choose to present your idea—including a sample paragraph or two or closing with a series of questions as Deidre Sullivan does—remember to keep the letter as short as you can. One page is preferred (remember how busy the editor is), and the query certainly shouldn't go more than two pages.

Remember that the two basic things a good query letter must accomplish are to convince the editor that your idea is right for his or her magazine and convince the editor that you are the right person to write the story.

January 5, 1995

Sally Smith
Editor
Water Magazine
1234 Haggis Avenue
New York, NY 10000-0000

Dear Sally Smith,

Despite more than 50 inches of rain a year, parts of Florida are turning into a salt-laden desert. Overpumped wells, poor conservation practices, heavy runoff from paved areas, a burgeoning population, and a thirsty agricultural sector all combine to drain Florida of its fresh water.

I'd like to send you a story about Florida's water problems.

The piece focuses on the unusual combination of events that result in the state's adequate rainfall's still not being able to meet the fresh water demand.

My recent writing credentials include stories on Florida's various environmental problems for Florida Yesterday, Florida Environmentalist, National Water Resource, Sunshine in Peril, and others.

I am a student in the Environmental Studies program at the University of South Florida, where I also write for the student daily newspaper.

Thank you for taking a look at this idea, and I look forward to hearing from you.

Sincerely,

Ann Student Writer

Ann Student Writer
12345 Epsilon Hall
University of South Florida
Tampa, FL 33620
(813) 555-0000

To do that, a good basic structure should have two parts.

An opening section that presents the idea: This might be one or more paragraphs long and may or may not use the actual opening of the story.

A second section that establishes your credentials: This might be anything from one sentence to one or more paragraphs long.

You might close the query with a sentence that says you look forward to hearing the editor's response.

A typical query letter might look like the one on page 226.

This letter is purely an invention, of course, but it does show the basic format. Note, as well, that it meets Deidre Sullivan's basic requirements of stating the proposal, giving a bit of background, and giving some of the writer's credentials.

Remember that Sullivan advises beginning writers to take advantage of any expertise in a given area because that can compensate for lack of writing experience. So, if our mythical writer didn't have any previous writing successes, that section of the letter could be rewritten this way:

The piece focuses on the unusual combination of events that result in the state's adequate rainfall's still not being able to meet the fresh water demand.

I have a deep interest in Florida's various environmental problems and have written several in-depth articles on those issues for our student daily newspaper, The Oracle. A clip of one of those stories is enclosed.

I am a student in the Environmental Studies program at the University of South Florida and will graduate with honors from that program this spring. I will start my graduate studies in water resource management in the fall.

Notice how Ann Student Writer has emphasized her strengths (her studies and her work for the student newspaper) and included one relevant clip. Even though she has no experience writing for magazines, if the idea works for the editor, her academic work and her writing for the school paper may be enough to get her at least a chance to write the story on a speculation basis for the magazine.

ON SPEC

There are three different responses you can receive from a query. The most likely, unfortunately, is a rejection. The best response, of course, is an acceptance that includes a contractual commitment from the magazine to publish the story. The third, and a common occurrence, is a request to see the story on spec (shorthand for "on speculation"), which means the editor is making no promises to buy the story but is interested in seeing it.

There is a lot you can learn from a rejection letter, and they come in various ways. See chapter seven for more information on how to respond to rejections.

Receiving a contractual acceptance from a magazine in response to your query is unlikely for a beginner but does occur from time to time. That means the idea is a good one for the magazine, and the editor is willing to commit to you as the writer. The typical contract for a story assignment will set out the payment, the word count expectations, the copyrights assigned, your deadline, and probably a kill fee (normally half of the payment) for a story that doesn't meet the editor's needs.

A letter that requests the story on spec is the most you can reasonably hope for. In such a letter the editor admits to liking the idea, thinks well enough of you to ask to see the story, but makes no commitment to buying it.

Receiving that sort of letter in response to your query is a major success for a beginning writer. It lets you know that you're on the right track in terms of your ideas, at any rate, and makes sure that your story will get a good, sympathetic read from the editor.

Remember that the editor *wants* to buy your story at that point, or the letter asking to see it wouldn't have been sent.

If the story is rejected, then it's time to revise it and send it out again, since you know the idea has merit.

COVER LETTERS

Cover letters follow much the same format as query letters, though their purpose is very different. A cover letter accompanies a story submission and should be helpful to the editor's reading of the story without trying to do a hard sell on the piece, because most editors emphatically want the story to sell itself. In other words, a great cover letter won't compensate for a poor story.

But a cover letter can certainly help your story get a good read. If you have some credentials (either through previous relevant story sales or through expertise), then the cover letter is the place to put them.

Again, any good business letter format is fine. Basically, like a query, the cover letter should contain the following information:

Section one: A simple statement about the story's topic.
Section two: A statement of your credentials and /or expertise.

A good sample cover letter might look like this:

January 5, 1995

Sally Smith
Editor
Water Magazine
1234 Haggis Avenue
New York, NY 10000-0000

Dear Sally Smith,

Despite more than 50 inches of rain a year, parts of Florida are turning into a salt-laden desert. Overpumped wells, poor conservation practices, heavy runoff from paved areas, a burgeoning population, and a thirsty agricultural sector all combine to drain Florida of its fresh water.

The enclosed story talks about Florida's water problems, focusing on the unusual elements that contrive to combine what seems to be adequate rainfall with a surprising fresh water shortage.

My recent writing credentials include stories on Florida's various environmental problems for Florida Yesterday, Florida Environmentalist, National Water Resource, Sunshine in Peril, and others.

I am a student in the Environmental Studies program at the University of South Florida, where I also write for the student daily newspaper.

Thank you for taking a look at the piece, and I look forward to hearing from you.

Sincerely,

Ann Student Writer

Ann Student Writer
12345 Epsilon Hall
University of South Florida
Tampa, FL 33620
(813) 555-0000

Again, just as in the query letter, the paragraph that talks about Ann's writing credentials could easily be rewritten to focus on her other relevant credentials.

PUT IT INTO PRACTICE

Discussion

1. One of the nagging ethical issues of query letters is the matter of multiple submissions. Many editors feel that writers should not do multiple submissions on query letters. Discuss why you think the editors feel this way.

   Many writers, on the other hand, feel it is perfectly ethical, and good business, too, to send out multiple queries. Why do you think the writers feel this way?

   In the discussion, can you arrive at any middle ground that seems acceptable to both writers and editors?

2. Discuss what a typical day must be like for an editor at a regional or national magazine. How much time do you suppose the editor has to read query letters? Suppose that editor has a stack of 15 query letters on the desk. Which ones might prompt the editor to give an assignment? To which ones might the editor write back with an encouraging note asking to see the story on spec? Which ones won't work for the editor at all? Why?

3. Have a member of the class or writers' group take the role of an editor. Take several of the query letters written by class members and have the editor read through each one and then discuss the query with the writer and the rest of the class. Does that discussion lead to some changes in the idea or in the letter's presentation of the idea? Why?

   Discuss how you can incorporate into your own query letters and their ideas and angles what you've learned from that discussion process.

Exercises

1. You are a beginning freelance writer who would like to break into print in your local city magazine. Do an analysis of the magazine that includes your assessment of the following:
   a. Who do you think the typical readers are? Can you describe them? List five qualities of the typical readers. Compare your five to those listed by others in your class or writers' group.
   b. What kind of feature articles does the magazine run? Using some of the things you have learned from this textbook, can you describe them? List five. Compare your list to the lists of others in your class or writers' group.

c.   What kind of articles has the magazine *not* run? Put together a list of five strong possibilities. Compare that list with other lists in your class or writers' group. Are there similarities? Differences? What do the similarities tell you about the magazine? What do the differences tell you?

2.   Write a good first draft of a query letter to a local or regional magazine, building upon an idea that you've come up with based on these exercises.

Before sending that query letter, trade it with a similar letter written by a classmate or other member of your writers' group. Put the query through the editing and revision process and see how it can be improved.

Analyze the letter for its professional appearance. Then analyze the idea for its appeal to the magazine. Does the letter seem to indicate that the writer is a professional and capable of writing the story? Is the idea or the angle a fresh one? If not, how could it be improved?

Trade the queries back, revise them, and get them into the mail. Don't forget your SASE.

TRAVEL WRITING

It's the middle of February, and you're avoiding the noontime heat by sitting in the thin shade of a casuarina tree on Grand Cayman Island's Rum Point beach while your wife and baby girl play a few yards away in the crystalline, shallow water. In the distance, breakers roll over the reef that guards the entrance to North Sound.

With a sigh, you decide that it's time to get back to work. You pull on the mask, snorkel and fins, trudge down to the water, wave once to the family, and then swim out into the lagoon to do some more reporting for your travel story on the Cayman Islands. It's a tough job, you think, but somebody has to do it.

Or, you're on the ferry that crosses the dark waters of the Northumberland Strait. It's been an eventful few days in New Brunswick, and now you're on your way to Prince Edward Island to continue your leisurely drive through the Canadian Maritimes. On your itinerary is a lobster supper at a favorite restaurant and then a few days spent taking notes on the relaxation that's possible at a favorite seaside resort. You wonder how the next few days will go. At most of the restaurants you've visited so far, the wine, in general, has been a disappointment. But the meals, you've noted, have been fine.

You keep your eye on the sights and sounds of the ferry crossing. Ahead is the small port of Borden, and beyond that the pastoral appeal of Prince Edward Island. You jot down a few notes. It's a shame, you think, to have to work this hard every time you travel. But, you admit with a smile, there are worse jobs out there.

Or, you're worried about your small boat's stability as your Italian fisherman/guide, Antonio, takes you across the water toward the tiny Italian island of Lisca Bianca. The water is choppy, the breeze stiff, and you're a bit nervous, but Antonio is blasé as he nonchalantly pushes the tiller with his foot to guide the boat, so how dangerous could it be? The view, as he promised, is spectacular. Bouncing along, you scribble down some notes on the moment. Maybe, you think, this will be your hook for that Aeolian Islands story that's planned for the June issue.

Ah, the difficult, demanding life of the travel writer, struggling to take notes in the middle of a choppy sea, or wading out into the Caribbean for another round of snorkeling, or taking the ferry across to Prince Edward Island.

If only it were really that way all the time.

To nonwriters, travel writing may seem like the perfect job. To travel the world and then get paid to write about it sounds too good to be true.

And it is. Most travel writers, most of the time, are lucky to get a few hundred dollars for a story that sells, and they aren't traveling on a lavish expense account, either. Typically, ethical freelancers pay for their own trip, write a story about it, and then market that story. The pay, when and if the story sells, hardly begins to pay for the trip, much less compensate the writer for the hard work of writing and marketing the piece.

Certainly, the majority of travel writers aren't in it for the money. Beginners need to realize that while there are some compensations for travel writing (including financial), it isn't a shortcut to free travel and easy publication. In fact, most editors and writers surveyed for this book said that the market is tighter for travel writing than it is for many other kinds of nonfiction writing. There are a lot of markets but also thousands of would-be travel writers trying to fill them with stories.

Still, like many freelancers, you may find that even though travel writing is an exacting, difficult craft, it offers enough rewards to make it worth your while should you decide to learn the field's demands.

Importantly for beginners, one of the best things about travel writing is that the skills involved are exactly those you'll use in a wide variety of stories later in your writing career—and travel writing is a fun way to learn them.

Most travel stories can be categorized into three basic types. They are *destination/informational stories, specialized stories,* and *literary/escapist stories.* There are subdivisions under each of those headings, as well, and in many cases the headings overlap. For instance, most destination stories are informational in nature, but they can also be escapist or specialized and even, in some cases, literary.

To further complicate things, a newspaper or magazine that uses informational stories might very well also use an escapist piece, and a magazine that needs a specialized story might very well want one, too, that is informational, escapist, or even literary. In your marketing efforts, you'll need to be aware of that.

Each of these kinds of travel story has special needs and a particular kind of audience, and each offers its own kind of opportunity for a freelancer.

DESTINATION/INFORMATIONAL STORIES

Most destination/informational travel stories are descriptive, factual, and explanatory. They are meant to provide a service for the reader as well as to entertain. Destination/informational travel writing is found in such magazines as those distributed by the various auto clubs and in the Sunday travel section of most newspapers (and this is one of the very few places in this text that we are able to talk about freelancing to newspapers, since travel sections constitute one of the few places in newspapers where there are markets for freelance magazine writers).

While these kinds of stories are frequently packed with information, it is always important to remember that they need to be entertaining as well. In many cases, the needs of the magazine call for a kind of writing that not only informs and entertains but fulfills some other purpose for the magazine, too. For instance, many of the auto club magazines serve a readership that is made up almost exclusively of members of the club. This makes service a must for stories in those magazines.

Michael Wright, editor of the Auto Club of Missouri's *Midwest Motorist* magazine, puts it this way: "We have a dual purpose. First, we want to entertain, to get the readers into the magazine through some entertaining. Our second purpose is to inform them about destinations, travel modes, cost of travel, and related services that the Auto Club might bring to assist them."

In other words, the stories are meant to entertain and inform, but they also serve a marketing purpose for the Auto Club. The idea is to tell readers about a destination that they can then contact the Auto Club's travel agency about visiting.

Wright wants his magazine both to serve the general purposes of the Auto Club of Missouri and to inform readers of the services the club offers. But he knows that "If you don't entertain them they won't get informed. You just can't put out a series of facts, of dry information. People won't even flip the cover open if you do that. So we try and give them a variety of diverse writing, all with a travel theme, and most of them destination stories."

It's important to note that you can't expect to write a general destination piece and really expect to sell it. Broad, general destination stories are too simplistic, too clichéd, and too ordinary to have much chance with most editors. Remember previous discussions in this text about finding a fresh angle, and remember you're in competition with thousands of other writers. You need to find a new perspective on the destination if you hope to interest an editor in your story.

Jack Schnedler, travel editor of the *Chicago Sun-Times,* puts it this way: "In 1991 I received 1,200 unsolicited manuscripts, and I bought 50 of them. So that's about 4 percent, which means 96 percent didn't sell. Of the ones that I bought, hardly any were traditional destination stories; I have those coming out of my ears. After all, I have destination stories on the wires [wire services]. I have my own stories. So it's just tough to sell that kind of story."

For Schnedler, most of the stories he bought were "in some way personal, idiosyncratic. One guy took a year off and traveled around the world. He wrote me a nice little essay about that."

For writers who can't arrange taking a year off to travel the world, Schnedler advises that "You need to try and develop a specialty, and then lock down some regular markets. I have one fellow who does stories on weekend tours from Chicago for me. He's passed the 500 mark in stories sold to me. He sells me one every week about Midwest travel, so, at least in theory, one kind of story that ought to sell is about travel in your newspaper's region."

Finding that fresh angle isn't as difficult as you might think. What you need to do is find a thematic hook to use for your approach to the place. Notice how the Cayman Islands piece reprinted at the end of this chapter found that special hook, that angle, into a story about an island that has already been written about in dozens of publications.

The story uses a narrative hook to establish that the primary character for the piece is an infant, and by the third paragraph the story makes it clear that the theme is the ease and safety with which parents can travel with babies and toddlers to Grand Cayman.

Dorothy Smiljanich, travel editor of the *Tampa Tribune,* bought this Cayman Islands piece precisely because "while we do a lot of pieces on the Caribbean, and we've done other stories on the Cayman Islands, this one had a new approach, and one that made sense for us with a family readership."

You'll need to find the same kind of fresh angle for your stories when you're trying to break into print.

Reporting for Destination Stories

To do your reporting for destination/informational travel stories, you'll need to bear in mind that you have to gather a wealth of hard data while you are there, as well as take notes on the sights, sounds, and people of the place you are visiting. Room rates and availability, restaurant quality and pricing, rental cars, air fares, admission prices for museums, parks, and other tourist sites, all are important in this kind of writing, so you can wind up spending a lot of time taking notes.

One hint to help you get around the time-consuming problem of detailed note-taking is to grab every free brochure you can find.

For the Grand Cayman story, for instance, the author collected enough material to fill a large manila envelope. The material included menus from restaurants, ticket stubs from tourist sites, receipts from shops and parks, copies of island magazines, and two books bought on the island that gave detailed information on the sea life and history of the Caymans.

It was a bit of a chore trying to fit the material into the crowded suitcase for the flight home, but the extra baggage made the writing of the story infinitely easier—as well as much more detailed—a week or two later back home.

Not only does this kind of brochure reporting make the use of pertinent detail much easier when it comes time to write, but it also frees the writer to take notes on the people, the sights, and the sounds that will help make the story come alive.

Notice how the following few paragraphs rely on those kinds of details to make the difference between general statements and exact information.

A rental car, at $20 Cayman per day for three days, unlimited mileage (which worked out to $80 U.S. for three days) was available from the Cico agent right next to the hotel.

That meant the family could drive the few miles into George Town, scoot past the high-rise banks that help fuel the island's economy (the Caymans have 500 banks involved in the tax haven business) and drive another mile south to Smith Cove.

There, in a little park, are picnic tables and plenty of shade from the wide-leafed grape trees that border the small beach.

The shallow water is just right for baby, and just offshore is some terrific snorkeling. So Mom and Dad took turns, with one of them playing in the shallows with Samantha while the other snorkeled the sights—plenty of parrotfish, some fan and brain coral and clouds of small tropicals.

The price and details about the rental car, the information on the island's banking, the name of the small cove and its trees, the details on the names of the fish and coral—all of that came from free brochures, receipts, or the two small books purchased on the island.

Writing for Destination Stories

To write the destination/informational story, you'll need to always bear in mind the balance between information, service, and entertainment that you're trying for.

You may find that your best bet is to build a structure that is a variant of the basic structure discussed in chapter five. You need to start with an entertaining hook, move to either a chronological or spatial main body, and then conclude with an ending that comes back to the opening.

The destination/informational story's hook must not only *establish the angle or theme* but also *establish the setting*. To establish the setting, if the destination is well-known a brief mention may do. If the destination is not well-known, a definer—something that names the destination and defines it as well—may be necessary.

Notice in the Cayman Islands piece that the first paragraph specifically names the site ("Rum Point on Grand Cayman") and then defines it as well ("shady picnic table" and "warm, shallow water").

The angle or theme of the Cayman Islands story is clear not only from the narrative hook, which is showing the reader a baby at play, but also from the third paragraph's explanation that "Rum Point—indeed, all of Grand Cayman—was an easy, comfortable spot in the Caribbean for a visit, even with a baby along."

The main body in all three types of travel stories will usually follow a chronological or spatial format; that is, either it will move the reader through the place in a time sequence (on the first day we . . .), or it will move the reader from place to place (there are four major sights to see . . .), or it will mix these two techniques. Occasionally, a literary/escapist story may use a structure built on characterization, as you'll see.

The Cayman Islands story uses a spatial format, talking in the hook about Rum Point, then backtracking to the hotel, Seven Mile Beach, Smith Cove, and other sites before returning the reader to more details on Rum Point.

It would have been just as easy, and probably every bit as effective, to do this story chronologically, beginning with day one at the hotel and Seven Mile Beach, and then running along through the next several days, mentioning all the same places but listing them in order.

SPECIALIZED STORIES

Most specialized travel stories are descriptive, factual, and tightly focused on a specialty.

Specialized travel writing is the sort of work that appears in magazines that occasionally or regularly use travel stories as part of their editorial mix, though their specialty is not travel.

Writer Catherine Merrill, for instance, has written many travel stories for *Food & Wine* magazine, as well as travel pieces for a wide variety of newspapers and magazines, including *Signature, Gourmet,* and the *Boston Globe.*

Merrill thinks of specialized travel stories as "a blend of art and service. The stories have to be entertaining, but also relate to the readers. *Food & Wine* readers expect to see some comment and criticism on the meals and accommodations, so I weave those into the story as cleanly as possible. Usually, the destination and its food and wine are pretty intertwined anyway, so it's a smooth connection to make."

Reporting for Specialized Stories

The reporting skills for specialized travel writing all relate to your awareness of the magazine's particular needs. For *Food & Wine,* for instance, Merrill needs to be a critic of, as well as a reporter of, the restaurants and inns that she visits. It is part of her job to criticize the meals she eats and to keep track of the availability and quality of wines at each place. Because this is done as part of a travel story, she weaves the information into the travel narrative, which, for her, is frequently in a chronological structure. After taking the reader to the town of St. Andrews, for instance, and discussing the tidal flows in the Bay of Fundy, Merrill moves into a discussion of the first night's meal:

But after a while, a funny thing happened: sometime over the Black Forest peasant bread and the complimentary spicy homemade pâté the gurgle of the lobster tank began to sound like a fountain. And the Swiss-training of chefs-owners Anita and Alexander Ludwig showed in nicely done sautéed scallops and panfried whole Arctic char.

(A caveat for oenophiles: L'Europe suffers the same limitations as do all Canadian dining establishments: retail-only liquor that is government owned and regulated. Every restaurant that I visited bewailed the inability to get a decent selection of wines at decent prices. Moreover, it's illegal for patrons to bring their own. On better wine lists you may find a Châteauneuf-du-Pape, a few serviceable wines from Drouhin vineyards, a variety of B&Gs, the odd Rioja or some mediocre Canadian Inniskillins from Ontario.)

This commentary, which comes early in the story, not only gives an assessment (a positive one in this case) of the meal but also explains the limitations imposed on the wine possibilities in the towns Merrill will visit during this trip.

Merrill avoids being too negative in her stories, since she's convinced that her readers "don't like to read negative criticism." But she does make sure to "try and steer the reader clear of negative experiences." In the Maritimes story, for instance, she notes the visual appeal of one hotel, but warns her readers about some problems, too:

The Algonquin looks beguiling, indeed—liberally gabled, turreted and iced with a long geranium-filled veranda—yet its appeal is deceptive. On a previous stay here I was kept awake most of the night by the raucous room parties of an auto dealers' convention. . . . I discovered afterward that the majority of the Algonquin's trade is convention and motor tours and that its walls are thin as wafers.

She then goes on to praise other aspects of her stay at the hotel, but the critical point has been made.

To do this kind of writing, it's necessary that Merrill keep copious notes.

"I do a lot of note-taking, typically. You have to have a pad with you at all times, and get used to jotting things down." In the interests of getting a fair assessment of a meal, she makes sure "to be very unobtrusive about my note-taking. I won't take the pad out until it's toward the end of the meal."

She then often finds it necessary to interview the chef, since "working with the chef helps me to understand what was in the meal, how it was pulled together."

She also practices the brochure collection technique, and "I try to keep menus, wine lists, and other relevant material when I can."

B O X   9 . 1

READING UP

Part of the necessary work of the travel writer is a good deal of background research about the place and its people before ever going for a visit.

As Joan Tapper explains, "It's important to know what's in the place. I once had a writer tell me, 'Oh well, I don't like to have story conferences beforehand or to discuss what I might be looking for. I just like to go and go into a bar and let the story happen.'

"Well, I never assigned him anything, because I don't believe that's the way to construct a good story. You have to know what people have thought about it, what historically has been there."

A visit to the bookstore or library, of course, is where you can begin this kind of research. But be sure not to limit such reading to almanacs or the travel writing of previous visitors.

Catherine Merrill does much of her background work not only by researching the facts but also by reading the literature of the place she has plans to visit.

"I try and read the poetry and native folktales of the place. It helps me get a sense of the flavor of the place, the mood of it," she says. "I've found that only in reading the poetry and fiction can you really find the heartbeat of a place."

For Merrill, this kind of reading helps get her "steeped in the culture of the people who live there."

For many out-of-the-way places, finding the literature beforehand may be difficult. In those instances, Merrill buys books while she's there and reads them during and after the trip, thus acquiring a valuable sensitivity to the culture through her reading.

The important thing to remember is that the greater your knowledge of the place and the more complete your information about the place and its people, the better the writing will be. So get your reading done before, during, and after your travels.

Writing for Specialized Stories

In her writing of these kinds of special travel stories, Merrill balances the needs of *Food & Wine* readers for information and criticism with their desire to be entertained and informed about the destinations, too.

"I do try to find a balance," she says, "between the information and the entertainment value. But, of course, if the story isn't fun to read then the information will never get to the reader, so keep it interesting above all."

So, right after a sentence that says, "With its stained glass, country furnishings and sunny courtyard, this bistro has an appealing air . . . [that] justifies a lunch or dinner time visit to St. John. . . ." Merrill makes sure to include a paragraph like this:

> That afternoon we drove 30 minutes east, past marshes and tide pools and shimmering lupines, to the tiny undiscovered fishing village of St. Martins for a fix of clean bay air. A haven for hikers, the area has several caves, cliffs and waterfalls to explore. We walked the rocky three-and-a-half-mile beach, pocketing odd little chunks of driftwood and smooth stones as we strolled toward an old wharf. We were alone on the beach, and the cliffs in the distance were as misty as Avalon's. Boats creaked in the tide, and an occasional car wound through two covered bridges.

That's nice travel writing in any sense, giving the reader a vivid description of the scene. The specific details help make this a memorable passage; the reader builds an internal picture of distant misty cliffs, an old wharf, and shimmering lupines (a kind of fern).

The basic structure that you may find most useful for this kind of travel writing is a basic weave of the chronological or spatial structure with inserted paragraphs that are specifically aimed at the needs of the publication.

When you can, weave the specialized material right into the sentence structure. Merrill does this in several spots. For instance:

> They endure a harsh economy and a harsher climate: long icy winters that linger from Thanksgiving to Mother's Day. Small wonder that when the summer season shines its first warm smile, the locals grin and sputter "Lord, thunder and Jesus, boy" at fair-weather tourists who come not in droves, but come nonetheless, for fresh lobster and salmon, plump strawberries and raspberries and crisp, clear weather that, even in the depths of July and August, turns its back on the rest of the continent's inevitable global warming.

Notice how Merrill has woven comments on "fresh lobster and salmon, plump strawberries and raspberries" into a passage that is really about weather and the local economy. By doing that, Merrill stays in touch with the special interests of her readers but gives them important cultural information as well.

LITERARY/ESCAPIST STORIES

Most literary/escapist stories are character oriented, subjective, and personal.

There is no argument over the literary merit of travel writing at its best; certainly the field's history supports that. Charles Dickens, Mark Twain, Stephen Crane, Ernest Hemingway, and many more are precursors to such contemporary literary figures as Paul Theroux, Jan Morris, John Updike, and others who produce travel pieces as well as novels, short stories, poetry, and other kinds of writing.

Joan Tapper, editor of *Islands* magazine, looks to this form of travel writing as the kind that her readers—a select, upscale, literate group— want in their travel reading.

"*Islands* showcases a particular kind of travel writing that we find is generally growing in importance right now, a literary style," she says. And that means that the stories in *Islands* "have a high fantasy component. Our features run the gamut, from places that people may actually travel to, to places they will just dream about. Our readers do travel, but they may not always be going to Tahiti.

"In choosing a writer," Tapper says, "I look for insight and literary style. Does this person tell you what a place is like? Can he or she make you see it, bring you there? There should be lots of information, but not presented in an encyclopedic or flat, informational style. I want the writer to make me experience the place with him or her, and to do so in a vivid, unusual way."

Finding that style is what you'll need to do if you want to write this kind of nonfiction. You might reread chapter six for a refresher course in high-style writing and ask yourself how you can apply that to your planned travel stories.

It's important to remember, too, that newspaper travel sections are also interested in these kinds of travel stories from time to time, and not all literary/escapist stories are lengthy, so the market is not as limited as you might think.

Tampa Tribune Travel Editor Dorothy Smiljanich says she likes to "have a mix of stories. We need the informational kind, certainly, but I also like to have the fantasy kind of story, the pure escapist story."

Smiljanich says that while "newspaper travel section readership is a general family market, those readers also want that vicarious thrill that you get from escapist stories."

In fact, Smiljanich thinks of the travel section of the newspaper as "the prime place in the newspaper where readers can turn to escape the dreary events of the here and now, and escape into the eternal."

Reporting for Literary Stories

Because this kind of travel writing is character oriented, you'll need to meet people and see them in their culture if you plan to get the kind of reporting done that's necessary. This kind of story requires a real immersion into a culture on the part of the writer, not just the sort of distant observation that might suffice for a more ordinary destination piece.

As Tapper says, "It is important for our writers to talk to people and experience things and not just be neutral observers, even if they choose to write it that way."

Tapper adds that two of the more famous travel writers in the world, Jan Morris and Paul Theroux, do things quite differently, but they share an ability to discover the reality of a culture in their travels.

"Paul Theroux always has characters in his stories. He's always encountering people. You can hear them talk, always filtered through his very particular filter."

Theroux sometimes uses quite a bit of dialogue in his stories, including a great deal of conversation as a way of illuminating people and a place. Jan Morris, on the other hand, says Tapper, "doesn't have a lot of conversations or dialogue in her pieces. Yet Morris is an acute observer. She has the ability to just pile up detail after detail after detail to reinforce her very subjective view of the place."

Morris's ability to see those details is a skill you want to acquire. When you're reporting for this kind of story, the little things begin to really matter. You need to look for small things that truly characterize a place. It's as if you're looking for the kind of symbolism that a fiction writer might use.

Tapper puts it this way: "Jan Morris, in one of her books, talks about her belief that you shouldn't try to tell everything about a place. You have to look at what there is that's unusual, that truly characterizes the place. And you do that not with a general description, but with the telling detail, the little things that make it special. Broad descriptions merely evaporate. You don't tell somebody that this island is beautiful, you tell them that this island has beaches so white that your eyes will be burned by the glare. The more unusual and subjective the detail the better."

This kind of reporting, then, places a heavy premium on your ability to interact with the place and its people, to get to know it and them, not just observe from a safe distance. If you do a good enough job of that, it will become clear in the story. Your research will pay off in a high level of believability and trust from the reader about your story. And that's necessary.

Tapper sums it up by saying, "We're looking for anecdotes, scene setting, narrative, and people." Notice how Tapper accomplishes many of these things in her reporting for her own story on the Aeolian Islands, reprinted at the end of this chapter.

In her opening scene, for instance, she introduces a character, Antonio, and begins an anecdote that tells us something of the scenery but also something of the people of the Aeolians. Within five paragraphs, she has given us mythology, history, and characterization for her story and has established a tone that she maintains throughout.

That took a lot of note-taking, as well as a talented eye (and ear) for observation.

"I take a lot of written notes," she says. "For me the Aeolian piece was difficult because I felt each island had its own character."

So Tapper looked on each island "for those things that I felt illustrated the specific scene."

She adds that "It's very important to do as much, to see as much, to talk to as many people as you can. You have to do your homework, have the background material, have a very good picture in your mind of what makes that place tick.

"You also have to pick up as much source material as you can. For example, local books that might not be available elsewhere. Read what people have written. Try to immerse yourself in information."

If you can do that, you'll be on your way toward writing a literary travel story.

Writing for Literary Stories

For some important hints on the structure of literary travel stories, take a look back at chapter six, and always remember that this is a very personal kind of journalism.

Tapper says, "When I send a writer on assignment, I say that what I'm after is the best mix of place and an author's personality. It's important to remember that the best travel writers are very subjective."

For her, it is important that the writer, as the traveler, be very obvious in the story.

"I think in travel writing you want the subjective viewpoint. It makes a story more believable when you know that somebody is there with prejudices and preconceptions. Travel is not bland. It's work. It can be funny or it can be dreadful. But you can't re-create that feeling with a neutral, omniscient tone. I think readers want to find out about a place from a friend who wants to tell them about it, and that's really the role a writer should play."

That sort of conversational tone is not only more enjoyable to read but often does a more effective job of informing the reader about a place and its people. As Tapper asks, "How much of what you read about a place in an encyclopedia really sticks? How much more memorable, though, is what a friend tells you. But you can't forget the importance of insight. You have to assume that the writer is smart enough to select the information that gives you the essence of the place."

Tapper says that "the best travel writers avoid rapturous, vapid descriptions. I can't tell you how many bad stories come across my desk beginning with the sentence 'Such and such is the land of contrasts,' or describing a 'picture-postcard town at the base of a mountain.'"

In other words, you'll want to avoid the obvious clichés and search for that something special about a place.

It's important in this kind of story, of course, that the various elements revolve around a theme. To do that, you'll want to write about those particular elements of the place and its people that support that theme.

As Tapper says, "You can't tell everything, so you have to tell a few specific things that will make this place appear a certain way forever in your mind."

Tapper establishes her theme in her extended hook, when she reminds the reader of the mythological connection the islands have to Homer's *Odyssey*. By the sixth paragraph she connects that myth to her own modern travels and establishes an odyssey theme this way:

> Thousands of years later the winds were still blowing, and the waves were still tossing little boats on the sea. But unlike Ulysses, I was in no hurry to go home.
>
> *   *   *
>
> My odyssey had started in Lipari, which buzzed with the energy and self-confidence of a central port with a place in history. Businessmen and students streamed off the hydrofoil as if they had just gotten off the subway. Taxi drivers accosted other passengers, "Do you need a ride? Do you need a hotel? I can show you a room." Boatmen offered sightseeing tours. Motor scooters zipped past like so many bees heading for a flowering bush.

From that point on the reader is prepared to follow the writer's thematic odyssey, traveling from island to island, town to town, getting a feel for the people and the places at each stop.

BOX 9.2

THE TOURISTIC EYE

One of the most difficult challenges facing the travel writer is finding a way to seem fresh and naively interested in a place and its people while actually being quite the opposite. After all, after a few years of travel writing you may well find yourself visiting some destinations for the second, third, or tenth time. And even on a first trip, a good travel writer needs to be so steeped in the background detail of a particular destination that things look familiar.

As Joan Tapper of *Islands* magazine puts it, "I want a writer who can be the innocent in a new place, somebody who will see a new place with fresh eyes, or who can approach a familiar place in a fresh way."

There's an interesting dichotomy that's needed. You need to be so well-informed about a place that you know exactly what to look for and what to avoid. But you also need to seem to be, for the reader, encountering the place with the excitement of the first-time visitor.

Call it the Touristic Eye. Much of it is internal. It has to do with your attitude as you travel. You have to make yourself feel as if it is all brand-new. You have to find ways to see Big Ben or the Louvre for the tenth or twentieth time as if you were seeing them for the first time.

Here are three hints for ways to find the Touristic Eye:

1. *Think photographically.* Try to see, in your mind, the photograph you would take of the place or its people. Try to discover unusual angles for the shot or an unusual element that you could take a picture of.
2. *Search for adventure.* Even a little adventure will do nicely. Get involved in conversations with the locals or with other travelers. Go for long walks at odd hours. Hop aboard a local bus and go for a long ride to nowhere in particular. Find your way into the places where the locals shop or dine.

    The author can recall when he and his wife took a long, late-night walk in a thick fog to the outskirts of the little Scottish Highland town of Drumnadrochit to Urquhart Castle, which overlooks Loch Ness. Stumbling along in the darkness, the two of them bumped—almost literally—into a pair of Norwegian adventurers who had traveled that day across the North Sea in a small boat and were camping that night in the castle's tumbled ruins.

For the next few hours the four of them chatted over a few pints of Scottish ale and a cup or two of mead at a local pub. That delightful chance meeting made for a wonderful anecdote that has since found its way into several travel stories. And it all came about from a quick decision to go for a brisk walk in the evening mist.

3. *Look for small but telling details.* Often, in travel writing, it is from the smallest of details that the best large picture is painted.

If you don't find such details when you are doing your reporting, you won't be able to relate them later as you write. So look for that small plaque on the side of the building that relates some interesting bit of history. Search for that paving stone in the street that marks where an event took place. Find that little fishing village just outside the well-traveled city, or that historic house that is rarely visited because the cavernous famous museum is just two blocks away, or that quiet little cove just a mile away from the busy beach.

It is these small places and things that add detail and give a fresh appeal to your writing—and make the traveling more fun and interesting for you as well.

■ ■ ■

A CANADIAN COASTAL GETAWAY

BY CATHERINE OSBORNE MERRILL

If it weren't for the Bay of Fundy's formidable tidal swell, the Maritime Provinces of southern Canada would remind me of Maine's coastline. The little fishing villages, the misty cliffs, the wildflower-covered hills and the sweater-cool evenings all seem as familiar as a Down East clambake.

But the Maritimes are decidedly not American. In many ways, the Maritimes aren't even Canadian. They are their own perplexing amalgam of French, English, Irish and Scottish influences—quite independent, thank you very much, and quite provincial.

New Brunswick, Prince Edward Island and Nova Scotia make up the Maritimes, and as much as I wanted to spend the summer touring them all, our four-day long weekend would allow only a brief ramble through the first two provinces. A previous trip had whetted my imagination and lured me back—this time with my husband—to reexplore these remote regions of rolling green farmland, gaudy in summer with purple and pink lupines that march down to a rugged, salty coast.

Thousands of United Empire Loyalists (we called them Tories) fled the States in 1783 and hightailed it across the Canadian border. In New Brunswick, they

built seafaring villages, and both St. Andrews and St. John still laud their heritage, proudly pointing to 200-year-old Loyalist homes, burial grounds, churches and blockhouses as living proof of their British patriotism. With all due respect, it's an odd feeling, as an American, to see the guns in St. Andrews pointing permanently at the States.

You must, however, respect the Maritimers' fortitude. These hardworking people are bound deeply to the sea, to shipbuilding and fishing, to long days of tangled nets, traps and rigging and to working-class industries. They endure a harsh economy and a harsher climate: long icy winters that linger from Thanksgiving to Mother's Day. Small wonder that when the summer season shines its first warm smile, the locals grin and sputter "Lord, thunder and Jesus, boy" at fair-weather tourists who come not in droves, but come nonetheless, for fresh lobster and salmon, plump strawberries and raspberries and crisp, clear weather that, even in the depths of July and August, turns its back on the rest of the continent's inevitable global warming.

Loyalists were not the first Maritimers, however. When they arrived, they ousted the native Micmac Indians, as well as the

French Acadians, who had settled the entire province and converted the Micmacs to Catholicism. The French fled to New Brunswick's northeast coast, now known as Acadia, and to Louisiana (the word *Cajun* is derived from Acadia). Officially bilingual, New Brunswick is still about 40 percent French speaking. After the Loyalists settled New Brunswick, thousands of Irish immigrants followed, adding a bit of the brogue to the Maritimes' unique mix.

We flew into New Brunswick's port city of St. John, rented a car at the airport and headed for St. Andrews, just an hour and a half west. New Brunswickers have an endearing expression, "Stay where you are and I'll come where you're at." Despite its skewed grammar, the phrase conveys my feeling about St. Andrews: "Don't move— I'll be right there." This lovely whitewashed village, which lolls along Passamaquoddy Bay, is a cluster of saltbox houses and seaside boutiques with the long arm of its wharf stretching out toward the sunset. You only have to walk into the Shiretown Inn on Water Street or the Algonquin on the hill to appreciate the century of resort patronage that St. Andrews has attracted. The Algonquin evokes an era when ladies swathed in white muslin and gents decked out in jodhpurs played croquet on the lawn, all bowlers and spats, white gloves and decorum, vestiges of another time.

It's a shame that neither hotel has maintained that elegant image. The Algonquin looks beguiling, indeed—liberally gabled, turreted and iced with a long geranium-filled veranda—yet its appeal is deceptive. On a previous stay here I was kept awake most of the night by the raucous room parties of an auto dealers' convention. (Vacation in hell?) I discovered afterward that the majority of the Algonquin's trade is conventions and motor tours and that its walls are thin as wafers. A heated pool, golf course, tennis courts and bike-rental facilities may, perhaps, make up for the hotel's lack of tranquillity. I can certainly recommend renting the hotel's bikes though.

My husband and I spent our first day riding the Algonquin's bicycles around St. Andrews. We went gliding like seabirds through the little town—down the wooden wharf, where our mountain bikes made deep rhythmic thumps on the boards, sailing along Water Street, dismounting only to duck into shops we liked. After checking out Tom Smith's Pottery, Stickney's Wedgwood, Cottage Craft's woolens and St. Andrews Antiques & Quilts—and finding good quality, albeit at resort prices—we stowed our bikes outside The Gables and grabbed an outdoor table by the bay.

There's something about having a cold beer and "u-peel-'em" boiled shrimp in the sunshine and salty air that cleanses your spirit and reconnects you to things elemental. I had chosen cooked rather than raw shellfish, recalling Woody Allen's memorable line, "I will not eat oysters. I want my food dead—not sick, not wounded— dead."

Afterward, I wanted to go whale watching on the Bay of Fundy, but alas, to everything there is a season, and we were too early for the whales. They come, along with the northern lights, in August. Cline Marine in St. Andrews takes groups out to whale watch or seal watch (they call seals sea dogs in these parts). Or you can deep-sea fish or go on lazy sunset cruises. The Bay of Fundy, of course, is a show in itself—the tides reach 52 feet at some points. Here in St. Andrews, about 25 feet of Fundy water spills into the Passamaquoddy each day, leaving wide strips of shiny sand and tide pools when it rushes out.

Since we couldn't see whales, we settled for landlocked sights. The 15-minute drive west to St. Stephen took us to Crocker Hill Studios and Herb Gardens—open to the public for $2 a head— where artist Steve Smith and his wife, Gail, have sculptured three acres of countryside into abundant gardens that flow down to the St. Croix River. Steve seems to enjoy taking guests on guided tours through winding paths, chatting energetically about herbal proper- ties and folklore. It's lovely, as well, to experience the garden on your own, strolling by ponds or under heavy fans of sumac.

We returned to St. Andrews in time for cocktails at the Rossmount Inn—and to the kind of salon- lounge that said to my husband, "Martini, please." Laden with mahogany sideboards and beveled mirrors, the boxy 18-room inn appears much older than its 22 years. Its reproduction decor borders on kitsch, but the Ross- mount is a pleasant place. We had reserved Room 20, the honeymoon suite, which has a rather short cherrywood bed (an idiosyncrasy that leads to some funny conversations at reservation time) and a spectacular view of the valley and the bay.

Fiddlehead ferns, parboiled and sautéed with onions, and poached salmon make up a traditional New Brunswick meal that's well prepared at the Rossmount. But dinner our first night was reserved for L'Europe. Frankly, it's not a spot I might have tried on sight—the exterior resembles a chalet-style schnitzel haven. But we chanced it based on Anne Hardy's high recommen- dation in *Where to Eat in Canada*, and we were glad we did. Although the restaurant, with its ex- tensive menu, promises the best meal in St. Andrews, its schmaltzy cuckoo-clock decor is even cornier than Rossmount's. But after a while, a funny thing happened: sometime over the Black Forest peasant bread and the complimentary spicy homemade pâté the gurgle of the lobster tank began to sound like a fountain. And the Swiss-training of chefs-owners Anita and Alexander

Ludwig showed in nicely done sautéed scallops and panfried whole Arctic char.

(A caveat for oenophiles: L'Europe suffers the same limitation as do all Canadian dining establishments: retail-only liquor that is government owned and regulated. Every restaurant that I visited bewailed the inability to get a decent selection of wines at decent prices. Moreover, it's illegal for patrons to bring their own. On better wine lists you may find a Châteauneuf-du-Pape, a few serviceable wines from Drouhin vineyards, a variety of B&Gs, the odd Rioja or some mediocre Canadian Inniskillins from Ontario.)

The next morning we drove east on Route 1, back toward the airport, to St. John. We joined a number of locals at Reggie's for a delicious breakfast of hearty Oktoberfest sausage, French toast and strong coffee. Our next stop was the block-long Old City Market on King Street, which was built in 1876. Here are row upon row of fresh mussels, oysters and assorted fish, as well as prime cuts, fruits, vegetables, cheeses, breads and pastries. Big bins of dried dulse, the purplish seaweed that Maritimers "eat like potato chips," invite the uninitiated. Tasting dulse was, for me, like being slapped in the face with a salty wave of seawater—it's kind of chewy and nothing like potato chips.

We continued down to King Square, a lovely city park, and explored the Trinity Royal pres-ervation area. We stopped in at the Loyalist Trinity Church, built extra long, I was told, so "brides would have plenty of time to change their minds." I found a few antiques bargains here in St. John: wonderful green Depression-glass goblets from Red's and an old quilt from Canterbury Antiques. New Brunswick and Prince Edward are both quilt country, but be prepared to spend between $300 and $1,000 for fine new work.

At lunchtime we walked around the corner to a restaurant on Princess Street that I'd visited on my last trip and found it even better than I'd remembered. Incredible Edibles offers such dishes as seafood remoulade, London broil roulade, manicotti and smoked sea trout. We started with generous Caesar salads, then split a huge portion of linguine and clam sauce that was tossed with bits of clams, mushrooms, bacon and scallions and flavored with sherry. For dessert, the house specialty is cheesecake: chocolate amaretto, French mint, pumpkin, Grand Marnier or blueberry. With its stained glass, country furnishings and sunny courtyard, this bistro has an appealing air. Incredible Edibles justifies a lunch or dinner time visit to St. John, an otherwise heavily industrial and sometimes smoggy working-class port.

That afternoon we drove 30 minutes east, past marshes and tide pools and shimmering lupines, to the tiny undiscovered fishing village of St. Martins for a fix of clean bay air. A haven for hikers, the area has several caves, cliffs and waterfalls to explore. We walked the rocky three-and-a-half-mile beach, pocketing odd little chunks of driftwood and smooth stones as we strolled toward an old wharf. We were alone on the beach, and the cliffs in the distance were as misty as Avalon's. Boats creaked in the tide, and an occasional car wound through two covered bridges.

Folks in St. Martins have always built boats, and better times are suggested by the many once-pristine Victorian houses along the coast road. The Quaco Inn, a pretty pale-yellow place just 300 feet from the beach, is a romantic spot for travelers, particularly if you get the Vaughan Room, which has a working fireplace, bay window and private bath. The inn hasn't quite worked out its culinary wrinkles, serving such retro-dishes as iceberg lettuce salads and lobster Newburg. But if you're more interested in hiking and picnics than fine food, you may enjoy the Quaco.

We chose instead the more formal Shadow Lawn Country Inn in Rothesay, a bit closer to St. John on Route 1. I'd stayed here before and loved this 120-year-old mansion. The large pink and burgundy dining room has two fireplaces and French doors, and the tables are set with silver and crystal. We had beef Wellington, and while this is hardly an imaginative offering, it was soundly done. After a brandy in the lounge, we retired to our spacious salon-bedroom, with its chandeliers and crisp white linens.

Breakfast the next day in the sunny bay-windowed morning room renewed us for the three-hour drive to the Marine Atlantic ferry at Cape Tormentine, which would take us to Prince Edward Island. Once we'd driven out of St. John, Route 1 became rural, hilly and forested. By the time we reached Sussex, about an hour northeast, we were ready for a light lunch at the Broadway Café on Broad Street. A busy, funky little eatery in the middle of an untrendy town, the café took a bit long to deliver our sprout-topped pita sandwiches, but we weren't in any hurry. Another two hours and we'd be at the ferry, where the wait could be 45 minutes for the next boat. The hour's ferry ride is quite an event. Hundreds of people and nearly as many cars are loaded on these tankers that plow surprisingly fast through the dark waters of the Northumberland Strait.

The ferry lands at Borden, on the south shore, in the middle of the crescent-shaped, 140-mile-long Prince Edward Island. Canada's tiniest province is also a pastoral paradise: fields of strawberries and potatoes square off against rows of tall spruce, and black-eyed Susans share the hills with cows and colts. In the midst of all this farmland, it's surprising to glimpse the sea at every turn and remember that you are indeed on an island.

It was close to evening by the time we checked into the Strathgartney Country Inn, located on the Trans-Canada Highway, about midway between the ferry and Charlottetown. Strathgartney is countrified to the extreme. Our dormered bedroom was wallpapered with a design that repeated "God Bless Our Home" and "Home Sweet Home" ad infinitum. But the white wicker and antique furnishings made up for the inn's decorating lapses. I liked this 150-year-old farmhouse, with its high ceilings and pine-planked floors, and I liked its prices. Our Royal Stewart Suite was spacious and romantically appointed with a fireplace and whirlpool bath. While the other rooms are quite a bit smaller, each is quaintly furnished and comfy.

We had planned to drive up to New Glasgow Lobster Suppers for one of Prince Edward Island's famous family-style lobster feeds that come with unlimited amounts of chowder, coleslaw and the like. But the smells from Strathgartney's kitchen were so enticing that we decided to stay at the inn for dinner. After a refreshing chilled raspberry soup, we ordered a bottle of Louis Latour Bourgogne and beef tournedos. If the bacon-wrapped meat hadn't arrived well-done (I'd ordered it medium-rare), I would have been happy. I can only conclude that Strathgartney joins the ranks of young, still-affordable inns that have yet to master their own menus.

Strathgartney does, however, offer a complimentary breakfast of freshly baked muffins, juice and coffee, which sent us on our way satisfied to Cavendish, the site of Green Gables House.

I was not reared on Lucy Maud Montgomery's girlhood classic, *Anne of Green Gables,* and this childhood deprivation has led, no doubt, to an untoward cynicism in midlife. But to me, it is bizarre the way hordes of young women from the world over—particularly from Japan—roam the house in Cavendish that was the inspiration for Montgomery's books. They walk from room to room, book in hand—some even insist on taking their wedding vows here—in order to retrace the tiny steps of their orphaned heroine. I found the attraction touristy, especially the gift shop, which sells Anne look-alike straw hats that come with sewn-in red bangs and braids.

We spent the rest of our day on Prince Edward winding through the middle of the island on Blue Heron Drive. We passed up the many roadside attractions: the Car Life Museum that claims to have Elvis's 1959 pink Cadillac, Ripley's Museum, replicas of a U.S. space shuttle and King Tut's Tomb, and even Fairyland. We did, however, stop at crafts and antiques shops. I liked The Dunes in Brackley Beach for pottery and Stanley Bridge Studios and the Old Stanley Schoolhouse in Stanley Bridge for crafts, particularly quilts. But the antiques are overpriced. Grant's

Trail Rides in South Rustico captured my imagination, and we found ourselves atop a couple of gentle mares for a sunny afternoon canter.

Prince Edward's roads are perfect for cycling; many bike lovers come here just for the rolling countryside that's so reminiscent of Ireland. I'm convinced that the best way to see this beautiful island, however, must be from the air. Pegasus Balloons (902-964-3250) at Hunter River takes adventurous tourists into the clouds. My husband had given me a choice: I could either get him on a horse or in a balloon, but not both. If we had planned ahead, the balloon would have won out.

We found our way back via the coast road to Brackley Beach, entered Prince Edward National Park and drove up to the place I'd been most looking forward to: Dalvay-by-the-Sea. As we sat in twig chairs on the plush lawn, looking out over sand dunes to the Gulf of St. Lawrence beyond, it was easy to imagine ourselves as guests of turn-of-the-century oilman Alexander MacDonald (one of John D. Rockefeller's chums), who built Dalvay in 1896 as his summer cottage. The 26-bedroom Victorian mansion reminds me of one of those Adirondack "camps," where the well-heeled roughed it during their summers in bygone days. Inside, Dalvay's grand foyer is distinguished by a wide staircase, balcony and huge sandstone

fireplace, where guests gather after dinner, reading, chatting and watching the fire.

Dalvay is such a discreet place that everyone seemed to know the rules except for newcomers like us. We had to ask where to get cocktails; there's no lounge proper, but at your request you'll be served anywhere on the premises. No one told us what time breakfast would be served, where to get mountain bikes, where the golf course or tennis courts were or what mystery sport a natty couple were playing on the lawn. We thought perhaps it was boccie; as it turned out, it was lawn bowling. We couldn't resist the urge to try a few rounds before dinner. Lawn bowling reminded me of trying to knock down a bunch of monster Milk Duds, and I imagine we looked quite silly. But no one really noticed or seemed to care. The occasional couple would wander by in tennis whites, or a family would stroll in from the beach. Then and there, I decided that this was my kind of place, the kind of "cottage" I'd like to return to summer after summer, asking for the same room.

One of the biggest advantages of staying at Dalvay is its almost-deserted beach and its vast windswept dunes. There are no billboards, no hot-dog stands, no parking lots, no ghetto blasters and no beach-blanket congestion. And the water of the gulf is surprisingly warm.

Back at the hotel, it seemed appropriate to dress for dinner, though many guests had not. Unless it's the beginning of the season and Dalvay is breaking in new waitresses, both service and cuisine are reliable. Our modified American plan included a four-course dinner, and this makes Dalvay-by-the-Sea, if not a bargain, at least a very reasonable destination. Our seviche and mussel bisque were both good, and the wine list, while still rather slim on fine labels, did have a better selection than most of the places we'd been to. A Joseph Drouhin Laforêt Chardonnay worked well with jumbo shrimp and asparagus tips wrapped in sole. My husband's lamb was generous and tender and was served with a mint-peppercorn sauce.

A final after-dinner walk on the beach brought our all-too-brief weekend into focus, and conversation drifted to ways we might return. For at Dalvay-by-the-Sea we felt as if we had come back to the "summer camp" we had never known. But, we agreed as we ambled down the moonlit shore, it is never too late to start a tradition.

■ ■ ■

This article first appeared in the June 1991 issue of Food and Wine. *Merrill is an English professor at Johnson State College, in Johnson, Vermont, and a part-time freelance writer.*

■ ■ ■

KIDS, PARENTS FIND ISLAND A HAPPY HOLIDAY

BY RICK WILBER

Fresh from a messy banana snack at a shady picnic table, 14-month-old Samantha ran down to the beach at Rum Point on Grand Cayman, chased a gull or two, and then plopped her diapered bottom into the warm, shallow water and declared the place perfect with a firm, declarative "Happy! Happy! Happy!"

Her parents agreed.

Whether taking solo turns on snorkeling expeditions into the stunningly clear water or just relaxing with a good book while keeping an eye on Samantha's efforts to fill a pail with sand, they found that Rum Point—indeed, all of Grand Cayman—was an easy, comfortable spot in the Caribbean for a visit, even with a baby along.

The family appeal of the place actually started in Tampa. The Cayman Airways flight from Tampa International Airport was nonstop, so gate-to-gate was under two hours.

The travelers had spent many a half-day or more in getting to island destinations in pre-Samantha days, changing airplanes in Miami or Antigua or elsewhere, so the hassle-free hop to Grand Cayman was much appreciated.

Samantha, in fact, barely had time to enjoy a cup of milk at takeoff and landing (to ease the adjustment to air pressure changes), take a short nap and listen to two or three readings of "Green Eggs and Ham" before she found herself strolling through the Caymans' mercifully quick customs and hopping into the taxi for a 15-minute ride to her hotel on Seven Mile Beach.

There, while Samantha was discovering that the Holiday Inn had an ideal baby pool, her parents were finding out that the hotel offered a baby-sitter service, high chairs in the restaurant and a baby-friendly staff.

Leave Stress at Home

It was a fine first day, with Samantha having a great time and her parents relieved to find that for a variety of reasons Grand Cayman offered as stress-free a trip as one could hope for with a baby along.

Part of the reason for that is the Caymans' enviable standard of living. With the highest per capita income in the Caribbean, almost no unemployment, a modern hospital, grocery stores filled with diapers and baby food (albeit with high prices) and not much of a crime rate, Grand Cayman doesn't challenge the traveler as many Caribbean destinations do. Instead, it strokes and coaxes.

That might not be adventuresome, but it's just fine for parents with young children.

Granted, there are no theme parks and no miniature golf courses, so perhaps a teen-ager might find it all rather boring.

But for the parents concerned about the safety, health and happiness of some pre-teens or babies, the place is darn near perfect. Heck, when young taste buds have had it with native cuisine, there's even a Burger King on West Bay Road near all the hotels, and Domino's delivers. For better or worse, you won't find that in tranquil hideaways such as St. Kitts or Montserrat.

The classic Caribbean is there if you look—it's just hidden behind the hotels and condominiums. On Seven Mile Beach, for instance, there are five miles (how five miles of beach got the Seven Mile name is another story entirely) of safe, panhandler-free sand and water. No one will try to sell you drugs or straw hats; you're not confined to the guarded grounds of one resort property; and if the quality of the sand really isn't up to Pinellas County standards, the startling clarity of the water more than makes up for it.

For instance, with Mom and Samantha walking along, Dad could, wherever it looked promising, pop on the snorkel and mask and head out for a quick look at the coral and the fish. On one such quick excursion on the morning of their last day, Dad saw a large— no, a huge—barracuda just 20 yards out, at the edge of the line of a coral reef. Samantha and Mom chose not to swim in that spot.

A rental car, at $20 Cayman per day for three days, unlimited mileage (which worked out to $80 U.S. for three days), was available from the Cico agent right next to the hotel.

That meant the family could drive the few miles into George Town, scoot past the high-rise banks that help fuel the island's economy (the Caymans have 500 banks involved in the tax haven business) and drive another mile south to Smith Cove.

There, in a little park, are picnic tables and plenty of shade from the wide-leafed grape trees that border the small beach.

Baby Water

The shallow water is just right for baby, and just offshore is some terrific snorkeling. So Mom and Dad took turns, with one of them playing in the shallows with Samantha, while the other snorkeled the sights—plenty of parrotfish, some fan and brain coral and clouds of small tropicals.

On another day, the family took a scenic morning drive south past Smith Cove and along the southern edge of Grand Cayman.

Just past Bodden Town (Grand Cayman's second city) and Frank Sound on that southern coast is a rocky coast where wave action beneath the rocks pushes sudden geysers of water 30 feet or more into the air from holes in the rocky surface.

The blow holes were interesting for the parents, who discussed how that pressure must have cut through the rock. Although Samantha was disinterested in the discussion, she was simply delighted with the spouting water and made that clear with a round of hand claps and squeals of joy.

Grand Cayman is only 20 miles wide and seven miles deep, so a drive around the entire island is the work of a couple of hours, even with frequent stops.

On a previous visit, the parents had driven past East End, where the sea can be considerably angrier than on the gentle west coast. Several wrecked hulks dot the horizon line there, and a locally famous story tells of the 18th-century Wreck of the Ten Sails, where a misread warning light led 10 vessels onto the rocks.

On this trip, the family took a road that cuts through the middle of the island and in a few minutes were on the north coast. A left turn there, another 15 minutes of leisurely driving and they were at Rum Point, which offers about as perfect a spot as the Caribbean has for a family day at the beach.

There is a rustic restaurant bar there, another snack shack next to it, some showers and toilets, a group of picnic tables and a nice stretch of beach with a wonderful view of the distant breakers and the calm lagoon behind them.

The snorkeling is terrific once you work your way out to the coral and rock outcrops, with frequent sightings of large rays, the expected variety of coral and any number of bright, tropical fish.

Back at the beach, the water is shallow and perfect for some baby splashing. If the sun gets to be too much, the shade offered by the trees is a welcome relief, and a bite of lunch or a soft drink, beer or something tropically icy is available.

Because it's away from the hotels on Seven Mile Beach, Rum Point never seems to be crowded. It is, frankly, a great way to spend a late morning and early afternoon.

On another day, Samantha thoroughly enjoyed a visit to the Cayman Turtle Club. The farm is on the coast just a few miles up the road from Seven Mile Beach and has literally thousands of sea turtles being raised in concrete tanks as well as one huge main pool.

One small tank has some mild-mannered green turtles that the visitors can pick up and hold. Samantha, cautious to a fault, managed to touch briefly the carapace of one such turtle when another visitor held it out for her to see.

The farm raises some of the turtles for "processing" into jewelry and meat, while thousands of others are released into the sea. The farm's primary focus is on the more common green turtle, but efforts are also being made to improve the odds for the endangered Kemp-Ridley.

Primarily a research site, the farm charges $5 U.S. for admission for adults and $2.50 for children. Turtle fans of Samantha's age get in for free.

Note that importation of any turtle products into the United States is banned. Based on its success in raising and restocking turtles, however, the turtle farm is fighting the ban, at last for turtle farm products.

The turtle farm is also a reminder that turtles were the primary source of income for Cayman residents until the tourism boom of the past 25 years. Reminders of that heritage are found at the new Cayman Island International Museum, which opened last year in George Town.

Scuba Divers' Paradise

Also on the "must-do" list for visitors to the Caymans is scuba diving, since the islands have a justified reputation for offering some of the world's best. The snorkeling, too, is outstanding at several locations, including Eden Rock or Parrot's Landing, both just south of George Town.

There is also a submarine dive available, on the Atlantis, which visits the famous Cayman wall and dives down to 150 feet.

Some of these things are easily done with a baby in tow; others are difficult or just not right for a baby. In the latter case, the hotel sitters can come in handy.

Samantha's parents never did find a need for a sitter, and instead traded off sitting duties while enjoying solo snorkeling trips or a quiet walk down the beach. But a surgeon and his wife from Houston vouched for the quality of the Holiday Inn's sitter, and all the principal hotels offer the service.

It is worth noting that the flight home was filled with Cayman islanders coming to Tampa to shop for things not available on the islands, including some baby items. A New Zealand couple currently living on Grand Cayman needed everything from a stroller to a high chair; those items are hard to come by for them at home. But all the basics are there for a tiny tourist.

A Few Tips

Should you decide to make the trip and take the baby along, here are some hints and reminders from Samantha's mom:

- Sun block for baby. Even Florida babies need protection from the Cayman sunshine. A coating of Water Babies sun block from Coppertone (and don't forget to coat the top of the head, too) seemed to do the job for Samantha, who spent a considerable amount of time in the water and on the beach without a hint of burn. There are several other brands on the market.

- Diapers. They are available in local supermarkets.
- Juices and formula. They are available but a bit expensive. Even Samantha's Isomil formula was there, though Mom had brought along plenty in powder form.
- Toys and books. Don't forget to bring along the favorites, including something to sleep with. Samantha's favorite "night-night" (a blanket) definitely made the trip, and helped make the nights in a strange room more comfortable.
- Cribs. The hotel crib was fine, if small, but had no bumper (for head contact, which babies like). Also, bring along crib sheets if they make the baby more comfortable.
- Stroller. Bring along a col-lapsible stroller. Although the sand on Seven Mile Beach is typically too soft for a stroller's small wheels, West Bay Road, which runs the length of the beach, has sidewalks and is perfect for a stroll.
- Beach ball. Deflate one, shove it in a bag and bring it along. Samantha got plenty of use out of hers.
- Car seat. Bring along the car seat for your flight. If the flight isn't full, the airline will let you set it up in an empty seat and use it for baby (it's better and safer than your lap), and then you'll have it for your rental car.
- Rental car. Spend the extra $25 a day or so for a rental. You'll enjoy seeing the island's other coasts and its historic sites. Rum Point and Smith Cove, in particular, are worth the drive.

■   ■   ■

This article, by the author of this book, first appeared in The Tampa Tribune *on Sunday, October 4, 1992.*

■ ■ ■

AEOLIAN ODYSSEY

BY JOAN TAPPER

For reassurance, I kept looking at Antonio's foot. He was steering with it, pushing the tiller to guide the small boat as we bounced on the waves. My own foot was braced against the side, and I was hanging on with both hands to keep from being pitched overboard. Still, if Antonio was steering with only his foot, how dangerous could it be? And the view was spectacular.

The Aeolian Islands stretched out around me, remnants of the volcanic history of this swatch of Mediterranean. Part of Sicily, visible on the horizon some 25 miles away, the Aeolians nonetheless retained their own identities, obvious even now. On my far left was Vulcano, aptly named though no longer active, unless you counted the steam rising above the whitish edge of the old crater. Closer was Lipari, largest of the group and at the center of everything. Directly in front of me was sleepy Panarea, its boxy white houses neatly arranged in front of red hills. To my right the symmetrical cone of Stromboli constantly renewed its mystery, erupting with dark puffs of smoke several times an hour.

Ripples caught my eye as several flying fish broke the water, adding a playful touch to this end of summer morning. Antonio was a fisherman, though these days he probably used his boat more to take travelers to rocky islets like Lisca Bianca, which we were now approaching. *"Quando il mare e calmo,"* Antonio said, "when the sea is calm, it's much hotter, this is a romantic island. People bring food, stay the day or into the evening, walking, talking."

I had once seen Lisca Bianca in the movies. It was the setting for Antonioni's *L'Avventura*, the place where a beautiful socialite disappeared, putting into motion the plot of the murky film. Lisca Bianca was so small that it was hard to imagine anyone getting lost there. But Antonioni's jet-setters had heralded a stream of later visitors—Italians mainly, other Europeans, a few Americans— who came to these islands in search of the same clear sea and romantic atmosphere that once drew sophisticated travelers to the Italian coast before it got too chic, too crowded.

Actually, the Aeolians have been welcoming wanderers since ancient times. Homer put the islands in the *Odyssey*, making them the home of Aeolus, god of the winds. (From my vantage point, amid whitecaps, it was obvious why.) When Ulysses showed up on Aeolus's doorstep, the god graciously sent him off with a bag of winds—tightly sealed so they could not blow the ship off a homeward course. Of course, curiosity got the better of the crew, who opened the gift—loosing the winds' full fury. Blown back to the Aeolians, Ulysses and company were fated to wander on.

Thousands of years later, the winds were still blowing, and the waves were still tossing little boats on the sea. But unlike Ulysses, I was in no hurry to go home.

■ ■ ■

My odyssey had started in Lipari, which buzzed with the energy and self-confidence of a central port with a place in history. Businessmen and students streamed off the hydrofoil as if they had just gotten off the subway. Taxi drivers accosted other passengers, "Do you need a ride? Do you need a hotel? I can show you a room." Boatmen offered sightseeing tours. Motor scooters zipped past like so many bees heading for a flowering bush.

Over the next few days I came to recognize the rhythm of that daily bustle, which rose in the morning and evening and slowed in the torpor of midday. My explorations took me up and down the narrow streets of Lipari's old town—into passages barely an arm's length wide—where islanders gesticulated in intense conversations that turned mundane exchanges into little street dramas.

One morning I climbed the stairs to the Castello, where the Cathedral of San Bartolomeo stood atop massive stone walls that dominated the harbor. Built on the site of an ancient Greek temple, the church's oldest walls were Norman, from the 12th century. Some 500 years later, in 1544, the pirate Barbarossa II besieged Lipari. "The town fathers thought they could make a deal," a local history buff had told me. "'Come in,' they said, 'take what you want, and leave.' Being a pirate, he paid no attention. He killed off the women and children and laid waste to the city."

Steps away from the church, tourists were filing in and out of an archaeological museum. Near the museum's main door, excavations had uncovered a jumble of stone ruins representing a series of civilizations—some lasting millennia, others only a few centuries.

The curator responsible for those discoveries was steely and passionate as she recounted Lipari's archaeological history. "What you have to know about Lipari," the woman told me, "is that here you have 6,000 years of continued habitation—layer on layer of settlements, one over the next. We knew that the settlements had been here, we just didn't know how rich the material would be. The museum started 40 years ago with just one glass case," she said.

"Then we had three, and gradually we expanded." Those collections now fill five buildings.

The exhibits represent the sweep of history in the Aeolians, beginning with obsidian—the hard, black volcanic glass that first attracted people here, around 4000 B.C. Obsidian was the crude oil of its time, highly prized for weapons and tools, and it made the islands a wealthy trading center until the dawn of the Bronze Age. Then, a thousand years passed before the islands regained their place as an important crossroads of the Mediterranean, by trading metals from Britain and the Near East.

Of the streams of invaders— Italian tribes, colonists from Greece, Roman conquerors—who left their cultures behind, the museum holds tantalizing traces, from massive sarcophagi to graceful painted vases, and from poignant baby bottles shaped like fish to models of theatrical masks, remnants of a cult of the god Dionysus in the fourth century B.C. Small enough to fit into my hand, the masks depicted individual roles like Oedipus or stock characters of drama—old harpies, pretty maidens, bragging soldiers. Eerily lifelike, they still, after centuries, spoke eloquently of the human spirit.

■ ■ ■

And what had become of that spirit? To see a more contemporary Lipari, I put myself in the hands of Marco del Bono—a Sicilian whirlwind disguised as a man with curly graying hair, blue eyes, and an exuberant affection for the place that has been his home for some 30 years. He had put up the first hotel on the island when Lipari was still rural, still undiscovered. "I built it in the style of the old island houses," he told me. "The maids were island girls. We had to convince them it was all right to ride the elevator.

"In 1960 there were only four cars on the island," he said, as we climbed into the shiny green Mini Moke that was clearly his new toy. "Mine was the fifth. Otherwise there were only donkeys. I had a donkey, too, named Toto, and I'd take him to the coffee bar and buy him an ice cream. The police would give him a fine. OK, I'd say, but you have to put the ticket on the donkey. After all, the fine is for him."

The warm afternoon sun heightened the dry Mediterranean landscape, turning stands of cactus into prickly pear reliefs, lengthening the shadows of fragrant eucalyptus trees, and adding brilliance to purple and fuchsia geraniums massed by the road. Offshore, beyond a scattering of rocks called the Formiche—the ants—rose the sulfur-coated flanks of Vulcano.

We bounced on around the island. In one village, whitewashed walls marked off vineyards and tidy patios, narrowing the road to a path just wide enough for our little car. Like a chute, the road eventually deposited us in a plaza with a domed church, gleaming white. A date in the lintel read 1646. From here the soft green hills on the neighboring island of Salina seemed close enough to touch.

"That's where malvasia is made," Marco said, naming the sweet golden wine that caps off Aeolian meals. "We call it God's nectar."

Beyond the square our road widened again, and we overtook a young couple on a motor scooter, then zipped past an old woman on a donkey. It was twilight, and we stopped for a moment on a bluff above Lipari's harbor to watch the evening lights flicker on. A hydrofoil, like some floating ornament, was pulling into port. Once again the island pulse quickened in the deepening shadows.

■ ■ ■

In classical tradition it was a boatman who took me to the other world of Vulcano. Stocky and good-looking, the boatman played guide as he detoured to show off the coastline of Lipari. Or perhaps he was practicing his pitchmanship. He had made a video of the Aeolians, complete with music, he told me, that he was willing to sell.

The water seemed fantastic that day, changing from gray blue in front of the hotel to azure in a grotto, becoming milky turquoise in front of the island's pumice quarry,

where the soft hillside sloughed its powder into the sea, leaving tiny rocks—bits of pumice—floating in the water. The Mediterranean darkened again to cobalt as we threaded our way around fanciful rock spires with names to match: Gate of Angels, The Mummy, Polyphemus's Eye.

Vulcano seemed raw and unfinished after Lipari. The volcano last exploded only a century ago, and even now the air smelled slightly of sulfur. Near the dock someone had posted a sign declaring this the realm of Vulcan: Dip into the hot springs, it promised, and the hand of the god would "sustain you sweetly, transforming your thoughts into balls of music and color." A little farther, a score of people were bobbing in a pool-size mud bath. As far as I could tell, only their bodies were being transformed, into cartoon figures of slimy gray.

At first the path to the crater was as paved as a Roman road, but it petered into gravel just as it offered up a panorama of the sun-browned islands in a blue sea. As the climb began in earnest, the landscape also altered: An array of pipe-organ fumaroles, warm to the touch, were spouting steam near yellow, sulfurous rocks that had cascaded down the slopes. Flints and shards of obsidian blackened the stony path marked here and there by a red line—which simply disappeared in a wall of boulders. I looked around. Across the water I could see the volcanic observatory on Lipari. If I couldn't find the path again, I wondered, would they sight me in their telescope, waving, worried, and lost?

I scrambled up a crack in the rock wall, and suddenly, there before me, was the trail, winding across a desolate plain toward the summit. As I kept climbing, noxious clouds of sulfur rose like fog from the center of the mountain, alternately hiding and revealing neon peaks in lime, lemon, and orange. Finally I reached the rim of the crater, which looked like a giant mud bath. Someone—guided not by Vulcan but by Cupid—had braved the fumes and descended into it; when the steam blew off, I could make out, printed on the crater floor far below, ROSA ♥ JUV.

■ ■ ■

"We call Panarea the bonbon," a friend on Lipari told me. I wasn't sure exactly what she meant, until I walked the length of the tiny, almond-shaped island. Purple bougainvillea draped bright villas with names like House of the Olives or The Pomegranate. Tall vases were artistically positioned around the houses, which had been painstakingly restored, and tapered columns rose from the corners of the patios, looking vaguely Egyptian in the sun. Precious, and achingly charming, I thought. Santa Fe comes to the Mediterranean.

Twenty years ago Italians from Milan and Rome had begun to buy up houses abandoned by islanders seeking jobs abroad. Panarea took on the stylish lassitude of a fashionable summer resort. I kept hearing about the August madness, when the island was full of boats and beauties and disco frenzy. But now it was late in the season, and I preferred the Panarea I saw. An easygoing village that sprawled beneath a hillside of impenetrable cactus. Sheltered coves that harbored a daily yacht or two. Paths just wide enough for the three-wheeled carts that substituted for cars here.

At the north end of the island I hiked another trail that hairpinned down a bluff to a rocky beach. There were thermal springs, I knew, but aside from some yellowish rocks, I couldn't see any sign of them. As I came closer, I noticed a curved wall of boulders against the hillside. A shovel stood to one side, next to a pair of loafers. Just then a man emerged from behind the rocks, clad only in a mustache. He turned out to be a Scot named Dave—a mechanic who had arrived on the island ten years ago and simply stayed. He genially donned a towel and showed me his handiwork—a natural sauna carved out of the bluff wall, fitted with a wooden slab over the opening. I stuck my head in. Sulfur fumes and steamy heat stung my eyes.

"Here," Dave said, reaching in,

"take some of the mud and put it on. It's good for the skin, for aches and pains." He plastered some on his own arm. "After you've had it on awhile, you can wash it off in the sea.

"There are hot springs in the ocean here," he said, stepping nimbly over the stony beach. "They warm up and cool down with the tides and the time of day."

He showed me three boulder-lined pools at the water's edge — more of his artistry. Steam was rising from the inland pool. I could barely put my foot in. The second one was cooler, except where a hot spring surged up from the seafloor. The third was washed by the waves, and it was cooler still. I told Dave I admired his exclusive health club.

"I keep the place up," he said, "move the boulders back when they fall over. People who know about the place come to use it sometimes."

As if to illustrate his words, a man in a skimpy bathing suit walked down the slope, introduced himself as Andrea, and headed into the natural sauna.

"He's a private pilot for an industrialist in Turin," Dave told me. "He owns a house on the island."

I bumped into Dave several times in the next few days, and saw Andrea again on the beach. The intimacy of Panarea comple-mented the routines of a beach resort. Every morning I swam at a quiet cove along with a standard cast of characters: the pilot; an artist in a pink feathered bathing cap; a lithe, bronzed lady — Signora Thong, we called her — with a beautiful young son; a French family laden with snorkels and fins; the honeymoon couple who kept bottles of champagne chilling in the sea. Just past noon everyone would disappear for lunch — back to a yacht, or into the villas, or perhaps to the trattoria next to the beach.

Afternoons were for lazing and reading, and a cone of *gelati* at the café near the harbor. There was time to watch newcomers arrive by hydrofoil or to see friends off on the ferry. Or to spend an hour in the Raya boutique, where the few Italian antiques were overshadowed by shelves crammed with Indonesian treasures and chairs draped with batiks — baubles of a jet set that is always looking to the next island.

Every night I returned to the same restaurant, where the lively young waitress offered the house specialty: spaghetti *alla fantasia*, "at the whim of the cook." It was always the same description, always a different dish.

Day after day I nodded hello to the same people; then, feeling that I knew them, started conversations. When I stopped to chat with a matron who was sweeping the walk, she showed me the house where she was born and introduced me to her 87-year-old mother.

A woman from Milan told me, as she sunned herself on a hotel balcony overlooking the dock, about her first trip to Panarea. "Twenty-five years ago there was no hotel here," she remembered, "only a garden. And there was a dance floor right at the edge of the sea. There was no electricity then, just candles. And at night people would dress up—for the islands, but not casual like today—and go dancing. It was such a romantic scene."

■ ■ ■

It was raining when I arrived in Stromboli, the first real rain of the entire trip. Under the leaden sky, all the color seemed to have leaked out of the landscape. The beaches were black—fine sand in some places, gravel in others, but always flat black. The familiar square houses had mostly black trim at the windows and doors, instead of the bright blue or green of the other islands. Even the grass that covered the perfect cone of the volcano was more gray than green. Along one ridge a flock of birds circled—crows, of course.

Only the smoke coming from the crater was white. Every few minutes the mountain would roar, and a new stream of clouds, like steam over dry ice, would flow down to be lost in the gathering fog.

It was no day for climbing the volcano. Instead I put on a poncho and went to town. In a broad plaza that served as a sleepy town center, one open-air café was blessed with a brilliant view. It was the Ingrid Club, named for the woman whose movie, and scandalous romance, had put Stromboli on the map. Just down the road a sign on a cherry-colored house explained the connection: "In this house Ingrid Bergman lived when she filmed *Stromboli* with Roberto Rossellini in spring 1949."

The next morning I sat over coffee in the Ingrid Club with wiry, bespectacled Prospero Cultrera, one of Stromboli's official guides. He was lamenting the hikers who ignored warnings and set off on their own to the top of the crater, some 3,000 feet high. "Lots of people go up and simply sleep there," he said. "It becomes a big hotel—the best hotel, because it's free," he added sarcastically. "I don't think that's right. It should be controlled. People bring food and bottles of water and toss them away, as though the volcano were a garbage dump."

Originally from Catania, Prospero had first climbed the volcano 15 years before. "The trail is sandy," he said, "and the higher you go, the more difficult it becomes. People can go up easily enough, but to get down at night is really a problem. This year a Czech girl died, and another boy fell."

After we finished our coffee, Prospero showed me photographs of some of the island's most spectacular lava flows. "Three years ago a seismologist set up a solar-powered monitoring system here," he said. "It shows there are roughly 7,000 eruptions a month on Stromboli."

That night I saw the volcano erupt—on film—as I watched *Stromboli* in the tiny community center. Black-garbed tourists sat at tables jumbled together, drinking beer and cognac and watching the Italian movie, dubbed in German, on a large-screen TV. Ingrid Bergman was less than convincing as a displaced person who marries an islander and returns with him to his remote village. But the melodrama had some wonderful scenes: Island women who shut the beautiful heroine out of their society and their houses—houses I'd seen as I walked around Stromboli. A magnificent fishing sequence of thrashing tuna and the harsh reality of a life dependent on the sea. A panic when the volcano begins to rain down boulders, and the villagers take to the sea to pray and await their fate. And finally the passionate climax, when Bergman leaves her husband and climbs the volcano. Pregnant, wearing high heels and a designer suit, she hikes, then scrambles, and finally claws her way up the cinder slopes, where she greets the dawn at the edge of the crater.

■ ■ ■

I was wearing stout hiking boots when I finally started my own

ascent, carrying a sweater, windbreaker, flashlight, food, mittens, and plenty of water as I joined a dozen others late the next afternoon. Our guide's name was Antonio. Fit, solid, and in his forties, he carried a reassuring walkie-talkie in his substantial backpack. He was born in Lipari, he told me, but he liked it on Stromboli. "It's quiet, except in summer, when there are hordes of people. But the rest of the time, you live well here. There are three or four hundred people. It's a family."

The path to the volcano was centuries old, he told us at the start of the hike. "You need to be agile, but it's still pleasant." His words proved true over the next, increasingly strenuous hour. Finally, overlooking the Sciara del Fuoco—the lava's path of fire— we stopped to catch our breath. Beyond the silhouetted edge of the mountain, against a sky that was a deepening pink, two islands shimmered, the divers' havens of Alicudi and Filicudi.

The trail crumbled to black sand, growing more precipitous until it was almost a series of steps. A half moon was rising over the flank of the crater, which now loomed over my right shoulder. Unsure of the path, I watched Antonio's steps intently and grabbed for support as the path ran upward over steep rocks. Very exposed rocks, it seemed to me.

At last we topped a ridge, and suddenly the volcano welcomed us with a show of sparks. "Is this it?" I asked Antonio. We'd been climbing for nearly two hours. I felt as if I'd been climbing for days. He gestured on ahead. On a distant hill I could see the ant-size shapes of other hikers. Half an hour later, after more slogging through ankle-deep sand, we reached the crater. By then the twilight was so deep it was hard to make out the natural amphitheater that fell away at our feet. But in the darkness the volcano's mouths glowed as though nature had kindled a magnificent campfire. One opening sent up frequent smoky bursts. Another blazed away like a log on some giant's hearth. A third punctuated the night with roars and explosions, shooting great towers of sparks into the air, bringing life and color into the blackness.

■ ■ ■

My Aeolian odyssey came to an end on Salina. From a quiet fishing village I made one last hike, to the saddle between the island's mountains, worn volcanoes of antiquity. Dogs barked, donkeys brayed. And with vineyards stretching beyond me, I looked to the sea at the island's far shore, then slowly started down.

Back at the tiny harbor, I asked in a grocery store for a bottle of malvasia, the sweet wine Marco had mentioned.

"Right there," the proprietress told me, pointing to an unlabeled bottle filled with a golden liquid and sealed with a plain bottle cap.

"Did you make this?" I asked.

"Yes," she said, "on my father's property. You have to grow the grapes specially, then dry them a little, and carefully press them." She demonstrated a wringing motion. "For a lot of land you get very little wine. And sometimes it doesn't come out well in any case."

The woman's words brought home all the hospitality of the islands. I remembered Marco's banquet on Lipari, a feast that began with a home-brewed aperitif, then went on to peasant salad, home-cured olives, sun-dried tomatoes, two pastas, a risotto studded with squash flowers, rabbit in hazelnut sauce, three desserts, and the cook's own grappa. All washed down with a series of *brindisi*—rhyming toasts that celebrated every guest at the crowded table.

I recalled the woman chef on Panarea, who insisted on giving me "little gifts" — a jar of pureed basil for pasta sauce, a container of *peperoncini* to be used as an appetizer, and a huge plastic bag of her own capers. "Just freshen them with water and put them on tomatoes. They have tomatoes in America, don't they?" she had asked.

And I thought of the woman on Salina who had come to her father's birthplace, served me a seaside dinner, and waved me off on the hydrofoil.

These people gave me friendship and a joy in the journey. So can you blame me for my wish, later, when I finally opened the malvasia and the capers and the other delicacies, that those little gifts, like the loosed winds of Aeolus, would carry me back to the islands?

■   ■   ■

This article first appeared in the May/June 1992 issue of Islands *magazine. Tapper is editor in chief and associate publisher of* Islands *magazine in Santa Barbara, California.*

PUT IT INTO PRACTICE

Discussion

1. In chapter fourteen there is a discussion of ethics for travel writers. Read through that section of that chapter and discuss its implications for beginning travel writers. How can you afford to get started in travel writing if you can't afford to travel? Are there ways to break into print that don't require exotic travel? If the Irish Tourist Board offered you an all-expenses-paid five-day tour of Ireland, would you go? What if the free tour offer depended on your having a contract in hand from a magazine to publish the resulting story? What if the tour were specifically with no strings attached?
2. Discuss those aspects of travel writing that you find applicable to other kinds of magazine feature writing. What aspects seem particularly useful? Discuss how particular stories that you've already read in class—either by classmates or from the textbook—could be improved using techniques discussed in this chapter. Cite specific examples when you can.
3. Read the short story found at the end of this book on page 395 and discuss the similarities you can find between that piece of fiction and the literary travel story by Joan Tapper. How do the uses of characterization compare? of setting? of specific detail?

Exercises

1. You want to write a travel story about the place where your campus or writers' group is located. At first, you don't think there's really much to tell (or, if you're located in a tourist area, you think it has all already been told), but when you begin to look for fresh angles, you realize there are several. List five of them. (Hint: If you're not in a tourist area, don't be afraid to expand this idea to your state or region, and then begin to look for the unusual angle.)
2. You are the travel editor of a large daily newspaper, and you receive numerous submissions from beginning writers. Using several stories by your classmates, choose one or two that hold particular appeal for you as the editor, and, in a paragraph or two about each story, explain why. If others in your class or writers' group haven't yet written stories, have them submit ideas (a few paragraphs long) and go through the same decision process.
3. You are the editor of an automobile club magazine. Go through the

same selection process for stories and/or ideas. How relevant are these stories for your readers? Why is one story chosen over another?

4. You are the editor of *Islands* magazine. Go through the same selection process for stories and/or ideas. Again, how do these stories seem to work for your readers? Why is one story chosen over another?

THE PERSONALITY PROFILE

WHOM TO WRITE ABOUT

IN-DEPTH PROFILES

SPECIALIZED PROFILES

Steve Friedman is senior editor at *Gentleman's Quarterly* magazine. A few years ago, serving in that same position at *St. Louis* magazine, he developed the habit of reading through the crime roundup in his local paper each morning over that first cup of coffee, looking for interesting ideas—those out-of-the-ordinary items that can sometimes lead to major pieces.

One morning, Friedman remembers, "I saw a tiny little item about this guy who'd been arrested for shoplifting and then he'd resisted being arrested and been sent to jail. It said the guy's name was Marshall Rogers."

That was a name Friedman recognized from years before, a name that had once really meant something to Friedman and to everyone else in St. Louis who loved the game of basketball.

"Marshall Rogers was a couple of years older than I am, and when I played high school basketball, he was the star of stars of high school ball in St. Louis," Friedman recalls.

"He'd played college ball after that and even made it to the NBA. This story mentioned he hadn't worked for three years before the arrest. I thought, well, what a great story, you know, the rise and fall."

So Friedman got started on a personality piece that he thought would be a moving, if unsurprising, story about a star athlete gone wrong.

Several weeks of interviewing and research later, Friedman found a very different story from the one he'd thought he'd find. There were, Friedman discovered, some tragic surprises involved in the fall of Marshall Rogers. In a lengthy, moving piece for his magazine, Friedman uncovered those surprises.

Jeff Weinstock is a successful freelance writer who often writes for *Sport* magazine. Weinstock, working on his own and frequently dealing with busy athletes during their season, rarely gets the kind of time Friedman had for research and interviewing. For his personality profiles for *Sport,* Weinstock is lucky to have an hour or two over dinner with a famous athlete. Still, Weinstock gets the job done, and with considerable style. He frequently focuses on those aspects of the athlete's life that most of the fans don't know about, and he tries to make the athlete a real person for the reader.

In much the same sense, *Ebony* writer Karima Haynes often has little time in which to get her information as she interviews famous personalities. As we found out in chapter one, Haynes had about a half-hour to interview Senate candidate Carol Moseley Braun, for instance, and had to do a taped interview over the rattle of the propellers on Braun's small campaign plane. But Haynes got what she needed, and she combined it with her extensive research to pull together an effective story that helped illuminate the soon-to-be Senator Braun for *Ebony*'s readers.

All of these writers were involved in one of the most common types of magazine stories: the *personality profile.*

As you've just seen from the examples that open this chapter, there is a wide variety to these kinds of stories. Access to the personality, available space in the magazine, the special needs of the editor, and a number of other factors all have an impact on the kind of story you'll write and how you'll structure the piece. But there are general areas of commonality, beginning with the idea that what most good profiles try to do is either expand the reader's knowledge about an already well-known personality or inform the reader about a previously unknown personality.

WHOM TO WRITE ABOUT

Tied in with the two foregoing items is the idea that there are basically two kinds of people worth doing personality pieces on, those with existing news value and those without existing news value who nevertheless who have something about them that makes them interesting.

Those with news value may be famous athletes, musicians, Hollywood stars, business executives, or even criminals. The key is that they are already well-known, and readers want to know more about them. Readers are eagerly waiting for you to expand their knowledge of the personality, as noted earlier.

In a sense, you're dealing with objectification when you write personality pieces on celebrities like these. Such persons have become objects of attention in the public eye, and in most cases that objectification tends to emphasize certain aspects of their character and de-emphasize others. The public gets a highly simplified version of these personalities (usually through brief stories about them in newspapers or on television).

This objectification works to your advantage as a magazine writer because it offers you the opportunity to find out the "real" personality and then tell your readers about it. And you'll find that there is always room for additional information on even the most famous of personalities. Take a look at Jeff Weinstock's piece on Charles Barkley at the end of this chapter as an example. Weinstock offers fresh insights into one of professional basketball's most famous players.

Beginning writers often find that the most difficult part of the reporting and writing process for personality profiles is simply getting to the personality for an interview. Finding access to a famous public figure long enough to do an interview can be difficult even for established writers, and downright impossible for a beginner.

There are two ways for beginners to solve this problem. The first is to *write about those famous personalities that you* do *have some access to.* Don't defeat yourself up front by going after a personality profile when getting an interview is highly unlikely. Instead, change your target to something more attainable. If you're a college student, perhaps your parents or their friends know a celebrity. Try that connection to get an interview and then work to sell that story. It's surprising how often such connections exist. The author has had students who had connections with major league baseball players, professional basketball and football players, Miss America winners, *Playboy* playmates, famous musicians, and top political figures. In most cases, it hadn't dawned on these students that the person they had access to would make for a good story. In almost all cases, however, once the student pursued it, the story came to life.

Later, after you've done a few of these and had them published, you'll begin to have a little more clout as a writer, and the access problem should begin to ease.

The second answer, assuming you don't have any connections to celebrities, is to *search for personalities who have undiscovered news value.* This isn't as difficult as you might think. There are any number of people with news value not because of their celebrity status but because of what they do, or because of something that has happened in their life, or because they are examples of something of news value.

These kinds of stories could include, for instance, a piece on a firefighter, a police officer, an AIDS victim, a homeless person, or a fighter pilot. Right in your neighborhood there may be a Holocaust survivor, or a World War II veteran of Pearl Harbor, or a Vietnam veteran who was there for the Tet Offensive of 1968. Handle it in the right way, bringing the memories and human reality of these people into the story, and you can write a personality piece on these people that has real merit for any number of magazines.

Think of the personality pieces found in the opening of this chapter and elsewhere in this book and ask yourself how each fits into these two broad categories.

Carol Moseley Braun, for instance, is certainly a public figure with established news value. Marshall Rogers held a great deal of news value at one point in time, though at the time the story was written he was more a symbol of the classic athlete's postcareer troubles. Charles Barkley is a good example of the news value of top athletes.

But several other stories in this book focus on people who are not in the news but are involved in something the writer (and the editor who bought the story) found interesting.

Think of John Morthland's stories on Habanero chile farmer Jeff Campbell, or musician Butch Hancock (at the end of this chapter), or John Calderazzo's piece on grave digger Tom Bridinger, or Deidre Sullivan's piece on intuition expert Bill Kautz, or Joe Bargmann's piece on the wrongly convicted Steve Ferndo.

None of these people were broadly known before these articles brought them to public attention, but each of them was involved in something the writer found newsworthy, and an editor agreed.

Once you know whom you are doing the story on, you need to realize that different magazines need different things in a personality story. Those needs are as varied as the magazines themselves, of course, but there are two general types to these stories. We might roughly break them into *in-depth profiles* and *specialized profiles*.

IN-DEPTH PROFILES

The *in-depth profile* is the sort of story that Steve Friedman got to write with some frequency during his time in St. Louis. This kind of lengthy profile has been a powerful, effective staple of the city magazines for more than two decades.

Recent trends toward shorter stories have cut into the depth that was once a hallmark of these stories, but even at shorter length, these kinds of stories are well liked by many writers, and for good reasons. In-depth stories give the writer the chance to combine lengthy interviewing and research with high-style writing. The result is often the kind of stylish writing discussed in chapter six.

The important aspects of reporting for the in-depth personality profile are those contained in your interviewing and research skills. Take another look at chapters one and two to see if you can't pick up some hints on how to go about finding the information you'll need to be ready to write.

The structure of the in-depth profile can be handled in several ways, including the *chronological approach,* the *day-in-the-life approach,* the *scenic approach* (that is, built around dramatic scenes), and the *historical approach.* Importantly, these approaches are frequently blended into one story. Steve Friedman's piece on Marshall Rogers is a smooth blend of several of these approaches. At first glance, the story seems to be chronological and historical in structure, incorporating a great deal of Rogers's background and bringing the reader from Rogers's youth to his current state. But there are a number of very vivid scenes, too, each of which tells us something important about Rogers and his mental problems. Listen to the simple, straightforward presentation of this scene:

> Rogers is standing at the free-throw line in the gym at Vic Tanny on Dorsett and I–270. His right arm is cocked in a U, and a scowl splits his face. He hits 34 free throws without missing, and without smiling. Then he hits 31 without missing, then 17. The only sounds are the clanking of the weight machines nearby and the rock music being piped over the fitness center's sound system. That and the occasional bounce of the basketball on the floor, and the swish of the net. And Marshall's muttering. He is talking to the voices.

Friedman recalls that as the interviewing went on for this story, "I knew I had some great scenes, when he was shooting baskets, when we were in the cafeteria, when we were in the car."

Friedman's writing technique consists of doing much of his outlining and note-taking on his computer, so, as he recalls, "I thought I'd just get those scenes into my computer. I wrote them and as I did I realized that this was a great story of rise and fall just using these scenes."

A short story writer might have left it at that, pulling together these powerful scenes into a story that slowly opens up Rogers's problems. But a nonfiction writer also has to *inform directly.* The reader needs to know enough about Rogers's life to make clear sense of these scenes. You can't let that material be in the subtext, to be guessed at or sensed subconsciously, as you might in writing fiction.

So, Friedman says, "I wrote them and then thought, well, I could just intersperse them. It seemed to come easily. Maybe it wasn't that easy—most of them aren't—but I remember it that way."

Friedman knew he had such strong visual and emotional pictures of Rogers that he could rely on them to carry nearly the full weight of the storytelling.

Importantly, looking back on the story now, Friedman sees that "There are some parts of the chronology where I really tried to put in some good language that now sounds contrived to me. They sound like I labored over them, which is probably a good lesson for writers. Just tell the story as simply as you can."

National judges of writing excellence disagreed with Friedman's assessment of that good language. It didn't sound at all contrived to them, and *The Sporting News* voted the story one of the best sports stories of the year for 1988.

Friedman basically breaks down the structure of this story into two elements—the *scenes* and the *chronology*—with one several-paragraph insertion coming right after the lead to inform the reader of the story's basic background. He also knew that as part of the chronology he had to insert sentences or paragraphs (called *nutgraphs*) of factual support for what he was saying about Rogers.

"I had the scenes, and I had the chronology of Rogers's life, but I also had to fit in this kind of nutgraph section—parts here and there where I just displayed the research—so the reader would know that the material is valid.

"You know," Friedman adds, "the very best magazine writers don't use that nut section, because the narrative is so seamless that it keeps it going. But I did in this. I felt like I wanted to tell the story from little boy to the present, and support that time line, and then insert those scenes from today to keep hammering home the pain and confusion and the drama of his life."

So Friedman built a structure that has each scene followed by a section of chronology. You can see the success of that structure in his story at the end of this chapter.

SPECIALIZED PROFILES

The *specialized profile* is that story written for a magazine with a particular focus into which the profile has to fit. Jeff Weinstock's personality profiles for *Sport* magazine are a good example. Readers of *Sport* magazine are fans, and the stories in the magazine have to give those fans the sort of information they expect about the athletes. Statistics, for example, are often important to sports fans.

There are quite literally hundreds of specialized magazines, focused on everything from road building to rock climbing to surfing to sailing. In each case, the personality profile published in that magazine has to pay particular attention to the expectations and needs of a specialized audience.

The best writers, though, use those basic expectations and needs merely as a starting point when they write a profile. Their stories certainly contain the information readers expect, but writers then go on to expand readers' knowledge of the personality, pushing the story in directions readers didn't necessarily expect. In that way, writers manage to build a sense of broad knowledge about a personality, making the person more real and less of a cardboard cutout.

It requires ambitious reporting and stylish writing to produce this kind of personality profile, and it entails a certain risk, since in some cases the personality (and even the readers) won't like the accurate picture you've portrayed. What they want is the cardboard construction the public normally gets to see. But many editors (and many readers as well) love these kinds of profiles, and if you do a good job of this type of story, assignments from grateful editors will come your way.

Jeff Weinstock enjoys writing this kind of personality profile. "I try to make sure and illuminate the athlete beyond the field or the court," Weinstock explains. "When you interview these athletes, you learn that they're complex persons, with a lot going on. I see my duty as trying to make the reader aware of those complexities."

Structure

For the structure of a specialized profile, Weinstock searches for those elements of the athlete that are unexpected, or unknown, to the reader, and he then builds a story that skillfully weaves the new information into better-known aspects of the player.

Notice how, in the story on Charles Barkley, Weinstock opens with a passage that meets the reader's expectations of the well-known "fire-breathing Phoenix Suns power forward [who] hates trespassers. 'If you mess with me, I'm gonna get you,' he warns."

Then, a few paragraphs later, Weinstock expands the knowledge of Barkley by adding that Barkley "has a sunny side, too, enough to warm a tribe of Iditarod dog-sled racers."

In the next paragraph he establishes a theme for the story by noting that, for Barkley, "One act of mayhem is countered by one act of kindness." Weinstock then gives examples.

This structure allows him to build a story that takes the reader into an expanded knowledge of Barkley, beginning with the flamboyance that is already known and adding on the new information about Barkley's softer side.

One of the problems in writing personality profiles for specialized readerships is that the similarities in focus make it difficult to find those elements of interest that make the story really come alive. There is often a wealth of information on the personality, but very little of it makes the subject different from a host of other basketball players or actors or rock climbers. *It is your job as a writer to discover that something that makes each personality special and to let the reader know about it.*

Jeff Weinstock finds that a large quantity of research long before he ever interviews the athlete helps him discover those special elements. In a story he wrote on basketball player Chuck Person, for instance, Weinstock recalls, "In the process of preparing for that interview I asked the PR person for the team who were Chuck's most important influences and was it OK with Chuck if I spoke to them. Chuck said it was, and they gave me some phone numbers, so I spoke to his wife and his high school coach, his college coach, his sister—all of those interviews came before I ever talked to Chuck."

It can be time-consuming, and sometimes a large amount of research produces a small amount of copy: "I interviewed Chuck's high school coach for 90 minutes," Weinstock says, "and I used one sentence from that whole conversation."

But it takes this kind of hard work to find those things that other writers haven't uncovered. In talking to Person's sister, for example, Weinstock came across a special family nickname for the player that wound up being an important part of the story.

"I just happened to ask her—that interview hadn't really gone very well—if he had any nicknames as a kid, and she mentioned 'Deeboo' and then told me the story about the name." The nickname, and its implications, constituted just the sort of thing Weinstock was looking for, and he used it in his opening.

"I always try to open up the story in a way that's an attention grabber, so the person doesn't just flip by and onto the next story, and also in a way that's going to capture the athlete and open up a theme I'm going to deal with.

"The main idea with Chuck Person is that he's two different people, and this nickname really talked to that. So I went with it."

In print, the story's opening looked like this:

Deeboo has them big eyes, see. That's how you know when he's around. Otherwise it's pretty much Chuck Person you're talking to, softspoken, serious, sadder, darker, unsatisfied. But when you see the big eyes and the head starts to juke a bit and the words come in tremors and sentences start spilling over each other in their haste to be heard and the big eyes, you know, kind of crackle, filled with a memory, you know Chuck Person has a second soul. He saves Deeboo for the right time. Else he might lose that edge. But Deeboo has the juice, has the stories. The big eyes are out now.

Validating the Story

In specialized magazines it is quite common to write stories about personalities without prior news value. In those cases, the story may be the first information that readers have received about the personality, and so more background and contextual material may be necessary. *This material helps validate the story for the reader.*

For instance, a major point for John Morthland's piece on singer/songwriter Butch Hancock is the artist's relative obscurity. Morthland makes this clear in the second paragraph when he calls Hancock "the best-known unknown on the folk circuit," even though the artist has no major record label.

In other words, it is entirely possible that even though the piece was written for *Texas Monthly* and Hancock lives in Austin, this will be the first acquaintance that many of the readers will have with this interesting, talented musician.

"For Butch Hancock, I had at least three or four hours of interviewing for a 1,500-word piece, so I knew I had a lot of great quotes to work with. But the whole point is that the guy is unknown, so I had to insert a lot of background material, too," explains Morthland.

Notice how in the second paragraph Morthland not only establishes Hancock's fame as "the best-known unknown" but also gives the artist credibility both by connecting him to a "gifted generation of Lubbock musicians" and by pointing out that many of the more famous singers use Hancock's material.

A member of the inexplicably gifted generation of Lubbock musicians that includes Terry Allen, the Maines Brothers, Joe Ely, and Jimmie Dale Gilmore, Hancock has been a critic's favorite and the Texas songwriter's Texas songwriter for the past fifteen years. Ely has recorded enough of Hancock's material to fill an entire album, and Emmylou Harris introduced his "If You Were a Bluebird" to the mass country audience. Hancock's remarkably broad but unified body of work has made him the best-known unknown on the folk circuit and has even won him write-ups in the *New York Times*—yet no major record label has ever offered him a contract.

This kind of validation is necessary in a personality profile that works to establish news value for someone not previously newsworthy. Morthland does a fine job of it: making sure the needs and expectations of the specialized readership of *Texas Monthly* are met and then accomplishing one of the roles of this kind of story that we talked about in the opening of the chapter—expanding the reader's knowledge of the personality. You can read the piece in its entirety at the end of this chapter.

■ ■ ■

PLAINS SONG

BY JOHN MORTHLAND

As always, Butch Hancock is doing two or three things at once. Sitting in his Austin office, dressed in cutoffs and a T-shirt from a Los Angeles guitar shop, he intently considers an interviewer's question, while just as intently strumming an acoustic guitar he is restringing and tuning. Then, getting up from his chair, he walks to a wall of twenty cassette-tape duplicators, opens each one up, and flips the tapes over two at a time, one with each hand.

A member of the inexplicably gifted generation of Lubbock musicians that includes Terry Allen, the Maines Brothers, Joe Ely, and Jimmie Dale Gilmore, Hancock has been a critic's favorite and the Texas songwriter's Texas songwriter for the past fifteen years. Ely has recorded enough of Hancock's material to fill an entire album, and Emmylou Harris introduced his "If You Were a Bluebird" to the mass country audience. Hancock's remarkably broad but unified body of work has made him the best-known unknown on the folk circuit and has even won him write-ups in the *New York Times*—yet no major record label has ever offered him a contract.

The cassettes he is making document the six nights of shows he put on at Austin's Cactus Cafe

in early 1990. During the stand, which Butch dubbed "No 2 Alike," he performed 140 originals, ranging from "In Another World," the fifth song he ever wrote, to "One Kiss" and "Unknown Love," both of which he was just finishing. Starting in September 1990, he has released one *No 2 Alike* cassette each month and sold them mainly by mail order. Butch expects to sell a couple thousand of each to his diehard followers.

Although he's a word man in song and a world-class talker, the lanky, sandy-haired Hancock is not an easy interview. He answers questions with parables or long, detailed explanations that sound like thinking out loud until he gets to his summation sentence, which invariably makes it clear that he has given the subject plenty of thought. But the explanation rambles too far to make much sense on the printed page, and the summation sentence doesn't stand on its own without the rest; quoting it alone would make him sound glib, which he definitely isn't.

When he talks about a projected trip to Lubbock, he speaks of "reinvestigating self-history." Then he explains his distrust of self-investigation: "It tends to get into egocentric lying to self, drifting off into reverie." This is a man who once photographed Austin crosswalks as they were distorted by the heat of car exhaust because he felt the images would reveal important truths about the land; he still believes the photos do just that, though he can't say what the truths are, only that they are there. "There's still life going on in the rocks and the trees and the hills," Butch declares. "It's sort of reincarnation, but it's more omni-incarnation. And it's not new-agey, it's ancient."

Talk like that sometimes seems a little too much to digest, but Butch's real gift is that when he sits down to write about those subjects, he is able to recast them into earthy tunes like "Fools Fall in Love." The life going on in those rocks and trees and hills is conveyed in a finely delineated borderland love story like "Leo y Leona." The weary western ballad "Only Born" somehow evolved out of his meditations on eternal recurrence, while "Real World Kid," a new one with a good shot at anthem status, captures the oppressive weariness of mainstream American politics. ("We got a vice president who can hardly read/We got another president we hardly need/I don't know how they got elected, but they did.")

And it's pretty near impossible not to warm up to a guy who writes an ongoing saga like "Split and Slide," a piece of slapstick storytelling that bounces words off each other for the sheer delight of seeing what happens when they collide. Amidst a comical overload of puns and alliteration, the characters Split and Slide wander into the song for no apparent reason, then drift back out. When he wrote "Split and Slide II," Butch borrowed characters from previous songs of his, as well as from Townes Van Zandt's "Mr. Mudd and Mr. Gold." Butch is now working on "Split and Slide III," which he envisions as a marathon narrative for live performances featuring several artists. To introduce a performer, Butch would do five minutes of "Split and Slide," using the artist's characters and imagery. Before the next act, Butch would do five more minutes of "Split and Slide," and so on.

Butch started writing songs back in the heyday of the sixties' folk movement, when he was driving a tractor near Lubbock for his father, an earth-moving contractor. He still calls his musical style—singsong talking blues with pinched nasal vocals—"tractor music." To Butch, his songs invoke the rhythms of life on the High Plains, and when you hear him moan "Wind's Dominion" or chortle through "West Texas Waltz," the description makes perfect sense.

Hancock has favored the Bob Dylan/Woody Guthrie guitar-and-harmonica setup from the beginning, inflecting his country-folk melodies with bluegrass and a dab of early rock and roll. But it took him a couple of false starts before he got serious about music.

First, he took stabs at architecture school at Texas Tech in between trips to San Francisco, where he concentrated on photography. Eventually, Hancock joined with Ely and Gilmore to form the Flatlanders in Lubbock in 1971. The novel folk-country outfit headed off to Nashville "to become rich and famous," Butch recalls. Instead, the Flatlanders wound up with one album (which was unreleased until last year) and a standing ovation at the 1972 Kerrville Folk Festival. Then they promptly broke up.

Butch moved to Clarendon, where he did construction work. By 1973, he was living in Austin, where he began to make music again while doing carpentry and redesigning a train station in Seguin, among other projects. In the mid-eighties, he even produced a cable live-music show, *Dixie's Bar and Bus Stop*. Meanwhile, Jimmie Dale Gilmore delved into mysticism and eventually wound up in Austin. After making two solo records for an independent label and *Two Roads*, a Gilmore-Hancock Australian release, Gilmore finally made his major-label debut, *After Awhile*, last July. Ely formed the Joe Ely Band, an endlessly resourceful group that was quickly recognized as one of the crackerjack bands of the era. The band's first album, released in 1977, featured four Hancock-written gems (including "If You Were a Bluebird," perhaps Butch's best-known effort). The next three Ely albums included nine more

Hancock tunes that were critically hailed. Butch watched with semidetached interest as the Ely band was torn apart nonetheless, with record-company politics widely cited as the main cause.

Though his music has taken him as far away as Europe and Australia, Butch remains committed to his photography and his architectural drawings. He has worked solo and with the Sunspots, an Austin rock band, playing mostly Austin clubs and international folk festivals. Occasionally he gets plum assignments, such as opening for the Cowboy Junkies, a popular Canadian folk-country band. Most recently, he has been performing with Gilmore again. Before *No 2 Alike*, he released eight recordings on his own Rainlight Records label, plus a British best-of set, which will soon be released in the U.S. on Sugarhill Records. Early this year, he opened Lubbock or Leave It, a small gallery in downtown Austin, where he displays his photos and whatever other art catches his eye; he also sells everything from his records to Stubb's Bar B Q Sauce, made by Lubbock barbecue legend C. B. Stubblefield. He has moved his tape-duplicating equipment and his darkroom to the gallery from the Airstream trailer that he lives in near downtown. Hancock insists that all of his pursuits reinforce each other and that his other projects keep him from burning out musically.

"There's incredible relaxation in

staying busy with so many different things. A lot of my work is a form of play," he says. "But now you're talking me into doing two things I hate to do more than anything else. One is being my own historian, and the other is talking about my own songwriting."

With all of his other interests, Butch Hancock doesn't need the validation of a major-label contract. Like other idiosyncratic artists who don't fit into today's mass-marketing systems, Butch has figured out that he can do just as well by doing it all himself. But anyone who is as prolific and popular as Butch Hancock has to at least consider the question of his own place in the record business. "I find it kind of interesting that no major label has ever approached me," he admits. "But really, I have never really pursued a major label either. Why do I want to sell more records? It's the old Groucho deal of not wanting to be in any group that would have me. But the whole question is not something I can spend much time thinking about, because you could drive yourself crazy that way. So I'm gonna go on doing what I'm gonna do, and if people pick up on it, that's wonderful. And if they don't, I can always drive a tractor.

"I mean, after all, I'm just in it for the cabrito."

■   ■   ■

This article first appeared in the November 1991 issue of Texas Monthly.

■ ■ ■

REBEL YELL

BY JEFF WEINSTOCK

Upon entering Charlesville, a word of caution: Step lightly. The proprietor, a Mr. Charles Barkley, fire-breathing Phoenix Suns power forward, hates trespassers. "If you mess with me, I'm gonna get you," he warns. He will too. Popped that beanpole Angolan last summer just for looking at him funny. And wipe your feet. He keeps a neat house.

Don't ask him any cotton-candied questions about being black in America, else you'll have to hear his whole Sidney Poitier spiel from *Guess Who's Coming to Dinner:* "I'm just a man. I'm not a black man, I'm not a white man, I'm just a man." Whatever.

And please, read the sign: Heckling is not permitted, no exceptions. Barkley's got an itchy spitter. Once, following a game in New Jersey, he approached a man who had dogged him all night, reached out as if to show there were no hard feelings, and when the man stuck out his own hand, Barkley spat in it.

A couple of seasons ago, in the infamous Night of the Wayward Loogie, responding to a spectator's string of obscenities, Barkley spat in anger. Regrettably, he soaked an 8-year-old girl. His image took a severe hit. Oh, just one last thing.

Charles Wade Barkley would like you to know that he doesn't give a plug nickel about image.

"What is image?" he says. "Image has nothing to do with life. Image don't mean anything to me. What is image?"

But Sir Charles, knighted, it seems, by popular demand, has a sunny side, too, enough to warm a tribe of Iditarod dog-sled racers. With his public, a finer fellow you will not meet, charming, civil, inexhaustibly gracious. Indeed, you cannot come to a full accounting of Charles Barkley until you have watched him work a room. In one two-hour lunch break, he received a steady stream of autograph seekers, handshakes, offers of sex (actually, there was just that one) and photo requests. In return, he accommodated every appeal, except for that sex one, and left all his well-wishers in brighter spirits than when they approached.

See, this is what we do with Barkley. One act of mayhem is countered by one act of kindness. It has become something of a game to try to figure out which side of Creation has control over his soul. And for all of his ravings about the rough treatment he gets from the press, it is Barkley's every intention to keep people guessing. He steals a moment to whisper, "Don't let 'em know I'm a nice guy."

■   ■   ■

"I didn't say anything bad in my book [his autobiography, Outrageous]."

You ripped players.

"Who did I rip?"

Armon Gilliam. You called him Mr. Macho Rebounder.

"No I didn't. Get the book. I guarantee you I didn't say that. I said he's a good scorer, he just doesn't want to rebound, which is just a fact."

Then you said he turned out not to be much of a scorer.

"No, no, now, that was one of the misquotes of the book. They just wrote the words wrong. I said he's just not a good rebounder, that's it. . . . I don't think that was bad enough to hurt a guy's feelings. If it offended him, sorry to hear that."

You'll speak your mind regardless if it insults your teammates?

"Why should I have to lie to people?"

You called [76ers director of player personnel] Gene Shue a caddie.

"He is a caddie. He deserves that. He said some things about me. An eye for an eye."

■   ■   ■

In conversation, Barkley says often, "Ask me a question, and I'll tell you the truth," brandishing the statement as if it were a sword. And if he feels pinched, he'll stick you with it. As his aggravation grew in his final two seasons in Philadelphia, Barkley called the owner cheap, his teammates stiffs and the city racist.

The thing about Barkley is, he doesn't run his words through the customary filters. In that way, he is childlike in his truth-telling. Barkley is the boy who says to the man with the big nose, "Hey, you've got a big nose," before his mother shoos him away. Where we pause or hedge or qualify, Barkley acts. Barkley speaks. No thought is reviewed or purified before it is sicked on the world. There are no speed bumps. He barrels from moment to moment, reverses, contradicts, denies, contradicts the denial, denies the contradiction, contradicts the contradiction and denies the denial.

But one can't help but love him for it, because there is something terribly appealing about someone brazen enough to, as Barkley did last year, deny having read or written parts of his own autobiography, although he did stop short of denying having lived them. Or maybe it's that round face, shaped as it is like a grin, which assures you that he means no malice. And at least in his own mind, everything adds up. "When I sit down to pray at night," Barkley says, "I say, 'God, I hope it's worth it, telling the truth all the time.'"

■   ■   ■

The Angolan incident.

"Anybody I play against is gonna get hit."

Your teammates didn't back you up.

"That's another misconception from the media. They pulled me aside and said, 'We don't need you getting thrown out of the game. We need you for this team to win.'"

David Robinson and Michael Jordan both said that your behavior reflected badly on the rest of the team.

"Well, I can't expect all those guys to stick by me. You've got some sellouts in the group. . . . If I hit a guy like that in the NBA, they would call it intimidating. But because they were trying to make money out of the Olympics, a couple of the brothers wanted to sell me out. I can understand that."

■　■　■

No one has ever quite wanted to deal with Barkley's excesses. The league hits him with fines, which Barkley pays off with as much pause as he does the cable bill. "They say that how you break into this league is how you will be your entire career," says Utah Jazz president Frank Layden. "I think when [Barkley] was a young player coming out of college, he had an awful lot of leeway and has never changed. If anything, he has expanded."

In Phoenix, the "incidents," the occasional fighting, spitting, after-hours dust-up, are seen as part of the package. "We take the total package," says his new boss, Suns president Jerry Colangelo, which is a coded way of saying, we'll put up with his eruptions as long as he delivers 25 points and 12 boards a night. Says his new teammate Danny Ainge: "I think a lot of people misinterpret his antics and his quotes. They read too much into them. I think Charles is just having fun."

Fine, but the problem in taking Barkley as entertainment is that he does have serious things to say. On these things, he is consistent. He continues to insist that some fringe white players make NBA rosters because management understands that an all-black team would offend segments of the league's audience. "I wouldn't expect Phoenix to have an all-black team," he says, echoing what he said of Philadelphia last year. "You just gotta accept what kind of country we live in. It's a racist country, and that's just the way it is."

He has a curious love/hate relationship with the media. We love him, he hates us. It's the devil media, Barkley says, who regard any opinionated black man as a renegade. According to Barkley, the press creates an athlete's public image by identifying him either as a "good guy" or a "bad guy" and then portraying him in that light.

"The black athletes know this," he says, "and they feed on it, trying to keep their image straight."

But the price of being Sir Charles, the personality, is that what you say is less important than the fact that it's you saying it. There was a poet who, comparing his own voice to that of a hawk, wrote, "I too am not a bit tamed, I too am untranslatable/I sound my barbaric yawp over the rooftops of the world." So it seems we now look on Barkley. Crazy Uncle Charles, howling off in the corner about something or other. Which, in Barkley's eyes, wouldn't be the worst way to view him. Better Uncle Charles than Uncle Tom.

■   ■   ■

"Don't give me that crap about leadership. You got good players, you're gonna win. Was Michael Jordan a bad leader when Chicago wasn't winning?"

But—

"There's no but. Michael Jordan is great. And he couldn't win a championship until he got better players around him. So was he a bad leader in the beginning? No. Thank you."

Well—

"When he criticized [Chicago Bulls general manager] Jerry Krause [a few years ago], was he a bad leader? No. When he said he needed some help, was he a bad leader? No. But Michael Jordan's a good guy by the press, he can say that stuff. Charles Barkley's outspoken, he's not gonna kiss the media's butt, so they're gonna get on him if something happens. OK. See, I know my stuff. They can't fool me. I know them guys. They're just a bunch of jealous nitwits, the media. They're jealous because you've got a good job, they have

to follow you around and be at your beck and call, and you make a lot of money. And if you don't kiss up to them, they don't like that.

"Michael's one of my best friends, but if he said some things that I said, it wouldn't be a big deal, because he's a good guy. Like if he said people would be offended by an all-black team, everybody would agree with that. I know he won't say that."

■   ■   ■

Once, when he was 8, a young Charles Barkley, convinced that he could fly, strapped on a Superman cape and leaped off the roof of the housing project in which he lived. When he awoke from the resulting concussion, he had learned otherwise. "I now know I can't fly," he says.

It's the only concession to limits Barkley will give. As he charts an earthbound passage to his first NBA title, one can expect him to continue to sound his barbaric yawp over the rooftops of the world, not a bit tamed, nor always translatable.

■   ■   ■

Do you worry that some people think of you as a loudmouth instead of a great basketball player?

"Man, let me tell you some- thing. When I quit playing basket- ball, I hope my teams won a lot of games and I hope I did the best I could."

But—

"Don't say but, 'cause when

you say but, you're trying to cover something up. I do the best I can. If somebody thinks I'm not that good a player, so be it. They're entitled to their opinions, but I'm not living by their expectations."

Do you want to be remembered a certain way?

"Hey, listen, nobody remembers you when you're gone, don't kid yourself. Don't kid yourself."

You don't worry about your legacy?

"Legacy? My legacy is that I did a helluva job as long as I was around."

■   ■   ■

This article first appeared in the February 1993 issue of Sport magazine. Weinstock is a full-time freelance writer in Los Angeles, California.

■ ■ ■

FALLING STAR

BY STEVE FRIEDMAN

On good days, Marshall Rogers can almost remember what it feels like to be rich and famous. Flipping through the scrapbooks he never allows to leave his room, he is struggling to make this a good day.

"I scored 58 here," he says, and stabs a finger at a yellowed clipping, then at me. "Here," he says, and flips the page, "this is where I scored my 1,000th point. There. That's Lamar. I used them up. I had 18 the first year we played them. The next year I had 44." He flips to another curled piece of paper. "I had 58 points here. This is important. Look at this."

It is late July, the kind of hazy, sweaty day when even little children in this North St. Louis neighborhood stay off the streets and cling to patches of shade on their front porches. We are sitting in Rogers' bedroom on the top floor of his mother's house. A fan blows hot, stale air around the cramped room, over the chessboard that sits on a footlocker between two beds, ruffling the pictures of naked women that plaster the walls. In a corner, nearly hidden, is a shiny, bronzed basketball engraved on its base. It says, "Marshal [sic] Rogers, The National Scoring Champ, NCAA

Division I 36.8." Rogers received it in 1976, the year he scored more points than anyone else in major college basketball. He picks it up, rubs the top of it, mutters something to someone who is not there.

Then he shouts. "Hey, you've heard of Willie Smith [former basketball player at Mizzou]? They retired his number, right? Willie Smith never scored 58 points. They're crazy. Don't you think so? See what I'm saying?"

■ ■ ■

People remember Marshall Rogers. He was one of the inner city's success stories. A role model. By the time he graduated from Sumner High School in 1971, he wasn't just a high school All-America basketball player. He was also the school's Scholar-Athlete. And when he left Pan American University on a spring day in 1976, he held, as well as a slew of scoring records, a bachelor's degree in history.

Did mothers tell their little boys about Marshall? Did they say it was OK to run outside and play, as long as they remembered to study—like Marshall? The children surely paid attention, because Marshall was living their dream. People paid him to play basketball. He was on television.

For a few glorious months in the winter of 1977, he worked for the Golden State Warriors, and on days he wanted to tool around the San Francisco Bay area, he hopped into a green Cordoba, or a lavender Mark V. Sometimes he tooled around in a yellow van with "Warriors" emblazoned on the side. He made $45,000 a year. That was a long time ago.

This past June, a downtown drugstore manager spotted Rogers stuffing something into his gym bag. When the manager searched it, he found a bottle of Mennen Skin Bracer, a stick of Adidas deodorant, a pair of white sunglasses and three Baby Ruth candy bars. Total value: $13.

Rogers has lived with his mother for at least three years. He hasn't worked steadily this decade.

Hometown heroes often fall, but rarely from such dizzying heights, and seldom to such public lows ("Ex-Sumner, Pro Player Held in Melee," said the headline in the *St. Louis Post-Dispatch*). Marshall Rogers seemed to have it all, and when he lost it, those who knew him groped for explanations.

"Living in the past," said a man who played against Rogers in high school. "Like a lot of inner-city kids," said one of his college coaches, "who can never give up that dream of playing big-time basketball."

Impatience, said his mother. "He always wanted to jump fast. You can't jump fast if you're new."

Pride, said one of his two ex-wives. "He probably feels that things should be better because they were better. . . . He will have to go back down, in a sense, to get back up."

Rogers is proud, of course, and impatient. Those qualities, as much as his enormous physical gifts, helped him claw his way to success. And yes, he clings to the past, and to the dream he should have long ago abandoned. But those are small problems. What's wrong with Marshall Rogers is more serious. And more frightening.

■ ■ ■

"I was drafted number 34 in the second round, but I would have been in the first round playing with the New York Knicks. But some important people didn't want me in New York."

We are sitting in Pope's Cafeteria in Central City Shopping Center. Rogers is halfway through his lunch—a pork steak, a plate of roast beef, a large salad soaked in Thousand Island and Italian dressing, a roll with six pats of butter, green beans, a large pickle, two cartons of milk, a piece of apple pie and a bottle of Budweiser. Before he digs in, he shakes salt over everything but the drinks and pie for five seconds, then pepper for three seconds, until there is a gritty layer of black and white covering his food. "Hey," he yells when a waitress walks by, "where's the ketchup?" She promises to bring some. "And bring some Tabasco and A-1 sauce, too."

Between huge bites, Rogers talks about basketball, and college, and women.

After he left the pros and before he returned, for good, to St. Louis, Rogers went back to Pan American University in Texas to take some graduate-level courses. He dropped out because "every time I went to take a test, they were using a machine to clear my mind."

"A machine?"

"Yeah."

"Who?"

"I can't tell you. You know what this place is called?"

"Pope's?"

"Yeah, exactly."

He attacks his pork steak, and we eat in silence. Then he tells me how he and his team almost defeated the University of Nevada–Las Vegas basketball team 12 years ago. "We were hooping 'em to death," he says, until "they were using some kind of animation machine to help them score in the second half."

"An animation machine?"

"They have these rays that grab the ball in midair."

"Who does?"

"I can't tell you."

Roast beef and green beans then, and more silence.

I ask how many children he has.

"I don't really know."

"Five?"

"No, about 12. I have some white ones, too. When I was

at Kansas, I had some white girlfriends, and they had my kids. They wanted some money for the kids, and cars, and stuff, and they asked the regime, and they got the cars and money and places to live."

"You mean the athletic department got that stuff for them? Coaches? Alumni?"

"No, the regime. Pope John Paul, Queen Elizabeth, King Arthur and Hercules."

■ ■ ■

Marshall Rogers was the sixth of seven children. A bright little boy, he paid attention and worked hard. Before long, he was riding the bus to Sportsmen's Park with all the other straight-A students to watch the baseball Cardinals. He decided he wanted to be a teacher when he grew up. That, or a professional baseball player. His heroes were Ken Boyer, Mike Shannon and Bob Gibson.

In third grade he discovered basketball. He was the best player in his class, "but the big dudes used to beat on us." For a while, anyway, Marshall stuck with marbles and hopscotch. But his mother bought him a shiny new basketball that year, and when he wore it out, she bought him another. By the time he graduated from Sumner in 1971, Marshall's mother had bought her baby boy 10 new basketballs. Every year, a new ball.

In the summer, he went to the baseball games with the other

straight-A students. In the spring, he set sprint and long jump records for the Sumner track team. And always, there was basketball.

He played for the state championship team when he was a sophomore; when he was a senior, he averaged 26.7 points per game and led his team to a 22–4–1 record (a near riot forced the tie with Vashon). When practice was over and the rest of the team had showered and gone home, Rogers stayed in the gym. Coach John Algee stayed, too, and when Rogers dribbled and shot, Algee slapped his star's wrist. Or he smacked his star's elbow.

"I wanted to make him get his rhythm down," Algee says, "to help him learn to shoot with people hitting him."

He learned—on the court and in class.

"My favorite course was probably history," Rogers says. "Math was good, too. Cutting class was the best, though. Just to talk about what happened yesterday, or last night."

John Algee: "I can't say enough about him as a high school athlete. He was one of the greatest basketball players that ever played for me. . . . He was a very good student, carried himself well.

"But he more or less was a loner—stayed by himself. I don't think he had any best friends."

■ ■ ■

"My mother stole one of my tank tops." He has finished everything

but the pie. He will take that home. He is sipping his beer and smoking a cigarette. "Someone probably called her—the Pope or the Queen, and told her, 'Steal Marshall's tank top, so he won't look so good.'"

■ ■ ■

Rogers left St. Louis and moved to Lawrence, Kan., where he had accepted an athletic scholarship at the University of Kansas. He led his undefeated freshmen team in scoring and assists and enjoyed the social opportunities available to a healthy young athlete in a college town. He averaged 24.3 points that year. His freshmen coach, Bob Frederick (now athletic director at KU), says he "really enjoyed" Marshall, but remembers that "he did have a little bit of a temper. He'd flare up pretty quickly."

He had plenty of chances to flare up the next year. The Jayhawks employed a slow-down offense which could not have been less suited to the insect-quick Rogers. His scoring average fell to 7.6. The team went 8–18. "I was unhappy," Rogers remembers. "We were winning quite a few games in the first half, then losing. There were some inner-squad squabbles. The teammates got upset."

During his sophomore winter of discontent, Rogers happened to pick up a magazine on one of the Jayhawks road trips. He spotted a story about a coach named Abe Lemons, legendary in basketball circles for his explosive offenses.

"Dear Coach Lemons," Rogers wrote, "My name is Marshall Rogers. I'm 6-foot-2-inches and 180 pounds. I averaged 24.3 points and 6.0 assists respectively for the Kansas freshmen team last year. My main strengths are speed and quickness. . . ."

Fourteen years later, Lemons still has the letter.

"I just thought he was the nicest kid," the coach says. Lemons was especially impressed that Rogers didn't badmouth his Kansas coach. "And he wrote a real nice letter."

After his sophomore season, Rogers left KU and transferred to Pan American University, where Lemons was coaching. When he showed up at the campus in Edinburg, Tex., and laid eyes on his new coach, the "nice kid" demanded money. "He asked if I was going to give him plane fare for his trips back to St. Louis," Lemons remembers. "I said no. He asked if that was the way it was for everybody on the team. I said yes. He said, 'Well, I can live with that.'"

While Rogers was waiting to become eligible to play for Lemons, he joined a city league in Edinburg. "They kicked him off," Lemons says, "and they told me he would never be able to play for me, because he shot too much."

They didn't know Lemons. Famous for his cowboy boots and his drawling one-liners, the coach never met a jumpshot he didn't like.

And if some of Marshall's shots were—shall we say, inventive?— well, Lemons took to splash and dazzle the way other coaches take to crew cuts and blazers.

For two years, the city kid and the country coach created a defensive specialist's worst nightmare. Their supporting cast could have been dreamed up by Ring Lardner. At one guard was Jesus Guerra, a short (5-feet-10-inches), skinny kid who grew up on the Mexican border. He penetrated and passed. Teammates called him "Chewey." Fans called him "Little Jesus." In the pivot was Pete "Pizza" Severa, a 6-foot-5-inch, 250-pound manchild who worked during the day at—where else?— Pizza Hut, then threw opponents around at night. "He was what we jokingly called our center," says Lemons, who now coaches at Oklahoma City University.

The Pan American Broncs often scored more than 100 points in a single game. And the biggest scorer and main attraction of the hardwood circus was Rogers.

"He was the best pure shooter I've ever seen," says Jim McKone, Pan American's sports information director for the past 18 years. Likeable? Rogers is one of two Bronc athletes McKone ever had to his house for dinner. Tough? McKone remembers a game—it was January 29, 1976—against Houston Baptist University. Rogers drove the lane in the opening minutes, and when he stretched toward the basket, Houston

Baptist's 7-foot center caught the nation's leading scorer in the jaw with an elbow. "He was out on the floor," McKone remembers, "absolutely cold." A minute passed. Rogers didn't move. Two minutes. Nothing. Three minutes. Rogers got up, walked to the free-throw line and sank two shots. He ended up with 45 points. Final score: Pan American, 81, Houston Baptist, 79.

Rogers averaged 26.7 points per game his junior year. The team went 22–2. In his record-setting senior season, he hit 36.8 per game. The team was 20–5.

"He was amazing," says Guerra, now head basketball coach at Roma (Tex.) High School, in the border town where he grew up. "Coach Lemons kept stats every day, and Marshall would shoot 40 out of 50, 25 out of 30. He was the most dedicated player I've ever been associated with."

"He was one of the best," Lemons says. "He had the size, the ability. There wasn't anything he couldn't do in the game. . . . He was what you'd call an All-American boy. He made his grades, worked hard, got along with everybody. He was a coach's dream."

■ ■ ■

Rogers: "We were playing the University of Hawaii. The Queen called me on the phone and said we had to beat them by 15 points. I scored 47 points, but we had to play them the next night again,

and I was too tired. So one of my brothers, who looks just like me, from Africa, he played."

■ ■ ■

Rogers was selected in the second round of the National Basketball Association's annual draft, and in the fall of 1976, he signed a $45,000 contract with the Golden State Warriors. He played in 26 games that year and averaged 3.8 points. "I was hooping 'em to death," Rogers says. "I should have been playing more."

The next fall, he attended veteran's camp, where he continued to ride the bench. In October 1977, the Warriors played the Los Angeles Lakers in an exhibition game in Reno, Nev.

"I should have been starting," Rogers says. "I got kind of upset. . . . You get real upset and feel like hurting somebody. It's best just to get away so you don't get into trouble."

He left the team.

■ ■ ■

We are driving to Shoney's, in North County. Rogers is in the passenger's seat, stroking an invisible baby he holds in front of him. He is talking out of the right side of his mouth, addressing something outside the car.

When we sit down, he calls to a waitress. "I'll have an apple pie a la mode while I order," he says. She brings it, and he asks for spaghetti with extra meat, and a turkey club sandwich, and the salad bar. He gives it all the salt and pepper treatment and asks for ketchup and A-1.

"On May 30, 1976," he says, "I went to the Olympic camp in Raleigh, N.C. There were two practices a day for three hours each time. It was grueling. It made you tired. And mean and mad. I did real well before the animation machine got in my way.

"Wait," he says, after we finish and I start to stand. "I have to do something." He stands in the aisle, turns and crosses his arms under his chin, elbows outstretched. He stands that way, rigid, for almost five minutes. "That was the Pope," he tells me later, "telling me to do that."

■ ■ ■

After leaving the Warriors, Rogers stayed in the Bay area. He played in pickup games, in tournaments. He was a substitute teacher in Hayward, Calif. And he was unhappy.

In September 1978, he tried out with the San Antonio Spurs. "I was doing good enough to be in the top seven. I didn't see anyone else hitting as many jump-shots as me. [But] people in the underground were saying, 'Marshall likes himself too much 'cause he scores too much.' That's why I didn't play. But I'm thinking about trying out again."

"The last I heard from him," says Coach Lemons, "seems like he was down in San Antone. He

called and said he needed $100, so I telegrammed it to him."

■ ■ ■

Rogers is standing at the free-throw line in the gym at Vic Tanny on Dorsett and I–270. His right arm is cocked in a U, and a scowl splits his face. He hits 34 free throws without missing, and without smiling. Then he hits 31 without missing, then 17. The only sounds are the clanking of the weight machines nearby and the rock music being piped over the fitness center's sound system. That and the occasional bounce of the basketball on the floor, and the swish of the net. And Marshall's muttering. He is talking to the voices.

■ ■ ■

KU's Bob Frederick heard from Rogers last winter. "He wanted to know if I could put in a word for him with" Topeka's semi-pro basketball team. "He told me how he and his friend were hooping everybody at Forest Park Community College."

Frederick clears his throat. It pained him to hear from Rogers. It pains him to talk about him.

"I don't want this to sound wrong," Frederick says, and clears his throat again. "It was like he was just a year out of college, instead of 11 years."

Roma's favorite son, Guerra, doesn't know what to say when he learns of his old teammate's troubles. First come the adjectives: "hardworking," "gifted," "dedicated." Then memories of specific games, particular feats of athletic heroism. There is a realization that "it was very rare when we got together" socially, and a few half-hearted attempts to understand why some people succeed and others fail. Finally, there is simply a request.

"Do you have Marshall's phone number?" Little Jesus asks. "I need to call him."

■ ■ ■

We are driving to O'Fallon Park with a photographer to shoot some baskets and some pictures. Rogers is expansive—laughing, smoking, jiving. He is telling us how he played one-on-one with a local teenager a few days earlier. "He was woofing on me. I smoked him. I'm gonna steal his mother from him now. She knows me from high school. She knows me from when I was a superstar."

It is Thursday afternoon, August 27. Today, Rogers turns 34 years old.

■ ■ ■

Narrating his own life story, Rogers will gladly rattle off dates and statistics. December 2, 1974: The Broncs steal the ball three times in the final 30 seconds to erase a 5-point deficit and beat Arkansas State in Jonesboro. January 3, 1976: The Broncs lose to the University of Nevada–Las Vegas,

and Rogers feels the "animation machine." May 16, 1976: Rogers graduates from Pan American University. September 1978: He tries out with the Spurs, but is cut.

And "that's it," Rogers says. "Right there. You don't need to write about any of that other stuff."

■ ■ ■

Kurt Gull used to work as a security guard for St. Louis Centre. He was on duty Wednesday, June 24.

"We got a call from Walgreens. They said they had a shoplifter in custody. I was the first person on the scene. When I got there, Marshall and the manager were arguing and pushing and shoving. . . . [The manager] explained that he had seen him take some items, and that he and the assistant manager had talked Marshall into going into the backroom, and they checked the gym bag and found the items. What they were pushing and shoving over was that [Rogers] didn't like the idea of them getting into his gym bag.

"I said, 'OK, I'm placing you under arrest.'

"He said, 'OK, what's going to happen now?'

"I said, 'I'll have to handcuff you until the police arrive, and you'll probably get a summons, and you probably won't have to go anywhere.'

"He said, 'OK,' and I put one handcuff on his left hand and he went crazy. He jumped back, *slammed me against the wall. He swung, he pushed, he shoved."*

By then, two more security guards and a police officer had arrived.

"I'm 5-foot-9, 225 pounds, 50 inches across the chest, and he was tossing us around like we were rag dolls."

In September, Rogers was convicted of assault. He was placed on probation.

■ ■ ■

After the Spurs cut him, Rogers returned to St. Louis. Except for a brief attempt to take graduate courses at Pan American in the fall of 1979 (where the machine "cleared his mind"), Rogers has never ventured out again. One of college basketball's greatest scorers hasn't done much the past 10 years.

He taught at McKinley High School and O'Fallon Technical Center in 1978–1979. He left McKinley because "the principal was upset . . . because the students were acting crazy, and one girl especially, and I started to curse her out." He has been married twice and has at least two children. His second wife, who asked that her name not be used, says "he probably feels that things should be better because they were better." His mother says he "does funny things with his hands." She wishes he would see a doctor.

Rogers spends much of his time sleeping and eating. He wakes up early every day—sometimes 5:30 or 6 A.M.—and makes breakfast. A typical meal is two eggs, two hot dogs, two pancakes, milk and Kool-Aid. After that, "sometimes I go back to sleep. Sometimes I cut the grass. Sometimes I just sit on the porch. Sometimes, but not all the time. Sometimes it's fun. Sometimes it's boring."

He usually skips lunch, and after a typical afternoon of "just relaxing," his mother cooks dinner. After that, he usually hangs around the house until he decides to go up to his room and go to sleep, which could be any time between 7 P.M. and 2 A.M.

"Sometimes I get mad at the voices," he says, "and I can't go to sleep. And I say, 'Leave me alone.'"

■ ■ ■

We are sitting in a courtyard on Laclede's Landing. Rogers is here with mixed feelings. He doesn't want anything written about his recent troubles with the law, and he would rather talk about how many points he scored against Lamar than his difficulties finding a job. On the other hand, without a car, he doesn't get a chance to leave the house much. And I'm buying lunch.

I ask who his friends are.

"No one."

"No one?"

"Sometimes, I'll be with friends, but not very often. Nowadays, I'll be by myself at home."

"You ever get lonely?"

"Sometimes. Sometimes. But not all the time."

"What do you see yourself doing in five or 10 years?"

"Some type of work. . . . With a job, I could get around and do more things I want. I could go to a discotheque and buy some drinks that I like—that's why I need to get some work. You know, I haven't been having a real good time lately."

"What plans do you have for looking for work?"

"I don't know. I haven't thought about it."

"You have any regrets about what happened at Walgreens?"

"It's over with."

"Do the voices bother you?"

"I'll be trying to lay down, and it really upsets me when I'm trying to lay down and go to sleep and I don't feel like standing up and they tell me to stand up."

"You told me you talked to a doctor about this once."

"That was someone else. That really wasn't me.

"Sometimes they say things to me that don't pertain to what I want to do. They tell me to do something while I'm playing and I don't feel like doing it, and I just say, 'Shut the fuck up.' Sometimes it gives me a headache."

"Do you ever think now about seeing a doctor?"

"I don't need a doctor. I just need to go to sleep and not talk to them anymore."

■   ■   ■

This article first appeared in St. Louis *magazine in 1987. Friedman is now senior editor at* Gentleman's Quarterly *magazine in New York.*

PUT IT INTO PRACTICE

Discussion

1. One of the more challenging aspects of writing personality pieces about famous people comes from the tug-of-war between the writer and the personality. The personalities typically hope the story will be a positive portrayal that helps promote their career, perhaps through increased record or book sales or the like.

    The writers, on the other hand, are typically trying to tell the truth as they see it but to do so in a way that is entertaining and informative. If it's well received as a story (and sometimes controversy can help that reception), then it helps the writer's career.

    Discuss the conflict in purpose between the writer and the personality when it comes to writing personality pieces for magazines. Whose story is it, anyway? Why? Do the needs of the writer and the editor outweigh the needs of the personality? Why?

2. Suppose you are writing a personality piece on a paraplegic artist. The artist is trying hard, no question about it, grasping the brush between the teeth and spending many hours on each painting. But, the resultant watercolors are, several critics tell you, ordinary at best.

    Discuss how you handle telling this story to the readers of the magazine you are writing for. Does your story's tone or theme vary depending on the type of magazine the story will appear in? Do you sidestep the issue of the quality of the paintings, or do you make note of their mediocrity? Why?

3. In regard to that same paraplegic artist, are you bothered by the idea that an award-winning story about the artist—which notes the painter's courage but also the lack of merit in the paintings—enhances your career? In other words, are you concerned that you have turned that painter's handicap into profit for yourself while not helping the painter's career at all?

    Discuss whether or not it is wrong for a magazine writer to profit from the troubles of others. Why? Why not?

    What if the paintings are truly outstanding and your story helps the painter's career? Does that change the equation at all? Is it all right now for the writer to profit from the painter's physical tragedy? Why? Why not?

Exercises

1. Look through the stories collected in this book to decide how many might be classified as personality pieces. Which ones are in-depth

profiles? Which ones are specialized profiles? Which ones are about people who are already well-known? Which ones are about people who were relatively obscure?

In those stories about famous personalities, what is it that makes the story interesting for the readership of the magazine in which it was printed? In those stories about more obscure personalities, what is it that makes the story interesting for the readership of the magazine in which it was printed?

In all this listing and organizing, can you come to any conclusions about whom you could do a personality piece on? What famous personalities do you have the possibility of access to? Whom do you know who may be obscure but worth doing a story on?

List three of each. For the more obscure personalities, write a short paragraph or two about each one, listing why a story on each would work for a particular magazine. Make sure to mention the needs of the magazine you have in mind and how this story meets those needs.

ESSAYS

Scott Russell Sanders opened the door to his Indiana home on a March morning and smelled the change in the air. The wind—cold and northerly the night before—had shifted to the south. The snow that had covered the backyard only a few days before was melting, and there, in a sunny corner of the yard near the shed, was the first sign of spring.

Sanders took a deep breath, walked down the steps and into the yard, and, lost in thought, bent over to brush the snow from those first hesitant crocuses that broke through the thawing soil.

An hour later, he was at his word processor, typing this first sentence: "The dirt in my neighborhood has begun to thaw, releasing a meaty, succulent smell that is older than I am, older than humankind, older than anything I can see from my window except the sun and moon."

There was something here that Sanders wanted to say, something he wanted to delve into, discover for himself and for others. He is a very talented, and well-published, novelist and short story writer, but this, he knew, had to be an essay.

One of the most challenging forms of nonfiction writing for magazines is the essay, challenging not only because it demands much from the writer in the way of research and writing skills, but also because the modern essay as it is found in many magazines demands that the writer be able to make a series of logical, thoughtful connections that help the reader gain new insight into a particular topic.

While modern magazine essays can touch upon any topic and can come in a variety of styles, they frequently fall into one of two major types—either *critical* or *personal.*

CRITICAL ESSAYS

Critical essays typically use a review of a recent book, play, film, or performance as the starting point for a wide-ranging discussion that illuminates, and critiques for the reader, an entire context for understanding the work at hand.

An assessment of a new murder mystery novel, for instance, might lead to a lengthy discussion of all murder mysteries, perhaps including the origins of the genre and certainly discussing the genre's current merits and demerits.

These kinds of essays are often found in academic journals and in relatively small circulation publications that cater to a specific readership. But they also appear regularly in large circulation national magazines such as *The Atlantic Monthly,* the *New Yorker, Esquire,* and *Playboy.*

The Atlantic Monthly, for example, ran a review of the book *At The Hand of Man: Peril and Hope for Africa's Wildlife,* by Raymond Bonner, about the decline of Africa's wildlife in general and of its elephant population in particular. That review, by author Kenneth Brower, quickly expands into a general discussion of the wildlife crisis in Africa and includes a significant amount of background information on both Bonner and environmental writing.

For instance, Brower says:

> Reporting on the environment is a departure for Bonner, who in the past has reported on politics. (His two previous books are on U.S. policy in El Salvador and the dictatorship of Ferdinand Marcos.) Departures of this sort are often advantageous: they permit a fresh eye, a freedom from dogma. Most books on the disappearance of African wildlife have been by people in the

"religion," as environmentalists sometimes call their movement. Bonner cannot be called an apostate—he was never even baptized. These departures, of course, may also have disadvantages. The fresh eye can be too fresh. The newcomer can be insufficiently grounded in the facts, language, history, and arguments of the field. In this book disadvantages overwhelm the advantages from the start. Bonner brings his own dogma to the writing, and his ignorance in environmental matters is profound.

The reader gets not only Brower's blunt assessment of Bonner's preparedness to write the book ("his ignorance in environmental matters is profound") but also the context in which that assessment is made.

Later, Brower discusses elements of the African wildlife crisis that are not found in the book, as well as information that disputes some of the book's assertions.

The overall effect, then, is not only to critically discuss the book in terms of matters such as its writing style or clarity of thought (though those, indeed, are evaluated) but also to discuss the very topic the book takes on. In so doing, essays like Brower's use the critical assessment as a starting point for a more ambitious discussion, one that contests and expands upon the book's content.

It is important to note that this kind of essay is, of necessity, highly personal and written from expertise.

Brower very much places his own credibility and opinions on the line, making it clear that his reaction is quite personal and based on considerable knowledge. Note that the very first sentence establishes both elements: "A year ago, in Cameroon, I accompanied a French doctor, François Morel, on some of the occasional visits he paid to a pygmy encampment in the rain forest of Campo Reserve, near the border with Equatorial Guinea."

Using the pronoun "I" and placing himself in Africa, Brower makes it clear to the reader from the very start that this will be a knowledgeable, first-person assessment of a book and its context.

It is worth noting that the critical essay is a good example of the kinds of differences found between magazine and newspaper feature writing.

Most newspaper critics are so limited by space constraints (and deadline pressure) that they are unable to move beyond any immediate discussion of the work and the artist. A movie review, for instance, will briefly discuss the acting, directing, and writing and then hastily conclude with some sort of handy (if often simplistic) scoring method.

Magazine critics, on the other hand, have more freedom to discuss the work fully, and that is where the depth of discussion offered by the critical essay becomes significant.

PERSONAL ESSAYS

The personal essay is similar to the critical essay in several ways and quite different in others.

As the name implies, this kind of essay is deeply personal in nature, and like the critical essay, it, too, relies on the writer's expertise for its impact. But this kind of essay doesn't begin as a review of someone else's creation. Rather, it begins with the writer's noticing something in the world and coming to conclusions about larger matters as a result of the thoughts that stem from that initial impulse.

Unlike the critical essay, which ultimately revolves around the book or play or film being discussed, the personal essay has no ready-made thematic core, nothing to necessarily tie everything together into a smooth whole. This means that the challenge for the writer is to make connections from the small to the large, keep the reader interested and involved while doing so, and emerge at the end of the essay with some worthwhile thematic point, something that is ultimately the purpose for the essay.

That theme usually emerges from the small event that started the writer's thinking in the first place. Whatever that something is, it serves as a metaphor for the larger themes being discussed, and it allows the writer entrance into those wide-ranging discussions.

Robley Wilson, editor of the prestigious *North American Review,* frequently uses essays by writer Scott Russell Sanders. Wilson says one of his reasons for using Sanders's work is "I love Scott's way of taking very small things and going cosmic with them."

Sanders himself sees it this way: "Usually what sets me writing is some incident, some event, some sense perception. From there the essay becomes an effort to think through some of my deepest concerns, the concerns that moved me to start writing in the first place."

As you saw in the opening scene of this chapter, in his essay "Ground Notes," written for *North American Review,* it was "literally the smell of the dirt thawing which set the writing in motion," says Sanders. From that single perception, Sanders began to extrapolate a wide variety of meanings, using everything from the Bible to baseball to do so.

"This became an essay about belonging somewhere with full awareness, what it means to inhabit a place," he explains. "And also, the essay was set in motion by the sense of transience and uprooting that is so common in our culture, and I was really reacting against that and asking myself what has made me feel grounded in those times of my life when I have been grounded."

The result appears at the end of this chapter.

STRUCTURE

It is the *connections between elements* that form the basic structure of the personal essay and that make it interesting to readers. The writer, in connecting these various ideas, incidents, people, or places, helps readers see how the interrelationship between one thing and another (or between one thing and many) has meaning for their lives as well as the writer's. You'll want to search for similar connections when you take on the essay form for yourself.

A typical structure, then, might be an opening that begins with the specific small thing that started the writer off on the discussion, followed by a discussion of those thoughts that stemmed from that initial impulse. The writer's musings on how these items connect, and the implications of those connections, are interspersed throughout, illuminating for the reader the importance of the seemingly ordinary.

Because the essay ranges widely, focus can be a real problem. It is all too easy to lose track of your theme while moving from one idea to another. As a result, you can wind up with a confused story, one that leaves readers scratching their heads in befuddlement instead of coming to the realizations you'd like them to have.

Remember, though, that the freedom to wander from idea to idea is part of the essay's appeal for both writers and readers. It makes for a difficult challenge: to both wander and stay focused.

Sanders puts it this way: "Focus is a problem, no question about it. But the fact that the focus can wander and still give the feeling of a coherent essay is one of the glories of the essay, for the writer as well as the reader."

Sanders says, "There's obviously not a single right way to give coherence to an essay, but, for me, when I go back and work over and revise, part of what I do is draw the essay together and try to make it feel like something that's whole."

A large part of the problem comes from the essay's freedom. After all, as Sanders says, "At any given point in the essay, at the end of any sentence or paragraph, certainly at the end of any section, you can go virtually anywhere, off to some new thought. But," he warns, "the reader is not necessarily going to go there with you, so you have to have some sense of what are reasonable connections, what leaps to make that the reader can still follow and be moved by."

See how Sanders helps the reader make sense of his "reasonable connections" in the following paragraph from "Ground Notes." In this section, Sanders concludes a section that has talked about all the various definitional uses of the word "ground."

> So much ground to cover! From this sampling, you can see that ground straddles a deep division in our feelings. It summons up contrary longings for support and liberation. It hangs in suspense between the freedom of flight—of balls, planes, teenagers, foxes, melodies—and the constraint of staying on earth. The ambivalence is not in the word, of course, but in us, for we desire to fly free, but also, when we land, to rest securely. We yearn to be held up, but fear being held down. The mind soars weightless through time and space, while the body answers to gravity and clocks. To lead a life that is firmly grounded means not only that one is supported but that one is constrained. Once you glimpse your true place, that vision begins to define how you should live.

This one paragraph does much to guide the reader toward an understanding of the thematic implications of what Sanders has been saying in the previous sections of the essay, and it also steers the reader toward a fuller understanding of what is still to come. In that sense, it is meant to help the reader make those leaps that are the main thematic appeal of the essay form.

RESEARCH

Research and reporting for the essay can be very different from what you're used to in other kinds of magazine writing. You're not likely to do a lot of interviewing, and the first thing you may have to learn how to do is *really "see" things and think through their implications.*

In fact, "implications" is a handy key word for you to remember as you go through the research and thought processes that will lead to writing an essay. Ask yourself about the implications of what you're sensing. Ask yourself where this occurrence, or this thing you've noticed, leads, what kinds of things connect up to it. In trying to answer those sorts of questions, you'll be on the way to the kind of discoveries that can lead to a powerful, interesting personal essay.

There is always a great deal of note-taking in the reporting process for an essay, for you'll find yourself jotting down all sorts of possible elements to the story as they occur to you. Many of them won't, in the end, pan out. But some will, and the more of them you have jotted down, the better the odds that the ones that survive your later scrutiny are likely to be worthwhile.

And there can also be a lot of library research involved, because following those implications will force you into some major fact-finding sessions.

Sanders does his reporting this way: "What's important to me when it comes to getting ready to write an essay is that I do a lot of very detailed, elaborate note-taking beforehand. I don't give a special structure to the notes, but for 'Ground Notes,' for instance, I have 15 pages of single-spaced typed notes."

Those notes, says Sanders, are "memories, impressions, things from reading. Sometimes they're just outright statements that I'm making; sometimes they're analogies that I've noticed, or etymologies—all of which are just things that feel to me as if they belong in the arena of 'Ground Notes.' I don't have a structure for it, but I'm building up a body of material. Gradually, as I soak in the notes, as I read through them and think through them, I begin to see patterns emerging."

It is from those patterns that Sanders begins to make a rough outline of the pattern he plans to use in his writing. Only at that point does he begin to seriously construct the essay.

Michael Martone, another talented fiction writer who also is an essayist for *North American Review,* usually finds himself in the library once he gets past the initial stages of the idea for his essays. For Martone, not only does a computer search at the local library fill him with facts, but also the search process itself begins to make any number of those interesting connections that make the essay form so enjoyable.

"What's really wonderful about the computer age is that for research you just punch in a key word and see what it brings you. I love to research that way," he says.

Martone recalls, "I did an essay once on windmills and did my research that way. I noticed that when you see a news program that talks about farming they'll always put up a windmill behind the news anchor or reporter. I wondered why. Why a windmill? Why does that mean farming? So I just wandered through the computer at Iowa State University, and I found wonderful books that hadn't been checked out since last 1965—no one had seen them in years. It gave me a wealth of information for that essay."

For another essay, one on the township structure that helps define the Midwest, Martone recalls, "I just asked the computer to spit out things just on key words. I put in 'township,' and I put in 'Northwest Territory' and 'Old Northwest' and I found a variety of books and sources."

The result of his search is reprinted at the end of this chapter and is part of his book *Townships* (University of Iowa Press).

WHY WRITE ESSAYS?

What is it about the essay form that attracts so many fine writers? Part of it is the personal nature of the form, which allows a writer to express deeply held opinions and feelings.

As Sanders puts it, "I feel a freedom in the essay that I don't feel even when writing fiction. I feel the opportunity to speak more directly about how I think and what matters to me.

"Obviously one can convey deep feelings and concerns in fiction, but there you have to do it through indirection. In the essay you can do it more directly, you can quote from other people, you can move from Yeats to Hopi myth, talk about science or religion or politics."

As Sanders notes, that very openness of form is what makes the essay so tricky and risky to write, but, he adds, "When you can handle it, it becomes a very free and exhilarating form. It's a bit like ice skating. You know, when you're out on the pond you can move in any direction, but you can also fall down. There's a great sense of openness and exhilaration.

"Also, I have written about a number of things through my essays that are either too personal or too urgent for me to camouflage them or transform them the way that one has to do through fiction. Anybody who reads all my fiction and nonfiction will see the same themes, the same preoccupations in both kinds of writing, but my nonfiction is, on the whole, much more personal and closer to the bone than my fiction is."

Martone, too, finds the essay especially appealing. Like Sanders, he also writes fiction and poetry. But, when it came time to confront some deeply held thoughts, he turned to the essay to express them.

"I'm a Midwesterner, and I had made a decision to confront this idea of Midwest. So I was looking for a metaphor to hold things together, and this thing that kept popping up was grids—how we impose a two-dimensional idea on a three-dimensional thing, which, to me, is a metaphor for the Midwest. When you talk about Midwesterners, you talk about flatness in several different levels. The flatness of the speech, the flatness of the emotional life, the flatness and boredom of life in general, and the flatness of the place itself."

Martone found that the nonfiction essay was his best entrance into those kinds of discoveries, realizations that led him from the seeming flatness of Midwestern life to an effort to uncover those aspects of the Midwest that aren't usually seen or known.

"What I really wanted to say was that there are a lot of secret things in this country, and the Midwest strikes me as a place where a lot of it goes on. Most of you don't know how your food is raised, you don't know about your schools, your factories, all of these essential things we've worked very hard to keep hidden from ourselves."

For Martone, "Nonfiction writing, or at least this essay type of nonfiction writing, can at least bring it to you. Really, my urging was for people to go and see these places for themselves. When you see 300 hogs raised, it's so startling to see a 19-year-old with a $3-million debt load out there raising 300 hogs for slaughter, for instance. The Midwest is the place where all of this certain death goes on, but it's all quite hidden. What nonfiction allows me to do is talk about these things that I think we take for granted and ignore though they're crucial to our lives."

GETTING STARTED

Modern magazine essays, whether critical or personal, aren't easy to create. The form is an elevated, challenging one that demands much from you as a writer.

Scott Russell Sanders recommends that if you're interested in writing essays you begin by "reading essays, of course. That's true for any art form that you want to practice. But also, you need to get in touch with your own experience, which means your memories, the incidents in your life and the lives of people close to you." Then, he adds, it is time for "practice, and the ideal medium for practice is *a journal*—not a diary, a journal, where you're reflecting on your experience as you live through it."

What you will want to do as a beginning essayist is follow Sanders's advice and read essays—both critical and personal—in magazines like *The Atlantic,* the *New Yorker,* and *North American Review.*

While you're at it, begin that journal. Simply writing down your thoughts and thinking them through (remember to look for those implications) will help you acquire the mental tools necessary to an essayist.

Remember that the introspection required by the essay begins with knowledge, so a wise beginner might want to start with an essay that discusses something already familiar, whether it's farming or life in the inner city. What are the implications of a late spring freeze? What are the implications of an outdoor basketball game on a hot summer day?

Think it through, come to some realizations of how that new fade-away jump shot connects up to life in America, and share those thoughts with your readers.

BOX 11.1

JOURNAL PRACTICE

One of the keys to writing essays is learning how to be introspective and then learning how to put that introspection into a logical discussion for the reader.

The writing of essays requires that you know how to reflect on your life and its occurrences and place them into a larger context.

Scott Russell Sanders advises that you start a journal to practice this kind of introspection. "You need to recall things from the past that you're reminded of by present things. You might find yourself, for instance, quoting from a book that you're reading and you're not quite sure why the passage sticks with you but it's exciting to you so you record it."

Journal writing is a habit that Sanders developed for his own work. Getting into the habit of frequently writing in his journal has been, he says, "a wonderful resource for all my writing, but it has been an especially valuable resource for the writing of essays because it's the closest mode to the writing of essays."

Sanders advises that you keep the content of the journal wide-open, knowing that although most of its material won't get into print anywhere, such a journal will, nevertheless, not only give you plenty of raw material but also give you a good place to practice your structural techniques for essays.

When you start a journal, you'll want to have the entries conform to some basic structural guidelines, perhaps making sure that each entry includes *an event or object that you notice, some musings on the broader implications of that event or object,* and *some conclusion about those broader implications.*

But make sure as you make your journal entries that you leave yourself plenty of time and space to wander in your thinking. It is, after all, from that kind of mental wandering that many of the most telling points of an essay may emerge.

■ ■ ■

GROUND NOTES

BY SCOTT RUSSELL SANDERS

The dirt in my neighborhood has begun to thaw, releasing a meaty, succulent smell that is older than I am, older than humankind, older than anything I can see from my window except the sun and moon. The smell promises the resurrection of the year. Soon the brown blades of winter will flicker with green. The purple buds of crocuses and the white of bloodroot will pierce the leaf duff and open their hinges to the bees. This fecund smell breaks my clocks, spreading me over all my ages at once, so that I am a toddler digging in the spring dirt of a Tennessee cotton field, and I am a teenager staggering behind a plow in Ohio on the lookout for arrowheads, and I am a lone young man lured to the melancholy roar of the ocean on the coast of Rhode Island, and I am a husband and father here in Indiana transplanting ferns and hepatica into my garden. Thawing dirt also breaks the grip of winter in me. The promise of new life in that loamy smell gives me courage to ask questions I have been afraid to ask.

What do I fear? A story is told of the physicist who, upon learning that matter is made up almost entirely of empty space, began wearing boots with enormous soles to keep himself from falling through the gaps. In cartoons, the hapless coyote races over the edge of a cliff and keeps on blithely running until he chances to look down, whereupon he plummets. I sympathize with coyote and physicist both. The void that opens beneath me is not the vacancy within atoms, nor the gulf of air, but the void of ignorance. I do not know where I am. I look down, and cannot say what ground is beneath my feet.

The ignorance I am talking about stretches from the dirt to the stars, and even beyond the stars to the source of music for this cosmic dance. Consider that lowly dirt. The soil thawing outside my window contains humus from generations of decay, silt from glaciers which visited these parts ten thousand years ago, and clay from the decomposition of three-hundred-million-year-old limestone. A handful of that soil may contain a billion organisms. I doubt these myriad beasties are troubled by their ignorance of me, but how can I live without giving them thought? Yet if I opened my mind to even one percent of those creatures, would I have room for anything else?

Ignorance is bliss only so long as you do not know how little you know. In the Genesis account, on the third day the Creator divides water from dry land. Now there would be a place for the grass to grow, the grains to lift their seeds, the birds to make their nests, a place for the four-legged beasts to slink and run, a place for us two-legged animals to walk. All very comforting, so long as one believes, as the people who recorded the story did believe, that the land visible within the horizon's hoop is a large proportion of all there is. Very comforting until one learns that land and sea stretch on and on beyond the horizon to form a globe, and this globe is but a speck in orbit around a run-of-the-mill star, and the star is caught in the outer arm of a spiral galaxy, and the galaxy itself is but a speck flung amid an untold dusting of other galaxies within a space whose outer limits we have not yet seen, and the space we see may be no more than one bubble in an ocean of universes. Who, grasping that, can avoid feeling vertigo?

I have had since childhood a recurrent dream, one of the commonest in the lexicon of dreams. I walk out along some high surface—an airplane wing in flight, the rim of a water tower, a windowsill on the top floor of a skyscraper. Unaware at first that a gulf opens beneath me, I move with assurance until, like the coyote, I glance down, and then I panic, lose my footing, and fall. As I tumble, I realize that I am dreaming, and that unless I wake before hitting the earth I will die.

So far, I have always managed to claw my way up out of sleep.

Awake or asleep, one day I *will* die, of course. That knowledge darkens the shadows over which I balance. In my waking hours, I have the dizzying sense of looking down into the abyss whenever I ask where it is I actually live, and what this broody "I" might be that does the living, and how both place and self are bound to the rest of the world. What is my true home? Is there solid footing anywhere? If so, how can I reach it? If not, on what shall I stand?

These questions are the ground notes of my life, playing beneath everything I do, like the steady bass notes in Bach's music that underlie the surface melodies. They are also questions *about* the ground, a reaching toward the outermost circumference and innermost core of things.

■ ■ ■

Because I live so much among words, I am prone to see patterns in language where there may be none, as a spy might see conspiracies on every street corner. But consider for a minute this word *ground,* and then decide for yourself.

Ground may be dirt, the stored-up fertility that feeds us, or it may be the earth itself. We think of the soil as stable and nurturing; but it is fluid, like the rest of creation, and it can easily slip away, as the topsoil of the Sahara blew away, as the loam of the American plains is fast eroding. Then surely the earth must be firm. We anchor our foundations in it. We ground our electrical systems and lightning rods by driving metal stakes into it. We say that a convincing argument is well grounded. A person whose feet are on the ground acts prudently. One possessed of ground sense is wise, knowing what to expect of life and how to behave. To prepare for any difficult job—building a house or running a campaign—we first do our ground work, clearing the ground, preparing the ground, breaking the ground. Our projects may fail to get off the ground. We gain ground, hold ground, give ground, and lose ground. Surely this vast globe that undergirds so many metaphors of security must be steadfast. And yet the earth, for all its seeming solidity, trembles and shakes, toppling cities, heaving the ocean into tidal waves. A ground swell in the sea or in public opinion can smash everything before it. Mountains erode, glaciers advance and retreat, the very continents drift about. On such a planet, are any foundations secure?

In physics, the ground state is the lowest energy level of a molecule, an atom, or a subatomic particle such as a proton. An electron, say, may be excited to a higher level of energy, but it will settle back to its ground state. That sounds reliable enough. But again things are shakier than they at first appear. For molecules will come apart, atoms are notorious for splitting, electrons fly away promiscuously after positive charges, and—recent theories predict—even protons, those seemingly durable lumps, will eventually decay.

We say that a ship hung up on a reef or a scheme hung up on a snag has run aground. A fox trapped in its lair, a fugitive trapped in his hideout, has been run to ground. A teenager confined to the house on weekends for misbehaving, or an airplane held on the runway for repairs, is said to be grounded. The dregs left behind after the making of coffee are grounds. In Elizabethan theaters, the groundlings watched plays from cheap standing room in the pit, by turns rowdy and rapt. This protean word is also the past tense of *grind*, meaning to wear down, pulverize. The most perilous spot of all is ground zero, where the falling bomb meets its own shadow.

Heard all by itself, the steady ground bass in music is a dull droning, yet it supports the towers of harmony and the flights of melody. In art we make this distinction over and over between figure and ground, between the pattern we notice and the setting against which that pattern stands out. In baseball, a grounder skips over the dirt and grass and stones, with all the unpredictable bounces of earthly existence. By comparison, a fly ball is nearly pure physics, a parabola bent only by gravity and air. But the batter who lofts the ball and the fielder who catches it must both dig their cleats into the dirt. Even astronauts in orbit must answer to ground control. Their flight is the drama, like the soaring of a melody or the arc of a homer, yet without the humdrum business at Canaveral or Houston there would be no adventure. No flight without control. No foreground without background. Against what ground do we shape the figures of our lives?

So much ground to cover! From this sampling, you can see that *ground* straddles a deep division in our feelings. It summons up contrary longings for support and liberation. It hangs in suspense between the freedom of flight—of balls, planes, teenagers, foxes, melodies—and the constraint of staying on earth. The ambivalence is not in the word, of course, but in us, for we desire to fly free, but also, when we land, to rest securely. We yearn to be held up, but fear being held down. The mind soars weightless through time and space, while the body answers to gravity and clocks. To lead a life that is firmly grounded means not only that one is supported but that one is constrained. Once you glimpse your true place, that vision begins to define how you should live.

■   ■   ■

Some years ago a utility company wanted to build a nuclear power plant on the sandy shore of Lake Michigan near Chicago. Their permit required them to set their foundations on bedrock, so down they drilled through the sand, down and down; but after excavating a very expensive hole, they had still not come to solid rock. Having made what they considered an honest effort, they petitioned the regulatory agency to allow them to anchor the foundations in a considerable depth of sand, and treat that as the equivalent of bedrock. The agency, to their credit (and to my surprise), said no. So the utility rolled up their blueprints and trudged back to the board room. But most of us, after failing in our own efforts to drill all the way to bedrock, give up and build our lives on shifty sand.

Ground, foundation, and *fundamental* all derive from roots meaning *bottom,* as in, "I'll get to the bottom of this." But *is* there a bottom, and even if there is can we ever get down to it? "There is a solid bottom every where," Thoreau assures us in *Walden.* That cantankerous book is a prolonged invitation to dig:

> Let us settle ourselves, and work and wedge our feet downward through the mud and slush of opinion, and prejudice, and tradition, and delusion, and appearance, that alluvion which covers the globe, through Paris and London, through New York and Boston and Concord, through church and state, through poetry and philosophy and religion, till

we come to a hard bottom and rocks in place, which we can call *reality,* and say, This is, and no mistake; and then begin.

I share his aspiration, but not his confidence. The aspiration is an old one. Twenty-five centuries before Thoreau, Lao Tzu wrote in *The Way of Things:*

By many words is wit exhausted. Rather, therefore, hold to the core.

Gladly: but how to find it, this core?

■ ■ ■

As a boy, I thought I might find the ultimate ground in the Bible. I studied the fine print with the urgency of a child lost in the labyrinth who is seeking the thread that will lead him home. With Job, I heard the Lord roaring from the whirlwind:

> Where were you when I laid the foundation of the earth? Tell me, if you have understanding. Who determined its measurements— surely you know! Or who stretched the line upon it? On what were its bases sunk, or who laid its cornerstone, when the morning stars sang together, and all the sons of God shouted for joy?

In the Psalms I heard praise for the Creator:

Thou art clothed with honor and majesty, who coverest thyself with light as with a garment,

who hast stretched out the heavens like a tent, who hast laid the beams of thy chambers on the waters, who makest the clouds thy chariot, who ridest on the wings of the wind, who makest the winds thy messengers, fire and flame thy ministers.

After combing through the Bible, I scoured the holy texts of other religions. Everywhere I looked, I came across rumors of the primal power. In *The Upanishads,* for example:

Just as a spider spins forth its thread and draws it in again, The whole creation is woven from Brahman and unto it returns. Just as plants are rooted in the earth, All beings are supported by Brahman. Just as hair grows from a person's head, So does everything arise from Brahman.

Or in the *Tao Te Ching:*

Before the Heaven and Earth existed There was something nebulous: Silent, isolated, Standing alone, changing not, Eternally revolving without fail, Worthy to be the Mother of All Things. I do not know its name And address it as Tao.

Eventually I realized that nobody knew its name. These holy texts could only gesture toward the source, whether they addressed it as Tao, Brahman, Yahweh or God, as Logo, Dharma, Atman, World

Soul, Manitou, or Spirit Keeper. In scripture after scripture, the ground I was seeking slipped through the white spaces between words.

So then I searched in music, painting, and literature. I read shelves of poetry and fiction, Auden through Zola. I hummed to the rapturous lines of D. H. Lawrence:

Put me down again on the earth, Jesus,
  on the brown soil
Where flowers sprout in the acrid
  humus, and fade into humus again.
Where beasts drop their unlicked
  young, and pasture, and drop their
  droppings among the turf.
Where the adder darts horizontal.
Down on the damp, unceasing
  ground, where my feet belong
And even my heart, Lord, forever, after
  all uplifting:
The crumbling, damp, fresh land, life
  horizontal and ceaseless.

I listened to Bach until my skull reverberated to his harmonics. I peered into Van Gogh's flaming sunflowers and starry nights until the air began to spark. But still there were gaps between notes, brush strokes, words. No screen was fine enough to catch the flow of reality, no frame large enough to contain it.

Next I tried science, beginning with biology, the squishiest of the hard sciences, then chemistry, that Erector set of atoms and bonds, and finally physics, which pursues reality with the butterfly net of mathematics, the finest mesh

of all. At least since Democritus speculated about atoms twenty-five centuries ago, scientists have been hunting for the ultimate building blocks and fundamental laws of matter. It is the same quest that Thoreau describes, a delving down through opinion and appearances to a "hard bottom," to *reality*. The scientific search, like the religious one, is inspired by a conviction that there *is* a ground, a single source underlying all the surface variety we see, and that we can apprehend it through the power of mind.

I remember encountering in freshman physics class the following simple and terrifying idea: Imagine all things spread out according to size upon a great ladder, with atoms and such minutiae toward the bottom, and galaxies and other giants toward the top, and us humans somewhere in the middle. Moving up one rung on the ladder means jumping to a scale ten times as large, and moving down means decreasing to a scale one tenth as large. For simplicity, as the scientists like to say—and also perhaps for humility—let us begin not with ourselves, an awkward size, but with an animal that is a meter long: a collie, say—my favorite dog. The step up from a collie would be a scale of ten meters, the length of a small whale, or, if you prefer, the height of a two-story house. Two rungs above the collie we would leave the range of animals entirely and reach the size of a football field. The next level would carry us to a thousand meters, roughly the length of three aircraft carriers placed end-to-end. Within only seven jumps of this sort we would rise to the diameter of the earth, and six more would carry us to that of the solar system, and so on rapidly up and up, beyond the scale of the Milky Way, then our local cluster of galaxies, then clusters of clusters, until our vision gives out somewhere in the neighborhood of twenty-five rungs above the collie.

Reverse directions, and the descent is just as dizzying. The step down from a collie would be one tenth of a meter, the size of a chickadee or a grapefruit. One more rung down and we reach the pesky house fly, the next lower and we come to the size of coarse sand. Again, after only a few more rungs, we fall below the scale of amoebas and bacteria, below the smallest microörganisms, into the domain of molecules, atoms, protons, electrons, quarks, until once more our vision gives out, roughly fifteen rungs beneath the collie.

From largest to smallest, the range over which we can presently see is about forty steps on the ladder. Whether going up or down, we eventually reach a level beyond which our instruments can no longer peer. How many levels there are, or whether they ever end, we do not know: and some theories—including a troublesome one propounded in mathematics by Kurt Gödel and the even more troubling uncertainty principle formulated by Werner Heisenberg—argue that in principle we *cannot* know. The farther out or the deeper in we look, the fainter and more ambiguous the information, and the greater the distortion imposed by our ways of looking. Heisenberg warned us not to mistake our descriptions of reality for reality itself: "[W]e have to remember that what we observe is not nature in itself but nature exposed to our method of questioning. Our scientific work in physics consists in asking questions about nature in the language that we possess and trying to get an answer from experiment by the means that are at our disposal." The point is that we will never see to the outermost circumference or innermost core of things with eye or instrument alone. Physics is a grand endeavor, one I follow with a fan's enthusiasm, but not even the most powerful accelerator will ever knock on reality's hard bottom, not even the subtlest equation will perfectly map the universe. And even the superb maps that physics does provide ignore too much of what we know by other means. To say, for example, that you and I and your cat and my banjo are just so many piles of quarks may be true, but it misses some crucial distinctions.

If neither scripture nor art nor science can lay bare the primal ground, where do we set our feet?

For all his crowing confidence, Thoreau himself was aware of the difficulty. In *Walden* he relates an anecdote about a traveler who comes to the edge of a swamp and asks a neighborhood boy if the swamp has a hard bottom. Sure does, the boy replies. So the traveler rides forward and his horse promptly sinks in up to the saddle girth. "I thought you said that this bog had a hard bottom," the man complains. "So it has," the boy answers, "but you have not got half way to it yet."

■ ■ ■

Note that in my example of the ladder I am talking about a hierarchy of size, not of importance. I do not mean to drag in the old notion of a chain of being, which would start down among the worms and ascend past us to the angels and beyond the angels to God. Even in the heyday of that notion, in the eighteenth century, the observant English vicar Gilbert White insisted that "Earthworms, though in appearance a small and despicable link in the chain of Nature, yet, if lost, would make a lamentable chasm." I would extend White's claim to say that there are no despicable links; the loss of any life would make a chasm. Whatever divinity there is runs through every step on the ladder.

To speak of divinity will make some readers nervous. It makes *me* nervous. But I cannot avoid religious language. The root meaning of *religion* is to bind together. The only way to avoid being religious, in that original sense, is to pretend that the universe does not cohere. It does cohere, beautifully. On every scale we have been able to examine, from quarks to supergalactic clusters, we find structure. Even what we used to label chaos now appears to obey rules. In the history of science, every time we have come up against phenomena that seemed haphazard, they turned out to be lawful on a scale we had not yet grasped.

To insist that nature is orderly is not to say it is tidy, like a billiard ball, or easy to grasp, like a doorknob, or that it has been set up like a doll house for our little human play. In *Moby-Dick*, Melville's narrator speculates that the whiteness of the whale terrifies us because it is a reminder of "the heartless voids and immensities of the universe, and thus stabs us from behind with the thought of annihilation." He describes the blank forehead of Moby Dick as an image of the "colorless, all-color of atheism from which we shrink." If the whale's whiteness fairly sums up the world, if reality is nothing but random collisions of particles, then the universe is absurd. For most of a century, it has been fashionable among intellectuals to say so. But not one of them could have stood upright, held a pen, or digested supper without participating in an exquisite and, for all we can see, infinite order.

Just because we cannot lay our fingers on the pulse, does not mean the universe is heartless. What presumption, to imagine that because we are bewildered the universe must be a muddle, or that because we cannot see a direction in things there must be no purpose. Even sober scientists have been known to project our uncertainties onto the cosmos. Steven Weinberg, a Nobel laureate in physics, concluded his account of the big bang with a sentence that sticks in the mind like a bur: "The more the universe seems comprehensible, the more it also seems pointless." Commenting on this passage in an interview, the cosmologist James Peebles said, reasonably enough, "I have never demanded that the universe explain to me why it's doing what it's doing."

If we gaze about us and see nothing but a shambles, we have not looked hard enough, we have not looked beyond the arena of human deeds and needs to the order that sustains us. We may appeal to the headlines, or cite a disaster fallen on someone we love, and proclaim that the world makes no sense. Yet how could we be troubled by cancer, by hurricanes, by war, by all the messy ways in which things fall apart, if things did not cohere so amazingly to begin with? Of course we seek patterns, but the universe answers our seeking. What we call constellations are human shapes imposed on the stars, with names and legends attached; but we did not invent the stars, nor their motions, nor their light. The question is not whether there is an order to the world, but what sort of order it is, whence it comes, how to speak of it, and how to live in relation to it.

■ ■ ■

A t-shirt design popular some years ago showed a broadside view of the Milky Way, a blurry swirl of dots, with an arrow pointing to an indistinguishable spot far out near the edge, and the familiar caption: "You Are Here." Humorous, but not sufficiently humbling, because only an infinite t-shirt would be large enough to map the true scale of our insignificance. And yet, there is the curious fact that we can summon all of this creation into our minds: not only can, but seem compelled to do so. The flowers outside my window thrusting up their snouts are not wondering about the dirt that feeds them or the urge that quickens them; the galaxies career without pondering their flight. But I sit here puzzling about crocus and constellation; and so can you, if you choose. Measured on the celestial scale, we are nothing, yet we can think of everything. Our minds stretch over all forty rungs of that ladder. The smaller we perceive our role in the universe to be, the more astounding that we can reflect on the universe at all.

We have stories aplenty, in addition to the gloomy one about the Garden of Eden, to warn us against trying to know too much. Even a sip of knowledge can make you tipsy. Remember when you realized for the first time that, since the earth is a spinning ball, everyone must flip topsy-turvy between noon and midnight, midnight and noon, and you suddenly wondered how you kept from flying off? When I saw that picture of myself whirling and whirling, I grabbed for the bedpost. I locked my door. Oh dear trees, I thought, lend me your roots. Over time, the earth reassured me by steadily drawing me to its generous bulk. Later, when I studied Newton's equations, I learned that we tug with equal force on the earth.

The billionfold clusters of stars that we call galaxies used to be known as island universes. Before Europeans misnamed this continent America after an Italian sailor, the native peoples called it Turtle Island: a dry land lifted obligingly from the sea. Anatomists refer to groups of specialized cells in the body as islands, such as the Islands of Langerhans in the pancreas. Islands within islands within islands. Given so little matter in so much emptiness, only by huddling together can the stuff of creation build up a world.

The galaxies are rushing apart, the astronomers say, and I believe them. But even as the universe expands, the fleeing galaxies still pull at one another. Every bit of the cosmos sways every other bit, either by the force of gravity, according to Newton, or by curving space, according to Einstein, or by the intertwining of strings, according to the latest theory. Regardless of the image you choose, it assures us that the whole cosmos is bound together. Astrology is bunk, yet it arises from a profound intuition: everything connects. The desire to trace what we can of this connectedness is the source of religion as it is of science.

If I am to grasp an idea the size of the universe, I need a picture. So think of going outside one damp morning and finding in the grass a spider's web glistening with dew. Now let this spangled web extend on and on, out to the frontiers of imagination, then add a second one intersecting with the first, then a third, a fourth, as many as your mind can hold, all interconnecting, until you have a vast, intricate three-dimensional web filling all of space. (Whether the outermost skeins eventually curve back to form a ball, or whether they trail on and on forever, I leave deliberately vague, since the cosmologists are still not sure if our universe is open or closed.) This web has no center, no privileged spot where the spider lurks. Everything is linked to everything else. Pluck any strand, wiggle any node, and the vibrations pass out through the whole web.

The more we learn about the world, the tighter the cosmic web appears. Consider again that lowly dirt, whose fecund smell has launched me on these reflections. Among those billion organisms in a handful of soil are anaerobic bacteria, creatures so successful that they have survived virtually unchanged since the earth was a quarter of its present age, for they date from the era before the atmosphere flooded with oxygen, that dangerous gas. These same bacteria flourish in the airless reaches of my gut, and in yours, nor could we live without them. They are part of the menagerie of creatures with which we share our sacks of skin. And every bit of us, skin and marrow, is made out of recycled materials. The carbon in our guts, indeed all the atoms in our bodies heavier than helium, were fused in the centers of stars. Physicists believe that the heaviest of these elements were made and scattered abroad by stellar explosions. The sun and moon and all the planets congealed from the dust of disaster. The oxygen we breathe, the phosphorus in our cells, the iron in our blood, the calcium in our bones are the debris of a supernova. According to the English scientist James Lovelock, "Within our bodies, no less than three million atoms rendered unstable in that event still erupt every minute, releasing a tiny fraction of the energy stored from that fierce fire of long ago." The radiation that warms the earth's core is a remnant of our violent origin. We have oceans and rivers

and rains because the heat of our beginnings boiled water out of rock. I think of this as I sip my tea.

My life, or any life, is a knot where an infinite number of threads lace together. If we tease out one of those threads, and trace it as far as we can, eventually we come up against the unknown, where even the experts fall silent. The universe is tied together quite firmly enough without any help from science, religion, or me. In a famous closing image from *The Origin of Species*, Charles Darwin likened nature to a "tangled bank." In our eyes it may appear tangled, and yet, no matter how numerous and fine the threads, they are not snarled.

■ ■ ■

Once when I asked my father if he had ever been lost, he answered, "No, but there's been a few times when I didn't know where anything else was." By that definition, I am lost for days and weeks at a stretch, aware of myself but of little else. The only ground I notice is the grit under my shoes. The world is gray cardboard. I trudge through dullness, as though deep in a trench, wholly absorbed in taking the next step. Chores, chores, chores. Places to go, things to do.

Then occasionally I wake from my drowse and for a few minutes every toad becomes a dragon, every lilac is a fiery fountain, and I am walking on pure light.

These luminous moments are the standard by which I measure my ordinary hours. It may be the oldest human standard, older than the desire for comfort, older than duty. As the maverick monk Thomas Berry put it in his stiff but dignified way: "Awareness of an all-pervading mysterious energy articulated in the infinite variety of natural phenomena seems to be the primordial experience of human consciousness." *Energy* is a word that scientists willingly use, but *mystery* is not. Let mystery into the discussion, they fear, and pretty soon you'll have astral travel and bloodletting and witch hunts. You'll have fanatics reading the future in the bones of birds. You'll lock up Galileo for saying the earth spins about the sun, you'll hoot at Darwin for tracing our descent from the apes. You'll sweep away the magnificent, meticulous theater of science and replace it with a Punch-and-Judy show.

Cosmologists have tried every way they can to avoid having to posit what they call "initial conditions"—those conditions that determine the features of our universe. Why, for example, does the proton have exactly this mass, why does the electron have that charge? Why does energy convert to matter and matter to energy? Why do the fundamental forces interact just so? Why does nature obey these rules, or any rules? Why are the parameters such that life could evolve, and, within life, consciousness? And how does it happen that consciousness has figured out so many of the rules? If you admit that you cannot answer

those questions, and simply appeal to initial conditions in order to explain fundamental features of the universe, then you raise the question of how those conditions were set. You bump into the old conundrum: How can there be a design without a designer? You can't do physics on God. So cosmologists have proposed a steady-state universe, an oscillating universe, or a universe with zero net energy sprung from quantum fluctuations—anything to avoid having to concede that reality extends beyond the reach of science.

With our twin hands, our paired eyes, our sense of a split between body and mind, we favor dualisms: design and designer, creation and creator, universe and God. But I suspect the doubleness is an illusion. "How can we know the dancer from the dance?" Yeats asked. We hear treble and bass because we have two ears; the music itself is whole and undivided. The wind and the leaves shaking on the tree are two things; but the wave and the sea are one. When I sit on the pink granite of the Maine coast looking out over the water, I see the ocean ripple and surge into whitecaps. Just so, the earth is a wave lifted up from the surf of space, and you and I are waves lifted from the earth.

According to Hopi myth, long ago, at the beginning of our age, people emerged from a hole in the ground. They looked over the earth and liked what they saw, so they stayed. But at the end of time the people will go back again into the ground. When buried in graves or scattered as ashes, we also return to the ground. The throwing of the first shovelful of dirt on the coffin or the flinging of gray dust into the wind is a ritual moment when the earth reclaims us. Writing about the ground is in part an attempt to come to terms with death, with my own return to the source. But it is at least as much an attempt to come to terms with life, with the issuing-forth.

This is the light in which I have come to see Thoreau's best-known sentence: "What I have been preparing to say is that in Wildness is the preservation of the World." "Wildness" here is usually understood to mean wilderness. But I think it has a larger meaning. I think it refers to the creative energy that continually throws new forms into existence and gives them shape. Thus "Wildness" is literally the "preservation of the World," because without it there would *be* no world. Gary Snyder may have had some such notion in mind when he insisted that nature is simply what is, the way of things: "This, *thusness*, is the nature of the nature of nature. The wild in wild." By keeping in touch with wildness, we preserve our sanity and the world's health.

Beneath or behind or within everything there is an unfathomable ground—a suchness, as the Buddhists say—that one can point toward, bow to, contemplate, but cannot grasp. To speak of this ground as a mystery is not to say that we know nothing, only that we cannot know everything. The larger the context we envision, the more tentative and partial our knowledge appears, the more humble we are forced to be. Merely think of the earth as a living system, taking the health of that system as the gauge of everything we do, and you recognize that our ignorance is profound.

■　■　■

The thawing dirt brings me a whiff of the world's renewal. The green shoots of crocuses breaking through are the perennial thrusting-forth of shapeliness out of the void. Breathing in the breath of soil, I feel the source of Thomas Berry's claim that "Our deepest convictions arise in this contact of the human with some ultimate mystery whence the universe itself is derived." The smell brings to my lips the words my Mississippi grandfather would say, of anything that especially delighted him: "That suits me right down to the ground."

And yet, for all my conviction, I still get dizzy when I look down. Where oh where is that solid footing? On what rock can I build? Philosophers and theologians speak of the foundation of things as the ground of being. They go about like dowsers with divining rods, alert to every twitch in the forked stick. Here it is, one of them proclaims. No, it's over here, another insists. No, no, any fool can see it's right *here*. The quarrel among the dowsers is as old as speech, and most likely will continue as long as our breath holds out. What a seductive phrase: the ground of being. But if you waited to plant your beans or build your house until you had dug down to that elusive ground, you would go hungry and cold. I'll make do with the dirt I can touch.

The dirt I can touch beside my front door, where the grass needles through, is a mousy brown. If I lived elsewhere, the soil could be red, yellow, buff, or black. The colors of dirt are roughly the shades of human skin. I scoop a handful of it, gingerly, mindful of those billion organisms. Then I lift it to my face, sniff the damp, fruitful smell, and am glad.

■ ■ ■

This article first appeared in the January/February 1992 issue of North American Review *and was later included in* Staying Put, *by Scott Russell Sanders, published by Beacon Press in 1993. Sanders is an English professor at Indiana University—Bloomington.*

■ ■ ■

CORRECTIONVILLE, IOWA

BY MICHAEL MARTONE

Pelisipia, Polypotania, Saratoga, Illinoia, Assenispia, Michigania, Cherronesus, Metropotania, Sylvania. . . . Thomas Jefferson drew up a list of names for the new states northwest of the Ohio River. Since 1776, the Congress had been promising land to the soldiers who fought the War of Independence and had considered the sale of land in the new region as a way to raise money for the war. Now, with the war over and the land being purchased from the tribes and ceded by the states with claims, Congress appointed two committees, one to plan for the governments of the new territory, the other charged with locating them and drawing up methods of their disposal. Thomas Jefferson sat on both committees.

I think of him sitting on top of his mountain in Virginia, not in the squat fireplug mansion of Monticello with its collections and contraptions, but in the little cubical cottage out back, the honeymoon house, the first building he put up after balding the hill. Through the mullioned windows he watched his slaves tend the lattice work of gardens that stretched along the ridge, square beds divided into smaller squares. Before him he had a rough map of the territory under consideration. For his purposes, it didn't matter how accurate that map was. He had never been there, though George Washington had actually toured Ohio and surveyed a few miles there. With a ruler, Jefferson drew a straight line north from the falls near what is today Louisville. The lakes, the rivers, the hills did not deflect the line. From his original meridian, he began to lay out squares of space that would eventually add up to new states that needed naming.

In Jefferson's list there is a goofy classicism. He screws the Latin endings on to the native names. Sitting in his little cottage, he is like a kid in a treehouse daydreaming about the secret club he is founding where everyone holds a title and everything is ordered and embedded in ritual. Of course Jefferson's musing isn't *like* the summer distractions of the neighborhood gangleader, it is exactly the same thing, the only difference being in the scale of the invention. It is not just a map of the backyards in the local cul-de-sac but a whole continent he is considering. I like very much the names he scribbled inside his neat squares. They contrast smartly with the severe and logical grid he generated to net up the beginnings of an empire. The names that did settle on those places are harmonics of those Jefferson toyed with. Michigan, Illinois echo the originals as if they are the final versions of copies of copies, only the main plosives picked out from the mumbling through time. But it is the chutzpah of the whole enterprise, the wicked inventiveness and brute reason that allowed him to sweep away the physical features of the west and coolly scale it down to human size.

There are compromises. Jefferson originally thought in hundreds, ten by ten mile squares. And his miles were the nautical kind, I don't know why. With the Ordinance of 1785, the Congress of the Confederation created the office of the Geographer of the United States, charged with surveying the new lands into six by six mile squares called townships. The land ordinances of 1784, 1785, and 1787 address how the recently independent colonies would handle their own colonial expansion and were platforms for confronting the issues of expanding slavery and extending human rights. Those laws prefigured the workings of the Constitution, being written in Philadelphia while the initial ranges were being surveyed in Ohio, and its first ten amendments. But I am more interested here in the physical residue of these acts, the scoring of the land with that waffle grid of true bearings.

∎ ∎ ∎

Recently, I came across a book by Joseph W. Ernst called *With Compass and Chain: Federal Land Surveyors in the Old Northwest, 1785–1816*, published by Arno Press in 1979. In it, Ernst explores how Jefferson's abstract ideas were made real. Ernst is consumed with procedure and the practical questions of implementing theory in the field. He records the surveyors' food and pay, their measuring instruments, their letters and notes, their payoffs and politics. These men walked every inch of the ground that would become the Midwest.

On September 30, 1785, Thomas Hutchins, the Geographer of the United States, sent his first survey notes to Congress:

Based on observations made while running the E-W line from the North bank of the Ohio at point due north from Western termination of a line run as a southern boundary of Pennsylvania. 46 chains and 80 links West of this point, lands disposed for growth of vines. Variety of trees and bushes. The whole of the above described Land is too rich to produce Wheat, but is well adapted for Indian Corn, Tobacco, Hemp, Flax, Oats, etc. and every species of Garden Vegetables, it abounds with great quantities of Pea Vine, Grass, and nutrias weeds of which cattle are very fond and on which they soon grow fat.

33 Chains, 14 links, which make a mile from the Meredian, High land.

22 Chains, 37 links, the land is extraordinary good, and in some places it is too rich for Wheat, where fine Meadow may be made. Timber Locust, Black Walnut, Mulberry, Hickory, Elm.

21 Chains, crosses a ridge, land between good, in several places it is tolerably free from brush or underwood.

6 Chains, 60 links, brook running South 20 degrees West.

14 Chains, 40 links, steep narrow ridge nearly 170 feet high, perpendicular. Covered on east side with many bushes and weeds. Golden rod, the latter when timely used and properly applied has been found efficacious in curing the bite of the most ven-omous Snake. Soil on the ridge equal parts sand and black mould.

13 Chains, gradual descent, thicket with trees, the whole of this distance was cut through for the Chain carriers to pass.

5 Chains, 63 links, makes two miles.

In the first two miles of his survey, Hutchins plows through a sheer ridge face, fords a stream, and clears a straight blaze through a thicket. As the geometry of this task draws him straight on, his eye is drawn to this new, new world in his periphery. He sometimes reports what he finds, but of course he sees deeper into what he sees to what can be used and exploited. He is musing on the proper order of domesticating the wilderness. It is another act of imagination. In his mind, he imports the grain and crops. A pedestrian Adam, he names the trees he finds while at the same time he pictures the lumbering. It goes without saying the timber's sectioning, milling, and planing follow. Its metamorphosis into furniture and into the wagons to haul it to new houses is the final destination. He brings the garden to the Garden. His vision even includes the metabolism of the native weeds into the fat on cattle. He gets carried away here, a touching flourish, empathizing with the livestock. He almost breaks into narrative. This flight of fancy is made even more tender when the reader remembers that its writer is mired down in mire, swamp and jungle, bitten by bugs and ever conscious of those venomous snakes. Linking it together is the stretching of the chain itself, inching along the ground, another snake, rattling over rocks and hollow logs and fresh cut stumps, sizzling through the grass as it is reeled back in. Sound has come to the forest, the haunting racket of the ghosts to come trailing the forged, precise shackles of their vices. There is someone here now who will hear the trees falling.

In the geographer's notes as well, there is another story. While he suggests the cultivation of Indian corn and tobacco, his eye is peeled for the Indian himself.

His survey had already been delayed by skirmishes, his stakes and corner markers would be destroyed once he moved on. The American incursion into the lands northwest of the Ohio river would proceed in its crystalline manner, square by square, but it was preceded itself by the most irregular pattern of purchase, conquest, or acquisition. In contrast to the logic woven by the patient web of townships, a Midwestern map of treaty cessations looks like the splotches of woodland camouflage. The patches of Indian territory sold or won were chewed away from the edges, eating their way towards the center. The water routes took the Europeans far inland where they struck out from the forts at Detroit, Chicago, Louisville, and St. Louis. The irregular shapes of the treaty lands, their borders fixed not by compass and chain but by the land itself, rivers, lakes, and hills, suggests the anarchy of their tak-ing, a swipe here, a swath there.

Which is more terrifying? This random rent or the steady quilting? Perhaps they were worse taken together, the chaos so reasonably ordered and camouflaged by the brand of that order which remains cut into the land today.

■ ■ ■

No other feature so marks the Midwestern landscape as the signature of townships. The six mile squares broke down into 36 sections of one square mile each,

and each square mile of 640 acres reduced to those plots of recognizable dimension, the 80, the back 40. There is nothing natural about it. It is not like the Spanish moss drooping from Southern trees or the dripping ferns of the Pacific Northwest, nor is it like the rocky scrabble in the soil of the East or the dusty reaches of buttes and mesas in the West. We know the Midwest by this arbitrary and artificial pattern that has been imposed upon it.

Though most of the public lands outside the original colonies and the south were surveyed into these grids, it is this chunk of land, stretching from Ohio west to Minnesota and Iowa where its pattern is most deeply inscribed. Here the subtlety and variety of the region's topography and ecology cannot suppress the imposition of the grid. Further west, the landscape becomes much more spectacular, space an identifying feature in itself. The people are fewer, and they begin to speak of the land in sections not acres. Historically, the Homestead Act of 1862 changed the focus of land claims. Individual settlement powered land acquisition west of the Missouri River, not the communal motives that informed the original ordinances. The grid "took" in those more eastern states, and, though the townships governing structure have withered away in many places, but not in all places by any means, what survives is the network of roads and fields oriented north to south and east to west, and measured out on a human scale of rods and acres that scores this place.

The Midwest, then, began as a highly abstract work of the imagination and lingers so today. The power of the grid that overlays it often prevents us from seeing the place itself. It has been characterized from its inception in two dimensions alone, flattened by fiat. At the same time, for those of us from the Midwest, this plane geometry that enmeshes us might be the only connection we have between us. What links the auto worker in Detroit with the actuary in Des Moines, the mussel digger near Galena with the strip miner near Athens? Perhaps it is only this thin tissue of coordinates plotted a long time ago that can tie together this region's inhabitants. We are Midwesterners because we think ourselves into the map of the place without having to fit into the place itself. We relate to each other on that mathematical plane alone.

■ ■ ■

I didn't know it then, but the borders of my own neighborhood where I grew up in Fort Wayne, Indiana, were streets that followed the original township grid. My mother had set State Street on the North and Tyler Street on the west as limits of my range. There was one exception. I could be ushered across those busy streets by watchful safety patrols to Price Elementary School, sited at their intersection. On the south was

Spring Street where we lived. On the eastern edge was the smaller square of Hamilton Park.

But within this one square mile border, developers had carved out streets with asymmetrical abandon. A map of those streets looks like the burrowings in cross-section of a colony of termites. Jefferson thought the grid to be the most democratic of forms. North Highlands, my neighborhood, the first suburb in town, was having nothing to do with democracy. Its larger houses, brick with drooping awnings, were perched on hills at the prows of parabolas. There were pockets of cheap ranch houses that looked like a sprouting of motel courts set off behind massive clapboard four-squares positioned off-center on oblong lots. The roads followed the contours of the land. The land had been bulldozed, before the subdivision, into the traps and bunkers, the roughs and fairways of a golf course. A friend of mine lived in what had been the club house. Its lawn still had patches of the practice green disrupting the bluegrass like a strange weed infestation. It seemed you were meant to get lost in the winding streets as if they were a defense against invading hordes from the greater city who could then be defeated in the maze of tree-lined streets. The neighborhood was a watered-down version of vernacular villages of Greek Islands where the dice-white buildings tumble down a hillside. Its warren of alleys and double-backs were defensive measures against pirates. Here, the houses were all detached, the only raiders the armies of children free to run wild in the yards between them.

Before the golf course, the land had been owned by the Hamilton family. Some of the street names were Edith, Alice, Ida, Jesse, names of the Hamilton children. Edith grew up to be the great popularizer of ancient Greek myths. We read her book, *Mythology*, in our Language Arts classes at school. Growing up in Fort Wayne, I read about Perseus and Medusa, Theseus in the labyrinth, Odysseus wandering home. I also marveled at the strange connection that had brought these old stories to me. I saw a picture of the ancient Miss Hamilton in the theater of Dionysus in Athens being named a citizen of the city. She wore the draping gown of the Golden Age. I'd sit on the steep banks of Hamilton Park, where we sledded in winter, and imagine it was another classical theater.

Hamilton Park had those steep hills because it had been, before it was grassed over, a trash dump. I played in a ruin. The grass covered the terraced steps of the sides where dogwoods, redbuds, and flowering crabapples had been planted. Rows of lilac outlined the square rim of its top lip. There were ball diamonds, tennis and basketball courts, and picnic tables where you could play Rook at the bottom of the pit. When it rained, water collected

on the floor of the sunken park, and, sometimes, the buried trash would work its way back to the surface. Burned and broken blue glass, smashed tin cans, rusted springs, buttons, plates and cups, bottle caps, nails, books with rotting pages. All the kids had collections of their finds.

I look back now and see how this little patch of ground surrendered up its history, how too it was a frame for the larger histories of the world. Somewhere along the way I realized that classical Athens was not much bigger than my own home town, and the stories I read of those golden ages, interpreted by someone from my town, were relentlessly local while they spoke to the larger human condition. I also realized that the stories of this place were just beginning to be told. Platting the landscape, sub-dividing the subdivisions of property would not be enough to kick-start the culture of myth. We who grew up in the Midwest would have to sit here awhile, within the borders of our own defined neighborhoods, on the banks of a natural theater, and watch as the junk of our too-recent past resurrected itself and appeared to us as treasure in the dust at our feet.

■ ■ ■

In Iowa, the idea of the township was raised to the *n*th degree. The squares of the sections quilt the larger squares of the townships that form the squares of the counties. It is a joke in Iowa that there is only one diagonal road. From the air, Iowa looks like a rumpled crossword puzzle. The squares spell out the season in an alphabet of three green letters—corn, beans, pasture—that alternate with the ink-black turned fields. Driving through the country on all those straight roads, I could check my odometer with the regular rotation of features. Intersecting road, corn field, soybean field, lane, corn, bean, house, bean, corn, road. A Midwestern mantra of quarter-mile heartbeats. When you drive long enough in Iowa you've strung together a rosary of small towns as well that punctuates the rhythm of the spaces between. Cottonville leads to Garry Owen, Garry Owen to Cascade, Cascade to Monticello. The towns are like knots in the chains the surveyors used. The towns can go together to form a kind of picaresque story line. Driving through Iowa can become a modern walkabout, the water towers painted with the pictographs of town names, booster slogans, and zip codes that rise up to meet you like giants on the horizon.

Once I strung together a story that drew me west. Starting from Spillville in the northeast corner of the state, I vectored to Hospers in the northwest. In between was the town of West Bend. It takes three points to draw a line, and the line I sketched followed U.S. 18 as it stepped occasionally north

or south shooting across the state. The towns were linked by an eccentric geometry. Each contained the life's work of bachelor folk artists. In Spillville, brothers had built gigantic wooden sculptures housing clocks. In West Bend, a priest had constructed on the lawn of the church a grotto dedicated to the Virgin. In Hospers, a citizen sculpted a garden of painted concrete statues for the town square. Each of these creations is amazing in itself, but I find the parallels of their creation more interesting.

You learn that the artists never traveled more than a few miles from their homes. The wood for the clocks, you hear, was shipped in. Butternut, grapefruit, mahogany, teak arrived by train whose conductors on their travels were always on the lookout for the fresh scrap of lumber, a new bark to peel. The shells and semi-precious stones that encrust the bubbling chambers of the grotto were also imported. Quartz and coal, fossils and pumice. The corals of the tropics grew on the thickening reef in West Bend. The artist in Hospers took his models from the books he read. Sculptures of Carrera marble were copied in the other medium of cement. The worldly contributions to the art came into the hands of resolutely local artists, and yet each of them included in their elaborate schemes a piece or niche or grouping dedicated to the act of travel itself. There is a History of Transportation clock, a tower of Babel wedding cake with marching bas reliefs of vehicles topped by the legend "Time Flies." There is also a clock commemorating Lindbergh, a globe carved up with latitudes and longitudes cutting through the swirling clouds of the wood's grain. The grotto blesses mobility. Do I remember a side altar of the flight into Egypt? In Hospers, another History of Transportation includes a green tractor in the evolution from dinosaur to rocket ship. The tractor is rendered most realistically. Its models burbled through the town as I toured. The artist swiped the paint for his tractor, the green Deere shade, from the local machine shop.

The clocks must stay in Spillville. They were willed to the town on that condition. The grotto is rooted to its lawn in West Bend. The garden of melting statues is cemented to its square in Hospers. I like how all of these artists had recognized their own boundaries and then constructed a few more but still managed to elaborate, to the extreme, their chosen art. Once they defined their labor to such narrow tolerances they seem to have found an infinite source of freedom. The clocks, the grotto, the sculptures are amazing, literal mazes of their creators' visions. They play all the variations within those limits.

Think of the Midwest as a vast plane studded with nodes of creation where artists are making

a place by staying in place, riddling it with possibilities. Some, like the artists in Spillville, West Bend, and Hospers, remain physically in the places they are creating, while others take their places with them. Those who travel still worry the fragments they take with them from their given coordinates, a piece of the true cross.

■ ■ ■

You can draw another line through Iowa from Dubuque to Sioux City. That line would be the western extension of the northern border of Illinois. It also forms the northern border of a tier of counties in central Iowa. Remember that in Iowa counties are laid out in a regular pattern of squares that replicates the township squares forming those counties. Just south of the Dubuque line there is a parallel line called a correction line. The county boundaries running north and south take a little jog to the west along this line so that this tier of counties isn't exactly square but whittled down a bit as they head north. The correction allows a two-dimensional surveying system to be placed on the spherical globe. Reading *With Compass and Chain*, I learned that not only did surveyors of the townships have to struggle with the physical burdens of their task but they also had to face the geometric paradox of their assignment. They were charged with squaring the earth. A correction line was one of their solutions.

Correctionville, Iowa, sits in the notch of correction between Ida and Woodbury counties. When I lived in Iowa, I always wanted to visit the place where theory butted up against reality. I never made the trip, but in my idle moments, I did like to speculate what the small town might be like. I imagined a main street filled with shops making minor adjustments to small engines, bicycle seats, and television sets. A town of photo retouchers, glass blowers, paint mixers, piano tuners, tree pruners, barbers and tailors. Every house would need fixing up. In my mind, Correctionville was a kind of rheostat regulating the flow of all the forces coursing through the Midwest. The Delphi of tinkering. The epicenter of alteration. The mecca of dentists.

"We don't have the prison, that's for sure!" Maude Schemmel told me. "People usually think we have the prison here."

I had called the town clerk in Correctionville thinking I could have a city map sent to me. I thought I could find out if there was a chamber of commerce and when the library was open. I called the clerk, but Maude Schemmel, the librarian, answered the phone.

"I answer the phone when the clerk is out of the office," she told me. "She answers the library phone when I'm not here." A cybernetic logic behind this, I thought.

I told her that I knew the town wasn't the seat of the penitentiary and that I called because I was interested in the correction line, in townships, and in mapping. We talked about the town name and its history. She would send me their Bicentennial booklet. Then we got lost while talking about geography and charts. I told her about the Greenland problem, how the island isn't as big as it looks like it is on certain maps.

"It depends upon the projection you use. Every map distorts the world some way," I said. "Iowa uses a different projection than Illinois or Indiana. They want their maps to be more accurate running north and south."

I continued. Not really knowing what I was saying. For a moment I became confused and suggested that the correction corrected something on the earth itself instead of on the map of it.

Maude said, "You mean if I started walking due north from Correctionville, the miles would get longer the farther I went?"

"Only if you were walking on a map," I said vaguely. I was distracted by the picture in my mind of the librarian striding across the map of Iowa, crushing the names and numbers, trampling the ideograms of campsites and rest stops. I also thought about Thomas Hutchins, the first Geographer of the United States, as he stepped off into Ohio dragging his chains behind him, the ones he would use to try to shackle the planet.

I had exhausted the limited expertise I had in the matter of cartography when Maude asked her final question. "But what if the map was as big as the world?"

■ ■ ■

I'd like to go to the real Correctionville someday. I have been living and working as a writer in the other Correctionville, the one in my mind. There, I am constantly tinkering with the maps of the Midwest, trying to damp the distortions as much as possible while realizing that each selected vision of the place is a map more detailed than the thing it represents.

The Midwest is unique for this framework of squares stretched across the landscape, this cage of reason that has never quite fit. It is ground that has been imprinted, literally. It comes to us with its own fractal geometry where the smallest of its parts replicates itself on ever larger scales. All the efforts of politicians and surveyors to net up the region in knowing has not begun to capture the spaces between the weave. To write about the Midwest is to cast a web in those spaces and then wait patiently for things to begin to stick.

■ ■ ■

This article first appeared in the December 1991 issue of North American Review *and is included in Martone's book* Townships (*University of Iowa Press*). *Martone lives in Syracuse, New York.*

■ ■ ■

TUSK, TUSK

BY KENNETH BROWER

At the Hand of Man:
Peril and Hope
for Africa's Wildlife
by Raymond Bonner.
Knopf, $24.00.

A year ago, in Cameroon, I accompanied a French doctor, François Morel, on some of the occasional visits he paid to a pygmy encampment in the rain forest of Campo Reserve, near the border with Equatorial Guinea. Dr. Morel is sixty. An old Africa hand, he killed many elephants in his youth, when elephants were everywhere in Francophone Africa. Now, with elephants scarce, he is full of regrets. On the path to the pygmies, Morel walked briskly but noiselessly, hoping always to surprise the pygmy *ganga,* the sorcerer, before the man could slip away. The *ganga* was Morel's competition as healer, and the doctor hoped to work out a rapprochement. The sorcerer was never home.

One day on the path we met a pygmy with a shotgun. The shotgun was French, an old engraved double-barreled Darne, and Morel exclaimed happily on seeing it. Taking it from the pygmy, he squinted down the barrel, broke the piece open, and peered inside the breech, all the while

making appreciative clucking sounds. The pygmy watched unhappily. He was a big man for a pygmy, and his teeth were bad. We had seen him each time we visited the camp. Once we had asked him the whereabouts of the sorcerer. He *was* the sorcerer, but we would not learn this until later. Morel, hefting the sorcerer's shotgun, told me that his own father had owned a Darne just like it. It was a gun too expensive for the pygmy himself to own, the doctor said. It belonged to the mayor of the nearest Bantu village. The mayor would give the pygmy a cartridge or two, and the pygmy would hunt in return for a percentage of the meat. I smiled at this theory. Morel was new to Campo Reserve. He had only just encountered this shotgun. How could he possibly know that it belonged to the mayor? *But it did! It belonged to the mayor!* And it was true about the two cartridges, as I would learn later from the mayor himself. It was a pattern so common in Francophone Africa, this poaching by proxy, that an old hand like Morel did not have to ask. He could read it as clearly as if it were engraved there in the scrollwork on the gun.

Another day, on a dirt road deeper in the reserve, Morel and

I saw a Camerounais soldier standing with some pygmies beside his car at the side of the road. The soldier, a Bantu in a camouflage uniform, stood head, shoulders, and chest above his companions, and was several shades blacker. Morel stopped our battered Renault alongside. *"La chasse?"* the doctor asked. Hunting? *"Oui,"* the soldier said. *"Pièges?"* Morel asked. Traps? Yes, the soldier answered, looking slightly uneasy now. Ah, Morel said, but this was a reserve, *n'est-ce pas?* No, the soldier lied; this section lay outside the reserve. We bid the man adieu, and Morel drove on down the road. Rounding a turn, we saw a pygmy with a shotgun over his shoulder. "Weapon of soldier," Morel told me in English, and we waved at the pygmy as we passed.

This is the reality of wildlife preservation in postcolonial Africa, and in most of the rest of the Third World. Parks and preserves are scattered all across the Dark Continent, but most are just paper parks, shaded portions on the map—illusions. The worst poachers in Africa, more often than not, are the game wardens. Africa's wildlife is in its most precipitous decline since the biosphere's last big collision with an asteroid. This is the catastrophe that Raymond Bonner seeks to address in *At the Hand of Man.*

■ ■ ■

Bonner's particular concern is the elephant, and his argument is wonderfully counterintuitive. The problem with the elephant is not so much the poachers and ivory dealers, he says. The problem is the conservationists. The World Wildlife Fund, the African Wildlife Foundation, and the other outfits concerned with the elephant have had their policies hijacked by the greed of their fundraisers. In contravention of sound conservation practice, oblivious of the wishes of the African people (or openly contemptuous), these rich white men have foisted a misguided ivory ban on Africa and the world. The elephant is, if anything, overprotected. The best way to save elephants, paradoxically, is to kill a percentage for their ivory.

Reporting on the environment is a departure for Bonner, who in the past has reported on politics. (His two previous books are on U.S. policy in El Salvador and the dictatorship of Ferdinand Marcos.) Departures of this sort are often advantageous: they permit a fresh eye, a freedom from dogma. Most books on the disappearance of African wildlife have been by people in the "religion," as environmentalists sometimes call their movement. Bonner cannot be called an apostate—he was never even baptized. These departures, of course, may also have disadvantages. The fresh eye can be too fresh. The newcomer can be insufficiently grounded in the facts, language, history, and arguments of the field. In this book disadvantages overwhelm advantages from the start. Bonner brings his own dogma to the writing, and his ignorance in environmental matters is profound.

Bonner is much more a reporter than a writer. Some authors are both, but Bonner is not one of them. His is not a prose style designed to give much pleasure. His writing is, among other things, totally without humor. For an evocation of the Africa he is talking about—the landscapes, the animals, the people—you need to keep the old, dog-eared Dinesen, or the Hemingway, or the Beryl Markham around. Bonner has not composed a single African image or description that will stick with you.

The elephant, central figure in this book, is among the missing characters. The first elephant we meet lies in a pool of blood, her face hacked off for ivory. All Bonner's subsequent elephants are faceless too, in a figurative way. The elephants of Raymond Bonner are all destroyers of the *shambas* of African peasants, uprooters of whole forests. We learn nothing at all about elephant behavior, society, lore. The most wonderful of recent discoveries about elephants—that they communicate over great distances by low-frequency sound—is never mentioned. Last year, on rain-forest paths in Cameroon, my French doctor, Morel, would drop to all fours occasionally to demonstrate the amble of the elephant. His performance was transforming. He *became* an elephant. Bonner never tries the equivalent thing in his prose, never drops to all fours to help us see and understand the elephant. This is partly because he is not equipped for it, as an observer or as a writer, and partly because undue sympathy for elephants would work against his thesis.

Bonner is an advocate of "culling" and of "sustainable utilization," as are, he claims, all conservationists with any sense. He seems to have no inkling of the history of abuses perpetrated in the name of those two concepts. Culling is often just killing. Sustained utilization has seldom been sustainable. The woods are full of calculated euphemisms—the "multiple-use" of our own U.S. Forest Service, for example—that sound wonderful but cannot be accepted at face value. Bonner writes of ecosystem "management" as if it were like managing a store. Human management of wild resources is a nearly unbroken history of hubris, miscalculation, and error. That nature manages ecosystems better than human beings do—an article of faith in the religion of the environmentalists, and a firm principle now of ecological science—Bonner seems not to have considered.

In one argument for culling he writes that "a herd of elephants goes through an area like a slow tornado, snapping off branches and uprooting trees, leaving devastation behind." That slow tornado of elephants—Bonner's finest elephant image—he uses to justify shooting elephants in order to save the forest. There exists, apparently unread by Bonner, a great and growing ecological literature documenting the importance of nature's various agencies of large-scale renovation—fire in forests of lodgepole pine, typhoons and crown-of-thorns starfish on the coral reef, herds of grazers on the grasslands, windfalls in the rain forest, elephants on the savanna. Has it not occurred to Bonner that his slow tornado of elephants might have a role? What does he make of all those hundreds of millennia in which Africa's elephants and Africa's trees coexisted somehow, before rifles arrived for culling? Bonner concludes his slow-tornado paragraph by complaining of "the general public, understanding little about the complexities of ecosystems." The party vague on ecosystems is Bonner himself.

■ ■ ■

In the great shuffling herd of conservationists, Bonner has found two or three heroes. One is Garth Owen-Smith, of Namibia. To Owen-Smith, Bonner suggests, goes credit for the idea that local people should be involved in parks, and that some of the benefits of wildlife preservation should accrue to them. "It is a principle few Westerners have

absorbed," Bonner writes. On the contrary, I know of no Western student of Third World parks who does not recognize this principle. It is the watchword now. A big literature exists on the need for local participation, and on how to achieve it.

Bonner complains that animal-rights groups, in their campaign for an ivory ban, "indulged in hyperbole, incited passions with horror stories, and leveled ad hominem attacks on anyone who disagreed with them." This is a fine summary of Bonner's own approach. His book is an edifice of ad hominem attacks on anyone who favors the ban on ivory. When not guided by "emotion," of which Bonner disapproves, the pro-ban people are fuzzy thinkers, or sometimes clear thinkers who in their hearts know better, in which case they are cowards. Often, on top of this, they are well-heeled.

The term "patrician" seems to have for Bonner the damning force that "pedophile" might have for the rest of us. He feels the same way about "elitist." When the conservationists really irritate him, he squeezes off both barrels, "elitist and patrician," simultaneously. One of the patricians Bonner goes after in the chapter he calls "Patricians" is Russell Train, the first chairman of the White House Council on Environmental Quality, the head of the Environmental Protection Agency under President Richard Nixon, and now the chairman of the World Wildlife Fund in the United States. Bonner lists Train's clubs, schools, and affiliations with a joyous, bloodthirsty pleasure, as if each one—St. Albans prep school, Princeton, marriage to a Bowdoin, the Long Point Hunt Club—were another nail in a tight coffin of Bonner's construction. Most of the "Patricians" chapter is an appeal to class prejudice, built on the assumption that we all share it.

That someone as new to the field as Bonner should even set out after Russell Train, a conservationist with more than thirty years of good work in Africa behind him, a principal architect of the World Heritage System, and the only bright light in what for environmentalists was the wasteland of the past three Republican administrations, is hard to take.

Sometimes Bonner's ad hominem attacks are laughable. His attempt to smear—or perhaps "tar" is the word—Charles de Haes, the director-general of the World Wildlife Fund, is one such. Of the sinister background of the director-general, he writes,

> De Haes's official résumé—that is, the one WWF distributes—makes a point of noting that he went to work for the tobacco company "although himself a non-smoker." It then says de Haes "helped establish companies" in Sudan, Kenya, Uganda and Tanzania. What it does not say is that these were companies that sold cigarettes. Maybe de Haes didn't

smoke, but he made money by encouraging others to do so.

Bonner has forgotten, perhaps, something he told us earlier about his paragon, the conservationist Garth Owen-Smith. Owen-Smith's volunteer rangers, he writes, "were paid the equivalent of $25 a month, and received rations of maize meal, sugar, tea, coffee, tobacco, soap, and milk powder." Bonner's hero, this is to say, did not stop at dealing tobacco to his African employees. He dealt them dental caries, jangled nerves, and probably—as many Africans are lactose-intolerant—curdled stomachs. In Owen-Smith the sins of Charles de Haes are virtues.

Sometimes the ad hominem is not so amusing. Throughout his book Bonner is very free with the accusation of racism. About Prince Philip, an important WWF figure, he reports, "At a meeting of the Commonwealth heads of state, most of them from the Third World and black, Philip said to an aide, 'You wouldn't think the peace of the world rested on this lot, would you?' On another occasion, he referred to the Chinese as 'slitty-eyed.'"

Bonner offers these items without citation. At which Commonwealth meeting did the first incident occur, and who was the aide, and who the fly on the wall? It seems an extraordinarily impolitic remark for Philip, the consort of the Commonwealth's Queen, to have uttered. And what is Bonner's source for the comment about Chinese eyes? Prince Philip has been a genuine small-*p* prince of a fellow in his dedication to environmental causes. For a man in a hopelessly elitist position, he succeeds remarkably well—from all accounts I've heard—at being a regular chap. If his name is to be maligned, it should be with a little documentation.

Bonner is lightning quick with the bold generality. "Making contact with Owen-Smith was not easy," he writes. "He does not live in the city or hang out at conferences, like most Western conservationists working in Africa." And later: "Owen-Smith cares about Africans, is not condescending toward them, and knows the value of listening to them, which sets him distinctly apart from nearly all other Western conservationists in Africa."

Africa is a big continent. There are more than fifty nations there, and hundreds of conservationists at work. Does Bonner really know where most conservationists in Africa hang out, and how they feel about Africans?

Bonner is forever claiming that "most scientists" and "most conservationists" believe as he does about ivory. He arrives at these conclusions by a journalistic technique that I guess we might call "intuitive polling." All of us who write—even the gum-chewing authors of two-page term papers—know about, and often use, this technique. We stumbled upon it while struggling with our first deadline in third or fourth grade. Few of us, however, indulge in it as frequently as Bonner does.

Bonner takes Africa's conservationists to task for the whiteness of their organizations, the leadership in particular. This problem is not unique to Africa's conservation movement, of course. Reasons for it are plentiful, and Bonner himself discusses some—the fact, for example, that few Africans of previous generations trained in the field. But it is shameful indeed, and the conservationists should remedy it.

I can't help noticing, though, that Bonner himself is white. Until recently a staff writer for *The New Yorker*, he lived for several years in Nairobi with his wife, Jane Perlez, then the East Africa bureau chief for *The New York Times*. When was the last time a *New Yorker* report from Africa was written by a black African? I'm drawing a blank. And "Jane Perlez" is not, I think, a Masai or Kikuyu name. Why wasn't an East African the *Times* bureau chief in East Africa? Shouldn't a black African be writing Raymond Bonner's dispatches from Africa—and writing this book, for that matter? Racial imbalances are always more galling and inexcusable in professions other than one's own.

Bonner faults the conservationists in Africa for failing to consult Africans about their fate. Indeed, he calls the first section of his book "Listening to Africa," and his complaint is that white conservationists never do. The curious thing is that Bonner scarcely consults Africans himself. He briefly quotes Perez Olindo, Kenya's foremost black male conservationist, and a few black Namibian game wardens, and a few Masai, but 90 percent of his voices are white. This is partly inevitable, given his complaint that all the major players are white. Still, I wish he had found a way to work in more nonwhite opinion. What do the small-time ivory poachers think about their trade? How do big-time traffickers (often government officials) rationalize it? What was going through the heads of those Ugandan soldiers who decimated their country's wildlife with automatic weapons, mostly just for fun? These are the people, after all—these black people—who are squeezing the triggers, not a handful of pallid conservationists.

Perhaps someone will come forward with good arguments against the ivory ban. If so, I am eager to hear them. They are not to be found in this book. Errors in fact, flaws in logic, and an unmitigated tendentiousness mar Bonner's case throughout. The World Wildlife Fund, for all its good works, does have flaws: too much secrecy, too much coziness with the powers that be. Somewhere in all the smoke Bonner smells there is clearly a little fire. But the fact that conservation organizations have flaws is not much of a revelation.

Africa is a tragic continent. Great, sad stories are unfolding there: war, poverty, famine, AIDS, drought, desertification, deforestation, the decimation of game. Bonner's angle, his stroke of genius in approaching this vast story, is an indictment of the World Wildlife Fund. It is as if Shakespeare had written *Othello* as an exposé of irregularities in Iago's bookkeeping. Bonner has fingered the wrong villains, examined the wrong psyches, written the wrong book.

■   ■   ■

This article first appeared in the April 1993 issue of Atlantic Monthly. *Brower lives in Oakland, California.*

PUT IT INTO PRACTICE

Discussion

1. Discuss what Scott Russell Sanders means when he says he feels a freedom in the essay that he doesn't feel when he's writing fiction. How can he find more freedom in writing nonfiction, where everything must tie in to something real? In writing fiction, Sanders is perfectly free to make it up as he goes. How can this be more confining than the essay? What do you think there is about fiction that a writer might find confining? What could Sanders mean when he says that in writing the essay, "I feel the opportunity to speak more directly about how I feel and think and what matters to me. Obviously one can convey that in fiction, but you have to do it through indirection in fiction."

2. Read the short story reprinted in the back of the book and compare it to the Sanders essay. Discuss any similarities you find either in theme or in the ability of the story to convey that theme. Do you think that the essays discussed in this chapter could be rewritten as short stories? as novels? Try inventing a story in your class or writers' group that incorporates the theme from Sanders's essay. Do the same with the Martone essay and with the Bonner essay. Does the material gain or lose impact from being turned into fiction?

   Now ask yourself which form appeals to you more. Which is more direct? Which has more emotional impact? Which is more difficult to write? Which is easier, do you think, to get into print?

Exercises

1. A reader of near-future spy thrillers for years, you have just finished reading a new one by author Tom Clancy, and the book has prompted you to ask yourself some questions about the whole genre. You decide to write a critical essay that starts with some criticism of the new Clancy novel and moves on from there to a general discussion of the genre.

   How do you go about placing the new book into a reasonable context, that is, what other books like it have come out in recent years? List a dozen.

   What attributes do the books share? What problems? List several of each.

   How has the world's changed political landscape affected these kinds of thrillers? Which authors have handled the changes well, and how have they done it? Which authors haven't succeeded as well, and why? Again, list several of each, mentioning in a sentence or two how the authors have succeeded or failed.

2. Using the notes and lists you've gathered for the first exercise, pull together a one-page outline of the critical essay that you would write.

3. As you drive your car home or to class or to work today, look for particular driving habits that seem common among the drivers in your area. Do the drivers use their turn signals to indicate a coming lane change on the freeway, or do they make abrupt changes without warning? Do they leave adequate room between themselves and the car in front, or do they tailgate? Do they allow you to change lanes when you use your indicator to say you'd like to change, or do they speed up to keep you from making the change?

   If you live in an area with good mass transit, can you compare it to other areas where most commuters are forced to drive? Perhaps you can comment on the way pedestrians walk down the street. Do they avoid making eye contact?

   Try thinking about how driving skills say something about most Americans. Driving habits differ in different parts of the country. What do the driving habits in your area say about the culture in which you live? If you've traveled abroad, tell how the driving habits of other countries compare to those in your area.

   Spend a little time in the library to find some statistical or sociological proof for what you think you've discovered.

   List the driving habits you've discovered, and give a short description of what you think each habit says about the people in your area. Then compare your list with those of your classmates or others in your writing group.

4. Using the notes and lists you've gathered for the exercise, pull together a one-page outline of the personal essay that you would write.

Careers

STAFF WRITING AND EDITING

FREELANCING

FINAL HINTS

Sandra Donnelly's career is following a classic path. After working on the student newspaper for a year or two, Donnelly applied for several different internships during her senior year and with her solid clips from the school paper, she won one with *Working Woman,* a major national magazine.

The internship turned into a job, and in time Donnelly became a full-time editorial assistant with *Working Woman,* frequently getting the chance to write for the publication as well. Several of those stories are reprinted in this book.

Later, Donnelly moved on to ZiffNet Information Service, an on-line company offering information about the computer industry. At ZiffNet, she figures to be on the front lines of the changes that are sure to come in the magazine industry.

Joe Bargmann was a young writer at his college newspaper when he got a chance to write for the local town's daily paper, covering the police beat. That turned into full-time work and was a great job. Bargmann was happy there, but he always felt constrained by the newspaper's tight space and tighter deadlines, so when the opportunity came to move on to a nearby city magazine, he jumped at it. Later he jumped again, this time to New York, where he is now a senior editor at *Seventeen* magazine.

Carol Hay began her career as a reporter for a small paper that published its own magazine for the local tourist industry in the Caribbean island of Grand Cayman. When that magazine went out of business, Hay and her friend E. J. Jarnigan pooled their resources, borrowed the rest, and started their own magazine. Now they have to do it all, from writing and editing to selling the ads. It's exhausting, difficult work, but it's their magazine, and despite the long hours, they love it.

John Calderazzo took the part-time path to writing success. He pursued a teaching career and now makes his "real" living in the classroom, which frees him up to be a part-time freelancer, writing the articles he chooses for a wide variety of national magazines. He wishes he had more time these days to do all the writing he'd like to, but hundreds of articles and two books later, he has to admit he's happy with his career decisions.

What all these examples—and thousands more like them—show is that there are as many ways to structure a career in magazine writing as there are writers. Full-time, part-time, staff writing, freelancing—all of these are common paths to writing success.

STAFF WRITING AND EDITING

As you have just seen in some of the previous examples, if you are interested in becoming a staff writer or editor at a magazine, there are several different ways to go about the business of getting your career under way.

Among the career paths for staff work, some of the most common are to start off with a journalism, magazine, or similar degree from college, then:

Move into an internship and/or part-time work with a magazine.
Find a job in the newspaper business, then later make a shift to a magazine.
Move into a magazine or newspaper before starting up your own magazine.

Sandra Donnelly provides a good example of the first career path. Donnelly began writing and editing during her undergraduate days at Hofstra University, where she worked on the school paper as editor in chief. Then, during her senior year, she took an internship with *Working Woman* magazine.

"I really enjoyed that internship," says Donnelly. "It taught me a lot and really put the pressure on me like school never had."

Donnelly met that pressure, and following her graduation was hired by *Working Woman* as a fact-checker, the classic first job at a large magazine (see chapter seven for more on fact-checking). Then, after several years on the staff, Donnelly thought it was time to do a self-assessment, asking herself where she'd like to be in five years, or ten. Though she then moved to Ziff Net, she's not yet fully convinced that magazines are where she'll stay.

"Well, I certainly see myself in the journalism field," she says, "but I'm not sure whether it will be magazines or newspapers. In college I did all newspapers and loved it, but I'd taken a magazine course and loved it, too. So, I thought when I got out that I wanted to do that. Now, as it turns out, I've really enjoyed the experience.

"I think if I stay in New York I'll stay in magazines. If I go somewhere else I'll probably go into newspapers."

Her advice to you? "If you can get an internship, do it. It really helps," says Donnelly. "And you have to immerse yourself in magazines. One of the reasons I got this job was that they asked me how I liked the magazine, and I said I liked the focus much better than other magazines. I was able to make an intelligent comparison to other women's magazines, which I said I felt insulted the readers' intelligence of a working woman. The editor who interviewed me had just come over from *Mademoiselle,* but she agreed with me. That displayed I was well-read in the field; I knew what was going on in magazines."

Donnelly points out, "When you first come out you'll take any job you can get in magazines, and that's good, to get your foot in the door. You can try and go for what you want—if you want *Newsweek,* go for it—but one of the things that's good about journalism is that you are able to jump from field to field and that's part of being a journalist. As long as you're able to put a story together from the experts, you're fine."

Donnelly's advice to take whatever is available is solid, because movement within the field is, as she points out (and as you'll see later), relatively easy.

Donnelly says she has a friend who's now with a computer magazine and who admitted, "If you'd told me two years ago when I was graduating that I would be working for a computer magazine I would have laughed in your face."

But Donnelly's friend has a good job now and knows it. She's getting valuable experience and is aware she can probably switch to another magazine later if she wants to.

Seventeen magazine Senior Editor Joe Bargmann took a more circuitous route to success, but one that is also reasonably common: coming to magazine writing through newspaper work. Bargmann began as a journalism major at the University of Missouri, working on the school paper and "Doing the regular clip-building that everyone says you have to do," he recalls.

After graduation, Bargmann moved into a full-time newspaper job, serving two years as police and court reporter of the Columbia, Missouri, *Daily Tribune,* a small afternoon daily. He wanted more time and space to work on his stories, though, and so kept looking for magazine opportunities. When one came up, he jumped at it, and was hired by *St. Louis* magazine.

As you've seen elsewhere in this book, Bargmann is an excellent reporter and writer, and within a few years he had risen to the position of senior editor at *St. Louis* magazine.

When *St. Louis* magazine went through a shake-up and Bargmann found himself out of work, he was ready to turn the disappointment into an opportunity—by using his clips and his résumé to win a job at *Seventeen* magazine, as senior editor in charge of fiction as well as handling nonfiction.

Echoing Donnelly's sentiments, Bargmann says, "One of the interesting things about magazines is that there is a lot of job movement, so it's not unusual to make a jump. And in my case, I'd won some awards for stories at *St. Louis* magazine and met some good people in the business at various conferences, so I was ready for whatever openings were out there.

"I was lucky to get the job at *Seventeen,* but then I was well prepared for it when the opening came up."

Carol Hay grew up in the Caribbean, on the small British island of Grand Cayman. After a college education in the United States, she became a reporter on the island's newspaper.

The Cayman Islands are a major Caribbean tourist destination, as well as a world banking center, and the paper published its own magazine for the tourist industry. When that publication went under, Hay and a friend, E. J. Jarnigan, saw their chance and took it.

"We just saw a chance to start up something of our own, and we took it," she explains. "We formed this magazine together and we haven't looked back since."

Their magazine, *Horizons,* is now the official in-flight magazine of Cayman Airways and also has some distribution elsewhere on the islands.

Hay and Jarnigan enjoy being their own bosses, of course, and living in the Caymans and working on their own publication may sound wonderful. But be warned: "It's very hectic," says Hay. "You'd better be prepared to work long hours. And if you don't love it, get out; it can be frustrating as hell."

Hay points out that the two of them must not only write much of the copy but also edit, design, and sell ads.

"Every day seems crazier than the last," she says. "And then it gets even worse at deadline time."

But when the presses roll (in Florida, for no presses on Grand Cayman can handle the magazine) and the 22,000 copies of *Horizons* are read by the thousands of visitors to the island, it makes the job worthwhile.

The kind of pressure that Hay talks about isn't limited to understaffed small magazines. Even on the large magazines, the pressure exists, especially early in a career, when you are trying to prove yourself. Openings are hard to find, and the competition is fierce. As Sandra Donnelly noted with a dry laugh during her time at *Working Woman:* "There's a lot of people ready to take your place. We have interns here—we don't pay—and they are willing to come here for no pay and then work hoping that one of the three of us [the current editorial assistants] will die."

FREELANCING

Full-Time Freelancing

Full-time freelancing has its own pressures and payoffs, as many a writer can tell you. For full-time freelance writers, the pressure consists in trying to write often enough, and well enough, to make a living. With the top magazines paying a few thousand dollars for a story, and most magazines paying far less, it takes a lot of copy to keep one's income at a reasonable level.

Most full-time freelancers, then, try to move from magazine writing into book writing as soon as they can. The income level from book-length manuscripts, while often not as high as you might expect, is at least livable.

"I always enjoyed writing just for the magazines," says freelance writer Michael Bane, "but even with writing for *Esquire* and places like that, the money just wasn't there."

Bane now ghostwrites book-length autobiographies for music personalities, writes specialty books for corporations, and works on a number of other book-length projects as well, as much for the income as the writing satisfaction.

BOX 1 2 . 1

ON GETTING STARTED

Comments on careers from Senior Editor C. Michael Curtis of the *Atlantic Monthly,* Writer/Editor Adrian Nicole LeBlanc, and Editor Mary Batten of *Calypso Log.*

ADVICE TO AN UNDERGRADUATE

C. Michael Curtis

I would say that in your senior year you need to do a couple of things. One is, do as much work as you possibly can with the periodicals your college has to offer. Do as much writing as possible; learn as much as you can about editing and proofreading; develop some skills. You need a lot of practice, and college journalism is a very good way to get it.

Second, understand that the better and more broadly based your education is, the more valuable you will be to any serious publication, anywhere. So, avoid too narrow a specialization; avoid vocational training, as distinct from broad liberal arts education. Consciously take subjects in areas where you have taken none, in order to broaden the base.

Also, begin thinking about graduate school as one serious option, and, again, not graduate school in, say, journalism or some other vocational specialty. If you want to go to graduate school at all, (a) seriously consider a field you haven't been exposed to; so if you're an English major, go into economics or history or government or something else; and (b) bear in mind that if you go to graduate school, you need not be a captive of your graduate committee and the needs for certification, the trap that ensnares most graduate students.

You can very profitably spend two or three or four years in graduate school aware that your purpose is to get better trained for journalism, and this will have a liberating impact on you, and it will also help you, encourage you, to take courses in other departments.

This is also an opportunity, while you're in graduate school, if that's where you go, to continue doing a lot of work with student publications or with the university press or with the alumni magazine or the university quarterly. All those things are helpful if you're learning how to be a proofreader and copy editor and so on.

And that isn't the only option. I see about three or four principal routes.

The second one is newspapers, which I favor most. If you're not going to go to graduate school, this is the best possible thing to do. It gives you the broadest kind of experience in a lot of different areas and teaches you disciplines that are enormously helpful in magazine work and newspaper work and book publishing and probably life in general.

Happily, it is widely viewed as good training, regardless of where you go next, as distinct from the third option, which is starting somewhere as a secretary and waiting for an opening. That, in my experience, is often very confining and doesn't help you learn a lot of skills that you need to learn unless you're lucky enough to land in a place where you're encouraged to do lots of different things and are trained.

The fourth way is to try to make it as a freelance writer. You have to be pretty mature and have a lot of staying power for that, and you have to be pretty good, or you won't earn a living. But almost all the people who have been hired here as editors have written for the magazine first, and I think that's probably true of a lot of publications.

It's a very good way to leap over a lot of those entry-level jobs. If you can do it well enough to earn a living, you can establish yourself as a professional writer and at the same time insinuate into the minds of those people who might hire you that you understand the kind of writing they need.

This is the connection for us: The people who write for us we come to think of as people who understand what we want and how we look at things, how we edit things.

All of that is good experience. It makes us begin to think of them as people who could be inside and editing instead of outside and writing for us.

Adrian Nicole LeBlanc

I decided after graduation to freelance and read a lot, so that led me to a decision to go on to grad school in literature. That helped me tremendously as a thinker, really in two ways: (1) It

Continued

Continued

helped me to express myself better. (2) It helped me to organize my thoughts and gave me access to a different world.

So, I went off to grad school in England. Then, after finishing, I came back home, and *New England Monthly* gave me an assignment. Then *Seventeen* magazine called. The editors there had seen the story on suicides that I'd done for *New England Monthly*.

Seventeen offered me some writing assignments, and so I worked for *Seventeen* for a while as a freelancer. I met my editor there, and we used to talk about short stories pretty frequently. When they needed a fiction editor, they asked me if I was interested. Well, I took the job, and it gave me a chance to learn about writing fiction, too.

SHOULD YOU PLAN YOUR NEXT FIVE OR TEN YEARS?

C. Michael Curtis

I think that if you're going on to graduate school, then give yourself four years in a Ph.D. program of almost any sort as long as it's serious. It's a very broadening and liberating experience, so the more of it the better, and if you go straight from undergraduate to graduate school, you're still only 25 or 26 and that's young.

Most people who get hired as editors get hired after they're about 26 or 27. Everyone thinks of those years after leaving school as a time to experience a lot of different things and different parts of the country, different professional situations.

So, I guess I would recommend to the college junior that he or she think of the five years after graduation as a time for experimentation and rolling around and trying new parts of the country, consciously going to parts of the country that are unknown.

When I've persuaded people to write to newspapers across the country, wherever they are, they seem to find that newspapers are intrigued by applicants from out of town.

Mary Batten

First of all, I wouldn't say that anyone should be in a certain place in ten years, because individuals differ. I would say that newspaper writing is a great place to start, whether it's the local newspaper, or the college paper, or in the college press office. I had a job in North Carolina where I was a student, writing in the college's news bureau, just items on the college that went into the local Greensboro newspaper.

That gave me a chance to work with a seasoned newspaper man who was in charge of the bureau. It was tremendous experience, so I would say that getting into some type of journalistic situation, whether it's a newspaper, whether it's a magazine, but where you're working with and learning from older professional writers, is invaluable. Make sure it's a place where you are also learning to write about a variety of subject matters. I think variety is the key, and do not allow yourself to get stuck in one slot.

Another good way to get experience in college is by getting an intern position for a magazine or newspaper. We offer internships here at the Cousteau Society, and we have each semester a young student from one of the nearby colleges that has an intern program working with us. We don't pay students anything. They work about 20 hours a week, and they learn everything we can teach them about how a magazine is put together, from sitting down and discussing the stories that will go into that magazine to actual production of the final magazine as it comes off the press. This is experience that people can't get any way except on this on-the-job apprenticeship.

That's an excellent way for college students to go, if they can afford it. A few internships pay a small amount; most don't seem to pay anything but it's a great help to people's careers. If they performed well in that internship they're going to get letters of recommendation from the editor that they can put in their portfolio when they graduate from college and are trying to get a job.

There's a huge transition from college to the work world. It's one thing to learn the skills in a classroom situation; it's another thing to put them into practice in a real situation; and that's a transition that college students have to be able to get over. An internship is that kind of on-the-job training.

SHOULD YOU SPECIALIZE?

Mary Batten

I would caution people who want to go into writing against channeling themselves into only one area. I have written in many fields: for television, magazines, books. I think it's very important

Continued

Continued

that you not put yourself into a slot too soon in your career. The pressure of the market out there is to try to put you into a slot, and that, of course, limits your marketability of yourself. If people get the idea that you can only write about birds in the short form for magazines, then it's easy for them to think that's all you can do.

My advice is to write about everything, to write in different forms, to write magazine articles, to try your hand at films, to try your hand at books, to try your hand at PR [public relations] writing. And newspaper writing is wonderful training for any writer. I know of no better training for any young writer than a job on a newspaper, learning to meet deadlines, honing your interview skills, learning to go out there in the field, getting a story and having it ready by that afternoon. That, to me—I did that one summer—was the most valuable career experience that I ever had.

Part-Time Freelancing

Part-time freelancing is the path that many writers take, especially early on in their career, working at another job while they continue to write on the side.

Certain real advantages accrue to part-time freelancing, including fewer worries about money. But there are drawbacks, too. The full-timers certainly seem to get more bylines, for one thing, so their careers seem to move ahead much more quickly. And part-time writers often envy the amount of time that full-time writers enjoy in which to get their stories done. Most part-timers have to struggle to find a few hours at night, or perhaps early in the morning, to get their writing done before the day's responsibilities come roaring in.

Still, if you love to write, then part-time freelancing is rewarding, not only in terms of the satisfaction of seeing your work in print but financially as well. That $500 check, which may seem very small to a full-timer, seems like fair payment to the part-time writer who is really in it for reasons other than money.

Freelancer John Calderazzo took the academic path to part-time writing. An English professor at Colorado State University, Calderazzo began writing magazine articles part-time early in his teaching career—more for the joy of writing them and the satisfaction of seeing them in print than for any other reason.

Later, as his stories began appearing in national magazines, Calderazzo's part-time satisfaction began to seem more and more important, and he, too, made the move into book-length work.

Many of the other writers quoted in this book have done the same thing—starting with a fairly low key, part-time commitment to writing magazine features and then moving into a deeper and deeper commitment to the writing as they became increasingly successful.

FINAL HINTS

As you begin your magazine-feature-writing career, there are a few hints to bear in mind that may help you achieve some success in the field.

Note that these career hints assume that you have the writing skill necessary to get the job done. Once you've attained that level of competence, there are a number of other factors, including blind luck, that start to figure in your career. In order to be in control of as many of those factors as possible, you need to start now.

Work for Your School Newspaper

The experience of writing to meet deadlines and space requirements will be good for you, and being published in your school newspaper and magazine will get you the clips you need to win a good internship.

If you can rise through the ranks at your school paper and become an editor, all the better for later work in magazines, because it will give you a chance to hone your editing and design skills. If a top editorial slot doesn't look likely, try for a spot as a copy editor, working with everyone else's stories, laying out pages, and writing headlines. It's terrific experience and will look good on the résumé.

Get an Internship or Part-Time Job

Internships, as the experts say in this chapter, are very important. Occasionally, they turn into permanent jobs, but even at those publications that make a point of never hiring interns, the internship will still serve its purpose by being a highlight on your résumé and a major factor in your acquiring the clips you'll need to get that full-time staff spot somewhere.

Part-time work, like an internship, will get you the clips you need and also look terrific on your résumé when you graduate. In addition, doing a good job in your part-time position may lead to that full-time spot once your college days are over.

Be Mobile

Be ready to move from magazine to magazine or from city to city. Many of the top national consumer magazines are in New York, with others in Chicago, Los Angeles, and a few other cities. If you want to work at that kind of publication, you need to be ready to make the move to those cities. Also, as you've seen in this chapter, movement from magazine to magazine is not unusual in the business, so be prepared to move several times before you find a publication where you can build a long career. Many staffers never do really settle down, and others have a long, stable career at a single publication.

Note that it is not at all unusual for magazine companies to be bought and sold these days with surprising speed. A new owner may want a lot of changes, and those changes could include you. Bring your résumé up-to-date once or twice a year, and keep tuned to openings in the field.

Get to Know Others

Make the effort to get to know other people in the field.

To help you stay in tune, make sure you build as extensive a network of professional relationships in the field as you can. It's a cliché perhaps, but also quite valid, that it is who you know as much as what you know that matters.

To expand your network, try to attend professional gatherings locally, regionally, and nationally. Join the various professional groups relevant to your work in the business. Go to writers' conferences when you can, not only to improve your skills but also to widen your network.

Get a Mentor

This is especially important early in your career. Find someone knowledgeable about the field, whom you can confide in and ask questions of. Once you've impressed the mentor with your abilities and attitude, you may discover the person has connections in the field and will use them to help you advance your career.

The mentor can be a professor, or a local writer or editor, or someone you met at a writers' conference. It should be someone you genuinely admire and can learn from, for falsehood is easily discovered. In turn, the mentor needs to see in you the promise of a good career.

Note: Years down the road, once your career is well established, pay back that mentor by helping other beginners in the same way.

Get Organized

One of the pitfalls for freelancers is lack of organization. Many writers pride themselves on that certain cultivated chaos that exists within their office setting: Piles of papers, stacks of books, hidden coffee cups with month-old stains in the bottom of the mug—these are the marks of a freelance writing career.

However, even at the risk of jeopardizing your artistic freedom, you'll need to establish a few basic minimums of organization. Among them are (1) relevant tax information (mail receipts, phone bills, and the like); (2) a record of what stories have been submitted where (some writers do a simple chart for this; others keep track nowadays on their computer; and still others keep at least one pile of papers strictly limited to photocopies of query and cover letters and another pile limited to acceptances and rejections); and (3) separate files for various stories in progress (this has been made easier by the computer, but your research needs to be kept organized, too, so a small filing cabinet is not a bad idea).

Be Prepared to Pay Your Dues

Have reasonable expectations. Magazine staffs are small, and the competition for jobs is fierce. When you get the chance for a job, you are probably wise to take it, even if it means starting on the ground floor when you thought your two years on the school newspaper had readied you for more than that.

Many writers start their career with five- and ten-year plans. Those kinds of goals are fine, but don't let them get in the way of opportunity when a job comes along that isn't in the plan, and don't let a plan discourage you when you haven't reached your goals. Learn to be patient and forgiving with yourself while also making high demands of your skills.

Be Ready for the Future

One of the most exciting things about the future of the magazine business is that a lot of changes are on the way, the great majority of them computer based. You need to be ready for those. For a first look at them, turn to chapter thirteen.

PUT IT INTO PRACTICE

Discussion

1. Beginning writers often join writers' clubs, in which they can trade information, learn from other writers, and find support for the hard, lonely work of writing. Discuss the positive and negative aspects of writers' clubs. Is the information you get there likely to be useful? In what ways? Can you learn from other beginners useful things about writing? Can you learn from veteran writers? Will the camaraderie you can find in such a group be helpful?

   Discuss what a writers' club could offer to increase its usefulness for beginning writers. If there are such groups in your area, do they offer those things?

   See if you can, through group discussion, design the perfect writers' group, listing the group's membership, its goals, its structure, and a typical meeting.

2. The chapter talks about your finding a mentor—a professor or an established writer—who can give you advice and some occasional editing guidance and generally support you as you start on your writing career. Discuss the mentoring idea. Is it fair to ask a busy professional writer or professor to give you free advice on your stories and your career? What is the best way to find a mentor? What do you think a mentor gets from the relationship? Discuss what reasonable guidelines for the relationship can be set by the mentor and the beginner.

Exercises

1. Where would you like to be professionally in five years? Whether your goal revolves around staff work or freelancing, outline a five-year plan, including goals for each year. Read through some of the advice from editors contained in this chapter, and then try to pull together some reasonable expectations for yourself. Be as specific as you comfortably can. Are there particular publications you would like to work for or sell to by the time that fifth year has arrived? What steps do you need to take to get there?

   As you begin to list the goals, year by year, include a paragraph or two under each that shows you understand what it will take to accomplish the goal.

2. What kind of opportunities to get started are available to you in your current situation? If you're on a college campus, is there a school newspaper? a nonfiction magazine? a literary magazine?

What kind of internship possibilities exist in your area? Have you researched the national possibilities for internships? Visit your department advisers or the nearest library and put together a list of internships that appeal to you, breaking the list down into local, regional, and national categories. There are dozens available, so your list should certainly be a reasonably extensive one.

An internship should fit nicely into most five-year plans, but certainly not all. What other possibilities are there in your area? Part-time newspaper work as a copy editor or stringer? Part-time magazine work? Breaking in as a freelancer? Again, list the part-time possibilities, with a descriptive paragraph under each one.

3. If freelance writing is your goal, look back over some of the advice given elsewhere in this book, and ask yourself which publications look as if they offer you the best chance to break into print. List the top five publications. Remember to think of areas of expertise as you construct your list. Write a descriptive paragraph under each possibility.

    Now make another list, this one of the top five magazines in the country that you would like to have stories in. As you've done before, write a descriptive paragraph under each possibility.

    Now take another look at exercise 1, and ask yourself what steps you might take to get from that first list to the second. During the first year of your five-year plan, what steps can you take to get ready professionally for freelancing for the top magazines on your list? during the second year? the third? the fourth?

C H A P T E R 1 3

THE FUTURE

Many magazine writers will tell you that the future is already upon us in the magazine business, but that a lot of publishers and editors haven't quite realized it yet. These writers know that the Information Age will probably bring radical change to the way magazines are produced and distributed, and the wise writer is one who is ready for that change and can use it to advantage.

Magazine staffers know that the days of typewritten copy and dummied layout pages that are carried off to a typesetter and printer to be turned into a final product are gone forever. Pagination, desktop publishing, on-line publications, and a variety of other innovations are either already here or are on the way and will be here soon.

Even though the new technologies offer improved ways to query and submit stories, however, most freelancers still send out queries in the mail, follow that by sending their manuscripts through the mail, and then wait patiently for an acceptance or rejection. That process, too, will likely be changing soon, and the writer who wants to sell regularly is the one who is computer literate, as well as ready to write, edit, query, and submit, all by computer.

If you're not sure what the difference is between hardware and software; if DOS, Mac, mouse, and WordPerfect don't mean anything to you; if you're still writing longhand and then laboriously typing a second or third draft on a typewriter before sending a manuscript out in the mail— then you're not ready for the future of magazine writing.

In fact, if you do use a computer for your writing, but consider the computer as only a kind of smart typewriter, useful for processing words but for little else, then you, too, aren't really ready. There is a lot more you can do with your computer right now, and the future will offer much, much more.

The wise beginning writer is the one who sees the coming changes and is ready for them.

TOOLS FOR THE FUTURE

As far as freelance writer Michael Banks is concerned, the post office is in the Stone Age—and most magazine editors are still back there with it. But the changes, he notes, are coming.

Banks is an expert in computer technology for writers. He is the author of several books on the subject and has frequent bylines in a variety of computer magazines. As someone immersed in the computer age, he wonders why more magazines haven't fully embraced the possibilities offered by modern computer technology, which can make the "snail mail" of the post office seem absolutely neolithic in its lack of immediacy.

Banks has been ready for the past several years to submit his queries and his stories electronically. He can write both the query and the story on his computer, using one of several software packages created specifically for word processing. Then, by having his own computer contact the computer at the magazine, he can send the query electronically, get an answer back from the editor, and then send along the manuscript in the same way.

It is quite possible for a writer like Banks to do his research, write and edit his story, query an editor, and then send the manuscript, all from his computer at home, and all without ever having once seen the story printed out in hard copy.

But although the technology is already here, this kind of communication between writer and editor is still unusual.

"To be honest," Banks says, "most magazine publishers have taken their time moving into the computer age. Most magazines," he adds, "now use computers for typesetting, layout, and page production. But the fact is that magazines that accept or require freelance submissions on disk or through electronic mail—E-mail—remain a minority, thanks in large part to the overwhelming diversity of computer types and word processing programs."

Such diversity may slowly settle out in the next few years, and more and more of the programs will be able to access and read other programs; so, that, too, will help the situation begin to stabilize.

For now, though, freelancers who are fully computerized and have a modem may still find themselves too far ahead of the curve. That is, while you may be able to create, edit, and then send a story off to the magazine completely by computer, the magazine probably isn't ready—yet—to accept the product from you in that mode.

"Magazines that accept manuscripts via modem—be it direct to their computer, or via an intermediary system like MCI Mail or CompuServe—are a definite minority and will remain so for some time," thinks Banks.

The reason, says Banks, is not just that there are too many various kinds of computers with incompatible formats; it goes deeper than that and really boils down to many magazine editors' still being intimidated by the seeming complexity of computers and of modems.

"It *is* ironic, to say the least. The situation is due mainly to the perception that if computers are mysterious and difficult, modems must be even more mysterious and difficult—a myth I try to dispel with my book *The Modem Reference*" (Brady, 1988).

Despite the fact that the magazine industry has been slow to embrace all that computer technology offers, you'll want to be computerized as soon as you can afford it (and, happily, the price seems to steadily drop as the technology steadily improves).

If you find a staff position, odds are (as many staffers have noted in this book) that you'll be working with computers routinely at the magazine's offices, doing research (see chapter two), writing, revising and editing, and these days even doing layout and design.

For freelancers, the benefits from computer technology start with your research and writing and then extend to the submission process for those magazines ready for electronic submission. In time, more and more magazines will be capable of routinely receiving electronic submissions. For now, even though you'll still have to send manuscripts through the mail to most magazines, a computer will still be of significant benefit to your career. And later, when editors and publishers catch up with the computer's potential, you'll be ready.

The Basic Home Computer System

The basics of a home computer system start with your hardware, which consists of a computer with a keyboard, a monitor, and a printer. From a writer's perspective, the computer—the brains of the system—immediately offers you a very intelligent, and helpful, typewriter. The monitor is the televisionlike screen, where you can see the copy as you write it. The printer is the device that actually prints out your stories.

Once you've purchased the hardware, you'll need to find the appropriate software for your needs. The software is the program that works inside your computer to actually handle the material you type into it. A good word processing program, for instance, not only converts your typing into words on the screen and then prints them out but also allows you to edit on the screen, change margins easily, add footnotes, number your pages, and do a host of other things, too.

There are a number of good programs available for writers. You'll want to ask around for the one that best meets your needs.

Finally, you may want to purchase a modem and its software, too. A modem is a device that allows your computer access to other computers, or to on-line services, through your telephone lines. Modem software is the program that enables the modem to do its work for you.

Advantages

What do computers and the appropriate software programs for word processing offer you that a typewriter can't? Well, even for the kind of magazines that now exist there are several things, including speed, ease of revision, ease of organization, and (someday) ease of submission.

Most writers find that using a computer for writing is much quicker than using a typewriter or writing things out in longhand. For one thing, you never have to put in a new sheet of paper, as you would with a typewriter. For another, you can easily correct typographical mistakes as you go and even move sentences or whole paragraphs around—thus avoiding having to retype pages or entire stories, as you might often have to do using a typewriter. Finally, if you are hooked into a computer network through a modem, you may also be able to do much of your research through your home computer, thus avoiding trips to the library.

You'll find that revising on a computer screen is much easier than working with a manuscript. Virtually all word processing software programs have the ability to "cut and paste" for purposes of restructuring stories. In fact, most also have a spell-check function, and some even check your grammar. All of this can be done right on the screen, so the copy is clean and ready before you ever print it out.

Even if you are the kind of writer who needs to see a hard (paper) copy and edit in your corrections and changes there (the author of this book sometimes works in that fashion), it is still a simple matter to transfer any changes onto the computer version of the story. After that, just hit "Print," and wait for the new draft to come out of the printer.

Once your career begins to take off and you are doing a fair amount of freelancing, you'll find that the automatic storage feature of the computer is a real organizational boon to writers. You can call up any story at any time, even saving separate drafts if you want. With a few quick keystrokes, you can add a notation at the top of the story that says when you sent it out and to what magazine. Or, if you like, you can keep a quick, easily produced separate file of your submissions and their dates of submission.

Printing out a clean version of a story for each new submission is a benefit of computer-generated copy.

And remember, as Michael Banks has pointed out, someday soon more and more magazines are going to accept electronic submissions, so with a computer and a modem, you're ready for that to happen.

To give you an idea of just how easy the process is, the author of this book has for some time edited a special fiction supplement of the *Tampa Tribune*, a large daily newspaper.

One writer sent a query letter to the editor by way of E-mail on a computer network that both that writer and the editor are on (the GEnie network). The editor agreed to take a look at the submission, and the writer then sent the story electronically from a computer in the Midwest to the editor's computer in Florida. The process took a few minutes. Within a couple of weeks the editor found the time to call up the story on the computer and read it on the screen; he liked it, and asked for some revisions. Over the next month or two the writer and the editor sent the story back and forth between them several times, working on those revisions and never once printing the piece on a printer. Finally, on about the third revision, the story seemed perfect and the editor accepted that draft for publication.

The editor then simply downloaded the story onto a disc and took the disc to the newspaper's offices, where the computer there accepted the material on the disc, downloaded it onto the mainframe of the newspaper, and then printed it out in that issue of *Fiction Quarterly*. From conception until printed publication, the story never existed in hard copy. It was all handled entirely by computer.

It won't be too long before most magazines begin to handle stories in this way.

NEW FORMS OF PUBLICATION

The advent of computer technology has meant a lot more than merely new ways to write and distribute stories. It has brought in a whole range of brand-new ways of dispensing information.

John Morthland, a freelance writer whose work is discussed elsewhere in this book, is one writer who's involved in the future right now, in the present.

CD-ROM

Morthland writes text for CD-ROMs for Warner New Media, a division of Time-Warner.

The acronym "CD-ROM" stands for "Compact Disc, Read Only Memory." "Basically," Morthland explains, "a CD-ROM is a compact disc [CD] that not only contains sound but also has written text. What you'll have is a CD player that ties into your computer so you can have text on your computer screen while the sound is on, the two things working in conjunction.

"For Warner New Media I'm working on a CD-ROM called 'The Birth of Rock 'n' Roll.' Basically, we've settled on 18 songs from 1954 to 1958, and I'm writing the text that goes along with the music. It's complicated, but in essence, I write something called spines. These are short pieces in real time that are coordinated to the music.

"There are two or three of them coordinated to the music so that one spine is about the artist and one, say, about the record. So, while the guitar solo to 'Maybellene,' for instance, is what's coming out of your speakers, what will be on one spine at that moment will be a couple of sentences about Chuck Berry's guitar influences, and on the other spine will be a couple of sentences of the history of the music, or perhaps some biographical material about Chuck Berry."

Using a mouse, the listener/reader can hop among the spines, explains Morthland. And, he adds, "There are also 8 or 10 sidebars that are not in real time that are just on the disc and in the computer, and you can call them up anytime as background.

"There's one on the rise of Top 40 radio, for instance, and another on the postwar rise of teenagers as a consumer class, and yet another on the anti–rock 'n' roll backlash."

You can see that each CD-ROM represents a challenging, exacting piece of writing for the freelancer.

Morthland's spines for the Chuck Berry section of the CD-ROM he talks about look something like this in manuscript form:

SPINE 1

0:00–0:06

Berry's hooky intro--a two-bar lick followed by two more bars of rhythm groove--establishes guitar as one of rock's lead instruments.

0:07–0:16

That jump-starts "Maybellene," rhythmically as the band chugs into a country two-beat on the chorus. But blues, Berry's other chief influence, is emphasized by the hard, fat attack.

0:17–0:28

Berry soars into the verse, simulating the racing cars. But because he phrases clearly rather than with slurred, blues diction, he doesn't "sound black," which helped him attract white listeners.

0:29–0:40

Listen to the band shift into high gear on the chorus, like a car reaching top speed and holding it, as Johnnie Johnson's splashy, barely audible piano lines provide variety and color.

0:41–0:52

Berry's raucous, trebly guitar, clashing sharply against the smooth country two-beat, heightens the impact.

And Chuck's vocals contrast similarly--though his phrasing remains country and his diction careful, he shouts like a bluesman.

0:53–1:04

Because the one-chord verses remain twelve bars in length, "Maybellene" retains some kinship with jump blues.

Unlike bluesmen, Berry avoided horns in favor of the simpler, stripped-down sound of the rock band.

1:05–1:17

Beginning with eight bars of one note, which creates a screaming effect, Berry's solo is inspired by the stinging, single-string runs of electric blues pioneer T-Bone Walker.

1:18–1:28

It's still essentially a country guitar line, but it sounds like it could careen out of control at any moment.

1:29–1:41

Except for the instrumentation, Berry's verses are nearly identical musically to those in "Ida Red," the country hit on which "Maybellene" is based.

1:42–1:53

"Maybellene" joined a growing body of blues and country songs celebrating the automobile. But by mashing words like "motor," "heat," and "highway" into a breakneck tempo, Chuck kicks the whole idea into rock 'n' roll overdrive.

1:54–2:05

Though this is now the fifth time around for the chorus, it still has a loose, raw feel. Repetition without tedium is what makes a great rock 'n' roll song memorable.

2:06–2:17

Played on top of the rhythm section's pounding, roadhouse beat, Chuck's final guitar line ties "Maybellene" up and eases the song into the "fade," sounding very much like it began.

SPINE 2

0:00–0:16

Berry was 29 and unknown outside St. Louis when he hustled Muddy Waters on a trip to Chicago.

Muddy urged him to give Chess Records his demo tape. It included "Ida Red," an unlikely country-blues hybrid that led homefolks to call Chuck "that black hillbilly."

0:17–0:28

Chuck pushed the conventional blues "Wee Wee Hours." But "Ida May" (complete with surreal, made-up words like "motorvatin") immediately gave Leonard Chess other ideas.

0:29–0:40

Chess had Chuck change the name to something with as much pizzazz as the hard-driving music and the story line.

"The big beat, cars, and young love," Leonard later explained. "It was a trend and we jumped on it."

0:41–0:53

Berry understood, inspired by his own high school days: When girls turned down rides from him, Chuck begrudgingly loaned his 1934 V-8 Ford out to football players so they could take cheerleaders cruising.

0:54–1:04

Pianist Johnnie Johnson, an unsung architect of the Berry sound, was the only St. Louis musician on the session. The Chess studio vets had more commercial savvy.

1:05–1:16

Running the session from his windowed office, which served as control room of the small studio, Leonard often speeded tapes up artificially to make Chuck's records more frenzied. This must be one of those cases.

1:17–1:28

But Willie Dixon, the black producer/arranger who was the white owner's liaison to the artists, shaped the sound. Leonard understood the importance of the big beat, but as you can hear, Willie knew how to get it.

1:29–1:42

But Chess had the last word, working the band through 35 takes of the tune before he was satisfied.

"Maybellene" and three others were finished between mid-afternoon and 8:30 p.m., and then the boss sprung for hamburgers.

1:43–1:53

Chess gave a dub of "Maybellene"--plus one third of the songwriting credit--to star-maker deejay Alan Freed. Promising Berry a hit, he gave one third more to another deejay.

Chuck won back full rights in 1968.

1:54–2:05

But the strategy, then a fairly common form of payola, helped. Freed made Chuck a star by "breaking" the single nationally late in the summer of 1955.

2:06–2:17

"Maybellene" identified Chuck as the first black rocker with a distinct persona. After quickly creating several more car-tunes, he moved on to such teen themes as school, young love, and rock 'n' roll itself.

You can see how different this kind of freelance writing is from the more typical magazine story. Instead of a structured, long story that illuminates Chuck Berry and his talents for the reader, Morthland is working in a medium in which the spines provide a quick bit of information while the music is playing.

It is worth noting that some of the material that Morthland is writing in the new medium—the sidebars that users can call up at any time to read in more depth about a musician, for instance—is longer and it more closely resembles current magazine writing. But much of the material is quite short (though packed with information) and dependent on what else is happening on the CD-ROM.

"It *is* a different kind of writing," Morthland says, "particularly the part that is synched to the music because you have to tie it in. You have three sentences, for example, of under 35 words that are on the screen for 11 seconds, and two sentences of 25 words that will be on the screen for seven seconds. This material that is in real time you really have to plan out, and that's why it's so involved. It's a completely different kind of writing for me, but it's really interesting."

Morthland's lengthy background in popular music helped put him at the front edge of this developing market for writers, and he is happy to have done the work.

"I'm not sure I'll do much of the typical magazine writing anymore," he admits. "For one thing, I'm really learning a lot about future media by doing this. For another, a lot of this kind of writing is going to be the standard form of dispensing information one day soon, and the kind of writing I've done in the past is going to have more limited application in the future."

On-Line Magazines

The growth in home personal computer use has led to one new aspect of the magazine business that is certain to expand: on-line magazines, publications that are available to home computer users through electronic transmission.

To receive one of these publications, you typically need to subscribe to one of the various on-line networks, though that may change, too, in the years ahead. One day soon you may consider it quite ordinary to dial a local phone number through your modem and download a particular magazine (or several of them).

With continuing improvements in laser printer technology, there is no reason why an entire magazine couldn't be downloaded into your home computer and then printed out (even stapled, for that matter) right at home.

Many experts think that this sort of distribution, or something very much like it, represents the probable future for both magazines and newspapers. According to one such expert, the distinction between magazines and newspapers will blur as computer technology makes home access to the computerized publication increasingly popular.

"I suspect that as more and more homes have home computers, an increasing number of publications—magazines and newspapers both—

will take advantage of the opportunity to put their publication on-line," says Karen Brown, dean of the Poynter Institute for Media Studies, a top media think tank.

"In fact," she adds, "this kind of technology will force newspapers to become more magazinelike, at least in the sense of reaching out to specialized audiences. The reader will be able to download any particular item of special interest that she wants, and then just print it out. Magazines have been taking advantage of this kind of specialized readership for a long time. Now newspapers will head in that direction, too."

Brown adds that although the technology doesn't change *what* writers must do (in the sense that stories still have to be reported and written, but the mode of distribution will have changed), it does change *how* they will do it.

In the near future, it is entirely possible that writers will do their research from home (through a database), write their story at home, and upload the story to the magazine's main computer, where an editor will work with it and then place it into the next electronic issue. A story will never see print unless a reader at home chooses to print it out. In fact, if a reader is content to view it on the computer screen and read it there, a story may never actually be printed at all.

FINAL HINTS

It all makes for a future that is ripe with opportunity for the beginning writer who is poised to take advantage of it. To do that, you might want to consider a few hints:

Invest in a Personal Computer

Despite the trend toward lower and lower prices of personal computers, the cost is still high. Throw in the additional cost of a printer, the right software for word processing, a modem, and a few instructional books, and there is no question that it becomes a major investment in your writing career.

But when the time comes that you can afford to buy a system, do it. Not only will it be useful for you immediately as a writer, but it will be your investment in the future of the business as well.

Get On-Line

Once you've purchased a system, you'll want to join one or more of the various on-line services. These services offer you access to various databases, helpful writing groups comprising other on-line writers, and, in many cases, some publications that are already on-line.

Work On-Screen

Learn to research, write, edit, and revise on the screen. You need to be able to think of your personal computer as a useful tool that can accomplish all the writing tasks involved in creating a solid story. Accessing databases, creating and then editing and revising your story, even, perhaps, submitting the story are all things that you should be comfortable doing from your personal computer.

From a staff viewpoint, by the way, more and more magazines are going to full pagination. That is, the design and layout of the publication are also done on a computer screen. If you are interested in staff work, familiarity with one or more of the design-oriented software packages (PageMaker or QuarkXPress, for instance) is a necessity.

PUT IT INTO PRACTICE

Discussion

1. There is probably someone in your class or writers' group who pays close attention to computer technology. Let that person lead the discussion, and ask yourselves where nonfiction writing might go in the next five or ten years. Are we approaching the era of the paperless magazine? the paperless book?

   Imagine yourself on assignment to do a magazine personality piece on a famous athlete in the year 2005. Discuss how you think the process will take place. How will you do your interviewing? How will you do your research? How will you write the first draft? How will you revise? How will you submit the story? How will it reach its audience?

2. Discuss the economic implications of the Information Age for writers. It's an expensive proposition—getting computerized and on-line to meet the future's demands in the magazine writing business. Does that expensiveness discriminate against writers who don't have the financial means to join the computer age? In the future, will the writer with the most money get the most, and best, assignments?

3. Discuss the technological implications of the Information Age for writers. Has the technology become a hindrance to some writers rather than a helpful tool? Can a writer who has a difficult time using computers and who prefers working in a simpler fashion stay in the field? Has the tool (the computer) become more important than the writer's talent?

   Finally, do the limitations of the computer define what you write, or do you feel that computers liberate your writing skills? For instance, do you overedit a story because editing is so easy with a word processor? Do you do a sloppy job on the first draft because you are aware of the ease of revision? And does that sloppy first draft mean the final version isn't all it could, or should, be? Do you rely too much on computerized research techniques and not enough on solid interviewing and observation skills?

Exercises

1. You have been assigned to write a story for a major writers' magazine, comparing the various software programs for word processing. Do some library research (no doubt using NEXIS or other databases), and then make some phone calls. Which programs seem to be the fa-

vorites of freelance writers? Why? Which ones are most commonly used by staff writers? Why?

Make a list of the major word processing programs and include a paragraph or two under each one that summarizes what you've learned about it from your research and interviewing.

2. Compare your list with that of someone else in your class or writers' group. Did the two of you generally get the same reaction from writers and editors, or was there a great deal of difference?

3. You have been assigned to write a story for *Omni* magazine on the future of magazine distribution, covering how the magazine will be delivered to the reader at home in five years, then in ten years. Do some library research (no doubt using NEXIS or other databases), and then make some phone calls. What do you think is likely to be the most common method of distribution? Do you believe it will be by mail and by sales from magazines racks, as it is today, or something else? Will one method of distribution dominate, or will there be a variety?

Will it make any difference if the magazine in question is *Sport* or *Sports Illustrated,* or *Gentleman's Quarterly,* or the *New Yorker,* or any other magazine? Will there be a difference in distribution methods between the local, regional, and national magazines? If so, what will be those differences?

Again, compare your results with those of a classmate and discuss the differences and similarities.

COPYRIGHT, LIBEL, AND ETHICS

COPYRIGHT LAW

A LIBEL PRIMER

ETHICAL CONSIDERATIONS

You've finally finished that personality profile that you've been working on for weeks, and now it's time to put it into the mail and hope for the best.

You're confident that this will be a breakthrough piece for you: You've interviewed the fellow who sold Elvis Presley his first guitar, and he was the most unusual character you've ever met. Certainly he said a lot of nasty things about several people in the record business, but you used a cassette recorder, and you're confident the quotes are accurate. No one, you're sure, has ever written anything like this.

You're just about to seal the envelope containing the story and its self-addressed, stamped envelope, when you realize that the editor might love this idea but not the way you've presented it. It's entirely possible, you think, that the editor at *Elvis Lives* magazine might steal the idea from you.

What to do to protect your copyright to the story?

You're thinking you might send to the U.S. Copyright Office for a registration form, but that may take weeks and you want to send this story off right away.

Well, here's what most writers and editors will tell you about your dilemma: Don't worry about it.

Most beginning writers don't realize it, but everything they've written is automatically copyrighted as soon as it is down on paper. There is no need, according to current copyright law, to send off to Washington, D.C., for special forms, no need to pay to register material with the copyright office, no need, in fact, to even put the copyright symbol, ©, with your name and date on the stories you send off.

Since the 1989 update of the U.S. Copyright Act of 1976, all of that is taken care of automatically.

COPYRIGHT LAW

According to the copyright act and subsequent decisions by the copyright office, everything you write is automatically copyrighted once it is in tangible form. Remember that you can't copyright ideas but that the way you present those ideas is yours and is protected.[1]

When you send that story off, the magazine that buys it will be buying the rights from you to print the story. Typically, the magazine will offer you a contract that stipulates which rights it is buying. At the least, there should be a letter of agreement from the magazine stipulating those rights.

If you don't receive a contract or agreement, then in order to protect yourself, you might want to stipulate in a letter to the magazine exactly what rights you are offering.

There are several basic copyrights that you need to understand for

---

[1]However, the copyright office recommends that you *do* use the copyright symbol, ©, with the year and your name if you have worries about protecting your rights. Also, the copyright office adds, filing the story with the copyright office will serve as important added protection should there be a legal wrangle over the copyright.

your work in magazine writing. They are first serial rights, second serial rights, all rights, and work for hire.

First Serial Rights

First serial rights means that you are selling to the magazine the right to publish your story once, after which occurrence the copyright reverts to you. These are called First North American Serial Rights when the rights include Canadian publication.

You will find that this is the norm for magazine publication. The majority of publications buy first serial rights from you and publish the story (often with a contractual commitment that you not republish it for some stated period of time); then the rights revert to you.

Second Serial Rights

Second serial rights means that the story has been previously published elsewhere and you are giving the magazine permission to be the one to publish the story for the second time. They are sometimes called reprint rights.

You will find this, too, is a common practice in the magazine business. In this era of specialized magazines there are many cases in which the readership of one magazine does not overlap the readership of another, and so the second magazine is quite happy paying you for the right to be the one to publish your story a second (or third, or tenth) time. Frequently, the payment for this kind of secondary publication is less than if the story were being published for the first time.

There are certain benefits to reprint rights—both for you and for the editor. From the editor's perspective, he or she knows the story is publishable (after all, it was already published once). If the editor likes the piece, and knows it is unlikely his or her readers have seen the initial publication, buying it saves a little money, for the payment is smaller, and it still gets a good story into print in the magazine.

From the writer's perspective, a smaller payment is certainly better than none at all, and the reprint does get your byline into the magazine that is reprinting the story. More readers will know your work. Also, the editor will now be familiar with your writing, and that can't possibly hurt your chances to sell more stories to that magazine in the future.

Similar in some ways to second serial rights are *simultaneous rights,* which involve selling the story to two noncompeting markets at once.

Again, the payment is quite likely to be smaller in both cases than First North American, but you gain through being published more than once, and the editor gains some small savings in payment.

All Rights

All rights means you are selling the story forever. You give the magazine all future rights to the story. It now belongs to the publication, not to you. Any subsequent publication of your story will bring in more money to the magazine, not to you.

You need to be very wary of agreeing to all rights, although there are times when it may make good sense for you. Commonly, if a publication wants to buy all rights, it will pay you considerably more for those rights than it would for first serial rights.

Work for Hire

Work for hire (which the copyright office calls "work made for hire") is a situation in which you agree to write material for magazines (or publishers) under their copyright. That is, the work is completely theirs, and you have agreed to have no copyright attachment to it.

Like all rights, the payment should be substantially higher than if you were selling first serial rights and had a chance to sell the piece again elsewhere.

The most important thing to remember about current copyright law is that anything you write is automatically copyrighted as soon as you finish writing it and getting it into tangible form. You can, if you choose, call or write to the copyright office for an official form, fill it out, pay a $20 fee, and get formal copyright registration, but it is not legally necessary in order to copyright your work.

For more information or to receive copies of the form, write to the Copyright Office, Library of Congress, Washington, D.C. 20559, or call 202-707-9100. If you write, the office advises that you include your ZIP Code in your return address and that you supply a daytime telephone number where you can be reached.

If you call, voice mail will take you through a process that ends with your receiving the forms in the mail about two weeks later. You'll probably want to ask for circular 1 (Copyright Basics) or circular 3 (Copyright Notice).

A LIBEL PRIMER

Knowing what libel is and knowing how to avoid being successfully sued for it are important to all nonfiction writers and crucial to those who want to write personality profiles, investigative stories, and the like.

Basically, libel causes injury to a person's reputation. A story that harms someone's reputation may be libelous, and you need to be wary of writing such articles. However, there are any number of cases in which such a story can, and perhaps should, be written. If, for instance, you are doing a magazine article that exposes fraud in a particular industry, you may very well cost some of the perpetrators their jobs—you've caused them harm. But you've done well in doing so.

The key element in U.S. magazine work is that the truth remains the great defense. If what you say is provably true, then you are safe in saying it. This defense for libel goes back to Colonial days, when an editor named John Peter Zenger worked for a newspaper that frequently tweaked the nose of the Colonial governor of New York.

The governor had Zenger arrested for libel, but Zenger's lawyer, Andrew Hamilton, argued that there should be no punishment for printing statements that were true. The argument prevailed, and Zenger was set free. At least philosophically, the U.S. standard that makes truth the great defense for libel stems from that case.

Remember that the things you say must be *provably true,* which frequently means that you'll have to have the paper trail to back you up.

Because most of the magazines that run stories with libel potential will require that you submit (for the fact-checkers) supportive materials as well as names and phone numbers, it should be unlikely that you run into a problem with truth in a printed story.

It is important to note that accuracy of quotation is not a defense for libel; that is, having a quote be accurate is not at all the same thing as having factual truth. Because you quote someone accurately does not protect you from libel. If what the person said is libelous, you can be held responsible for that libel.

In the example used at the start of this chapter, the writer was comfortable with libelous material in the story about Elvis's guitar because the quotes were accurate (from a recording). That kind of thinking can be very expensively wrong.

Another important defense for libel is called privilege, which revolves around our democratic form of government. Government officials in the United States have what is termed absolute privilege, which means they are free to discuss the issues of the day without fear of libel suits. That privilege extends from the U.S. Senate and House of Representatives to city council meetings in your small town, and it is designed to encourage the democratic process in government.

Writers who cover the news about public officials enjoy a watered-down version of that protection, called qualified privilege. This means that you may write what the officials say, but you are not as fully protected as they are. In other words, your privilege is affected by how you treat the material.

In general, if you stick to accusations that involve the facts on the issue at hand, you will be safe. If, however, two government officials get personal in their attacks and you have no evidence that supports the attack, you need to be wary of including such material in your story.

These qualifications vary from state to state, and you'll need to ascertain how complete they are where you are writing.

One of the most important protections from libel suits is contained in the First Amendment protection that centers on public figures.

Beginning with the Supreme Court's 1964 decision in *New York Times v. Sullivan,* the high court has consistently upheld a writer's right to talk about a public official's performance, as long as a story is not malicious (the court defined "malice" as "knowledge that it [the information] was false, or reckless disregard of whether it was false or not").

That 1964 decision, which established what journalists call the N.Y. Times Rule, was specifically aimed at stories about public officials, but subsequent cases expanded the definition to include public persons ranging from college football coaches to Hollywood figures and anyone else willingly in the public arena.

In recent years, the trend in Supreme Court decisions has been to contract, rather than expand, the N.Y. Times Rule, and the court seems to be changing the malice standard to one of negligence, which seems to be easier to stumble over for writers. However, there is still solid protection for writing about public figures.

The Associated Press (AP), in its *Stylebook,* summarizes the issue on public persons by classifying such people this way:

> *Public officials:* You have wide protection when you are writing about public officials. In order to sue successfully for libel, a public official must prove actual malice, that is, must prove that the writer either had knowledge that the facts were false or acted with reckless disregard.
>
> *Public figures:* The rule is basically the same as for public officials, but the danger comes in defining who is a public figure. The courts seem to say there are two types: (1) General Purpose Public Figures, or individuals who have assumed a role of special promi-

nence, and (2) Limited Purpose Public Figures, or individuals who have thrust themselves into public view.

Private figures: These individuals, defined in the negative, are those who are not public figures. Your protection when writing about them can be significantly less broad than for public figures. AP categorizes private figures into three basic levels of protection depending on the state where one lives. In some states, the level of protection is the same as for public figures; in New York State, the private figure must prove that the writer (or magazine) acted in a "grossly irresponsible manner"; and in other states, the private figures do not have to prove malice: they must simply prove negligence, a standard that is difficult to define but seems to be less protective for the writer than actual malice.

It is also most important that you remember that the courts' expectations for magazines are frequently higher than those for newspapers. That is, the daily deadlines for newspapers may factor into court standards of free speech. Magazines don't have that deadline pressure (at least in the eyes of the courts), and so the standards often seem tighter.

Another area of special concern for magazine writers is the issue of right to privacy. Generally, when you write about someone newsworthy, you are protected. When you write about someone with no timely news value, however, you may, in some states, be in trouble. The Supreme Court, in a 1967 case, ruled that "the constitutional guarantees of freedom of the press are applicable to invasion-of-privacy cases involving *reports of newsworthy matters,*" according to AP (emphasis mine). The actual malice standard also seems to apply.

Finally, a common defense for magazine writers is the Fair Comment and Criticism standard. Basically, the courts have long upheld that people who put themselves in the public eye for their performances knowingly take on the risk of a bad review. This is the basic standard that applies to critics, reviewers, sportswriters, and other writers who make value judgments about a performance.

ETHICAL CONSIDERATIONS

The copyright laws are reasonably straightforward, and libel law, even with its gray areas, is at least based on legal decisions.

A much trickier aspect of magazine writing that you need to pay particular attention to is ethics. What is ethical behavior for a magazine writer—especially one on a tight budget? There are several areas of ethical concern for you to consider as you set out on your writing career.

Freebies

This is a particular problem for travel writers, though to some extent any magazine writer may come across it. People or organizations that you are writing about may offer you free meals, trips, apparel, or other items.

You must learn to always turn these freebies down.

You are, of course, committed to ethical work, and a free meal here or there or a new briefcase or even an all-expense-paid trip to Hawaii won't buy you off. Just because you accepted something free from people doesn't mean you are committed to saying nice things about them that they don't deserve.

Appearances Matter

Knowing that you can't be bought is missing the point. It is the *appearance of influence* that you need to avoid at all costs. How can the reader trust you to write a fair assessment of a travel destination if it turns out that you stayed at the hotel for free, flew free on an airline that you mention in the story, and never paid for a meal?

Most travel editors are adamant about avoiding stories by writers who have accepted freebies for just that reason. And even if you come across an editor who doesn't mind, that won't change the basic standard you will have set for yourself by accepting a freebie, and so will tarnish your reputation for other editors. It isn't worth it.

If the magazine gives you an assignment, then the magazine should pay your expenses. If you are freelancing on your own, then pay your own expenses (and keep a record for tax purposes), and keep your reputation untarnished.

Multiple Submissions and Multiple Use of Reporting

It is considered unethical to submit a story to more than one publication at a time without informing the editors that you are doing so.

The editors who open your envelope and take a look at your story are operating under the premise that they are the only ones holding the story for consideration. If you submit elsewhere at the same time without informing them, you are lying to them, and that, too, can come back to haunt you later.

This is often a frustrating reality for writers, for it is all too common for a story to spend months at a particular magazine only to come back with a form rejection. This seems a great waste of time, and there is, as a result, a great temptation to send the story out to several publications at once, figuring that if one buys it, you can then inform the others that the story is no longer available.

Alas, such behavior, though it makes sense to the beginning writer, makes little sense to editors, who need to know that the stories under consideration haven't been published before and aren't about to be published elsewhere.

From an editor's perspective, it would be chaos to have to regularly deal with multiple submissions. Frequently, a great deal of time and effort is expended in making the decision to buy a story (the story may have been read by several editors before the decision is made, for instance), and then, once the decision to buy is made, the story immediately goes into the production process.

Finding out a few days, or weeks, later that a story has been sold elsewhere would be a major crisis for the editor. Multiply that possible crisis by dozens, hundreds, or thousands of submissions, and you can see why editors like to know the story at hand is theirs alone to consider.

Plagiarism and Proper Attribution

Plagiarism is the use of the writing of others without their permission. This is becoming increasingly common (and worrisome) for a variety of reasons, including the large amount of public relations material available to writers and because of the vast amount of research material available through such databases as NEXIS.

A travel writer who uses written material from a brochure found at the travel destination and who appropriates it without attribution is plagiarizing, and that's unethical.

Similarly, if you use stories, or sections of stories, that you found in your research—without giving proper attribution in your story—that, too, is plagiarism. Don't do it.

Public relations personnel will avow that they are quite happy to have you use their press releases without attribution; getting the material into print, after all, is what they seek. But by using their material as part of your story without informing the reader of it, you are cheating, even if that public relations professional is happy to have you do so. Attribution usually takes care of the problem. Just make sure that in every case you either cite the source or place the material in quotes and give attribution.

Even when you are merely using facts and information from a source and not actually using the same words as the source did to describe them, you are better off citing the source and thus giving proper attribution.

Fairness

This is a surprisingly tricky area for magazine writers. Unlike newspaper reporters, magazine writers are not writing for a general audience, so usually they are under no pressure to take a neutral stance on issues. Indeed, as you've seen in several cases cited in this book, editors frequently expect a strong, opinionated voice from the writer. But being strong and opinionated does not mean being unfair, either in your writing or in your reporting.

You must always strive for fairness in your use of quotes, for instance (bearing in mind such things as proper context and accuracy of quotation).

Similarly, you need to be fair not only in how you write the story but also in how you go about acquiring it. Hacking your way into someone's private computer file to find information is against the law, but that does not necessarily mean it is unethical. If the information you find is important to a story that you feel has overriding merit, then perhaps the hacking was a legal risk that you were willing to take.

Much more frequently, it is not a risk worth taking. Practicing deceit (when you pretend to be something other than a writer to do a story), practicing illegal computer hacking, getting quotes from people without their knowing you're a writer on assignment—all of these things compromise your standards as a writer. If you are going to do some of them, you'd better have a story of sufficient merit to be worth the risk to your career.

Finally, because magazines are so specialized, the editors typically have a very clear idea of what they need for their readers. This can put you in a bind when the story you find is not the story the editors wanted you to find.

Especially early in your career, you may find yourself facing a tough call. Do you write what you think is the truth, or do you compromise to meet the needs of the editor?

Freelancer Michael Bane recalls that during his undergraduate days, he was assigned a story that didn't turn out the way the magazine wanted, and he found himself in just such a dilemma.

"When you start out, you take what you can get, of course. One of the first stories I ever did taught me a real lesson. It was for a very liberal university-type publication in North Carolina, and they sent me out with [activist priest] Daniel Berrigan. They wanted a very adulatory piece on him, but I thought he was very shallow and really not much of a guy. I wrote that, and of course the story was killed. They wanted what they wanted, and so they sent somebody else out and got it.

"For a lot of magazines," Bane points out, "once the editors get it in their heads what they want, you either do it their way or they kill the story. I try to watch for that now and avoid those assignments."

You might not be able to do that as you start, so at the very least be aware of the potential for the problem. Your best bet will be to look for areas of compromise and to talk with the editor about what you are finding out.

PUT IT INTO PRACTICE

Discussion

1. Using the lists that you and your fellow writers will bring in from exercise 3 (see below), discuss some of the basic ethical issues that routinely arise in magazine writing. Are there some basic standards of behavior that you can recommend to magazine writers, or must ethical issues be decided case by case? See if you can, through discussion, compose a short paragraph that serves as an ethics guide for magazine writing.

2. Have you or the other writers in your group ever duplicated a tape of a pop group's recent compact disc? Is that fair to the artist (who, after all, makes no money from such duplication)? Have you or the other writers in your group ever made photocopies of a magazine story and shared it with others? Is that fair to the writer?

   Discuss the copying of created works (music, books, magazine articles) and the implications of such copying for the person who created the work. Consider some of the broader implications of the discussion, too: What about libraries? What about friends' sharing a copy of a new best-seller? What about passing around one copy of a recent issue of a magazine?

   Can you, through discussion, arrive at some reasonable conclusion about what is fair and ethical to the creator and what isn't? See if you can produce a short paragraph that describes your fair conclusion.

Exercises

1. You have decided that you want to register a story with the copyright office. Call 202-707-9100 to request the proper application forms or information circulars. Write a brief description of the phone process, and then keep track of how long it takes to receive the forms.

2. Many states have so-called sunshine laws, meant to promote open government. Look up the sunshine law in your state, and give a one-page summation of which records are open to reporters and which ones aren't.

3. There are enough ethical issues involving magazine writing to fill a textbook or two on their own. Go to a nearby magazine stand and select any five magazines. Read them through, looking for stories that have ethical implications. Does that travel story sound to you as if the writer had a free trip and now feels the need to promote the des-

tination? Did the writer of that personality piece on the pop music star go too far in invading the star's privacy? Has the writer of that piece that attacks the governor of your state been unfair in her attack?

List at least one ethical issue worth discussing from each of the five magazines, and give a brief description of the issue.

AFTERWORD

Some final thoughts on writing nonfiction —

There are a number of specialized kinds of magazine writing that this text hasn't touched upon, including science writing, how-tos, environmental writing, and many more. In an era of increasing specialization, it seemed best in this book to focus on the reporting, writing, and marketing skills that would translate well across the spectrum of magazine feature writing, rather than spend too much time on individual specialties. However, one of the most productive things a nonfiction writer can do to help hone the craft is to attempt some of those other kinds of specialties from time to time. Just making the attempt is worthwhile, for it helps to sharpen your appreciation for the specialized audiences that are increasingly important to the magazine business.

Another way to help sharpen your research and writing skills is to read, and to try writing, short stories and poetry. Short story writing teaches you some very useful things, including how to tell a good story, pay close attention to details, and achieve effective use of language by constructing metaphors, creating symbolism, and applying other devices.

Perhaps the most useful of all the things that you'll gain from writing short fiction is the experience of telling a good story — one that grabs the reader's interest right from the start and holds it all the way to a solid conclusion.

Storytelling has its roots in verbal communication, of course, when ancient cultures passed on their traditions through stories that became cultural myths. Modern short fiction comprises several kinds of storytelling. Some of the genres, such as science fiction and mysteries, depend heavily on plot and an interesting idea; other kinds of short fiction depend more on character and the subtleties of subtext (the story beneath what seems to be the main story). The very best popular short fiction, some might argue, is the kind that can do both, offering an intriguing plot with an interesting idea and also incorporating well-wrought characters and a useful subtext that complements the main story.

No matter which kind of fiction appeals to you, you'll find that for the short story to work, it has to have an interesting beginning, middle, and end, and there is usually some growth on the part of the main characters.

Ask yourself how the short story that follows this afterword accomplishes those things. Does it tell a story? Is there growth in the main characters? Are there any subtleties of writing, or is it heavy-handed in its thematic message?

In the writing of a short story, you will also find that the act of inventing details of character, setting, and plot (even if these start from reality, you must "invent" them as pieces of fiction to fit into your story) is good practice for you as a writer. This act of invention helps you see that it is often from the details that a sense of reality emerges in a story. What kind of word choice or verbal tics separate the dialogue of one character from another in your story? What particular articles of clothing do the characters wear? What kind of street do they live on? What kind of weather is taking place during the story? All of these details add a sense of believability to a short story, and you'll find yourself inventing them as you go. With practice, you'll find that you invent details that are more and more in keeping with the plot and characters that you've devised.

Finally, the writing of short fiction will help you polish your use of the language. When you realize that virtually everything you say in print has a certain value as a symbol (what does it say about a character who drives a Porsche? a Volkswagen bug? a minivan?), you will begin to effectively incorporate those symbolic values into your short story.

Judicious use of linguistic devices such as metaphor, synecdoche, and personification will help you improve your fiction by adding useful, subtle detail to a story. As with the other elements mentioned here, as you apply these devices more and more, you'll begin to see better and better how they improve your story—and your writing.

To translate these kinds of fiction-writing skills into nonfiction is not as difficult as you might think. The major difference, after all, is that in fiction all you have to do is "invent," or make up, a useful verbal tic for a character, or a particular article of clothing, or bit of dialogue, or a rainy day, to find it improves a story.

It is, you might think, going to be another thing entirely to use these things if you can't invent them. But many of the elements are there if you do enough reporting. Remember that fiction works best when it seems real; that in many cases, these kinds of details do, in real life, surround the characters and things you are writing about; and that it is simply up to you to do enough good reporting that you notice them, jot them down, and then incorporate them into the story.

In writing fiction, you will use a lot of little lies—made-up things— to tell an effective truth-in-fiction. In writing nonfiction, you can use the same techniques to reveal something true, but you must find the actual, real things to use, and that means solid reporting. Think of doing a personality piece on an athlete, for instance. What kinds of clothes does she wear when she's not in uniform? What do those clothes say about the person? What kind of car does she drive? What is the weather like on the day of your interview? Does the weather fit into the story?

If you ask yourself a constant stream of these kinds of questions—the very questions a fiction writer might ask while working on a new story— the answers will help you write a better piece of magazine nonfiction.

Fiction is a tough market, much tougher in many ways than nonfiction, and so you may find it difficult to sell. But that's not really the main point. It is in the writing of fiction that you'll stretch yourself, making yourself a better writer of nonfiction.

Poetry, too, is helpful for the nonfiction writer to attempt, not only for many of the same reasons that short fiction is but also because poetry, especially narrative poetry (the kind that tells a highly condensed little story), teaches you the art of concise writing. A good poet can say in just a few words what a nonpoet might take pages of prose to get around to discussing. It is the *essence of the message* that poetry strives to express, and it is good practice indeed for you to find, and then express, that essential message of a story.

For purposes of improving your nonfiction, you may find it most useful to try writing poetry that does not rhyme. Though there is nothing at all wrong with rhyme and meter in poetry (and the resurgence of formally structured poetry in recent years is an indicator of how effective, and popular, rhyme and meter can be), striving to find the right rhyme is not going to be as useful to you as a magazine writer as is finding the exactly right word, whether it rhymes or not.

What you want to recognize from writing poetry is, first, how difficult it is to say things this concisely and, second, how rewarding it can be when you can see that in just a few words you have written paragraphs' worth of information.

Think of a poem as the tip of an iceberg. If the reader can sense that the rest of the iceberg is underneath the waterline, then your narrative poetry is beginning to succeed. For practice, try taking any one of the magazine articles that you have written while reading this book, and reduce it to a 15-line poem. You'll be surprised, perhaps, to find that you can do it, and much of the essence of what it took you several thousand words to say comes through in those 15 lines.

Take a look at the three poems reprinted at the end of this afterword to decide whether they accomplish any of the things you've just read about. Can you sense a greater story underneath the poems? Can you imagine how the poems might work as short stories? as novels? as non-fiction magazine pieces?

Finally, notice that the setting for the short story and the poems is Scotland. The author of this book spends a considerable amount of time in Scotland and often fixes short stories, poems, and nonfiction magazine articles (usually travel articles) in that setting. In fact, the setting for the poem "Running in the Rain, Cramond, Scotland" is exactly the same small fishing village as the one used in the short story "Bridging." Though the poem and the short story were written years apart, you might find it worthwhile to think about ways the poem and the short story are similar in how they use that setting for effect.

■ ■ ■

BRIDGING

BY RICK WILBER

It is the dying hours of the twentieth century, and Paul Doig would rather be home in the Florida sunshine to wait out the epochal madness than be standing here in the rain where he is tired, wet, and cold. Only Julia, even in death, could have brought him here.

He began this odyssey with an afternoon flight from Tampa. After two plane changes and that dizzying false night of travel over the Atlantic he caught a taxi from the Glasgow airport to his hotel. A few hours there for a nap, and then it was time to drink a cup of wretched and overpriced coffee and come across to Edinburgh for Julia's funeral.

To clear his head he didn't take a taxi but, instead, took the risk of walking through several dangerous blocks of miserable Glasgow poverty to Queen Street station for the train across to here.

On the way he was nearly caught by some endtimers, four young toughs dressed in monk robes and carrying staffs so they could cudgel anyone they could catch into donating to their cause.

Paul was dressed down to avoid trouble. He wore blue jeans and an old rain jacket, but something about the way he carried himself or perhaps the way he checked street signs for directions gave him away as an American, and the endtimers zeroed in on him as soon as he stepped into the Sauchiehall Street pedestrian precinct.

He carried a stasprod and might have used it to stun all four of them, but several policemen were walking the beat together near Buchanan Street as Paul rounded that corner, and the endtimers pulled to a halt when they saw the police. There was some jeering and yelling, but Paul got to the station easily enough after that and was on the five P.M. train when it pulled out. He treated himself to a first-class ticket and sat alone, avoiding any conversations.

He wasn't sure why the endtimers were out to get Yanks; certainly life in the States was just as miserable for most people as life in Scotland these days. If they were going to beat someone up out of sheer envy, they should take on some German or Japanese tourist. Or beat up an Englishman; at least there was history behind that sort of action.

Still, he wasn't about to argue points of economic logic with four of that sort, so he counted himself lucky as he settled into the seat for the fifty-minute run over to Edinburgh.

The train guards checked his credentials three times during the ride, making sure he was legal to carry the stasprod, which was powerful enough to kill if he set it that high. He had it on the middle levels, though, and had his papers straight as well, so there was no problem. Truth was, he had owned the stasprod since it had first come on the market, five or six years ago now, and had never used it once.

From Edinburgh's Waverley station he caught a taxi that avoided the worst of that dying city's danger spots by weaving through the narrow streets of Old Town to eventually bring him out here to tiny little Cramond. They crossed several bridges on the way, and now he wonders how Julia managed crossing them for all those years. Her fear of bridges, her terror of them, was legendary. There must have been other ways for her to get here from the city.

He watches the black hulk of the taxi disappear around a corner and shakes his head. The driver had tried to get him chatting three or four times, and Paul's ignoring of the remarks didn't seem to work. Finally Paul asked him to please be quiet and then had to suffer the driver's foul mood for the final mile or two. It is good to be out of the noisy, smelly old taxi, nasty weather or no.

Paul turns and walks to the guard box where the letter from Julia's daughter will get him through the newly bricked city walls and down into the village for the service. He has never met the daughter and hasn't seen Julia in fifteen years, not since the one time he came here to visit.

He wonders what kind of service it will be. Julia's eccentricities were famous, so almost anything at all could take place this evening—a High Mass, a loud party, a quiet gathering. Who knows?

Nothing would surprise him, not after what he knows of her and what he's read about her in the magazines—the reclusiveness, the bitter hirings and firings of her staff, the manic jet-setter parties, the binges with alcohol, the paranoia and the phobias. There was so much pain that accompanied her success.

He thinks of her fear of bridges. That one, at least, he understands. He was there when that began for her. Her rise and his decline started on that terrible day.

He shoves that memory aside, doesn't want to think about it. Instead he prefers to remember the years with her this way:

■ ■ ■

Those small, perfect breasts that rose and fell in rhythm as she moved above him. Beads of sweat on her upper lip, though the window unit labored to cool the beach cottage bedroom. She would smile that slight smile that started at pale blue eyes and gathered together those high cheekbones, the upturned lips, the almost open mouth. She would arch her back to ride him as they moved together in waves that crested with her cries of passion and joy. They were nineteen and very much in love.

■ ■ ■

The comfort of a shared life with her as they made the long drive through the American West, listening to bad pop and country on the tape deck and stopping to climb the peaks and walk the valleys.

Once, at a place called Mosquito Pass in Colorado, they drove their beat-up old Volksie bus up the jarring narrow gravel road nearly to the top before the engine ran out of air and the Volksie stalled.

They got out at the entrance to an abandoned lead mine there, and Julia, always the one in good spirits to contrast with his dark moments, told him it was fine, just fine that the bus gave out. They weren't meant to go over that pass, that was all. Fate.

A four-wheel-drive rescue jeep came by, and two women got out. "You two okay?" one of the two women asked Paul and Julia. And Julia laughed. "Of course," she said, "why wouldn't we be?"

"We heard someone went over the edge up there about an hour ago," the woman said. "Tough winds today, gusts to eighty. You were smart to stop here with that thing," and she hooked

her thumb toward the unstable old Volkswagen bus.

Julia said nothing as they drove back down from the pass. She just stared at him, and smiled, and nodded her head. Fate.

■ ■ ■

Or the time, years later, toward the end, when he was pitching for that semipro baseball team in the championship finals of their summer league.

It was a miserable Florida August day, unspeakably hot, with no breeze from the nearby Gulf of Mexico, no hint of shade from clouds or the thin palms. Just heat.

In the top of the ninth, up by a run, he had to get through the last two hitters to win it. The first grounded out to short on the second pitch, a flat slider that Paul was lucky to get away with.

The second was stepping in when Julia pulled up in the little Toyota they shared, beeped the horn, and got out waving a piece of paper in her hand.

Paul took the sign, nodded, and went into the windup as Julia ran from the car and headed toward the field. The pitch, a tired fastball, reached the plate as she ran out from behind the backstop. The batter, swinging under it, tipped it almost straight back, and Paul watched in horror as the ball arrowed toward Julia's smiling face.

At the very last moment she saw it enough to begin to duck, and the ball grazed her left temple instead of hitting her full on the forehead. She dropped like a sack.

Paul ran to her, yelling in fear, afraid for her life. When he reached her she lay silent, eyes closed, and he thought for a single insane moment that she'd been killed and it was his fault. Then she opened her eyes, smiled, and said, "You've got to see this. Look."

It was a letter from *The Atlantic Monthly*. "We are pleased to accept 'Greggie's Cup' for publication in . . ."

Her first sale. The start of everything for her. The start of nothing, of his collapse, for Paul.

A few minutes later, while she sat with ice on her head, he got the last man to fly out to left, and they won the championship for the summer league.

That night they toasted each other. He for his championship, she for her sale. It was, he realized now, about the last time he'd won anything. For her, it was barely the beginning.

■ ■ ■

She was a wonderful lover, taught him everything at age nineteen. They met at college in Tampa, sat one desk apart in a creative writing class. The professor wrote stories for *The New Yorker*, and Julia thought him wonderful. Paul thought he was a pompous old fool, and *The New Yorker*, which Paul despised as unreadable, pretentious drivel, deserved him.

They argued about it after class, then took the discussion to a local bar. A week later they were making love, and a week after that he was reading the professor's stories while Julia lay next to him and watched approvingly.

That, too, she said, was fate. He'd write for *The New Yorker* one day; they both would. And *The Atlantic*, and the *Paris Review*, and novels and poetry . . . she just knew it was their fate.

It was the start of five years of heaven. That's how he thinks of it now. It was heaven, and he didn't know how special it was, thought it would always be that way.

He was drifting into newspaper work by then; someone had to pay the bills for them, and he was good at it, from news to features to columns. He liked it, too, when he admitted it, though he never told her.

They were good years, fine years. They talked about finally getting married, having children.

Then came that day on the bridge, when so much of it died.

■ ■ ■

Standing there, just inside the city walls, cold rain on his face, he remembers how that happened.

He'd been late at the paper, finishing a piece for the Sunday feature section, a story on the area's growing violence, the steady march toward a big-city crime rate.

She had come by to pick him up at ten, and they'd gone home, parked the car, and then walked out to the beach for drinks and a late meal. It was a safe, pleasant one-mile walk across the Bayway bridge to the Seahorse bar, where they had grouper sandwiches and a couple of Heinekens.

Paul remembers parts of this in agonizing detail. Thirty years later, and still he recalls the details with startling, painful clarity. The beads of sweat on the green Heineken bottles. The sound of the waves against the restaurant's seawall. Julia's hair against the backlighting from the bar across the room. So beautiful.

On the walk home their timing was bad. That was how the police put it. Just bad timing.

A sailboat just returning from a month in the Keys putt-putted up the channel, signaled for the bridge to open, and then slowly moved through while the bridge was up.

A single car waited for the bridge. Inside were three young men in their early twenties, two of them in the backseat. They were high, giggling, bouncing around in the seats. They had just robbed a gas station convenience store a few miles up the beach, had shot the attendant and left him for dead. Their world was hilariously simple, was all theirs for the taking, as they waited while the center span opened and raised itself high. There were no other cars coming from behind.

Paul and Julia walked along the bridge's sidewalk, coming up close to the draw so they could watch the sailboat pass by below.

They were arm in arm as the boat passed beneath them. They waved at the man at the helm, who waved back.

Paul was just telling her about his feature story on the victims of crime when they were attacked.

Paul's memory is sketchy on this part of the night. There are hazy images of a beating, fists into his side and into his cheeks. Boots kicking into his ribs. Not much pain, really, not then.

He was sitting on the sidewalk, watching, helpless, as the two from the backseat dragged Julia away and into the car.

Paul tried to rise and then discovered the pain. Still, he managed to get to his feet, managed to step over the metal barrier that separated the sidewalk from the road, managed to take four steps toward the car, his arm raised.

The two in the back, busy raping Julia, paid him no attention at all. Their friend in the front opened his door, stepped out, said "Stupid fuck," and shoved Paul back over the barrier and onto the sidewalk. He lost consciousness at that point.

Another minute or two later, no more than three, the span came down; they tossed Julia out the car door and drove off. The bridge tender, an elderly man, could see Paul and Julia then and phoned for help.

The whole thing took a few minutes, a fraction of time from a lifetime of fifty-five years, thinks

Paul. But Julia never crossed a bridge again without knowing what her various psychologists and psychiatrists and counselors and friends all called that "irrational" fear.

Paul didn't find it irrational at all.

■ ■ ■

It was all so long ago.

The rain is light but insistent. He pulls up the hood on his jacket, and it focuses his sight on the road ahead, the peripheral vision nothing but gray plastic. That is something the wise person never does these days, close off the side vision. The wise walker keeps an eye out for trouble, for the proddy boys with their joysticks, the druggies needing cash, the endtimers with their profitable fervor, the simply vicious.

But this village is walled and guarded; he feels safe enough. And though he has only been here once before, years ago, and can barely see the buildings that line the road, he knows this place well enough. This is where he came to beg, years after she left him.

That memory hurts, like a lot of them. She was always reminding him of their past, using him. He's seen himself in dozens of her stories since those early days, known himself in four of her novels. He saw himself there all the time and hated her for it, the way she made him into the hero he wasn't that night when she needed him.

As he walks, through the gray plastic and the rain he recognizes landmarks from her stories and poems.

On his right is the old church, Cramond Kirk, where she had her hero, him, finally kill the madman who'd pursued that poor woman through three continents and a handful of time zones.

Beyond that is Cramond Inn, where that same hero two books later sat in the dark corner by the fireplace and hatched the plan that saved the world and rescued the kidnapped heiress.

He laughs. She made him a hero known all over the world, a dashing figure capable of winning through against all odds. Handsome, talented, rich beyond all need, this make-believe man grew more popular each year even as the world declined into depression and violence-and fear.

But the real man, the figure on which all this is based, can only smile at that image. He is a lonely columnist for a local daily paper, nothing more. He writes about local politicians and greedy business executives and how it's the little people who always get hurt.

He is very good at this, and very popular. Not many people know how solitary a life he leads. He is handsome enough, tall, a bit thin, bookish with his reading glasses. But he dates only when he must, so women think him gay or asexual. He almost wishes that were so; the first would at least be companionship, and the second a relief.

But it isn't so. He is, instead, isolated; can't seem to reach out. He finds ways to ruin any relationship he might drift into. A shrink he spent two years visiting said that he was into self-defeat and needed to work through why that was.

Paul smiles at that thought. He has come to accept that only through his column, through the safe distance of words on recycled paper, can he reach out to people, talk to them, try and know them.

And he is, at least, very good at that. He is popular, well read, well known in the city. Successful in his own way.

But it isn't what he thought he'd do, not back then with Julia, back when they planned the future.

Once, talking to her on the telephone, listening to the weird satellite echo that repeated his anger, he tried to defend himself, to tell her that he'd won a prize that year for his writing, and at least what he did was write about reality, at least it wasn't the invented pabulum of the cheap thrillers that she'd turned to writing.

She laughed at him, agreed. Just cheap thrillers, she said. That was all. Millions and millions of them.

■ ■ ■

Paul walks into the churchyard of the old kirk. A low stone wall there marks the ruins of a Roman fort from the second century. The rain is easing off, and as Paul pulls back the hood of his jacket the sun pokes through the clouds, and there is a moment of almost warmth.

In "Hope as an Element of Cold, Dark Matter," a story she wrote that won her prizes, Paul read of himself walking into this same place, walking along the same low stone walls that were the farthest extent of Empire, the very edge of Rome at its height of power.

He stands now atop the wall that once held the armory and looks to the north and west, where the mean waters of the Firth of Forth, the mountains beyond, and the simplistic brutality of the Picts just didn't seem worth it to Septimius Severus in the second century when he, emperor of all Rome, came here to visit. This, thought Septimius, was far enough.

The sky is clearing from the northwest, and there, its great girders rising over the hills, Paul sees the rail bridge over the Firth of Forth.

It was the wonder of the world in 1890, the greatest achievement of the age, a symbol of an empire's power and might at the height of its influence.

Paul wonders why Julia chose to live almost in the shadow of the bridge, why she would want to see it daily, this thing she never dared cross, this ultimate horror, this reminder.

"The bridge?" he hears a voice

say from behind him. "I think she actually enjoyed seeing it out the front window. She once said that because she could see it she always knew where her enemy was."

Paul turns, and a young woman is there. Julia at twenty, he thinks for a crazy moment, and then he realizes it must be the daughter, the one who called him two days ago in Tampa, telling him of her mother's death.

This girl is beautiful. Not her mother's beauty, not really, he decides as he looks at her. She is darker than Julia's pale beauty, and stockier in build, more athletic. But the short, dark hair suits this girl, and the smile seems genuine enough, given the grief, and the eyes are her mother's, pale blue and haunting, perceptive.

He's never known much about this daughter, never met her until this moment. He remembers that the girl's father—Julia's first husband, the one who came within the year after she left Paul—died a few years ago in a boating acci-dent. This poor child is alone now.

"Hello, Angela," he says. "I came as quickly as I could."

"Thank you," she says simply. "I'm glad you could come all this way on short notice. Mother made it clear that you were the first I should call after she died."

She walks over to him, takes his two hands in hers, holds them for a moment. "Mother told me a lot about you."

"She was a wonderful woman. A wonderful writer."

"She was a hack, actually," Angela says, smiling. "That's what she always said, just a hack grinding out novels to make a living."

Angela shakes her head as if to clear it of that kind of memory, drops Paul's hands, turns toward the water, points to it. "Beautiful view when the sun's out, isn't it?"

"Yes, beautiful."

"She loved this place. The village, this old ruin. She hated leaving it when she had to tour. Toward the end she even had me go into the city for her when she needed things."

Angela turns. "It was awful, Paul. Toward the end. The wasting away. That vital woman, eaten away like that."

"You were with her?"

"I was with her the past year. Quit my job and came home when she called and told me how it was."

There are no tears as Angela says this. Paul suspects the tears have already come and will come again later. Now she is being strong, lucid. She needs to tell him this. He listens.

"She's left me plenty of money, Paul. And two manuscripts, too. That's something we have to talk about, the manuscripts."

"We have to talk about them? Why? Surely she left instructions on when to publish."

"She asked that you be involved with them, help cut them

down to size. She said you're a wonderful editor, and that you understood her, and the work."

He laughs. Now? To ask this?

"You don't need me to do this, Angela. Hire someone, or just let her publisher handle it. I won't do it. I can't."

"It's not charity. She says this is something she should have done long ago but couldn't. She didn't tell me why."

Paul knows why, of course. The bridge. When he couldn't save her, couldn't help. She knew, in her head, that he did the best he could, couldn't have been expected to do more. He knows it, too.

But in their hearts, for both of them, he is to blame.

And now this is Julia, asking for a kind of forgiveness. She reaches out to him from wherever she is now, crosses that thing that divided them for all these years.

He smiles. "I'll think about it, okay?"

She nods. "It will be getting dark in another hour or so. That's when the funeral procession will take her to the cemetery. She asked me to take you for a walk first. A little stroll along the shoreline. Is that all right?"

"Fine," he says. "Down this way?" And he looks toward the shore. There is a path there, he can see it from here, edging along the Firth of Forth. In the distance is a ruined castle, remnant of other violent times. They head that way.

First there is a ferry across the River Almond. The ferryman lives on the far side, in a small brick home. Angela rings a bell to summon him.

A face peers out the front window. Angela smiles, waves.

"Thomas will be here in a minute or two," she says. "He makes it a point never to be in a hurry." They both laugh, almost nervously.

They say nothing, the silence a strain, as the front door creaks open and the ferryman comes out smileless, turns to slowly shut the door, and then walks down the low ridge to the dory that serves as a ferryboat.

"It's a new ferryman," Paul notes. "Fifteen years ago it was an older man. Looked a bit like Popeye."

"That was Jordan," Angela says. "He died a few years back. Bad heart. This is his son, Thomas."

In five long, slow minutes Thomas has the boat over and, in another equally slow five, takes the three of them back to this side of the river.

Paul thinks that Thomas is every bit as slow-moving as his father was but doesn't voice the thought. Instead, as they walk along, the rain returns, spitting at them, cold despite the calendar.

He shakes his head. "I never understood why she lived here, Angela. She could have lived anywhere, her own private island in the sun somewhere, or Canada perhaps, or, hell, anywhere but here."

He waves his hand vaguely in the direction of Edinburgh. "Why did she feel she had to live like this? God, the place is getting outright dangerous. Glasgow's fallen completely to pieces; Edinburgh's not much better. Hell, I avoided London entirely, too many gangs, too much violence. The whole U.K.'s a mess."

Angela picks her way over a fallen log as they enter a small woods. The leaves drip but block the worst of the rain. "It's like this in the States, too, isn't it, Paul? That's what our nets tell us, that it's even worse over there."

He nods his head. "A lot of places, yes, it's worse. Some places, like where I live, it's not too bad yet. Other places"—he shrugs—"it's anarchy. The government has given up completely in some of the big cities."

"You know she liked to face things head on, Paul. She always told me she liked to see the enemy, know where it was, and then she could deal with it."

Which is a lie, Paul thinks, but he says nothing. Some things, maybe, she faced, like having that damn bridge out her front door to stare at each day.

But other things, no, she dodged them as the rest of us do. The big things, the ones that really hurt. She stayed away from those if she could.

Angela leads the way, and they emerge from the woods onto a small stone beach. A large stone outcropping sits there in the tidal pools.

"She wanted me to make sure you saw this," Angela says, and she walks carefully around the pools to stand by the side of the outcropping. She points.

"That's said to be a Roman eagle carved into the side of the rock."

Paul walks over and looks at it. Perhaps. Worn away by two thousand years of miserable weather, but yes, perhaps it is an eagle cut into the stone. Some Roman, or a mercenary tied to Rome by profit only, spent the hours here to carve that, a symbol of how far the Empire had come.

"Remember in *Words of Praise* how the hero came here and saw that eagle?" she asks him.

He nods. Another book where she made him the hero. "And then he traveled to Rome, found the drug lord and killed him, rescued the girl he loved. Yes, I remember it."

She laughs. "Silly stuff, I suppose. But it pleased millions of people, Paul. It made them happy for a time. That's all she said she wanted."

He nods.

■ ■ ■

An hour later they are at Julia's home. It is a small stone cottage that sits on a bluff overlooking the firth. To the west is the rail bridge. To the north is Fife. To the south is Edinburgh.

The cemetery is in the small churchyard in Cramond, where Paul's evening began. They will return to it with a two-mile walk along the old main road. Halfway there, crossing the River Almond, is Cramond Brig, the old stone bridge over the river.

It took death to make it happen, Paul thinks when he hears Angela explain the procession, but at last Julia will conquer a bridge, cross one calmly, easily, and reach the other side.

It is dark outside when they leave her home. The casket, in a horse-drawn hearse, comes first. Angela and Paul are next, walking behind it, and friends and admirers fill in behind. They all hold candles because Julia wanted it so. In *The Compass* there was a funeral procession like this, and now is her chance to make that scene real.

The rain has slackened again, but a fog rolls in from the firth as they walk along the old macadam. Paul can see the casket in the glassed-in hearse ahead, can see Angela next to him, can hear the muffled footsteps of the two dozen or more behind, and that is that. Things twenty or thirty feet away are invisible, or brief murky snatches of them appear and disappear in the swirl, a dark branch of a tree, the shadowy form of a small house, the hulk of an automobile.

In the five years he was with Julia he saw things clearly, felt them sharply, knew their edges.

Not like now, here, where everything is hidden and muddy, obscure in the damn mist that swirls and hides and confounds.

His life is like that, he admits. Muddy. Obscure. It is his job to make things clear for five hundred thousand readers of the paper he works for, four times a week, fifty weeks a year.

That is what he does. Clarify.

But he has never met another Julia, and now he never will. The clarity he gives to others will never be his. Ever.

There are shouts from up the road a bit. Yelling, muffled in the fog. Paul peers forward, moves to his left to see past the hearse. The horse is shying away from the clamor ahead, trying to pull up.

There are torches. It is past eight P.M. on the final night of the millennium, and the endtimers are on the march, perhaps a dozen of them, two dozen, marching straight toward them.

The hearse jolts forward onto Cramond Brig, the driver clucking and urging the horse onto the stonework of the old bridge. On the other side, waiting, are the torches and the quiet group of endtimers. No one is saying anything. The people behind Paul and Angela don't know yet what is happening.

"Endtimers," Angela says. "They're out early. I thought they had a rally planned for the High Street at eleven to get ready for the end of it all."

"They might be here for us. It'd

be easy to know we'd be here," Paul says. "I read about this funeral in the *Glasgow Herald*. It was probably in the *Scotsman*, too. They were no great fans of hers, you know, these endtimers."

"She hated them," Angela says. "Talked about them all the time in interviews, said they were just using the millennium as an excuse for violence and thievery."

"She was right, for what it's worth," says Paul, coming to a halt as the hearse finally pulls up to a stop halfway across the bridge.

The torches come forward.

One of them—a teenager, a kid, really—speaks. "Tonight's the night, you lot. You shouldna be here. You should stay at home or get down to the Tron for the hour to come."

"Out the way, lads," the hearse driver says in even, quiet tones. "This is a funeral. There'll be plenty of time later for the New Year."

"It's not just the New Year, you stupid fool, it's the almighty end," the endtimer says. He raises up his torch to see the driver more clearly. "And we think you should turn this thing around now and go back. We won't let you cross this bridge."

"You *must* let us across," says Angela, walking past Paul before he can stop her, and then moving around to the side of the hearse as she speaks to them. "This is my mother's funeral. You must respect that, even you."

"Well, well," says the endtimer. "Look at this," and he walks

toward her, holding the torch high.

"That's her daughter," says one of the others from behind him.

So, Paul thinks, they did know what the funeral was about. This is a planned confrontation.

"And a beautiful thing she is, too," says the endtimer by the hearse.

The group from behind the hearse is caught up by this time and beginning to make comments. There are several prominent people in the group, and many of them have personal phones on them. Paul knows the police are probably already on the way.

On a normal night the police would arrive in a few minutes. This isn't the States yet, where the police might or might not arrive at all.

But this is no normal night. This is the end of the millennium, and the crowds in the city might already be in full riot. Paul wonders how long it will take for the police to get out here to Cramond to help. He wonders if he can stall these crazy young endtimers for that long, long enough to get Julia across this bridge in peace, finish the funeral procession, get on with the next thousand years.

Then the endtimers answer the questions. The one in front, the one doing the talking, walks up to Angela, holds his torch up high, and says, "Why don't we just celebrate right here, eh, daughter?"

And he grabs her by the right arm and starts pulling her back to his side of the bridge.

The hearse driver and Paul react at the same moment, both yelling and starting to come to Angela's aid. But the driver suddenly staggers, jolts upright, and shakes. A bolt protrudes from his leg, and a thin wire trails back to the endtimers—someone has a wire stunner and has used it on the driver. The electric shock might kill him if it goes on for long, and Paul knows he can't do anything about it except try to sever the wire.

Angela, meanwhile, is yelling for him, and the crowd from behind is starting to yell and scream as well, some of them running past the hearse and throwing their fists in the air to threaten the young toughs.

But threats won't work here. Paul sees one of the people from the crowd slip on some gloves and start to tug at the wire from the line stunner, and that frees Paul up.

He runs hard at the endtimer with Angela, who now has two friends with him who are holding her down on the ground, where she is kicking and struggling. The endtimer is pulling down his pants. A few more endtimers are coming up to watch.

It is all chaos and shouting and murky shadows in the flickering light.

It is violence and screaming.

It is Paul not stopping, not slowing down as he runs full tilt into the endtimer whose pants are half down. Paul throws a cross-body block into him, and the endtimer's left knee pops as Paul rolls through him, and there is a howl of pain.

Paul, landing on all fours, scrambles to his feet to take on the other two. He is crazy, insane with fear and rage, ready to take on anyone, do anything, kill them both if he has to. He has completely forgotten the stasprod in his coat pocket.

He gets to his feet, is ready for the two of them, but discovers there is only one. The other is on his back, and Angela leans over him, her arm pulled back. A vicious stab forward and blood spurts from the endtimer's nose. Another howl of pain.

Paul thinks of the stasprod, pulls it out, holds it forward to show to the final endtimer. This one holds his hands up, palms out, and mumbles something incoherent about just having some fun before turning to run.

Paul and Angela stand together and look toward the other endtimers. There must be twenty of them, maybe more, standing there at the end of the bridge, torches in hand, staring at them.

Paul starts walking toward them. Behind him Angela has walked back to take the horse by the halter and lead him forward. The hooves clop against the stone bridge.

"We're coming through," Paul says, simply. "Just step aside now, we're coming through."

And they do step aside, pulling their wounded with them. The funeral procession passes through them, crosses the bridge.

■ ■ ■

At the cemetery the ceremony is simple, brief.

Later, as the crowd walks down to Cramond Inn, the fog rolls back, disappears into the firth, and a full moon seems nearly blinding by comparison.

Paul Doig, walking beside Angela, sees the old Roman fort clearly as they walk through it on the way to the inn. In the distance, reflecting the moonlight, is the huge shadow of the rail bridge.

Tomorrow, he thinks, the sun will rise on schedule, and the endtimers will have to find a new excuse for living. For himself, this clarity right now is enough. It is hard earned. It is years in the making.

■ ■ ■

This short story first appeared in the anthology Phobias *(Pocket Books, 1994). Rick Wilber is the author of about one hundred published short stories and poems as well as hundreds of nonfiction magazine and newspaper feature articles.*

■   ■   ■

THREE POEMS

BY RICK WILBER

Running in the Rain, Cramond, Scotland

We warm nicely in the rain,
stride by stride as
we run that bouldered shore

where the legions faltered
and ceased at last
the outward surge of empire.

Fortress remnants
reduced to low stone walls
mark our path through churchyard,
   field,
and down to tidal shore—

   Low stone walls,
   once bastioned strong
   by proud cohort
   expecting state visit
   from the ambitious
   Septimius Severus.

We slap the sturdy rock
as we jog by
and talk of weather, football
and Labor's new losses
to the ever Iron Lady.

We slap the stubborn walls
that once were Rome's farthest citadel,
its final barrier against the savage
   north,

which we plan to visit tomorrow,
weather and football permitting.

■ ■ ■

Waverley to Leuchars in the Thickening Snow

I watched you, unobserved,
reflected in the train's window.

We sat opposite,
knees careful not to touch.
You looked out to winter
and I seemed to look out, too.

I seemed,
as I so often do,
to be doing the one thing
while actually lost in the other.

Then you smiled at me;
the eyes I'd watched reflected
met mine in the glass
so that I had to smile, too,
and admit my falsehood.

You discovered me,
found me out
and simply smiled
before looking down to your
   magazine.

I glanced across to see you truly there,
but your eyes sought the page
and your smile was gone;
and, when I looked back to the
   window,

the sun had cracked the clouds to blind
   the snow,
and your reflection was gone in the
   hard glare.

That is how I came to lose you,
as I so often do.

The one thing led me into another
until both, finally, disappeared.

Hi-Speed Ektacolor
Alan's father died on a day as
   innocent as this,
the 'Bonnie Lass' creaking in the
   swells
of St. Andrews Bay before putting
   out.

The 'Lass' rode empty and high
on her way to the fishing grounds.
The wind backed East,

the sea shifting and mounting,
and the 'Lass' disappeared.

Later, they found her battered dinghy.

Alan won't tell the tourist,
who's taking snaps for the slide show
   in Des Moines,
safe Des Moines,
that more have gone missing since the
   years have swept by:
two uncles, a friend, and Alan's boy,
his own strong boy.

Instead, he looks past the lens
to where he'll take 'Lass II',
her battered dinghy secure in its davits,
her hold empty for the long ride out
to the grounds on the calm and
   innocent seas.

The poem "Hi-Speed Ektacolor" first appeared in the Winter 1990–91 issue of the Scottish literary magazine Cencrastus. "Running in the Rain,
Cramond, Scotland" and "Waverley to Leuchars in the Thickening Snow"
first appeared in the Winter 1987–88 issue. Rick Wilber is the author of
about one hundred published short stories and poems as well as hundreds
of nonfiction magazine and newspaper feature articles.

Acknowledgments

Michael Bane, "Randy Travis: On the Other Hand," first published in *Country Music*, 1986. Reprinted by permission of the author.

Joe Bargmann, "The Wrong Man" and "Twice a Victim," first published in *St. Louis Magazine*. Reprinted by permission of the author.

Brian Brooks and James Pinson, "The Summary of Common Mistakes," from *Working with Words*, 2nd ed. New York: St. Martin's Press, 1993. Reprinted by permission of the publisher.

Kenneth Brower, "Tusk, Tusk," first published in *Atlantic Monthly*. Reprinted by permission of the author.

John Calderazzo, "Come Spring and High Water" and "Eulogy in a Churchyard," first published in *Ohio Magazine*. Reprinted by permission of the author.

Sandra Donnelly, selections from "25 Hottest Careers for Women," first published in *Working Woman*. Reprinted by permission of the author.

Steve Friedman, "Falling Star," first published in *St. Louis* Magazine, © 1987. Reprinted by permission of the author.

Karima A. Haynes, "Will Carol Moseley Braun Be the First Black Woman Senator?" Copyright 1992 Johnson Publishing Company, Inc. Reprinted by permission of *Ebony* Magazine.

Adrian Nicole LeBlanc, "You Wanna Die With Me?" first published in *New England Monthly*. Reprinted by permission of the author.

Michael Martone, "Correctionville, Iowa," first published in *North American Review*. Reprinted by permission of the author.

Catherine Osborne Merrill, "A Canadian Coastal Getaway," first published in *Food & Wine*. Reprinted by permission of the author.

John Morthland, "The Birth of Rock 'n' Roll," published by Warner New Media. © 1992 by John Morthland. Reprinted by permission of the author.

Robert Plunkett, "Pee-Wee, Paul, and Sarasota," first published in *Sarasota*. Reprinted by permission of the author.

Scott Russell Sanders, "Ground Notes," from *Staying Put* by Scott Russell Sanders. Copyright © 1993 by Scott Russell Sanders. Reprinted by permission of Beacon Press.

Bill Smoot, "The Fakahatchee Strand State Preserve." Reprinted by permission of the author.

Joan Tapper, "Aeolian Odyssey," from the May/June 1992 issue of *Islands* magazine, © 1992 Islands Publishing Co. Reprinted by permission.

Jeff Weinstock, "Rebel Yell," first published in *Sport* magazine. Reprinted by permission of *Sport*.

Rick Wilber, "Bridging," first published in *Phobias: Stories of Your Deepest Fears*, Pocket Books, 1994.

Rick Wilber, "Hi-Speed Ektacolor," "Running in the Rain, Cramond, Scotland," and "Waverley to Leuchars in the Thickening Snow," first published in *Cencrastus*. Reprinted by permission of the author.

Rick Wilber, "Kids, parents find island a happy holiday," first published in *The Tampa Tribune*. Reprinted by permission of the author.

INDEX